CRUDE
VOLATILITY

—

CENTER ON GLOBAL ENERGY POLICY SERIES

CENTER ON GLOBAL ENERGY POLICY SERIES
Jason Bordoff, series editor

Making smart energy policy choices requires approaching energy as a complex and multifaceted system in which decision-makers must balance economic, security, and environmental priorities. Too often, the public debate is dominated by platitudes and polarization. Columbia University's Center on Global Energy Policy at SIPA seeks to enrich the quality of energy dialogue and policy by providing an independent and nonpartisan platform for timely analysis and recommendations to address today's most pressing energy challenges. The Center on Global Energy Policy Series extends that mission by offering readers accessible, policy-relevant books that have as their foundation the academic rigor of one of the world's great research universities.

ROBERT MCNALLY

CRUDE VOLATILITY

———

The History
and the Future
of Boom-Bust
Oil Prices

COLUMBIA UNIVERSITY PRESS
NEW YORK

Columbia University Press
Publishers Since 1893
New York   Chichester, West Sussex
cup.columbia.edu
Copyright © 2017 Columbia University Press
Paperback edition, 2019

Library of Congress Cataloging-in-Publication Data

Names: McNally, Robert, 1963- author.
Title: Crude volatility : the history and future of boom-bust oil prices /
Robert McNally.
Description: New York : Columbia University Press, [2017] | Series: Center on
Global Energy Policy series | Includes bibliographical references and
index.
Identifiers: LCCN 2016040220 | ISBN 9780231178143 (cloth) |
ISBN 9780231178150 (pbk.) | ISBN 9780231543682 (e-book)
Subjects: LCSH: Petroleum industry and trade—United States—History. |
Petroleum products—Prices—United States. | Petroleum reserves—United
States. | Organization of Petroleum Exporting Countries.
Classification: LCC HD9565 .M29 2017 | DDC 338.2/32820973--dc23
LC record available at https://lccn.loc.gov/2016040220

Cover design: Noah Arlow

For Denise, my sweetheart

The problem of oil, it might be tersely said, is that there is always too much or too little.

–Myron Watkins, *Oil: Stabilization or Conservation?*, 1937

I am opposed to too much government in business. But conditions have changed . . . it looks like we must have some government in business. We will have to forget what we used to believe improper.

–Texas Governor Ross Sterling, July 22, 1931

. . . the price of oil must go to $1 a barrel; now don't ask me any more damned questions.

–Oklahoma Governor W. H. "Alfalfa Bill" Murray, after declaring martial law and ordering troops to shut down oil wells, August 5, 1931

We don't care about oil prices—$30 or $70, they are all the same to us.

–Saudi Deputy Crown Prince Mohammed bin Salman, April 21, 2016

CONTENTS

PREFACE

My inspiration to write this book stemmed from a lifelong passion for history and a professional career as an analyst, official, and consultant involved with the global oil market, energy policy, and geopolitics. My introduction to oil was somewhat accidental. After serving as a Peace Corps volunteer in Senegal, West Africa, I headed back to school to pursue a master's degree in international economics and U.S. foreign policy. My plan was to become a history teacher after graduating. But I needed a part-time job to help pay graduate school expenses, and was hired as a research intern at an oil consulting firm.

My unplanned exposure to energy started during a tumultuous period in the oil market and an active one in energy policymaking. The 1990–1991 Gulf War had just ended and the George H. W. Bush administration was beginning to implement new oxygenated fuel regulations on gasoline. Daniel Yergin's magnificent history of oil, *The Prize: The Epic Quest for Oil, Money, and Power*, had just been released and, like many, I devoured it with relish. In the course of punching oil market data into spreadsheets and analyzing OPEC and energy regulations, I realized the historical and contemporary oil market combined my main professional interests—economics, policy, and geopolitics—in a thrilling fashion. So my career path changed. I joined the firm after graduating and began a rewarding journey in energy. (Though I still would like to be a history teacher one day.)

This book elaborates on analyses developed over the past ten years and shared mainly with my colleagues and clients. My central thesis is the recent dramatic swings in oil prices, including the bust since 2014 but also the mid-2000s boom and bust in 2008, need be understood in the historical context of the broader economic and policy drivers that impact the oil market. This required a fresh look at oil's history, focusing on the critical role that *supply control* played in achieving the widely cherished goal of stabile oil prices. This focus led to my conclusion that, amid the boom in Asian demand in the early to mid-2000s and the more recent, surprise arrival of U.S. shale production, the most important feature of today's oil market is the absence of a swing producer able and willing to adjust supply to keep oil prices stable. Since the early 1930s, as this book details, someone has been trying to manage supply to keep oil prices from behaving as they have in the last ten years. No longer having such a swing producer implies a return to price volatility for which we have all but lost living memory and which we will find troublesome to manage. I presented these ideas at academic events and in congressional testimony, published some of the key themes with my coauthor Michael Levi in *Foreign Affairs* in 2011 and 2014, and wrote a paper synopsizing this argument in December 2015 for the Columbia University Center on Global Energy Policy, where I am a fellow.

I decided to write this book to explore more deeply how oil's history can clarify recent trends and shed light on tomorrow's path, and to present my findings to the general reader as well as the energy expert.

Tackling this topic presented formidable challenges, not the least of which was getting good historical data and information. For "barrel counters," the search for better data is a never-ending and arduous quest. Historical data on prices and spare production capacity—central to this book—are especially scarce and patchy. I am therefore delighted and proud that my able research assistant Fernando Ferreira and I were able to unearth historical data and present two novel data sets, neither of which (to my knowledge) existed until now.

The first data set is a continuous, market-based price series for U.S. crude prices extending back to 1859 and continuing to the present on a monthly basis. Constructing this series entailed digging up prices based on field quotations, exchange-traded pipeline certificates (a proxy for crude oil prices), prices paid by Standard Oil's purchasing agency, and data from the American Petroleum Institute and the Energy Information Administration.

The key issue here is frequency of the data. BP helpfully publishes historical crude oil prices back to 1859 on an annual basis. But annual averages fall short of illustrating boom-bust price trends as more frequent and dramatic price swings—daily, weekly, monthly—get lost in the annual average. Unless otherwise noted, all prices cited in this book, including this new monthly historical price series, are in nominal instead of real or inflation-adjusted terms. Using real prices would not change the story from a volatility perspective, but I decided to use nominal prices to better connect the prevailing historical narrative with price changes. This monthly crude oil price series is presented in figure I.1.

The second unique data set developed for this book is for U.S. spare production capacity extending back to 1940 and continuous data on U.S. and global spare capacity since 1955 (that is, including the Seven Sisters until the early 1970s and OPEC afterward). This entailed exhuming information from various government and industry reports and publications. Currently, EIA's published OPEC spare production capacity extends back to 2003.

My goal is to contribute to our understanding of the economic and political forces that shaped oil prices in history so as to better understand them today and tomorrow. Whether I have succeeded I leave to you, dear reader, to judge.

ACKNOWLEDGMENTS

I have been blessed all my life with supportive and talented family, friends, and professional associates, and the recent period spent writing this book is no exception. My expression of thanks cannot suffice but begins with my wife Denise Montroy-McNally and old friend Erwin Grandinger (an author himself). Both urged me to stop talking about writing this book and just do it.

Fernando Ferreira, my intrepid and astute research assistant and Rapidan Group colleague, contributed countless hours researching, reviewing, and improving this work, from diving deep into history to organizing and analyzing price and other data.

My extraordinarily talented editor at Columbia University Press, Bridget Flannery-McCoy, cheerfully encouraged and deftly fortified the manuscript's organization, development, and refinement at every step.

My brilliant and meticulous fact checker, Krista Dugan, provided invaluable assistance not only in spotting errors, but also by making substantive improvements.

Finally, my friend and fellow White House energy policy staff alumnus (if under different presidents), Jason Bordoff, encouraged me to write this book and introduced me to Columbia University Press. Jason and his colleagues at the Columbia University Center on Global Energy Policy, where I am a proud nonresident fellow, provided superb counsel and advice along the way.

Without significant and steady collaboration from Fernando, Bridget, Krista, and Jason this book would not have been possible and I deeply appreciate their steadfast support.

Several friends who are also accomplished energy and economic experts took the time to review the manuscript and contributed, improving the book with their seasoned expertise and perspectives. Greg Ip, an accomplished journalist, author, and economic commentator, provided invaluable recommendations. Nathaniel Kern, Jason Bordoff, and one anonymous expert also reviewed the entire manuscript and provided superb feedback and suggestions. Two anonymous reviewers reviewed an early manuscript and provided outstanding guidance.

In addition, I deeply appreciate insights and contributions from Daniel P. Ahn, Robert L. Bradley (whose magisterial *Oil, Gas, and Government* I relied upon considerably for historical information and insights), Allyson Cutright, Carmine Difiglio, Ramón Espinasa (who shared his outstanding, unpublished dissertation on Gulf-Plus pricing), Mark Finley, David Fyfe, Garrett Golding, Larry Goldstein, Antoine Halff, Paul Horsnell, Theodore Kassinger, John Kemp, Michael Levi, Kenneth B. Medlock III, Michael Miller, Scott Modell, Fareed Mohamedi, David (Mack) Moore, Campbell Palfrey, and Matthew Robinson. Thanks go to my daughters Grace and Emilia, who spent many hours transferring reams of old price data from dusty books to a spreadsheet. And I greatly appreciate Molly Ward's expert and careful copyediting and Noah Arlow for the terrific cover design.

I thank my family—Denise, Grace, Emilia, and Grant—as well as friends and colleagues at the Rapidan Group for encouraging me and tolerating my absence over the past two years. Finally, thank you Nancy Accetta, Rob Dugger, Sarah Emerson, Alan H. Fleischmann, Paul Tudor Jones, Larry Lindsey, and Dafna Tapiero for granting me over years—in some cases decades—your confidence and inspiration that made this book possible.

Whatever positive contribution this book makes to our understanding of oil market history, prices, and policy is the result of collaboration with and contributions from those mentioned above. Any errors, shortcomings, or omissions are entirely mine.

Robert McNally

AUTHOR'S NOTE

Throughout this book, unless otherwise specified, crude prices are in nominal terms and refer to the prevailing monthly U.S. spot prices. I created a continuous, monthly, market-based U.S. crude oil price series beginning in 1859 and continuing to the present.

1859 to 1874 prices are approximate and based on field quotations.
1875 to 1894 prices are based on pipeline certificates traded on the
  Oil City Oil Exchange.
1895 to 1899 prices are those paid by the Seep Purchasing Agency.
1900 to 1912 prices are based on field-level quotations collected and
  aggregated by the author.
1913 to 1982 crude prices are midcontinent 36 degrees American
  Petroleum Institute (API) crude.
1983 and forward prices are spot West Texas Intermediate (WTI) prices.

CRUDE VOLATILITY

—

INTRODUCTION

The Texas Paradox

O f all the things Texans are famous for, limiting government and producing oil might be paramount. Therefore, it is all the more remarkable that some eighty years ago Texan officials and oil drillers devised
and imposed the most heavy-handed, government-imposed quota regime
the world has ever seen. Moreover, fiercely independent officials and
oilmen welcomed help from the avidly interventionist Franklin Delano
Roosevelt administration in imposing and policing quotas not only in
Texas but also in other oil-producing states. OPEC would have been
envious at the scope, stringency, and compliance of oil quotas practiced
by U.S. oil states and backstopped by federal authority. Indeed, OPEC's
Venezuelan founder, Dr. Juan Pablo Pérez Alfonzo, was envious of U.S.
state quotas and tried to copy them. The United States was the world's
first and most powerful OPEC for 40 years.

Why would stalwart freedom lovers in the Lone Star State and other
oil states acquiesce to heavy-handed government central planning over
oil? The answer is, in short, to vanquish chronic price booms and busts
and to keep oil prices stable. This Texas paradox is of more than just
historical interest. It bears directly on an epic, structural shift currently
underway in the global oil market, with far-reaching repercussions
not only for oil and energy, but also economic growth, security, and
the environment.

The need to reexamine oil price stability arises from oil prices' wild ride
over the last ten years. After spending most of two decades below $30, in
2004 crude oil prices starting rising and by late 2007 they had reached $99.

By the summer of 2008 they soared above $100 and peaked at $145.31 in July 2008 in the biggest boom ever recorded—and then abruptly crashed back to $33 in less than six months. Prices rebounded to around $100 in 2011, and averaged about $95 over the following three and a half years. But from June 2014 to February 2016 prices crashed once more, from $107 to $26—a bust of over 75 percent.[1]

Two spectacular boom-bust cycles within ten years, after decades of relatively stable prices—what is going on, and should we care?

This book will address those questions by reviewing the history of the modern oil market through the prism of oil price stability. Most contemporary discussion of the oil market starts with the energy crisis of 1973 and the subsequent rise of the OPEC cartel, with the preceding 114 years ignored or glossed over. That will not do. Understanding current and prospective oil prices requires a more probing and dispassionate look at oil market history, starting with E. L. Drake's first well near Titusville, Pennsylvania, in 1859. (While James Miller Williams dug the first successful commercial well in Enniskillen, Ontario, in 1858, Drake's well ignited a drilling boom that revolutionized the oil industry.) By beginning the story of oil prices with the birth of the industry, we can better appreciate why oil prices are naturally volatile and why that volatility has posed an enormous problem not only for the oil industry but broader economy, causing oilmen and officials to go to great lengths to stabilize oil prices. How successful were they in leveling prices? Were they motivated by greed, nobler sentiments, or both? What do price gyrations in the last decade tell us about whether oil prices are successfully being stabilized today, and if not, what does that imply for the future? Has OPEC (or Saudi Arabia) permanently lost control of oil prices and is that a good or bad thing? Can U.S. shale oil replace Saudi Arabia as the guarantor of price stability? If not, how should we think about coping with much wider oil price fluctuations? These are portentous and complicated questions, and this book can only scratch the surface in terms of providing answers—but hopefully by providing some historical perspective and framework for understanding current and future oil price gyrations, it will contribute to a discussion that others will deepen and enrich. Although this book aims to contribute insight and raise questions for energy market and policy professionals, it is written and intended primarily for the general reader; no prior experience with oil history or markets is assumed or required.

NO OPEC, NO PEACE

Extreme price volatility, we shall show, is an intrinsic feature of the oil industry. Historically, oil prices have experienced multidecade eras of relative stability and wild boom-bust gyrations. Stability depended on a group of oil companies, officials, or both regulating supply through mandatory quotas on production or through cartels. When no one controlled supply, oil prices fluctuated wildly. Boom-bust oil prices between 1859 and 1879 prompted John D. Rockefeller and his Standard Oil Company and Trust to create a refining monopoly and collaborate or integrate with railroads and pipelines, resulting in stable prices from 1880 to 1911. Boom-bust prices returned after Standard Oil's dissolution, prompting major international oil companies to establish a cartel over Middle East oil fields while U.S. officials imposed quotas; prices consequently enjoyed their most stable era from 1932 to 1972. In the early 1970s, OPEC wrested control and played the stabilizer until, this book will argue, about ten years ago. Since 2008, monthly crude price changes have averaged 38 percent, on par with that last boom-bust era from 1911 and 1931. Recent fluctuations mark the return of a free and unfettered market for crude oil, and as a consequence boom-bust oil prices are making a return after eight decades. (See figures 1.1 and 1.2.)

WHY OIL PRICE STABILITY MATTERS

Should we care if oil prices have entered a new and much more volatile era? Absolutely, for notwithstanding sustainability concerns, oil is and will, for the foreseeable future, remain the lifeblood of advanced civilization. As a strategic commodity oil has fueled the engines of economic growth, accelerated technological change, and increased productivity. Abundant and affordable oil increased wealth and living standards in advanced countries in the twentieth century. Advanced economies are using less oil to generate growth, but still depend on it, and oil is currently essential to sustain fast-growing, emerging economies in Asia, Latin America, and Africa.[2]

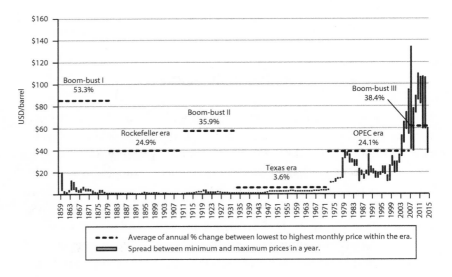

FIGURE I.1

Annual ranges of monthly U.S. crude oil prices, 1859–2016.

Source: *Derrick's*, vols. I–IV; API, *Petroleum Facts and Figures* (1959); Dow Jones & Company, Spot Oil Price: West Texas Intermediate; and U.S. Energy Information Administration, Cushing, OK WTI Spot Price (FOB). © The Rapidan Group.

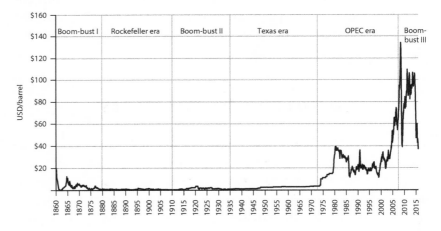

FIGURE I.2

Monthly U.S. crude oil prices, 1859–2016.

Source: *Derrick's*, vols. I–IV; API, *Petroleum Facts and Figures* (1959); Dow Jones & Company, Spot Oil Price: West Texas Intermediate; and U. S. Energy Information Administration, Cushing, OK WTI Spot Price (FOB). © The Rapidan Group.

While petroleum yields hundreds of common products, from medicine to plastics, oil's critical importance stems from the fact that nearly all vehicles on the planet run on it. Without well-functioning transportation, societies suffer extreme damage or grind to a halt. Oil market turbulence quickly spreads pain and uncertainty in wider commercial and industrial sectors that depend on the steady flow of affordable liquid fuels. The economic and geopolitical energy crises of the 1970s still haunt us. The oil price boom from 2004 to 2008 inflicted great hardship on consumers, oil-dependent industries and contributed to the Great Recession. The price bust since 2014 triggered not only unemployment in the oil patch but raised concern about broader stability of the financial sector.

Given oil's critical role in the economy, just about everyone cherishes stable oil prices and abhors volatility. Sustained oil price volatility reduces planning horizons, deters investment in machinery and equipment (especially for long-lived equipment), and increases unemployment.[3] Volatile oil prices make everyone cautious about investing and spending: producers contemplating the next billions of dollars in exploration and production (low cost but unstable Middle East, or high-cost Arctic?); motorists shopping for a car (Leaf or F-350?); airline executives in the market to buy jet planes (thirsty big planes and long-distance routes, or fuel-sipping planes and shorter routes?); or a delivery fleet purchaser (stick with gasoline and distillate or convert to natural gas vehicles?).

For government leaders and policy makers, gyrating oil prices are a major headache. They complicate monetary policy, such as in 2015 and early 2016 when crashing oil prices delayed plans by the Federal Reserve and European Central Bank to raise interest rates. To a greater degree than most commodities, petroleum is a "major factor in international politics and socioeconomic development." Petroleum is the largest single internationally traded good and "petroleum taxes are a major source of income for more than ninety countries in the world."[4] The impact of oil price volatility on developing countries has enormous repercussions for international trade, finance and policymaking. Government budget planning becomes more difficult for countries that subsidize energy consumption or that rely on energy exports for revenue.

Oil impacts not only the health of the economy, but access to oil and dependence on its revenue critically drives international affairs and geopolitical trends. Booms can embolden oil-exporting adversaries like Russia and enrich Daesh terrorists. Busts can trigger social unrest in oil-dependent countries.[5] Oil price gyrations destabilize producing countries in the Middle East, North Africa, and Latin America and can help trigger wars, revolutions, and terrorism.

So if troublesome boom-bust oil prices are back after a long absence, why can't we just get off oil? After all, the oil intensity of the economy has been falling as efficiency improves and substitutes for oil have been found.[6] Cars use less gasoline and oil has been to a great extent displaced by natural gas, coal, nuclear, and renewables in power generation. Looking forward, the International Energy Agency (IEA) and most analysts assume energy intensity per unit of GDP will likely decline as efficiency and substitution improve. Coupled with this, of course, are concerns about the impact of oil production and consumption on the environment and climate.

But even if some think we should, we won't get off oil any time soon, for several reasons. For one, energy efficiency does not improve overnight. Fuel efficiency of new U.S. passenger cars, even excluding gas-guzzling sport-utility vehicles and pickups, increased at an annual rate of just 2.5 percent since 1973.[7] And efficiency gains are partly offset by consumer preferences (such as for bigger cars and SUVs) and what economists call the "rebound effect"—higher efficiency lowers the cost of driving, inducing motorists to drive more.[8] So while oil has been displaced in electricity generation, there are no scalable substitutes on the horizon for oil use in transportation, which accounts for 55 percent of world consumption.[9] Oil's strong and likely enduring advantage in transportation stems from its application in a variety of vehicle types, cost competitiveness, infrastructure availability and supportive government policies.[10]

Scale also is critical to thinking about energy transformations. The larger the scale of prevailing energy forms—in this case, the near-total dominance of transportation by gasoline and diesel—the longer energy transitions will take. "Even if an immediate alternative were available," leading energy researcher Vaclav Smil has written, "writing off this colossal infrastructure that took more than a century to build would amount to discarding an investment worth well over $5 trillion—but it is quite obvious that its energy output could not be replicated by any alternative in a decade or two."[11]

As for policy, and the call that we *must* stop using oil because of climate change: Although elected officials from many nations pledged to reduce future carbon emissions in Paris in 2015, we are not going to see a forced march off of oil in the foreseeable future. The Paris agreements included no enforcement mechanism, and dramatically cutting oil consumption in transportation—given the absence of cost effective and scalable alternatives—would require extraordinarily costly taxes and subsidies or intrusive mandates and restrictions on consumption and production. There is little evidence that any country is ready to impose severe restrictions on oil or other fossil fuels, much less an "induced implosion" of the fossil fuel industry, as one influential climate scientist and government advisor called for.[12] Environmentalists and policymakers concerned about climate change frequently complain that current policies are woefully insufficient,[13] and nearly all leading analysts—even those who tout the economic, security and environmental benefits of radically reduced oil use—agree that oil won't soon be driven out of the market. For example, the latest long-term energy outlook from the International Energy Agency, an energy watchdog composed of advanced countries and that strongly favors reducing carbon emissions and transitioning to clean energy, concluded: "For all the current talk about the imminent end to the petroleum age, hydrocarbons will continue to play the leading role in meeting the world's growing hunger for energy for at least the next quarter of a century, and probably well beyond."[14]

Whether we like it or not, society's continued heavy dependence on oil—at least in the near future—is basically ensured. The main reason is that, other than in wartime, elected officials do not like to ask voters to pay now to fix a problem in the future. This is readily apparent in fiscal policy. Compared with the complexity, scope, and cost of policies needed to wean the world off of fossil fuels, fixing Social Security and Medicare is a walk in the park—only straightforward tax hikes and benefit cuts are required. But those comparatively simple solutions are extremely difficult politically, so elected officials avoid doing or saying much about them. So while political leaders may continue to talk about climate change, there is no indication yet that they will do anything drastic about it. Blessing or curse, oil will play a leading role in shaping our economy, security, and environment for the foreseeable future.

GETTING OVER THE MONOPOLY MAN

If we are going to need oil for many more years, and if its price is going to be harmfully unstable, we need to upgrade our thinking about the causes and cures for oil price volatility. The demise of OPEC and return of boom-bust oil prices calls for a more nuanced and balanced look at oil prices from the perspective of stability. We are accustomed to painting oil market managers (most today will think of OPEC, and some may recall its predecessors the Seven Sisters, Texas and other oil state regulators, and before them John D. Rockefeller's Standard Oil Trust) as a greedy group with a stranglehold on the global oil market, dictating prices to gouge consumers. But this common caricature is incomplete and misleading. It overlooks the way in which price stability has been supported—often through government support of or partnership with these groups—in the service of a well-functioning economy and global community. After all, the FDR administration was no natural friend of the oil industry—but to protect the economy, it helped enforce oil state quotas that not only stabilized but raised oil prices, benefitting the domestic oil industry. Democratic and Republican administrations alike tolerated and often supported the Seven Sisters' oil cartel that dominated Middle Eastern production for decades. Clearly they were not doing so simply to gouge motorists and line the pockets of oil barons. We need to understand why these officials gave a green light to the control of oil production.

To be clear, this book does not recommend that OPEC or other regulatory body reimpose oil supply quotas for the sake of stable oil prices. It does argue that we are going to be unpleasantly surprised by chronically unstable oil prices and will be looking for shelter from them. So it's time we asked: What *were* those Texans *thinking*?

1

THE LONG STRUGGLE FOR STABILITY: 1859–1972

1

AND THEN THERE WAS LIGHT

From Chaos to Order in the Kerosene Era (1859–1911)

I t is difficult for those of us lucky to live with electricity today to comprehend how miraculous the possibility of artificial light was to people who lived 160 years ago. Over the preceding millennia, the great bulk of human activity had been limited to daylight hours. By the mid-1800s, fast-growing literacy, industrialization, and urbanization required cheap, bright, and safe sources of illumination. Prevailing illuminants included animal fats, such as whale oil, or camphene, an explosive mixture of alcohol and wood turpentine—but these were in limited supply, dangerous, or both. "Artificial light," energy historian Robert L. Bradley, Jr. noted, "was a luxury waiting to become a necessity."[1]

Liquid petroleum—"crude oil"—was the solution to humanity's craving for cheap artificial light. Crude oil effusing from pores in the earth was hardly new: Humans had been scooping, digging, and mopping up oil from aboveground seeps for ages (the word "petroleum" derives from the Latin words for "rock" and "oil") and using the meager amounts they could gather for construction, medicine, and, later, lighting. However, in the late 1850s, inventors figured out how to tap into and unlock vast reservoirs of underground oil and thereby enable millions of families, workers, and investors to conquer the night.

Crude oil, often called "black gold"—unlike the yellow metal—is essentially valueless and even dangerous in its raw and unrefined state. Turning crude oil into useful consumer and industrial products requires distillation, a process of heating the liquid to a boil and then capturing the valuable, boiled-off subcomponents or "fractions" used to make consumer products. The most important consumer product in the first fifty years of the oil industry was kerosene, which shone brighter and was less explosive than competing fuels distilled from coal or turpentine.[2]

But since crude oil appeared only in seeps and small puddles, it had to be ladled or wrung from blankets, and so was in very short supply and an expensive luxury only the wealthy could afford. By 1858, the United States burned nearly 500,000 barrels of whale oil and 600,000 barrels of lard and tallow oil, compared with a paltry 1,183 barrels of crude oil.[3] As extensive whale harvesting sent whale oil prices skyrocketing, the rapidly industrializing world cried out for a cheaper and superior replacement for lighting and lubrication. Kerosene seemed to be the answer, but the problem remained—how to obtain enough to replace coal or whale oil in millions of lamps? By the late 1850s, the race was on to discover how to coax a much larger and sustained flow of "rock oil" from the earth.[4]

In 1855, a prominent Yale University chemist named Benjamin Silliman, Jr., issued an analysis prepared on behalf of two investors who had leased tracts of land near the remote village of Titusville, nestled in a valley and along a creek flowing south into the Allegheny River in western Pennsylvania. Dubbed Oil Creek by early European explorers, the valley's creek bed had long oozed with oil from natural springs and had been used by Native Americans for medicinal balms and personal decoration. Silliman's clients were eager to satisfy the fast-growing illumination market and sought validation that Oil Creek's crude yielded high-quality kerosene.

After distilling his clients' crude sample, Dr. Silliman concluded, to their delight, that it yielded not only high-quality kerosene for lighting, but also other products such as lubricants and paraffin for candles. "In conclusion, gentleman," Silliman summed up in a report that quickly turned into an advertisement pamphlet and became an epochal document in the history of the oil industry,[5] "it appears to me that there is much ground for encouragement in the belief that your company have in their possession a raw material from which, by simple and not expensive process, they may manufacture very valuable products." Dr. Silliman then joined his overjoyed clients, becoming president of their newly formed Pennsylvania Rock Oil Company of Connecticut to exploit the promising find.

But a central problem remained: How to obtain more oil from the springs around Titusville? At the time, producers simply dug trenches that filled with water and oil; it took a whole day of trenching to produce six gallons of oil.[6] In 1857, Silliman's successor at the company, a New Haven Banker named James Townsend, suggested boring for oil, using techniques employed by salt producers.[7] The boring technique, invented in the Sichuan province of China over two thousand years ago, uses an iron drill bit and a wooden rig to repeatedly lift and drive a shaft into the bedrock, crushing it.[8] The boring process (often conflated with the term "drilling" which will be used hereafter) was later adapted and adopted by Europeans and Americans, and had been used in the United States since the early 1800s. Borers innovated and improved techniques, such that by the 1830s salt wells in the United States reached 1,600 feet.

Salt and petroleum were commonly found together. Aboveground effusions or oil seeps would often signal the presence of more valuable salt, and salt borers considered it to be a great misfortune when they encountered the brownish oil as they drilled, as it could ruin the well.[9]

The idea of drilling for oil was not met with universal enthusiasm. "Oh, Townsend," his friends chided him, "oil coming out of the ground, pumping oil out of the earth as you pump water? Nonsense! You're crazy."[10] But the intrepid Townsend and coinvestors decided to dispatch thirty-eight-year-old former railroad conductor Edwin Laurentine Drake to visit their property and explore the possibility. They christened Drake with the unearned title "Colonel" to impress the local inhabitants. Sociable and adventurous, "Colonel" Drake made a quick reconnaissance trip to Titusville, confirming ample effusions of oil and visiting salt drilling sites on the way back to Connecticut. Drake's enthusiastic report moved the New Haven investors to action. They formed a new company—Seneca Oil Company—and relocated Drake and his family to Titusville.

Drake secured equipment, hired workers, and began drilling efforts in May, 1858. After a year he still had not managed to bring oil out of the ground; skeptical local villagers told him he was hopelessly chasing "merely 'the dripping of an extensive coal field.'"[11] But on August 27, 1859, down to his investors' last dimes, the tenacious Drake sunk a well sixty-nine and a half feet deep and struck oil that flowed to the surface at the rate of first ten and then, with the help of a pump, forty barrels per day.[12] The oil age was born—and all hell broke loose in western Pennsylvania.

"Word of Drake's discovery," historian, journalist, and John D. Rockefeller biographer Allan Nevins wrote, "flew like a Dakota cyclone."[13]

Drillers and prospectors swarmed to Titusville and surrounding areas—immediately dubbed the Oil Regions—establishing new boomtowns and throwing up thickly clustered forests of rigs. Maniacal drilling ensued. Prices offered for land previously worth little more than any lumber it might yield suddenly soared, making poor farmers and workers who struck black gold spectacularly rich overnight. One, a blacksmith named James Evans, spent $200 drilling a well eighteen miles from Drake's well on the Allegheny River and promptly received an offer for $100,000 after it struck oil. As word of overnight riches like Evans's spread, more prospectors, speculators, and drillers flocked into the Oil Regions, which became a bustling beehive of road building, land clearing, and drilling.[14]

But drilling for oil soon revealed itself to be a risky and uncertain endeavor. Not all wells struck oil (in 1867 half of the new wells were dry), and some that did soon tapped out. A few lucky investors struck and made a killing, but many drilled dry holes and lost fortunes. The unluckiest oilmen, and more than a few bystanders, were incinerated in frequent and often catastrophic fires and explosions.[15]

Early oil drillers and landowners focused mainly on drilling *fast*. The need for speedy drilling stemmed from the prevailing legal principle known as "rule of capture," which held that the owner of surface property owned any resources collected from his property, regardless of whether or not they migrated from someone else's adjacent property. Rule of capture originated in English common law, and was frequently associated with owners of land enjoying the right to "capture" deer or other wild animals that migrated onto their property. The first landowner to harvest, extract, or "capture" the natural resource won ownership rights.[16]

The law of capture also applied to underground resources. At the time, geological understanding of oil deposits was poor, and oil was thought to lie in underground pools (later the industry learned oil was trapped in rock and sedimentary deposits). To legally own the oil, drillers had to drain the underground "pool" before someone else did. Both drillers and eager leaseholders had an incentive to drill fast. As one expert described it, the scramble to drain subterranean deposits resembled two thirsty boys, two straws, and one glass of lemonade. "It becomes a sucking contest in which the one who sucks the *least* is the bigger *sucker*."[17]

The result was manic drilling and overproduction in the western Pennsylvania Oil Regions.[18]

To capture the lion's share of oil from underground pools, operators drilled extra or "offset" wells on the edge of their property and as close as possible to wells on adjacent properties in order to intercept and drain subterranean oil before it could migrate to the other side. (Water often intruded into well bores and could damage or destroy a well if it entered the pool. If a nefarious operator really wanted to play hardball, he would sink a shaft very close to a well on an adjoining property and threaten to damage their shared reservoir by removing tubing in his own well shaft, thus allowing water to enter connected substrata channels and ruining the well.[19])

The drilling scramble soon created major problems for those who handled the oil on the surface. Operators never knew where the next gusher would be discovered, and so when it was found there was often no storage or, until the late 1860s, small diameter, short-distance "gathering" pipelines nearby to contain or move the crude. At first, operators used wooden whiskey and wine barrels to hold the oil,[20] carting them away to local refineries in booming towns along Oil Creek or, more often, to navigable stream or river landings or more distant railheads, for onward shipment to larger refineries starting to spring up both in booming towns along Oil Creek as well as in nearby cities, principally found in Pittsburgh and Cleveland and later in New York and New England. But early transporters could not build barrels, pipelines, and barges fast enough to keep pace with new flowing wells. Enormous waste resulted as oil poured from the ground and was run into the creek or fields. One of the oil industry's earliest trade press, *The Derrick's Handbook of Petroleum* (hereafter, *The Derrick*), recorded that in October 1861 "[s]o much oil is produced, it is impossible to care for it, and thousands of barrels are running into the creek. The surface of the river is covered with oil for miles below Franklin."[21]

With crude oil production exceeding storage and transportation capacity, prices collapsed. From January 1860 to January 1862 oil prices crashed from $20 to as low as 10 cents per barrel,[22] forcing many oilmen to close their operations and abandon drilling. This was the first of many epic price busts in oil's history.

Soon after prices collapsed, persistently strong demand and temporarily shuttered supply quickly sent oil prices skyrocketing. Demand for oil steadily rose as the Civil War cut the North's supply of southern turpentine, used to make camphene. Wartime taxes on oil's competitors and a brisk export market to Europe also boosted demand. By the end of 1864 crude oil prices were back to $10 per barrel. All told, the price shock of the early 1860s was bigger in real-dollar terms than those during the "energy crisis" of the 1970s. However, since petroleum was in its infancy and played little role in the national economy, the shock had little macroeconomic impact.[23]

And so, almost immediately after Drake bored his first well and spawned the industry, the oil market saw the first of what would soon establish itself as a pattern of boom and bust prices, reflecting inherent characteristics that still vex oil drillers today—there was either too much oil or not enough.

Supply and demand were chronically out of balance and the result was widely gyrating prices. On the one hand, demand for kerosene and other oil products were growing at home and abroad. Within a year of Drake's discovery in Pennsylvania, oil was being marketed in Paris and London, and by 1866 two-thirds of Cleveland's kerosene output was shipped abroad.[24] On the other hand, discovery of new oil pools expanded but in "an irregular and capricious pattern."[25] Entering the new drilling industry was cheap and easy. While not all drillers struck oil, those that did produced more than could be stored, carried away, and refined. The result was price collapses, which would abruptly halt drilling until prices—as they always did—rose again. Cheap entry and the promise of astounding financial rewards attracted a torrent of new investment in drilling, "takeaway capacity" (barges, wagons, and later trains and pipelines), and refineries. New supply would then race ahead of demand, triggering a price crash. The result was a repeating, self-reinforcing boom-bust cycle in oil prices.

Indeed, crude prices tanked again in 1866 and 1867 as overproduction forced the shutdown of numerous wells and slowed the new drilling of others. At times, the wooden barrel used to hold crude was more valuable than the contents.[26] In the years following, oil price volatility abated somewhat compared with the first few years but market conditions could drastically vary week to week. An entry from *The Derrick* for August 7, 1866, reported that "the market is booming; the question with buyers is not what to pay, but where to get oil"—but just a day later "a sudden relapse; the buyers are all gone."[27]

Despite the wild price gyrations, excitement and confidence in the oil industry mushroomed. Demand for oil products—mainly for residential and office lighting and for factory and railroad lubrication, but eventually for manufacture of other products such as paint—was persistent and insatiable.[28] Exploding demand and price booms motivated investors to build more storage facilities, better transportation systems, and more refineries. Crucial transportation bottlenecks were steadily removed, especially after railways, and then pipelines connected wells to terminals and refiners. The massive, if chaotic, expansion of drilling, transporting, and refining transformed kerosene and other petroleum products from a rare luxury to a staple of mass consumption.

TAMING THE BEAST: CARTELS, STABILIZATION, AND JOHN D. ROCKEFELLER

Despite rapid growth in the demand for oil, everyone involved in the new oil business—drillers, transporters, and refiners—were constantly tormented by the fear of price instability caused in large part by unstable crude oil production. Excess supply stemmed not just from impatient property owners and frantic drillers operating under rule-of-capture competition. Investors and operators in every stage of oil production, transportation, and refining were compelled to produce all—out to generate returns on capital, often borrowed, that had been invested up front to drill, transport, or refine the crude. Once those drilling rigs were bought, pipelines were laid, and refineries built, operating them was comparatively inexpensive. The combination of high upfront capital costs and low operating costs induced producers and refiners to continue pumping and refining oil—even at a loss—to generate cash flow to cover at least some of their sunk costs. The result was sustained overproduction that led to ruinous, protracted price slumps, culminating in widespread bankruptcies that wiped out producers big and small, efficient or not. When demand picked up, the supply would be insufficient and prices would sharply rise, repeating the boom-bust cycle.[29]

After the first price bust in 1860–1861, mortified Oil Region drillers responded by attempting to form "cartels"—groups of competing firms that coordinate to restrict production and thus, raise prices. Cartels are often "children of distress,"[30] born during periods of ruinous price competition, and tend to develop when demand for a commodity is steady, the product is standardized, and capital or transportation costs are heavy relative to operating costs such that firms cannot respond quickly to changing conditions. Oil met these conditions. But there is one other necessary feature that enables cartels: A natural inclination (ideally by a relatively small number of producers) toward integration and collective action when oversupply develops. Cartels work best when there are a limited number of producers, barriers to entry are high, and patented or elaborate technology is required to produce. In the case of oil, conditions in the early Pennsylvania oil fields were decidedly not favorable to the formation or success of a producer cartel. New drillers were as numerous as they were independent, barriers to entry were low, and oil drilling was neither sophisticated nor subject to technology patents.

Despite an unfavorable atmosphere, early oil drillers tried to form cartels out of desperation to escape price crashes.[31] But their efforts did not last long and ultimately failed, mainly because members succumbed to the temptation to cheat as hordes of new drillers, eager to strike it rich, continued discovering new gushers.

For example, in what may be the earliest ancestor of Organization of the Petroleum Exporting Countries (OPEC), in November 1861—in the midst of oil's first price bust—Oil Creek drillers banded together to form the Oil Creek Association and promised to limit production. Its articles of agreement stated that no producer would sell below 10 cents a gallon or $4.00 per barrel.[32] That was quite ambitious, as crude was selling for as low as 10 cents a barrel just two months before.[33] The goal was to find a means by which "the price and supply of crude oil could be so regulated as to ensure remunerating rates to the well owners, and at the same time prevent the immense waste from flowing wells," the *Pittsburgh Gazette* reported.[34] Members agreed to appoint an inspector who would ensure that wells produced no more than demand. But the

Oil Creek Association was foiled by poor compliance, and did not succeed in pushing oil prices out of their slump. As we've seen, in January
1862 barrels were still changing hands for only 10 cents a barrel.[35] The only
thing that worked effectively to lower production was oil prices remaining low enough for long enough that they would force some producers
to plug their wells. In March, *The Derrick* noted that some drillers had
begun "shutting in" production, waiting for better prices.[36] (In the industry's parlance, a "shut-in" well is a well which is capable of producing but
is not producing.) Many small drillers were ruined, and simply walked
away from their rigs. It would take strong wartime demand in 1864 to lift
prices once more.[37]

In February 1869, with prices back up again following the industry's
second price bust of 1866 and 1867, some Oil Region drillers formed the
Petroleum Producers' Association of Pennsylvania. The original purpose
of the group was to oppose state oil taxes and gather industry-wide data
on production, inventories, and demand.[38] However, by 1870 prices weakened, convincing drillers to turn the Association into a supply-restricting
cartel, and on June 29, 1870, the Association resolved to stop drilling
for three months. Compliance was weak: just one day later, *The Derrick*
recounted there was "more wildcatting in progress than at any time since
the discovery of oil."[39] In the end, operators ignored the Association's call
to halt and new drilling soon broke new records.

Thus, from the earliest days, oil cartels have suffered from poor compliance with voluntary output restraints. The more successful a cartel is at
raising prices, the bigger the payoff for producers who refuse to join the
cartel as well as members who decide to cheat by exceeding agreed limits,
and so the agreement collapses.[40]

Cartelizing thousands of drillers proved futile, but the scourge of
chronic price busts and booms continued to afflict the infant industry.
If the fledgling industry was to save itself from chronic instability, drillers,
transporters, and refiners would have to target some other bottleneck in
the oil industry's supply chain—and this is where a bold, farsighted, and
industrious Cleveland refiner enters the picture.

John D. Rockefeller started out as an assistant bookkeeper for a produce shipper and merchant in 1855, but he went out on his own as a produce merchant in Cleveland in the late 1850s. Uncommonly intelligent

and "methodical to an extreme,"[41] he was intrigued by the reports of oil gushing out of western Pennsylvania, some 100 miles to the east. He investigated, and quickly recognized the enormous potential of the oil refining business. Small refiners setting up shop in Erie, Pennsylvania— about 50 miles from the oil wells around Titusville—were buying crude for around $15 per barrel, incurring another 30 cents to refine it, and selling refined products to marketers at $52 per barrel, for a profit of over 70 percent.[42] In 1863, Rockefeller and his business partner dipped their toes in the infant oil-refining business by investing in a Cleveland refinery.

Like all refiners then and since, Rockefeller depended on a continuous and reliable flow of crude oil, ideally at steady prices. What he found instead, biographer Ron Chernow wrote, was an oil industry that "tended to oscillate between extremes: gluts so dire that prices plummeted below production costs, or shortages that sent prices skyward but raised the even more troubling specter of the oil running dry."[43]

Rockefeller firmly believed in oil's long-term role as a massive consumer product. He dismissed concerns that arose from time to time that oil would "run out." For Rockefeller, the biggest threat to oil's future was its chronic instability and the resulting price gyrations that cascaded from pell-mell drilling down through the transportation and refining and marketing segments.[44] Control and order were urgently needed to bring stability, he concluded, and that would require combining small firms into large ones that could regulate supply and investment in order to avoid the ruinous cycle of overproduction, price collapse, and price boom.

For the oil industry, the competitive free market was a recipe for chaos. Leonardo Maugeri noted:

> [Rockefeller's] world was not Adam Smith's. In Smith's world each person contributed to the overall progress of society by embarking on and competing in economic activities, while the steady working of an invisible hand corrected all imbalances. But Rockefeller . . . saw only the world as it was: a brutal blind struggle fueled by rapacity and greed. To his mind, there was no "invisible hand" at work behind this world, which—in the case of oil—was moved by irrational people, whose addiction to building castles in the air brought disaster on themselves and on the whole oil business.[45]

A massive new oil field discovered in Pithole Creek, Pennsylvania, in 1865 encouraged the twenty-five-year-old Rockefeller to shed his other business activities and exclusively focus his talents on the refining industry. Aided by his shrewd new partner Henry M. Flagler, Rockefeller's superior investment and management prowess catapulted him from Cleveland's largest refiner in 1865 to the owner of nearly all the city's refineries in less than a decade.

Yet just as with drillers, the problem of too many refiners—concentrated in two geographic centers, one inland (Pittsburgh, Cleveland, and the Oil Regions) and one in the seaboard cities of New York and New Jersey as well as Philadelphia—tormented the industry and preoccupied Rockefeller. Building and operating a refinery required more capital, technical skill, and business prowess than drilling, but it was still relatively simple.[46] By 1870, U.S. refining capacity exceeded crude production by a factor of three, and nearly all refineries were losing money.[47]

Transportation, on the other hand, was a much more difficult segment of the market to enter cheaply. At first, crude oil had been moved out of western Pennsylvania in wagons and barges, but these were soon replaced by the railroads. Railroad cars collected oil from terminals connected to wells by short-distance pipes called gathering lines. With the entry of railroads, the transportation of crude became a bulk business. Until long-distance pipelines began to proliferate and eventually dominate in the 1880s, railroad companies dominated the "midstream" or transportation segment of the industry. (In the oil industry's jargon, drillers constituted the "upstream," transportation the "midstream," and refining and marketing of refined products the "downstream" part of the business.)

Unlike drillers and even refiners, the number of railroads was very small and new entrants were limited. Their limited number and economies of scale gave railroads, vis-à-vis upstream producers and downstream refiners, enormous leverage and market power.[48] (Market power is a firm's ability to raise and sustain prices above levels that would prevail under competitive conditions.)

Drillers and refiners scrambled to secure reliable and competitive transportation. In those days railroads commonly granted "rebates"—lower than advertised fees—to customers who shipped in bulk. Drillers were too numerous and small to bargain successfully for rebates with railroads.

But refiners, fewer in number and operating at a much bigger scale, were able to obtain them. Favorable transportation prices were crucial for Cleveland—based refiners like Rockefeller, who were at a geographical disadvantage compared with their competitors in New York or the Oil Regions. They had to pay for two trips instead of one: One, to bring crude oil west from Pennsylvania to Cleveland's refineries, then another to send kerosene east to consumption centers and export terminals on the coast. So Cleveland relied on its numerous transportation linkages, for easy access to railroads and waterways.

After the Civil War, competition among refiners in Cleveland was stiff. Rockefeller owned the largest refineries, but he competed with almost fifty others, and even more in Pittsburgh.[49] Convinced that future success in the oil business required managing capacity and lowering costs by achieving economies of scale, Rockefeller and Flagler pursued a dual track strategy of absorbing or driving their competitors out by operating most efficiently and therefore, at lower costs, and of winning rebates from the railroads.

Rockefeller excelled at low-cost operating. He prioritized standardization and other efficiencies, produced his own barrels, and cut out middlemen by sending purchasers directly to the fields in Pennsylvania to purchase crude oil feedstock for their refineries. While sweating his refining competitors in Cleveland, Rockefeller warily eyed the railroads as a major risk and opportunity. The risk was oil drillers and railroads might unite and gang up on his refineries. If his refineries could cooperate with railroads, Rockefeller could not only drive less efficient refiners out of business more quickly, but also limit the flood of oil out of the Oil Regions, thereby stabilizing crude oil prices.

Rockefeller had good reason to fear the railroad barons, who recognized their market power stemming from oil's transportation bottleneck. While the refining industry was brand new, railroad companies shared a tumultuous history as fierce competitors but also occasionally as cartel operators in the passenger, livestock, and bulk goods markets (such as anthracite coal in the late 1860s and early 1870s). This cooperation took the form of "pooling agreements," which entailed dividing traffic (or revenues from traffic) according to market share agreements. In theory, every member of a transportation pool received a fair, guaranteed share of business in return for agreeing not to undercut others by slashing prices.[50] But these pooling agreements suffered from the same problem the new drillers faced—cheating. Railroad pools usually collapsed as the temptation by one or more members to cheat proved too alluring.

Thus, with the railroads more often competitors than collaborators, Rockefeller and Flagler's initial strategy was to deftly play one off against another by dangling the prospect of large, steady traffic in oil to and from Standard's growing network of refineries. In 1868, Rockefeller and Flagler quietly approached two railroad companies—Erie and a subsidiary of New York Central named Lake Shore—that were both archrivals of the Pennsylvania Railroad (which aimed to weaken Cleveland as a refining center). With a verbal agreement and handshake,[51] Rockefeller and Flagler won extremely favorable rebates from their Pennsylvania rivals. To ship crude oil to Cleveland and then refined oil to New York, Rockefeller paid only $1.65 per barrel compared to an officially listed rate of $2.40.[52] In return for the cheaper transportation fees, Rockefeller promised continuous high traffic and agreed to lower railroads' costs by investing in warehouses, loading platforms, and other rail shipment facilities.[53] Rebate deals like these greatly strengthened Standard's leverage in the refining business and enabled it to weaken and either acquire or destroy its competitors in subsequent years.[54] The Lake Shore deal made Rockefeller a titan in Cleveland, which soon overtook Pittsburgh as the main refining center. Rockefeller began to attract the notice of journalists and detractors, who would later make secret rebates a top political controversy.[55]

Even after Rockefeller and Flagler hammered down transportation costs, the problem of too much refining capacity remained. Just as excess capacity drove drillers try to form cartels, it drove beleaguered refiners into discussions. Rockefeller and his remaining Cleveland competitors met at a picnic in 1869 to discuss unifying against rival refiners in Pittsburgh as well as oil drillers, but little came of it. Rockefeller grew increasingly skeptical that cooperative attempts would work and became convinced that involuntary control by one supreme company would be required.[56]

Thus, in 1869 and 1870 Rockefeller, possessing "ceaseless enterprise, ceaseless vigilance, and ceaseless economy,"[57] set about an audacious plan to dominate the entire oil industry. The strategy was based on nearly complete monopolization of refining and cooperation with, if not direct control of, transportation. Rockefeller pursued the same dual track strategy he had used to date—leverage superior efficiency, combined with common if ruthless tactics of the day such as predatory price wars, threats, and intimidation, to absorb or ruin competitors while integrating with railroads that moved oil.

In 1870 he incorporated as Standard Oil Company (Ohio) and targeted competitors first in Cleveland, with ultimate sights on overtaking the New York, Philadelphia, and Pittsburgh markets. Aided by an economic depression in the early 1870s, Standard Oil swiftly succeeded in purchasing and shutting down small, inefficient refiners or driving them out of business. By April 1872 Standard Oil owned or controlled over one-quarter of the country's refining capacity.[58]

As Rockefeller was cementing his control over refining, downward pressure on prices raised the specter of financial ruin with which drillers, refiners, and railroads were by now uncomfortably familiar. In response to the economic pain, refiners, railroads, and drillers stepped up efforts to cooperate among and against each other.

By November 1871 the head of the Pennsylvania Railroad, Tom Scott, was promoting a plan for cooperation among his rivals at Erie and New York Central as well as a small number of refiners, including Rockefeller—somewhat ironic, since the railroad magnate had just tried but failed to ruin Rockefeller and other Cleveland refiners. But with Rockefeller openly working to capture the bulk of the nation's refining capacity, Scott had to work with him.

While leery of Scott, Rockefeller was willing to try cooperation to stabilize raucous Oil Regions. Scott proposed a scheme centered around the South Improvement Company (SIC). Railroads and refiners who joined the SIC would agree not to compete with each other by cutting prices, ensure each other a steady flow of oil, and charge nonmembers higher freight rates. This way the railroads would divide and share the freight market, with refiners acting as "eveners," that is, making sure each railroad member of the pool received its agreed share and steady flow of traffic.[59] In return for evening the flows of oil, refiners would get up to 50 percent rebates from railroads, as well as "drawbacks" or a share of the revenue that railroads received from non-SIC members who were forced to pay higher prices. As a bonus, railroad companies would provide member refiners with information about oil shipped by competitors—valuable intelligence that Standard and other member refiners could use to undercut their rivals.[60] SIC members were sworn to secrecy.[61] "All in all," Rockefeller biographer Ron Chernow noted, "it was an astonishing piece of knavery, grand-scale collusion such as American industry had never witnessed."[62]

At first, Scott hoped drillers could be enticed to join the SIC as well, expecting they would see the need to rein in supply to stabilize the industry. Rockefeller did not oppose cooperating with drillers in principle. His motivation in joining the SIC was less to depress crude oil prices and more to *stabilize* prices and investment returns.[63] But Rockefeller harbored doubts that masses of fractious, independent drillers could be corralled into a disciplined body—and his doubts, as it turned out, were justified. As SIC conspirators finished their secret negotiations in early 1872, western Pennsylvania drillers got wind and grew agitated. When the higher railroad freight rates were released in late February, drillers exploded in anger. Thousands of drillers and their supporters in Titusville, Oil City, and other parts of Pennsylvania's Oil Regions "stopped work and poured into the streets" in protest.[64]

Vowing to fight "monopoly with monopoly," angry oil drillers met under the auspices of the Petroleum Producers' Association of Pennsylvania and planned a counterattack.[65] The new union agreed "to start no new wells for two months, to stop work on Sundays," and most importantly, to sell no oil to companies participating in the SIC.[66] At first the embargo achieved some success, partly due to the threat of personal injury or property damage for anyone who defied it. Horseback patrols monitored against unsanctioned drilling. Crude shipments fell from 400,000 barrels in February 1872 to 276,000 in March. Cleveland and Pittsburgh refiners saw their supplies drop to a trickle.[67] Rockefeller was forced to temporarily lay off 90 percent of his refinery workers.[68]

Under this fierce pressure from the oil drillers, the SIC buckled and then collapsed at the end of March 1872. While victorious, Pennsylvania drillers brooded and kept a wary eye on Rockefeller, fearing another plot by his increasingly powerful Standard Oil conglomerate.

And indeed, immediately after the SIC unraveled, Rockefeller attempted to unite refiners. He and his partner Flagler visited their rivals in Pittsburgh and then Titusville to propose a National Refiners' Association with the purpose of collectively bargaining with the railroads and drillers. The so-called Pittsburgh Plan would establish a collective board to set prices, purchase and allocate all crude for refiners, and negotiate with railroads for freight rates.[69] Not all refiners liked the idea. Titusville refiners were especially skeptical, suspecting a gambit by big-city rivals to undercut the advantage of proximity they enjoyed. A regional newspaper editorial warned, "It is to be hoped [the Regions'] refiners will not allow themselves to be soft soaped by the honeyed words of the monopolists and conspirators."[70]

While most Oil Region refiners shunned the Pittsburgh Plan, Rockefeller won over a few of the most powerful. In August 1872 they established the National Refiners' Association, headed by Rockefeller and open to all refiners in not only Cleveland, but Pittsburgh, the Oil Regions, New York, and Philadelphia as well. However, the Association was riven by cheating and free riding, with members routinely exceeding their production quotas and nonmembers benefiting from higher prices without sharing the burden of limiting production. As the Refiners' Association struggled to get off the ground, Pennsylvania drillers were preparing to launch a scheme of their own to cut production and raise prices.

Encouraged[71] by their shattering victory over the SIC, the drillers were also motivated by yet another price bust, as large new oil discoveries in Clarion County, Pennsylvania, sent prices in the Oil Regions plunging to $3.67 in August of 1872, $1.13 lower than the prior year. Storage tanks and pipelines filled to capacity and some drillers resorted to dumping oil into rivers. Yet throngs of new drillers kept coming. Amidst the chaos and demoralization, desperate drillers decided to give cartelization another try, this time on a bigger scale.[72]

In late August 1872, operators, imbued with "crusading spirit,"[73] promised to stop drilling for six months beginning on September 1, 1872. Their intention was to prevent another 500 new wells from being drilled, calculating that—once older wells began to decline—overall production would fall from 5,000 to 3,000 barrels per day, resulting in crude oil prices back up to $5.00 per barrel. The Titusville *Courier* hailed the supply cuts as "the only true remedy to the great evil of overproduction."[74] Leaders of the Association toured the oil fields, securing a pledge from drillers to halt new drilling and to pay a fine of $2,000 for each new well they drilled.

There was just one problem: New drillers making big strikes in Clarion County refused to go along. Why, they asked, should they be required to forgo exploitation of their lucrative new finds just so earlier drillers could feast on higher revenues? And so drilling continued to rise unabated. Prices fell to $2.75 per barrel by mid-September.

Despondent, drillers agreed to stop producing from *existing* wells for thirty days. By the end of September, some three-quarters of existing wells stopped flowing. To enforce compliance, "toughs" were dispatched to noncompliant drillers to close wells by force, though drilling often resumed after enforcers departed. The *Pittsburgh Gazette* reported that "[w]ell rigs were burned and engines destroyed by sledge hammers, and oil tanks tapped."[75] Even with this heavy-handed regulation, compliance was not universal. A drilling firm in Triangle City, Lavens & Evans, sent a proclamation to the Association: "Resolved, that we don't care a damn!"[76]

The thirty-day shutdown movement achieved some success. Activity in the Oil Regions ground to a halt and production in September fell to 16,651 barrels per day (b/d) compared with 18,816 b/d in the prior month. In October supply fell to 14,308 b/d. But once the thirty-day embargo was lifted, production rose back to over 23,000 b/d. And as oil production rebounded, oil prices nosedived again.[77]

Producers went back to the drawing board in late October, quickly hatching a new cartel scheme. The head of the Petroleum Producers' Association proposed a Petroleum Producers' Agency, which would be capitalized with $1,000,000 and would buy as much oil as necessary in order to raise prices to $5.00 per barrel. Excess oil would be stored in tanks the Agency would control. The Agency would also consider "such measures as may be practicable, necessary and lawful to prevent the drilling of oil wells" while allowing wells under construction to be completed when demand permanently exceeded supply and investing in local refining capacity to soak up excess supply if necessary.[78] In other words, the Agency would try to establish a total monopoly on the production, storage, and even refining of crude oil in the Pennsylvania Oil Region. The proposed Agency would also collect and share data, so drillers could understand market conditions better than speculators, the railroads, and refiners.

By the end of October 1872 organizers had raised some $200,000 in capital. When they gathered on November 6, confidence was high that the Petroleum Producer Agency scheme would work. *The Petroleum Centre Daily Record* of Cornplanter, Pennsylvania, exulted, "[W]e shall soon have the pleasure of announcing—'Oil, Five Dollars per Barrel!' and an appropriate obituary notice of the death of the Refiner's Combination alias South Improvement Co."[79] Oil consumers and refiners in New York that had been gleefully gorging on cheap oil grew concerned at signs the restive drillers might this time succeed at limiting supply and raising prices.

Notwithstanding the animosity Oil Region drillers felt toward refiners, some refiners—including Rockefeller—strongly supported efforts by the drillers to control production and stabilize crude prices. While, naturally, refiners preferred a lower crude oil price, hard experience with wild boom-bust prices induced them to desire price *stability* above all. Though they had just fought a nasty "oil war," many refiners and drillers realized cooperation of some form was necessary to achieve this stability.[80] The failed SIC reflected an attempt by railroads and refiners to collude. Now refiners and drillers were willing to try it. The two shared a loathing for speculators—middlemen who traded in early versions of oil futures contracts and who, drillers and refiners believed, were distorting oil prices and adding to volatility.[81] By negotiating a mutually agreeable price and enforcing production discipline, refiners and producers hoped to cut out the speculators and finally usher in the stability they cherished.

Thus, Rockefeller enthusiastically responded to the formation of the producers' new cartel, sending its leadership a message of goodwill, and ordering one of his buyers to buy crude from the new Agency at $4.75 per barrel.[82] By December 1872 Rockefeller and his new Refiners' Association reached an agreement with the producers, dubbed the "Treaty of Titusville." Under the terms, the Producers' Agency agreed to limit crude oil production to around 15,000 barrels per day and to sell exclusively to the Refiner's Association, which in turn would exclusively buy from the Agency. Refiners would pay drillers $5 per barrel, $4 immediately and the balance conditionally, depending on the retail prices of the refined product sold in New York. If New York kerosene went for less than 26 cents a gallon (equal to $11 per barrel) refiners would pay the Agency $4 per barrel, but for every penny refined products sold for above 26 cents a gallon producers would receive an additional 25 cents per barrel up to $5 per barrel ceiling.[83]

But just as the Treaty of Titusville was inked, discipline among producers once again collapsed and wild drilling resumed. Supply began an upward march toward 22,000 b/d, far above the promised 15,000 b/d. Oversupply obliged refiners and drillers to reduce the $4.00 per barrel price floor to $3.25 per barrel. Rockefeller duly put in orders for $3.25, but cash-strapped well owners started offering discounted prices of $2 per barrel to buyers outside the agreement.[84] Boston refiners had been excluded from the Treaty of Titusville and vowed to buy oil from independent producers at prices below the $3.25 target. By January 1873 public market prices had fallen to $3.29 per barrel, with some producers selling oil for as little as $2.60.[85] On January 14, 1873, the *Titusville Herald*, decrying overproduction and glutted oil inventories, pleaded on behalf of small producers for a "summary, decisive, continuous, and universal shutting down of the entire production for sixty days."[86] But such discipline was beyond the means of an industry numbering some 10,000 operators.

Rockefeller attended raucous producer meetings and was disgusted by their indiscipline and refusal to respect covenants. He later recalled a meeting at which a tobacco-chewing producer was asked to explain why he sold over the agreed limit and said: "Well, I thought it would be a fair commercial transaction!"[87] Depressed at disunity and treachery, the producers threw in the towel in the middle of January, declaring the Treaty of Titusville null and void.

Voluntary efforts by desperate drillers in the Oil Regions to control supply would extend through the 1880s. Some would achieve very short-lived success but each would end in defeat. There were too many new finds and too many eager drillers. The lure of profits from sunken wells and the payoff for new ones was far too great. "It was evident," Rockefeller biographer Nevins wrote, "that only a comprehensive, highly centralized, and permanent organization could control the glut in the market."[88]

Refiners had no more success in organizing themselves than producers. By 1873 the Refiners' Association itself was too small and weak to exert discipline and control dissolved. Instability returned to the entire oil industry. Rockefeller now discarded any hope of voluntary combination with drillers and transporters, and resolved to proceed with what he called "our plan." First envisioned back in 1869–1870, the strategy called for monopoly control and hard economic pressure to consolidate refiners in one single organization and integrate with transportation. The entire system would be supervised by a core group of managers who, not incidentally, could get rich in the process. As Nevins wrote, Rockefeller's "imagination had shown him that if the amorphous, overdeveloped, wasteful refining industry, prolific of bankruptcies and ruin, could be unified and firmly controlled, it might become an efficient source of wealth to the small group which reorganized it."[89]

To expand Standard Oil's empire beyond Cleveland to New York and other states, Rockefeller used the same tactics he perfected in Cleveland. Whether targeting firms for horizontal or vertical consolidation, Rockefeller typically tried persuasion first, imploring their leaders to sell or merge (often rewarding them with positions in Standard Oil), or—with independent refiners—striking agreements whereby he would guarantee a profit if they limited output during periods of overproduction. Producers and refiners who did not work with his system found themselves priced out of the market. He would obtain a critical mass of ownership or control in a particular market, and then leverage it to pressure remaining companies to fold.

As he had in Cleveland, Rockefeller skillfully and decisively leveraged his superior management and organization skills, while again resorting to industrial espionage, predatory pricing, and secret and deceptive ownership of ostensible competitors. He and his associates exploited rivalries and weaknesses among refiners and railroads. By 1879, Standard Oil controlled over 90 percent of the entire refining sector in the United States.

Standard Oil's growing presence as a monopoly began to exert itself on crude production and prices. Its leverage over ownership, or control of notoriously rivalrous railroads and the large-diameter pipelines that by the 1880s had superseded railcars as the principal means to transport crude, enabled Standard Oil to jam producers, forcing them to cut excessive supply. In some instances, Standard Oil–affiliated pipelines would refuse to transport crude oil from drillers unless the driller had already secured a buyer or had adequate storage, both of which were often beyond the means of the unlucky producer and both of which were, in some cases, controlled by Standard Oil.[90] Rockefeller refused to buy excess crude supply in the Oil Region, and at times of oversupply his refineries would curtail production to maintain product prices.

Despite these aggressive tactics, Standard's relationship with oil drillers was not always adversarial. From November 1887 to November 1888 they cooperated in what became known as the "Great Shutdown Movement," one of the early period's most successful voluntary efforts by drillers and refiners to curtail supply and stabilize prices.[91] Rockefeller suppressed his deep distrust of drillers partly because he himself was starting to get into the drilling business. The continued glut of Pennsylvania oil threatened Standard Oil's new investments in massive—but sulfurous and therefore relatively costly to process—oil fields in Lima, Ohio. And Rockefeller faced growing competition from foreign crude supplies, especially from Russia. As usual, Oil Region drillers clamored for relief from low oil prices. Thus, for once Rockefeller and the oil drillers were united on the need not just to stabilize prices, but to raise them.[92]

Under the terms Standard Oil signed with the organization representing the producers, drillers would stop drilling new wells and take other steps to cut supply from 60,000 to under 45,000 barrels per day. In return, Standard Oil would buy and store crude to be sold later at higher prices, sharing part of the proceeds with drillers thrown out of work by the shutdown. The Great Shutdown Movement lasted for one year and was a success. Some 85 percent of the Oil Region's 14,000 drillers took part; while new producers in Washington and Greene counties added production, overall supply fell to the 45,000 barrels per day target. Prices rose from 70 cents per barrel to 90 cents per barrel during the same period.[93] The yearlong agreement won Rockefeller and Standard Oil some uncommon friends and praise among producers. As intended, the shutdown achieved its dual aim of reducing the near-term glut of oil and raising prices which in turn made it profitable to invest in new fields that came onstream in the 1890s—such as Standard Oil in Ohio.

If convenient, the alliance between Standard and Pennsylvania drillers was also temporary. Crude oil prices started declining in 1890, falling to between 50 and 60 cents per barrel in the early 1890s. Standard Oil and the drillers went their separate ways—Standard Oil put its new Ohio crude on the market and Pennsylvania drillers decided "to compete with Standard Oil by developing their own transport, refining, and marketing organization."[94]

STANDARD OIL'S IMPACT ON PRICE STABILITY

By the mid-1880s, Standard Oil dominated all aspects of the oil business, from crude production to the marketing of refined products.[95] The order and stability Rockefeller imposed on the oil industry enabled it to enormously grow in the United States and increasingly in nascent markets in Europe and Asia. Monopolization of refining and vertical integration with railroads and pipelines sufficed to indirectly limit the flow of oil from the wells and thereby abolish pre-Standard Oil boom-and-bust price cycles, even if Rockefeller's control was insufficient to solely set oil prices or entirely eliminate oil price volatility.[96] During the twenty-one years preceding Standard Oil's dominance, crude oil prices gyrated on average about 53 percent per year (figure 1.1).[97] During Rockefeller's period of control, prices fluctuated by about half as much—24 percent. Of course, consumers paid a higher price for oil than they would have under pure competition—but since oil prices fell on trend during the Rockefeller era, the public did not notice what it was missing.

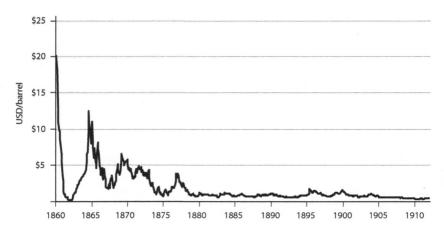

FIGURE 1.1

Monthly U.S. crude oil prices, 1860–1911.

Sources: Derrick's, vols. I–IV; API, *Petroleum Facts and Figures* (1959). © The Rapidan Group.

Rockefeller's empire centered on refining, transportation, and—indirectly—crude oil production in Pennsylvania, the northeastern states, and later the Midwest. But by the turn of the century, crude oil production was fast spreading nationally and globally to areas outside Standard Oil's reach into Texas and Oklahoma, where Standard Oil was not welcome.

The discovery in 1901 of Spindletop, a monster gusher near Beaumont, Texas, by a tenacious prospector named Pattillo Higgins, marked a watershed in the history of the oil industry. Flowing at 100,000 barrels per day, the great Spindletop gusher launched the Texas oil boom as well as two famous companies, Gulf and Texaco. While overdrilling caused Spindletop to dry up in a year, other enormous new finds soon followed in Texas and Oklahoma. The arrival of massive Texas and Oklahoma oil fields dispelled perennial concerns in the oil industry that domestic oil supplies might "run out."

While new competition emerged in Texas, international threats to Standard Oil's dominance mounted. Texas and Oklahoma discoveries also propelled the United States ahead of Russia, which had briefly overtaken the United States as the world's top producer. In the early 1870s, large-scale oil production began in what was then Russian Baku, in current-day Azerbaijan, on the shores of the Caspian Sea. Robert and Ludwig Nobel, the Swedish brothers of dynamite-inventor Alfred, quickly developed Baku-based oil production and refining and became a major supplier to Czarist Russia. Initially limited by Baku's distant location and the absence of large-scale tankers, the French Rothschild family stepped in to finance a railway west to the Black Sea in the 1880s that would enable Russian oil to compete with Standard Oil for the kerosene market in Europe. Baku proved extraordinarily prolific; production rose tenfold between 1879 and 1889, when it amounted to 57 percent of U.S. production.[98] Just like their western Pennsylvania counterparts, Baku well owners scrambled to find new markets for their massive finds.

Alarmed by the threat from these large oil discoveries overseas, Rockefeller's typical first instinct was to buy his foreign challengers. Standard Oil tried to come to terms with the Nobels, but were rebuffed.[99] Having failed, Standard engaged the Russians in a brutal price war—the same strategy it adopted at home when it wanted to give the competition a sweat. To end the bloodshed during what became known as the "oil wars" in the 1890s, Rockefeller's Standard Oil attempted to come to terms with its Russian rivals—companies owned by the Nobel family, the Rothschild family, and others. In 1892 and 1893 a deal involving all U.S. and Russian companies fell through when Standard Oil could not secure support of all independent U.S. refineries and producers. After a price war in 1894, Standard Oil and its Russian competitors tried again in 1895. They inked a deal that would grant American producers "75 percent of the world export sales, the Russians 25 percent." But before the agreement could become effective, the deal collapsed apparently due to objections from the Russian government.[100] Voluntary efforts to combine were proving just as difficult internationally as they had at home.

Meanwhile, another major threat to Standard Oil's global dominance was brewing in Asia. London-based trader Marcus Samuel won the right to sell Russian oil in Asia, designing ingenious tanker ships that could cut costs, especially when routed through the newly opened Suez Canal. Samuel's company, named Shell in honor of his father who had sold ornate shell gift boxes, declared total war against Standard Oil; the two companies were soon pouring resources into refining and distribution infrastructure in order to capture market share.[101]

Standard Oil and Shell actively sought to acquire stakes and develop large oil fields in Asia, closer to consuming markets. Both eyed a promising oil-producing venture based in Sumatra, in the Dutch East Indies, called Royal Dutch. This company was led in 1900 by hard-charging Dutch banker Henri Deterding. Deterding had a lot of crude oil near lucrative Asian markets, but he needed to integrate with firms with marketing networks. Like Rockefeller, Deterding loathed price competition and was open to combination. Shell opted to combine with Royal Dutch, though largely on the latter's terms. Initially Shell's head Marcus Samuel did not want to surrender too much operational control of his firm, but Royal Dutch preferred joint management and their negotiator, Fred Lane, convinced Samuel that such a joint management was necessary to avoid ruinous oversupply of oil. Once again fear of oversupply and price collapses helped shape one of the oil industry's momentous alliances. Shell and Royal Dutch agreed to joint management in 1901 and eventually amalgamated into the Royal Dutch Shell Group in 1907. The new powerhouse was financially backed by the Rothschild family, who pressed to be part of this new "offensive and defensive alliance" against the Standard Oil empire. Soon after the merger, Shell head Deterding ordered production declines and imposed quotas to prevent oversupply in the Dutch East Indies.[102]

But for Standard Oil, the biggest threat came neither from Texas nor Shell, but from Washington. In turn-of-the-century progressive America, monopolies and trusts—large business combinations—that had sprung up after the Civil War were the subject of widespread public distrust and scrutiny. Monopolies were (and remain) unpopular because they raise prices, restrict competition, produce inferior goods, resist and prevent innovation, and enrich a small number of owners. (Some industries are considered "natural monopolies" if they have high entry costs, or provide a good whose price the government wishes to regulate, or if one big firm is more economically efficient. Examples include water or electric utilities, which are usually state-owned or regulated.) Industrialization and the expansion of transportation in the mid-to-late 1800s spawned many monopolies, and by the end of the century the public was pushing back.

Trusts had been devised as a workaround for large corporations that operated across state lines—like railroads and oil industries—because, in late nineteenth-century America, there was no federal incorporation law and states generally restricted companies from owning out-of-state enterprises. Such corporate trusts, holding interests in dozens of companies through a complex system of equity holdings and control, were often established secretly. The nation's first was spearheaded by none other than Rockefeller, whose lawyer Samuel C.T. Dodd came up with a plan to secretly establish the Standard Oil Trust in 1882.[103] Under the trust agreement, all of Standard Oil's burgeoning affiliates, acquisitions, and assets would be held in trust of a committee of nine trustees. By having nine trustees, including Rockefeller, hold the assets of the Standard Oil empire in common, they could legally claim no single company owned any other. But as a practical manner, the trust agreement brought the Standard Oil empire under clear, uniform direction and control.[104]

The public and elected officials regarded trusts as monopolistic conspiracies. Anger and scrutiny started in earnest in the late 1870s. The initial targets were railroads, which attracted notice and suspicion because they colluded with many industries besides oil, including meat and salt packers. Media reports of rebates and other widespread anticompetitive

practices incited public attention, and by the mid-1880s Standard Oil—
not only the country's first but also its biggest trust—came into the
crosshairs.

John D. Rockefeller was pilloried as "the father of trusts, the king of
monopolists, the czar of the oil business."[105] Trusts in industries like lumber or machinery were at a distance from the public, but Standard Oil
was well-known to the late nineteenth-century consumer: it sold common and essential goods like kerosene and ointments for use in everyday
households. Oil was familiar, and so was Standard. As media vilification
of Rockefeller intensified, familiarity turned into contempt. Even Standard Oil's supporters acknowledged secret operations, cooperation with
railroads (including launching predatory price wars in certain markets
to ruin competition), and the employment of spies to gather intelligence
against competitors.[106]

State and federal officials started probing Standard Oil's activities. In
February 1888, the New York Senate's Trust Investigation Committee
called Rockefeller and his associates to testify, though the probe ended
inconclusively. In April 1888, after lambasting the sugar industry, a House
of Representatives trust-investigating committee trained its sights on
Standard Oil. Though Rockefeller was treated with respect and no new
laws resulted directly from the investigation, the House committee generally sided with the litany of complaints from producers, refiners, and
small distributors who had chafed under Standard Oil's market domina-
tion. Testimony about Standard Oil's large profits, coercive tactics, and
secrecy stoked public ire, prompting congressional action. Many states
strengthened laws against tricky business activities and both candidates in
the Cleveland-Harrison 1888 presidential election campaign denounced
trusts. In 1889 Senator John Sherman introduced a bill "to declare unlaw-
ful, trusts and combinations in restraint of trade and production."[107]
President Harrison signed the Sherman Antitrust Act into law in 1890, at
which point there were some fifty trusts operating in the United States—
but Standard Oil was viewed as the main culprit.

Ohio declared the Standard Oil Trust illegal in 1892, forcing Rockefeller
and associates to reorganize. In 1899, Standard Oil reestablished headquarters in New Jersey to take advantage of the state's accommodative

holding company laws. But while turning from a trust to holding company resolved immediate legal issues, it hardly lessened the intensity of its critics. Rockefeller's ruthless (although then commonplace) business practices had spawned legions of aggrieved parties over the years. None did more to tarnish Rockefeller's reputation and precipitate Standard Oil's downfall than the forceful journalist Ida M. Tarbell.

Tarbell was raised in the western Pennsylvania oil towns of Titusville and Pithole, and was the daughter and sister of independents stung by Standard Oil. She became Rockefeller's nemesis; her book tracing the life of Rockefeller and the history of the Standard Oil Company, serialized in *McClure's* magazine starting in November 1902, "turned America's most private man into its most public and hated figure."[108] Tarbell charged Rockefeller with debasing American business morality.[109] Her devastating critique hit the public just as furor against trusts and robber barons was peaking and "became the most spectacularly successful example of 'muckraking' journalism" during the Progressive Era.[110]

Rockefeller was also the ideal bogeyman for progressive leader Theodore Roosevelt, who became president upon President McKinley's assassination in 1901. Roosevelt excoriated Standard Oil and between 1906 and 1909 targeted it with several investigations, winning some prosecutions.[111] In November 1906 the Roosevelt administration sued the Standard Oil Company of New Jersey, other corporations it allegedly controlled, and seven individuals—including Rockefeller—for conspiring to control the oil industry by restraining interstate trade. While legal proceedings reaching the Supreme Court would drag on for five years, the game was over for Standard Oil. As Rockefeller biographer Nevins noted, by this time "[t]he Roosevelt administration, the officials of a dozen states, and the great majority of the American people had decided that the [Standard Oil of New Jersey] combination was a pernicious monopoly and must be broken up."[112] In 1911, the Supreme Court ordered Rockefeller's trust dissolved, breaking it up into thirty-four separate companies.[113] Among the notable "children" of Standard Oil were Standard Oil of New Jersey (today's ExxonMobil), Standard Oil of New York (Mobil, which later merged with Exxon), Standard Oil of California (Chevron), and Standard Oil of Indiana (Amoco, later acquired by BP).

THE PRICE OF STABILITY

Crude oil prices were doubtless more stable during the Rockefeller era than before. But the extensiveness of Rockefeller's influence over crude oil prices is debatable. The percentage change between the lowest and highest monthly average price, within each year between 1859 and 1879 averaged 53 percent. But during Rockefeller's reign, the percentage change was only 24 percent (see figure 1.2). Subsequent and contemporary historians also credit Rockefeller and Standard Oil with heavily influencing the amount and price of crude oil from the Oil Regions that was refined and marketed.[114] Rockefeller's influence over crude production and prices was mostly indirect, because Standard Oil never dominated crude production as it did refining and transportation, but Rockefeller did enjoy powerful leverage through his ability to change the cost of storing oil in the pipelines and storage tanks he controlled.[115] If he wished to counter a rising price

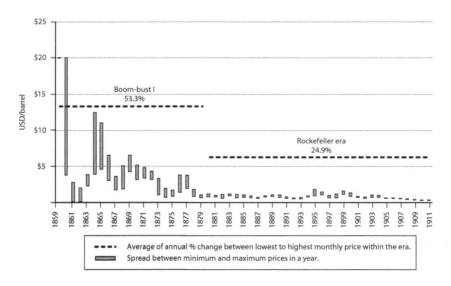

FIGURE 1.2

Annual ranges of monthly U.S. crude oil prices, 1859–1911.

Sources: Derrick's, vols. I–IV; API, *Petroleum Facts and Figures* (1959). © The Rapidan Group.

trend he could lower storage costs, inducing drillers to produce and store more oil. In periods of oversupply, he could raise storage costs or limit storage availability, leaving hapless drillers with little choice but to throttle back production.

Ida Tarbell described Rockefeller's influence over crude oil prices as at times dictatorial. "[B]y virtue of [Standard's] monopoly of the business of refining and transportation of oil," Tarbell concluded, the trust "had been at times almost the only buyers in the market, and at such times had been enabled to dictate and establish a price for crude oil far below its actual value."[116] As biographer Ron Chernow noted, Tarbell overstates Rockefeller's influence: "We must retire one common canard about Rockefeller: He didn't set crude oil prices through blanket edicts."[117]

It is impossible to know if technology, law, or patterns of oil production and demand would have developed toward a more stable oil business in the absence of Rockefeller. What we do know is that the oil industry was prone to intense instability, creating an impulse toward integration, and that prices were more stable during periods of production control.

Did Rockefeller use his power to keep oil prices high, stable, or both? In designing and executing "our plan," Rockefeller arguably showed more concern with *stable* prices than high ones. He agreed to pay the Petroleum Producer Agency's above market price of $3.25 per barrel in 1872 in support of its brief attempt to cartelize production. And just as crude oil prices were more stable under Rockefeller than they had been before (and, as we shall see, afterward), kerosene prices were both more stable and lower than in the pre-Rockefeller period, falling from 45 cents (without taxes) to roughly 6 cents per gallon from 1863 to the mid-1890s.[118] Remarkably, price stability occurred despite the size of the kerosene market exploding domestically and internationally, from zero in 1859 to sixty million barrels per year by the end of the century.[119] While oil use was expanding rapidly, industry continually achieved cost savings by introducing new technologies and becoming more efficient, especially in bulk transport methods such as pipelines and larger capacity railcars and tankers. That said, in the early 1900s a Bureau of Corporations report concluded most of the fall in kerosene prices stemmed from falling crude prices, not Standard Oil's efficient management of the refining sector.[120]

Whatever the cause, Chernow noted in 1998, "In general, Standard Oil did an excellent job at providing kerosene at affordable prices . . . [which] inoculated the public for a long time against the anti-standard venom."[121] Rockefeller's preference for low kerosene prices did not stem from altruism but instead from his obsession with being the big, low-cost supplier who dominated market share.[122] While as a monopoly Standard Oil sold high and low, on balance Chernow concluded "the trust wielded its monopolistic power to keep prices artificially low to forestall competition."[123]

Standard Oil was destroyed because of antipathy toward trusts, Standard's hardball business practices, and the extreme unpopularity of its founder, not its results in terms of making wildly popular petroleum products available to consumers at generally stable—often declining—prices.

2

NO ROCKEFELLER, NO PEACE

Boom-Bust Returns

The breakup of Standard Oil in 1911 marked a milestone in the history of the oil industry, but its importance was rivaled if not exceeded by a sweeping transformation in how oil was being used. For the fifty years after Drake's first commercial well in 1859, oil was primarily valued for kerosene for lighting, with lubrication a close second. But when running crude oil through their stills, early refiners could not avoid producing some lighter, more flammable gasoline, regarded as less valuable because it had fewer commercial applications (solvents and limited use in home cooking and portable space heaters) than kerosene.

But late nineteenth-century innovations involving electricity, the incandescent light bulb, and the internal combustion engine shifted oil's main use from lighting to transportation. Significantly improved by Thomas A. Edison in 1879, electric bulbs started being used commercially in 1880, and Edison opened the first electric power station in New York in 1882. Electric illumination provided better light than oil or natural gas, and without the dangers of an open flame. Electricity could also be used safely where oil could not, including in places like "flour mills, chemical plants, libraries, and even petroleum refineries."[1] However, the proliferation of electric generators and transmission lines took more than two decades, slowing kerosene's replacement with electricity until well into the twentieth century.

As one door closed for oil, another was opening. In 1885, German engineer Gottlieb Daimler and his partner Wilhelm Maybach patented the first gasoline-powered prototype of modern internal combustion engines still in use today. The following year the German inventors built the world's first four-wheel automobile, and Rudolf Diesel introduced the first diesel engine in 1897. Improvements and expansions followed quickly, with Europe taking the lead and the United States lagging by about a decade. France began commercial scale manufacturing of automobiles in 1890 and the United States began after the turn of the century, with Oldsmobile selling 425 cars in 1901.

At first, it appeared that oil would lose out to older steam or new electric engines in the new personal vehicle business. Steam-powered cars were built in the late 1890s but proved only moderately popular as they suffered from a variety of technical challenges, including an inability to operate below freezing temperatures. Streetcars and railroads had been adapted to electric use, and the first electric car was demonstrated in 1884. While pleasingly quiet, smooth, and easy to operate, the electric car suffered from one major pitfall that remains to this day: limited range.

Thus, early inventors soon concluded that internal combustion engines running on liquid fuels were the most practical for automobiles. Liquid fuels packed more energy and could be more easily stored and transported than electric batteries. Among liquid fuels, gasoline's chief competitor was ethanol, an alcohol obtained from fermented sugars and starches. While alcohol had been widely used as fuel in lamps and engines, it was more expensive than gasoline, even after the Civil War tax was lifted in 1906. Gasoline was also superior to alcohol fuels because it took less energy to produce and contained more energy per unit of volume.

In the automobile's early days, scientists worried that oil would not be plentiful enough to support a mass vehicle market, and Henry Ford envisioned cars he would begin mass producing in 1908 would run on ethanol. But Spindletop and other massive new finds in Texas and Oklahoma helped convince the burgeoning automobile industry that oil supplies were plentiful enough to serve as a reliable fuel source. Oil was headed for vehicle engines.

Whereas kerosene had been the most prized product obtained from refining crude oil during the industry's first fifty years (and as noted above gasoline was considered a dangerous and useless byproduct), henceforth, gasoline would be the most prized product of an oil refinery in the United States.

Oil's first major transportation use was in ships. Shell's founder Marcus Samuel strongly promoted oil, and began converting Shell's tankers from coal to fuel oil in the late 1890s. In addition to Spindletop in 1901, the discoveries of large new oil supplies in California and Mexico around the turn of the century convinced shipping interests to convert vessels to oil;[2] the opening of the Panama Canal in 1914 swelled maritime trade, with fuel plentiful on both coasts.[3]

U.S. Navy officials had also considered switching from coal to fuel oil, but progress was slow. The idea had come up during the Civil War, when the Union navy realized it would confer several tactical advantages. Fuel oil's higher density and thermal efficiency enabled warships to remain at sea longer and operate more independently; while refueling coal-powered vessels required port stops, oil-powered ships could be refueled while at sea. Fuel oil was also much easier to store and manage; up to three-quarters of the crew of coal-fired ships were needed to carry fuel from storage to the furnaces—a drawback that was especially onerous during longer battles.[4] Finally, oil-powered ships could travel faster and carry more cargo than their coal-fired counterparts; however, early evaluations concluded fuel oil was too costly. It was not until 1913 that Winston Churchill convinced Britain's navy to switch from coal to oil, and the U.S. Navy soon followed suit.[5]

While ships got the jump on oil use, automobiles quickly caught up and soon became the dominant users of oil in the transportation sector. Henry Ford, with the introduction of the assembly line and interchangeable parts, made the first mass-produced, affordable cars and catapulted the United States to the top of the world's automobile producers and consumers. The Model-T appeared in 1908; in 1910, gasoline sales outpaced kerosene and other illuminant products for the first time. The amount of gasoline refined from a barrel of crude oil (the "yield") increased from 10 percent in 1880 to 35 percent in 1926. Over the same period, the average yield of kerosene fell from 75 percent to 8 percent.[6]

NEW "GUSHERS" AND RISING INDUSTRY CONCERN WITH OIL "WASTE"

While demand for oil shifted to the booming transportation sector, on the supply side the industry success at finding new oil continued unabated.

The geographic expansion of large new oil production was greatly aided by the invention of rotary drilling, which replaced old boring techniques.[7] While Pennsylvanian fields were in decline by the turn of the century, new oil was being discovered and produced all over the country.

The gargantuan Spindletop discovery in 1901 put Texas on the world's oil map. Within five years, prolific new wells sprouted up in a 100-mile radius of Spindletop, including in the oil-infused underground salt domes of Louisiana. Oil wells in the Gulf states tended to produce a lot of oil initially but then quickly decline. But just as these Gulf state fields were starting to taper, new finds to the north in Kansas and Oklahoma started up, making the midcontinent the top-producing region by 1919. California's production, meanwhile, grew sixfold between 1900 and 1903 and doubled between 1907 and 1911. As noted earlier, oil production soared in Mexico after 1910, much of it for export to the United States; Mexican oil amounted to less than 1 percent of U.S. production in 1911, but rose to 14 percent by 1919.[8]

The large new oil finds put downward pressure on crude oil and refined product prices. Consumers were delighted, but drillers dismayed. The combination of large new discoveries and the weakening of Standard Oil's firm grip on refining and transportation made oil price plunges more frequent. The oil industry, two Cornell professors wrote, was butting up against "the stubborn economic fact that continued to plague the industry after the 1911 [Standard Oil] dissolution . . . there was no foretelling when a new well or a new field would be discovered and there was no way, short of monopoly, to curb the flow of oil once its presence had been revealed."[9] Crude oil prices fell by about one-third from 1913 to 1915. Drillers again became "demoralized by a superabundance of oil."[10]

Standard Oil Trust was dead, and the old ghost of price instability was returning to haunt the industry. Too much oil was coming out of the ground too fast. The same problems that had traumatized early Pennsylvania drillers remained. Exploration and production remained open to new entrants big and small now equipped with better technology and improved exploration and production methods. Small and independent drillers did not have deep pockets and required quick payback. "Wildcatters"—prospectors who drilled wells in places where there was no obvious indication of the presence of oil—drilled as fast and as often as cash would allow

NO ROCKEFELLER, NO PEACE

and bridled at any interference with their quest for the next opportunity. Larger, better-capitalized drillers could afford to sit on their oil longer and were more open to production restraint; however, relentless wildcatters kept finding and bringing on new supplies, causing prices to crash.

After Standard Oil's demise in 1911, drillers and oil state officials scrambled to find an answer to the unwelcome return of price busts. They had to find a way to restrain supply growth. Industry could not do it alone. Cartels were illegal and the industry's practices were now carefully policed by state and federal antitrust authorities.

At first, both industry and government ruled out any form of supply control for the explicit purpose of regulating prices. That would violate cherished free-market principles and confer excessive power on either industry or government. So they found another justification to restrict supply: to prevent waste and promote conservation. How industry and officials defined and viewed these terms played a significant role in shaping early efforts to stabilize oil prices, and requires some elaboration.

In the opening decades of the oil industry, state and federal regulation was limited to the protection of drillers' property and safety improvements to refined petroleum products. To protect property owners from being blackmailed or ruined by unscrupulous drillers threatening to flood their wells from adjacent boreholes, well tubing and plugging regulation was proposed in Venango County, Pennsylvania, in 1867 (although it did not become law until 1878).[11] Other states enacted similar measures. To promote safety, rules set minimum ignition or "flash point" temperatures for kerosene and prescribed kerosene storage zoning and construction.[12]

At the federal level, officials were chiefly concerned with husbanding supplies for federal use by preventing production on some federal lands— a friction between western producers and Washington that lasts through today. In September 1909 President Taft ordered three million acres of oil-bearing federal lands in California and Wyoming be reserved for federal use, cheering the U.S. military but angering western oil producers. With Standard Oil dethroned, the public's attention moved on to supervision of business practices such as the regulation of child labor and sanitary standards in the food industry.[13]

Although safety and property protection were the primary objectives of early regulation, some industry experts were concerned that rampant drilling wasted valuable resources.[14] This early definition of waste concerned *physical* waste through evaporation, overflow, or dissipation of underground gas pressure that left oil unrecoverable. Some warned (rightly so, as geologists later confirmed) that frenzied drilling could permanently decrease the amount of recoverable oil.[15] As early as 1861, some drillers fretted that excessive drilling would soon exhaust oil supplies and bring the oil industry to a crashing halt.[16] Waves of what today is called "peak oil" fear occasionally swept through the industry. But neither peak oil nor waste worries held sway for long or led to regulation in the early decades.[17]

After the turn of the century and amid general interest in regulations to improve industry practices, mounting government focus on conservation of resources dovetailed with growing industry concerns that rampant competition and overproduction destabilized oil markets and prices. For their part, drillers were more concerned with *economic* waste in the form of financial losses due to price crashes. Peak oil worries picked up as oil's importance in transportation grew.[18]

Thus, government anxieties about conserving resources and industry's worry about ruinous price decreases converged on a dual definition of waste—physical and economic. With this shared concern, conservation and stability became intertwined and the tone of government-industry relations turned less adversarial and more cooperative. Government and industry drew closer in a search of a solution for a common problem.

As usual, the discovery of prolific new oil wells drove events. The development of Oklahoma's enormous Glenn Pool, first discovered in 1905, prompted local crude oil producers to petition the state legislature to prevent unmarketable surpluses and waste. The Oklahoma Corporation Commission (OCC), a state government body established in 1907 to regulate businesses whose activities were deemed essential to public welfare (like transportation and electric transmission companies), held hearings on the link between fast flowing or "flush" new production and plummeting prices. The result was an OCC order that Glenn Pool oil be priced at no less than 65 cents per barrel. With no enforcement mechanism, the order was ignored, but the move presaged subsequent state regulation in coming decades.[19] Indeed, when the bountiful Cushing field started flush production in the state in 1912 followed by the Healdton field in 1913, Oklahoma's oil industry spiraled into crisis.[20] Oklahoma producers banded together in an Independent Producers League in April 1914 to pressure state authorities for control. The OCC responded in May 1914 by issuing the first of what it called "proration" orders or production quotas (henceforth I will refer to proration orders as quotas) on oil purchased from the Healdton and Cushing fields.

The OCC had no direct legal authority to regulate oil production, so it relied on applying a general antitrust statute to pipelines by prohibiting the purchase of oil from the two fields at less than a fixed price.[21] But in 1915, the state enacted an oil and gas conservation act authorizing the OCC to restrict production whenever it deemed that "waste was evident in a particular field," or that oil demand was insufficient relative to supply, or that prices had fallen below production costs.[22] The act thus recognized both definitions of waste: physical and economic. This noteworthy statute marked the first attempt by government officials to use public policy to stabilize oil prices by directly regulating the output from oil wells. Arkansas followed Oklahoma's lead, enacting a conservation statute prohibiting underground waste in 1923.[23]

While unprecedented in reach, the Oklahoma law was toothless and weakly enforced. State oil companies initially clamored for supply controls after the Healdton and Cushing field startups triggered a price bust. But subsequently oil drillers grew divided on the need for prorationing, with their position largely driven by whether they stood to gain a commercial advantage.[24] OCC officials, for their part, found it difficult to enforce prorationing orders. There were too many operators, economic incentives to exceed production limits were large, and when one driller exceeded his limit pressure his neighbors would feel pressure to follow suit.[25]

Nearby Texas also implemented conservation laws in 1919, but more cautiously than Oklahoma. Whereas Oklahoman producers wanted to prevent big oil companies from driving the little ones out of business by driving down prices, in Texas "an opposite view of the majors held sway. Texans feared that if the regulators were given the authority to [regulate supply to match demand with the goal of controlling prices], the majors would eventually control the regulators and engage in trust-like activity that would raise prices too high."[26] The Texas Railroad Commission or TRC, established in 1891 to regulate railroads and later other quasi-public companies, was authorized to limit oil production only in cases of underground or surface waste. Unlike their counterparts on the OCC, Texas officials initially took pains to avoid appearing to regulate production for the sake of price stability. Texas law deliberately excluded economic waste, defined as supply that exceeded marketable demand or that resulted in prices below production costs.[27] The TRC implemented its first quotas on companies producing in the Burkburnett field in north Texas near the border with Oklahoma.[28]

In setting quotas, state regulators were trying to resolve two conflicting legal doctrines that had been enshrined into law. One was the rule of capture: "What you can draw out of the ground beneath your feet is yours." Since oil moves underground toward a wellbore, the law incentivized drillers to drain the pool before others could drill to it. The other legal principle was called correlative rights, which stated "no-one person could act in a manner that inured the property rights of other landowners in an oil field."[29] Correlative rights came into play when laying pipe in a field; if the pipeline owner served just one producer but not others, those not able to access the pipeline would suffer loss of property rights. Thus, the correlative rights doctrine required pipeline companies to service all producers. And if there was not enough pipeline capacity to handle all the drillers, pipelines were obligated to take some oil from each producer, with the amount determined by that producer's percentage of the total field's output.[30] Requiring each well be allowed—and limited to—a certain amount served the same purpose as quotas.

The combination of anything goes capture and restrictive implication of correlative rights had mixed implications for oil production. In one sense correlative rights supported high production because drillers knew that state authorities would compel pipelines to service at least some of their production, reducing the risk of striking oil but having nowhere to put it.[31] But correlative rights also served to limit unbridled production by individual producers in the name of conservation, since regulators could cite the doctrine to defend quotas on grounds production in excess of pipeline takeaway capacity was wasteful production.

Early quota setting was light-handed and decentralized. Regulators were treading on new legal ground and were not sure of their authority, and the public was wary. Companies were allowed to police themselves, with private sector "umpires" hired to enforce quotas, to arbitrate and to determine how much oil would flow from which wells on which days.[32]

As oil industry and oil state officials found themselves drawn together by a common problem of contending with physical and economic waste—and with oil price instability, which was both a cause and a consequence of such waste—the United States' entrance into World War I in 1917 drove the oil industry and federal government into even closer cooperation. World War I was the first conflict in which belligerents depended substantially and increasingly on oil-powered vehicles, and the need for petroleum to power ships, airplanes, tanks, and motorized trucks cemented oil's importance as a strategic commodity. Almost as unheard of as a transportation fuel less than 20 years before the war, oil, French Prime Minister Georges Clemenceau put simply, was "as necessary as blood."[33] France's oil czar stated that the pivotal battles of Verdun, the Somme, and Aisne could not have been won without motorized transport.[34]

The war-driven thirst for oil meant that officials wanted high production, and fast; meeting the military's needs while preventing economic harm would require stable oil prices. To this end, President Wilson hired a petroleum engineer from California named Mark Requa to serve as wartime oil czar. Passionate about industry-government collaboration, Requa's Oil Division of the U.S. Fuel Administration closely worked with oil companies to ensure maximum output, improve operational efficiency, and standardize refined products. Requa reserved the threat of direct federal supply and price controls, but he preferred for oil drillers, shippers, and refiners to integrate voluntarily and (with government backing) to maximize production and stabilize prices. He set up regional committees of oil companies to plan for maximum production hikes and asked the industry to pool fuel oil supplies, intervening on behalf of oil producers to prevent the Railroad Administration from implementing a 25 percent increase in freight rates. Requa also ran interference for the oil industry with the competition watchdogs at the Federal Trade Commission (FTC), who noted increasing industry cooperation with alarm, accusing drillers and refiners in 1918 of profiteering.[35]

During World War I many of the strategies Rockefeller had employed to stabilize oil markets and prices returned, this time by order and direction of the federal government. Oil industry officials were delighted by the new industry-government cooperation to stabilize their turbulent industry. Wartime needs encouraged the oil industry to combine, pool and stabilize oil production and pricing. "What pools, trusts, and mergers had been unable to accomplish because of the antitrust laws," historian Gerald Nash noted, "could be achieved under this new device for intra-industry cooperation."[36]

WORLD WAR I USHERS IN A BOOM, NEW DRILLING, AND A BUST

As the war drew to a close, so too did the period of relative calm and harmony in oil prices and industry-government relations. Oil prices rose sharply due to spot shortages, pent-up civilian demand, and developments in oil-fueled technology. For example, coal-to-oil conversion and postwar replacements of shipping losses during World War I brought oil-fueled ships, as a percentage of the world's merchant marine fleet, up from 3.5 percent in 1914 to 16 percent just four years later.[37]

Midcontinent crude oil soared from the depressed, prewar price of $0.40 cents per barrel in March 1915 to $3.50 per barrel in March 1920—a jump of 775 percent, to a level that would not be exceeded for fifty years.[38] "Oil industry booms throughout nation," blared the *Pittsburgh Press* on January 2, 1917, as oil producers suddenly enjoyed the soaring prices amid a feeling of "certainty" that they would continue.[39] "No one can foretell," another newspaper reported at the same time, "when the market price of crude oil will decline."[40] In 1917, crude oil prices hit the highest level in a generation and for the first time in the industry's history all price changes were *up* and none down.[41]

Gasoline prices followed crude oil up, although pump prices did not rise as much as crude oil, largely due to rapid increases in refinery efficiency. For example, nominal midcontinent crude oil prices rose by more than 300 percent between 1914 and 1918, whereas, Chicago gasoline prices rose by less than half that amount.[42]

While gasoline prices may have been rising less than the prices of crude oil and other goods, they caused dislocations in industry and triggered

many complaints from all over the country. In Kansas City, meat packers discarded trucks and went back to horse-drawn wagons: "Price of
Gasoline Putting Horse Back in Harness Again," one Indiana newspaper
reported.[43] Consumers insisted that gasoline prices were excessively high
and that refiners and others were practicing price discrimination. The
uproar began in 1915 and triggered Senate resolutions and an investigation by the Federal Trade Commission (FTC). The FTC concluded prices
were "necessarily and naturally somewhat higher" in 1915 due to surging demand outpacing production, requiring inventory draws.[44] The FTC
cautioned that it was not clear how much higher gasoline prices should
have been based on market conditions.[45]

Rising pump prices sparked rumors of pending bigger price jumps
and shortages.[46] In 1918 car dealers placed ads in newspapers to assure
their customers that gasoline production and inventories were adequate
and to "kill this gasoline shortage myth."[47] Motorists were outraged and
officials launched investigations of industry practices, especially on the
West Coast, where actual shortages developed.[48] "Gasoline prices follow
crude," Standard Oil of Indiana tried to explain to the public in 1920,
promising it was "straining every fibre of its highly specialized [refin-
ing] organization to meet [gasoline] demand."[49] In June 1920, the Federal
Trade Commission again reported to Congress that rising gasoline prices
were due "more to varying conditions of supply and demand in the light
of emphasized and pessimistic statements as to the future supply than
to a combination in restraint of trade."[50] This was the second such FTC
investigation prompted by rising gasoline prices but certainly was not the
last. As we shall see in recent years rising pump prices induced Congress
to demand another FTC investigation of anticompetitive practices in the
oil industry, and the Commission invariably concluded there are none.

Postwar economic growth and burgeoning vehicle demand on the West
Coast led to real gasoline shortages that became known as the West Coast
Gasoline Famine of 1920. Then, like now, the West Coast was somewhat
isolated from the rest of the United States by the Rocky Mountains, which
limited pipeline and refinery linkages: The West Coast had a lot of drivers
but relatively limited supplies of oil and refining capacity compared with
other regions. In Oregon, officials relaxed quality standards on gasoline
expecting that would result in lower pump prices. When prices went up

instead, they launched investigations of oil company practices.[51] In other areas, actual shortages and rationing were imposed. Professors Paul Rhode and Alan Olmstead recount:

> In the spring and summer of 1920 a serious gasoline famine crippled the entire West Coast, shutting down businesses and threatening vital services. Motorists endured hour-long lines to receive 2 gallon rations, and, in many localities, fuel was unavailable for as long as a week at a time. . . . Drivers in the Pacific Northwest endured 2 gallon rations for several months, and even with these limits stations often closed by 9:00 A.M. In San Francisco, gunplay erupted in a dispute over ration entitlements.[52]

Not everyone was unhappy with soaring gasoline prices. "Electric car makers see big field opening," one Ohio newspaper cited a local electricity utility distributor in April 1920, who cited "uncertainty of gasoline supply [as] evidence of electric car's new day."[53]

Booming gasoline prices and temporary shortages (especially on the West Coast) provoked alarm throughout the country's business and political establishments that oil supplies would be exhausted. Peak oil fears following World War I amounted to a full-blown panic, at least among government officials. Dread spread like wildfire in 1920 when the U.S. Geological Survey (evincing, as would later be recognized, a lack of knowledge about the extent of underground resources) reported that 40 percent of the nation's oil supply had been used up, that the nation's production could peak in three to five years, and that relatively secure supplies from Mexico (which had risen to about 20 percent of U.S. consumption) would soon slump as well.[54] Conservation and new discoveries, they said, were imperative to avoid exhaustion.[55]

Perhaps no institution was more worried about price increases and possible supply exhaustion than the U.S. Navy, which had just converted its ships to oil. Confronted suddenly with the prospect of a fuel supply crunch and soaring prices, the navy's first instinct was to follow the lead of their British counterparts and take control of oil supplies. Even before prices rose, the navy chafed at the high cost of oil. In December 1913, U.S. Navy Secretary Josephus Daniels said in his annual address, "The only possible relief from . . . a staggering item in the expense account of the

Navy in the future is in the control of oil wells and the refining of its own oil."[56] Facing acute oil shortages and price spikes, in 1919 Daniels ordered navy officers to commandeer supplies if sellers did not offer reasonable bids. In the summer of 1920, the commander of the Pacific fleet went so far as to send six destroyers to forcibly seize oil from a San Francisco-based supplier, if fuel could not be obtained at the price of $1.72 per barrel as the navy wished. Market prices at the time were around $2.00 per barrel. The threat worked. The navy ships berthed at the fuel company's wharf and, "after a brief parley" with company workers, the vessels obtained the fuel.[57]

The oil price boom of 1918–1920 attracted a lot of new drilling. Between 1915 and 1920, the number of wells drilled grew to nearly 34,000 and production soared by roughly 45 percent.[58] The discovery of large new fields in California in the 1920s, particularly in the Los Angeles basin, triggered a stampede of new production that quickly dissipated fears of shortages.

New supplies turned the postwar price boom into a bust. Whereas, in 1920 a desperate West Coast had been forced to import expensive oil by train from the midcontinent, a few years later there was a glut in California. Crude started to flow back east through the Panama Canal, eliciting complaints of "unfair" prices from Oklahoma and Texas producers.[59] Prices nosedived from $3.50 at the start of 1921 to $1.00 six months later.[60] Euphoria vanished and as boom turned to bust, gloom once again descended over the oil industry (see figure 2.1).

By the mid-1920s, geologists understood unrestricted drilling of an oil reservoir caused a loss of pressure. The perforation of underground reservoirs quickly and prematurely dissipated the pressure (or "drive") from trapped gas or water that forced oil to the surface. Moreover, some geologists suspected over drilling could result in the *permanent* loss of recoverable oil. Restricting well flow increased pressure in an oil field and thereby increased the total amount of oil that drillers could bring to the surface.[61] The return of price busts in the 1920s triggered much stronger support within the oil industry for supply controls. As Bradley noted, "Now the previously vague terms 'underground waste' and 'economic waste' could have meaning, the former being the dissipation of crude oil-recovering reservoir energy and the latter unnecessary drilling costs."[62]

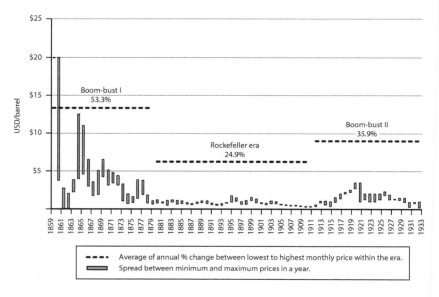

FIGURE 2.1

Annual ranges of monthly U.S. crude oil prices, 1859–1933.

Sources: Derrick's, vols. I–IV; API, Petroleum Facts and Figures (1959). © The Rapidan Group.

As the need for supply restraint intensified, the question became how to achieve it. Since the 1860s, voluntary efforts to stabilize oil supply and prices had repeatedly failed. Rockefeller's strategy of monopolizing refining and integrating with transportation worked, but trusts and other similarly collusive industry actions were now illegal. The state conservation laws that had been enacted in 1915 and 1919 were ineffectual. With peace and lower oil prices, government-sanctioned pooling and industry cooperation abated and Washington switched back to policing the industry for anticompetitive practices.

Yet many oil industry and oil state officials increasingly believed some form of compulsory supply control would be required to save the industry from itself. One option, called "unitization," entailed replacing rule of capture with a legal requirement that all the landowners over a large reservoir operate the field as one unit, with one operator deciding how and when to drill in order to maximize efficiency and economic returns. In return for losing the right to drill, the landowner receives a pro rata share of income of the unitized operation. Unitization was patterned after similar irrigation planning systems in the parched American West.[63]

The industry champion for unitization was Henry L. Doherty, a prominent industry figure in the interwar period. Doherty had become a believer in unitization after the deluge of new Californian oil cut his midcontinent oil company's profits by 50 percent. In 1923, Doherty warned his industry colleagues that regulation in some form was inevitable; if industry did not accept compulsory unitization, direct government regulation would be the alternative. Unitization, Doherty insisted, was the lesser of two evils.[64]

Doherty's pleas received a mixed response from his oil industry colleagues. Many saw mandatory controls as the only way out of "intolerable market instability; others saw in them intolerable restrictions on their freedom of action."[65] While instability harmed the entire oil industry, attitudes varied on the type of control that should be used to prevent it. Generally, bigger and more integrated firms were more in favor of stabilization efforts and more willing to accept the necessity of state intervention than their smaller, independent competitors.[66] And while some saw unitization as a way to stave off both ruinous price collapses and direct government control, others were skeptical of mandatory unitization because of its administrative complexity. Determining property rights and sorting the interests of operators and leaseholders in an oil province whose resource base was not clearly defined presented tremendous challenges.

Other oil executives went further, vigorously opposing compulsory unitization as a violation of property rights. They preferred cooperative industry integration, ideally with immunity from antitrust regulation. Most of all, they opposed federal imposition of unitization. If chronic instability made supply restrictions unavoidable, the thinking went, better to have friendly state commissions impose them.[67] With response to unitization decidedly mixed, a committee formed by the oil industry's main trade association to examine Doherty's plan, the American Petroleum Institute (headed by an opponent of unitization), resulted in a stalemate.

Stymied by his oil brethren, Doherty turned to the federal government, approaching President Coolidge directly to plead for compulsory unitization. The Coolidge administration was at first skittish: The Teapot Dome corruption scandal (a bribery incident involving the secretary of the interior in President Harding's administration, who became the first cabinet member to go to prison after he accepted grafts to allow acquaintances to drill on oil-bearing federal land set aside to fulfill naval fuel requirements in the event of a national emergency) was still on the front pages. But in 1924, after Teapot Dome had died down, Coolidge tasked a cabinet-level Federal Oil Conservation Board with probing oil industry practices and determining what federal steps could prevent waste and promote conservation.[68] Coolidge did not explicitly refer to an economic meaning of conservation, much less call for policies to promote price stability, but he made clear his concern that excessive oil production would lead to future shortages.

Coolidge pointedly warned that Washington would not remain aloof, since "the supremacy of nations may be determined by the possession of available petroleum and its products."[69] For President Coolidge, whether or not the oil industry could be left to the private sector was an open question:

> The oil industry itself might be permitted to determine its own future. That future might be left to the simple working of the law of supply and demand but for the patent fact that the oil industry's welfare is so intimately linked with the industrial prosperity and safety of the whole people, that Government and business can well join forces to work out this problem of practical conservation.[70]

Despite Doherty's activism and Coolidge's supply concerns, industry divisions and Washington's inattentiveness left matters in limbo. A brief period of tightness in the oil market—and resulting drawdown of inventories —in 1925 and 1926 further stoked concerns about the adequacy of future supply.[71]

While President Coolidge expressed concern about future scarcity even when supplies were abundant and prices weak, as a general rule other policymakers and elected officials lost interest in oil unless prices were rising sharply. Price busts generated alarm in the oil industry and among oil state officials, but less so in Washington, and Washington's attention to oil policy began to fade after World War I. It would take the experience of new, greater instability caused by new oil finds and price collapses to push the industry and oil state officials into action.

3

WHY ARE OIL PRICES PRONE TO BOOM-BUST CYCLES?

By the mid-1920s, oil had completed a major transition from lighting to transportation. Both industry and government regarded oil as a vital and strategic commodity. While as we have just seen the intensity of Washington's focus on oil waxed and waned, oil's increasingly central role in the economy meant that oil prices were becoming a broadly shared concern, outside and inside the oil patch.

Some circumstances that exacerbated oil price volatility in the early decades had been ameliorated—for instance, take-away infrastructure had improved, and the number and efficiency of pipelines, tankers, and other storage methods had greatly expanded and new finds were more quickly connected to refineries and marketing centers. However, the fundamental causes of oil price volatility remained. Massive new fields were being discovered by drillers who had every incentive to produce as much as possible—as fast as possible. The industry was getting better at connecting new wells to major pipelines and refineries, but new finds still overwhelmed local storage and take-away capacity. Even as it matured, the oil industry suffered from a chronic inability to handle supply surpluses well. New discoveries prompted price plunges. And after busts, prices soared as steadily growing demand outstripped available supply, triggering price rebounds and sparking anger among consumers and elected officials and panic about looming exhaustion of a critical resource. Clearly something particular to the oil industry and market made price volatility a structural feature.

Before we continue with our chronology, let's dive into this key question: Why is oil structurally prone to price volatility?

The answer, in a nutshell, is that oil demand and supply are insensitive or "sticky" in response to price changes. That is, when oil prices change, supply and demand do not adjust swiftly in response. Therefore, even small imbalances between supply and demand require large price moves to enforce an iron law of economics: that you cannot consume what you do not produce, and that whatever is produced must be either consumed or wasted.[1] Some of the specific factors that make oil supply and demand especially sticky have changed over time, but this basic volatility-inducing characteristic of the oil market has endured. Let's take a look at the supply and demand sides of oil in more detail.

YOU GOTTA DRIVE

Oil is a must-have commodity. Society craved illumination and transportation and these quickly became necessities, not luxuries. Demand for necessities—think about baby food, tap water, cell phone service, or to some extent housing and clothing—tends to remain steady even when the price changes because by definition consumers have little choice but to continue consuming them. Economists refer to such consumption patterns as "inelastic," and to such continued demand despite higher prices as "sticky."

Another factor that makes demand for commodities like oil insensitive to price changes—when the price goes up, demand does not quickly go down—is the lack of substitutes.[2] If the price of beef goes up, a shopper can buy chicken. But if the price of gasoline goes up, drivers still have to buy gasoline, although they may not be happy about it. After all, even if the prices of gasoline and jet fuel rise, school buses still need to take kids to class, workers still need to commute and travel, and the military still needs to fly jets. Most users of oil cannot cut their consumption quickly when the price goes up. The stickiness of demand in response to pump price changes holds when prices fall as well as when they rise. Veteran oil economist Paul Frankel's description 70 years ago remains apt today:

> If the price of beer or cigarettes were halved, it would probably result in an immediate and considerable increase in consumption, but this would

not be the case with petrol. Would people who were already running a car be likely to double their mileage?[3]

Or, as Howard Gruenspecht, one senior EIA official remarked, "it's not like $2 diesel is going to convince UPS trucks to drive in circles in the parking lot."[4]

Finally, the cost of fuel is relatively small in comparison with the up-front cost of the vehicle that runs on it. Once a motorist buys a car, subsequent operating costs like gas and the occasional tune-up are relatively low and the driver will use the car as much as needed.

This is not to say a fuel price change never impacts consumption. But changes in the short term—days, weeks, months—will be small. Large pump price changes that motorists regard as permanent, however, can dramatically affect consumption in the long term. We saw this in advanced economies like the United States after the 1970s oil price shocks, when high prices helped phase out fuel oil consumption in some areas (such as electricity generation and space heating, where fuel oil was replaced with natural gas, coal, and nuclear power), or in the 1990s, when sustained low gasoline prices helped launch the sport-utility vehicle craze.

While difficult to determine precisely, surveys of the academic literature suggest the short run demand price elasticity of crude is around −0.06.[5] That is, a 1 percent change in price would yield a −0.06 percent change in demand. So a 100 percent increase (doubling) in the price of crude would reduce demand by only 6 percent.[6] Compare crude oil's −0.06 price elasticity with goods whose demand is more sensitive to price changes like restaurant meals or fresh tomatoes, which one study estimated had price elasticities of demand of −2.3 and −4.6, respectively.[7] Thus, whereas a 10 percent change in the price of oil would only cause refiners to buy 0.6 percent less crude to turn into gasoline, a 10 percent change in price would cause consumers to buy 23 percent fewer restaurant meals and 46 percent fewer tomatoes.

Because demand is so sticky, a relatively small change in supply or demand can trigger a drastic price change to bring markets into equilibrium, as we can see by imagining how the elasticities above play out. Let us say a destructive storm knocked out an island's crude production as well as the tomato harvest, reducing the supply of oil and tomatoes in our imaginary island community by 5 percent each. Inventories of oil and tomatoes were low before the storm hit, and no other outside supplies were quickly available. Therefore, prices must rise to prevent consumption from exceeding supply. In this case, consumption of both must fall by 5 percent. To induce consumers to cut consumption of must-have oil and nice-to-have-but-not-essential fresh tomatoes by 5 percent, these elasticities imply crude oil prices would have to rise by 85 percent, whereas tomato prices would only rise by 1 percent.[8]

Our concern here is extreme volatility or relative stability in the "short run"—a couple months to a couple of years. In the long run (many years, decades), crude oil demand price elasticities are bigger (around −0.3 to −0.2) because producers and consumers of oil have more time to respond to price changes by altering consumption decisions.[9] This suggests that if crude prices rise by 50 percent followed by a 25 percent increase in gasoline prices, the owner of a sport-utility vehicle won't immediately run out and swap her Tahoe for an electric-powered Leaf. But if that 50 percent price increase sticks for a few years, she is more likely to do so.

Academic experts believe that demand has only gotten "stickier" in the United States, meaning price elasticity has fallen, between 1980 and 2007. One possible reason oil demand grew less responsive to price changes is that oil is no longer widely used in electricity generation (where substitutes to oil were available) and use is more concentrated in transportation, where there are fewer alternatives.[10] Moreover, oil's share of consumer spending has fallen. As oil's share of spending goes down, consumers can afford to ignore oil price changes more so now than they did then.[11] Outside the United States, in places where taxes and subsidies limit the direct transmission of crude price changes through to refined products prices, inelasticity of demand is even more pronounced.

While demand for oil may not respond much to price changes in the short term, it does respond quickly to changes in income, or GDP.[12] While income elasticity (like price elasticity) is difficult to measure, surveys of experts assess it at around 1.0 for oil.[13] That is, a 10 percent change in income (GDP) should lead to a 10 percent change in demand for oil. Income elasticities greatly vary depending on the country. Advanced economies have lower income elasticities when it comes to oil because they have relatively smaller energy-intensive industrial sectors and larger energy-efficient service ones. Two analysts estimated income elasticity to be 0.55 for advanced economies and around 1.1 for rapidly growing ones.[14] Rising oil prices themselves will not kill demand for oil, but a recession will do so, and quickly. Though effective, economic recessions are brutal and unpopular ways to reduce oil demand in a hurry.

All in all, while in theory oil prices would rise until they reached a level that made substitutes for gasoline, diesel fuel, and other petroleum products economical, the reality is that in the short run, there are no substitutes for gasoline and diesel. Therefore, in practice, oil prices will rise until energy expenditures become a big enough burden on the consumer and broader economy that they contribute to or cause a recession. The precise level at which oil prices would become an intolerable burden for growth is not known, as economic growth depends on many other things besides oil prices and energy expenditures. But recent experience shows that the economy can grow with oil price well above $100 per barrel, suggesting oil's price ceiling is in the triple digit range. In 2011, the Obama administration reportedly considered oil prices above $125 as putting the economy in peril.[15] That same year, analysts and banks considered $120 to be the ceiling beyond which oil threatened the global economy.[16] In 2012, IEA warned that oil price increases to about $120 could "plunge the world economy back into recession."[17] Fortunately, we did not find out as oil prices did not exceed $120 for long after 2008.

OIL SUPPLY IS ALSO STICKY IN RESPONSE TO PRICE CHANGES

The supply side of oil, too, is "sticky" or unresponsive to price changes, particularly in the short run. As long as prices are above the low costs of operating fields, most oil producers will keep producing all they can. And when prices are high, operators producing at maximum capacity cannot quickly increase production to take advantage of this. Nowadays bringing on new oil supplies takes many years, as it often requires exploring for and developing new fields. (U.S. shale oil, which is discussed later in this book, is an exception to that rule.) Current estimates of the elasticity of crude supply are estimated to be on par with that of demand—around 0.04 in the short run and 0.35 in the long run.[18]

The structure of the oil industry helps explain why oil supply is sticky and why each key segment tends to operate at full capacity regardless of prices. As we've seen, the supply side of the oil industry is broadly organized into three sectors: "upstream" explorers and producers who search and drill for oil; "midstream" transporters such as pipelines, railroads, and maritime tankers who transport the oil from fields to refineries; and "downstream" refiners and marketers who produce and sell final products that are used in the economy, such as gasoline, heating oil, and petrochemical feedstock.

Across all sectors, from drilling to refining, the oil business is very capital intensive, requiring large up-front expenditure. Moreover, the specialized equipment used to extract, transport, and store oil—purpose-built drilling rigs and wells, storage tanks, pipelines, ships, etc.—is expensive to build and is not good for anything else but crude, a toxic liquid. If oil was a solid, it could be produced and transported using prevailing, multipurpose equipment. "The history of petroleum would have been different," Frankel noted, "if the material to be burned in lamps or in internal-combustion engines could have been made into a powder, packaged, and sold in general stores."[19] Vehicles and containers that ship potatoes can also carry diamonds. But the equipment in the oil industry is only good for one thing—producing, transporting, and refining oil.

Looking at the upstream, the focus of this book, the bulk of outlays needed are spent up front and sunk before any barrels are produced and sold. Once wells are producing, the variable costs—that is costs that vary along with the amount of oil produced such as operating expenses (labor and materials) and taxes and royalties—are relatively low.[20] Once all that money is spent finding and developing new wells, oil companies do not turn off supply like a spigot because oil prices fall sharply. As long as oil prices cover relatively low variable costs, producers produce.[21] This is especially true for small operators, whose need to generate revenue immediately to cover expenses, debt service, and royalties is higher than for larger, better capitalized firms.

Midstream transportation and downstream refining operators also have an incentive to run their equipment at full capacity. Pipeline costs are generally unrelated to how much oil flows through; once the pipeline is laid, operating costs comprise of relatively minor supervision, inspection, maintenance, and power for pumping stations.[22] Reducing the amount of oil passing through the pipe does not help much to cut costs.

Refineries also have high fixed up-front costs. However, refineries enjoy more flexibility than their drilling and transporting counterparts. They turn crude into hundreds of products, from asphalt and heavy fuels for space heating to lighter materials used to produce medicines, candles, cosmetics, and waterproofing goods. Refineries have some flexibility that drillers do not have, as they can adjust the type of crude they refine to respond to market demands.[23] Refinery flexibility mitigates but does not eliminate the sector's heavy fixed-to-variable cost ratio, however.[24] Indeed, seizing opportunities to dynamically shift crude and product slates often requires new capital equipment. Once built, the refiner has incentive to use the equipment at maximum rates.

Finally, petroleum marketers—the people who distribute and market petroleum products—also want to operate their tanks, trucks, and filling stations to the maximum extent. Marketing is a highly competitive margin and volume business. While demand for gasoline overall is insensitive to pump price changes, drivers are happy to comparison shop among filling stations and fill up at the cheaper alternative. Therefore, a few pennies' change in prices makes a great difference to a single marketer's sales. Thus, the marketing sector tends to quickly pass changes in crude prices on to customers while running its facilities all out.

There is one segment of the oil industry that while also carrying high up-front costs can help reduce oil price volatility—storage tanks held by upstream producers, midstream transporters, and downstream refiners and marketers. Price volatility imparts an incentive to build storage[25]—to profit by buying and storing crude when the price is low and using it or selling it in the future at a higher price. The availability of storage plays a large role in shaping oil price volatility. As we saw in the early days, the lack of storage near many early western Pennsylvania drill sites meant that new discoveries caused oil prices to crash to nearly zero. Storage hardly guarantees price stability, however. It is costly to build storage tanks, so storage capacity is neither cheap nor unlimited. Tanks can be located far from gluts, or be expensive, and storage capacity can fill up. But since storage is the only place to really bottleneck excess oil supply or quickly access oil when demand is great, storage capacity and the amount of oil in storage has been one of the most important segments of the oil system, avidly monitored to the extent data would allow, from the earliest days to today.

Turning back to oil producers, we see the only time oil companies will seriously consider shutting in wells is when prices drop below the operating costs for crude wells. Even then, oil producers will resist, resorting instead to other means to lower the cost of production still, say by squeezing cost cuts from subcontractors or reducing royalties. Operating costs vary widely and are not transparent. In today's oil market, operating costs for major sources of oil range from $5 to perhaps $30 per barrel.[26] And recent experience shows that oil may still flow even when prices fall below these costs.

Indeed, we can see the stickiness on the supply side with what has happened recently in the global oil market. Crude oil prices dived from $105 per barrel in June 2014 to $30 per barrel in February 2016. Yet despite the unexpected collapse, enormous quantities of new oil had been arriving on the market, including from expensive oil projects that likely would not have been approved had investors foreseen collapsing oil prices. For example, several large and expensive new production facilities in the U.S. Gulf of Mexico that were built several years ago when oil prices were around $100 are just now being completed and oil is starting to flow into a glutted oil market, with inventories at record levels and rising. Even though these massive offshore oil rigs are not economically viable below $60 per barrel,[27] their owners will be very slow to turn them off; producers will resist shutting in at all hazard, especially if they are convinced the price swoon is temporary and a rebound will shortly follow.

Other high-cost producers like Russia have not reduced their production in the face of excess supply. In fact, Russian production hit a post-Soviet record level in September 2016. This was partly due to projects that were begun in recent years and also due in a large part to the ruble devaluation, tax cuts, and the oil companies' desperate need to repay loans. Even in the United Kingdom's North Sea, where oil supply had been falling since 1999, production posted an increase in 2015 because of investments made in preceding years when oil prices were near $100.[28] In both cases, the capital to develop these big projects has already been sunk. The cost of operating the new fields is relatively low. Their owners are going to keep oil flowing, even though the world oil market is saturated and prices have been plummeting.

The combination of sticky demand and sticky supply means that when the oil market is unbalanced—supply exceeds demand, or vice versa—large oil price moves are necessary to force changes in consumption or production. Consider a case in which a war in the Middle East suddenly disrupted 20 percent of the world's oil supply but demand elsewhere kept humming. After inventories were run down, the law of supply and demand says someone needs to consume less gasoline, diesel fuel, and home heating oil. But who would it be? How high would pump prices have to be before you would be willing to carpool or take public transportation to work? Or consider the opposite situation, when oil supply exceeds consumption; say due to large new supplies of U.S. shale oil along with rising Iraqi and Saudi production as happened in 2015. Supply exceeded demand, inventories swelled, and the price fell toward the cost of production, somewhere below $30 per barrel.

As with demand, supply will eventually respond to price changes, but with a multiyear lag. These multiyear lags can reinforce price boom and bust price cycles, for the future supplies being delayed or cancelled now will not be available in the future, when demand may be stronger. Thus, excess supply and price crashes today sow the seeds of inadequate supply and price booms in the future.

Oil's inability to self-balance without massive price shifts and a multiyear time lag creates within and between its producing segments—drillers, transporters, refiners, and marketers—an impulse toward integration, horizontally (among firms in the same sector, like refining) and vertically (across sectors). Within each sector, firms are wary of investing in excessive capacity that could result in lower prices and profits. As we have seen, early drillers attempted to reach horizontal agreements to restrain drilling and production, and Standard Oil approached horizontal integration with the more aggressive method of buying and closing small, competing refineries, as well as vertical integration by controlling pipelines and drilling wells. By integrating, oil companies could naturally hedge themselves against price fluctuations elsewhere in the supply chain. In addition to securing supply chains, integration dampened the tendency of individual oil companies to drill too many wells, build too much refining capacity, and erect too many bulk transportation and storage facilities. And perhaps most important for the industry and broader economy, integration enabled firms to avoid "disruptive fluctuations in prices which would raise costs to both producers and consumers."[29]

Thus, integration became a way of life for the oil industry since the earliest days.[30] Rockefeller was the first to successfully integrate key segments of the oil business, but his monopoly of refining and cooperation with railroads was denounced and outlawed. During World War I, Washington temporarily shifted priorities from regulating oil industry practices in the interest of promoting competition to directing companies to pool resources and collaborate in the interest of maximizing output quickly. But by the 1920s, the Standard Trust and World War I were history, and the oil industry found itself largely ignored by Washington, policed by competition authorities, forbidden from forming cartels, and afflicted by the same conditions that prevailed at its birth—massive new discoveries and price busts. By the mid-1920s new crises loomed that would totally reshape the oil industry and usher in extensive supply regulation.

4

THE TEXAS ERA OF PRICE STABILITY

U.S. Supply Controls and International Cartelization (1934–1972)

n the late 1920s, domestic and global dynamics forced oil prices down. There were the new gushers in Texas and Oklahoma and a kerosene price war in India, an important market for refined Russian crude, which became the site of an escalating contest between Royal Dutch Shell and Mobil[1] that spread to American and British markets and forced all major marketing companies to reduce prices to maintain market share. These price busts set in motion a chain of events that by the early 1930s would result in the most aggressive system of supply regulation and cartelization ever seen—and usher in four decades of oil price stability the likes of which the world had never seen before or since.

Texas and Oklahoma together accounted for 55 percent of all U.S. production in 1927.[2] Their local economies became extremely dependent on healthy oil operations and state budgets relied on revenue from taxes on the industry. While wary of appearing to favor monopolies or interfering in the free market, state officials were just as anxious as drillers were about oil supply and price stability.

Major discoveries in central Oklahoma in 1926, collectively named the Greater Seminole field, tipped oil prices into another super-bust cycle. Seminole produced an astounding 500,000 b/d by July of 1927.[3] Total production in the state soared by 55 percent between 1926 and 1927.[4] The deluge, along with other discoveries in Oklahoma as well as the Yates field in Texas, hammered midcontinent crude prices. The pricing of Oklahoma oil fell as low as $0.17 per barrel.[5] Producers howled for relief. "Once more," noted oil historian Norman Nordhauser, "the fundamental perils of price and production instability reappeared.

Suddenly, the gospel of conservation began to make converts among major petroleum executives."[6]

Prior to the Seminole field, many Oklahoma drillers and officials opposed mandatory controls on oil production. But the deluge of new supply triggered what Nordhauser called a "Great Reversal"[7]—oilmen now clamored for government regulation of supply. "Those optimistic [drillers] who had, a few months earlier, testified that there was neither waste nor shortage of American oil, now cried that there was an urgent need to check overproduction."[8] Initially the Oklahoma Corporation Commission (OCC), producers, and pipeline companies formulated a plan to limit the transportation of oil from Seminole and restrict new drilling of most new wells. Nevertheless, production continued to mount, inventories swelled, and prices crashed. On August 9, 1927, the OCC held a hearing, determined "waste" was occurring, and issued its first major mandatory quota under the 1915 Conservation Act, imposing a limit of 450,000 barrels per day on Seminole production. New drilling continued however, frustrating the OCC's attempt to rein in production. To prevent other fields in the state from benefiting by increasing output and concerned the federal government could step in to impose order, on September 9, 1928, the OCC took the "drastic step" of imposing a statewide quota of 700,000 per day, the first instance of wide-scale quotas to restrict production. While the OCC struggled to enforce its orders over the large number of oilmen, tighter controls began to impact production modestly in 1929.[9] Oil prices rose to $1.45 by mid-1929.

But just as Oklahoman drillers were catching their breath, in December 1928 a new and massive field started up, called the Oklahoma City Field (they would eventually drill under the capitol). Voluntary supply restraint was tried first and failed, and in July 1929 the OCC began issuing quotas for the field that ranged between 2.75 percent and 40 percent of potential production.[10]

With the OCC imposing quotas well below the total capacity of their wells, Oklahoma City Field drillers who had previously been unified on the need for supply controls now divided into two camps that would mark a broader disagreement about quotas among oilmen. Quota opponents, especially those with flush wells situated near transportation or refineries, responded harshly to officials' mandatory supply cuts. Refiners also chafed at being forced to purchase higher-priced crude. But drillers with relatively poor wells or far from takeaway capacity continued to favor production limits—they were not well situated to produce more anyway. Opponents launched legal challenges to Oklahoma's restrictions, but were rebuffed by the Oklahoma Supreme Court in 1930.[11]

Despite Oklahoma's mandatory statewide quotas in effect, oil prices began to slip, averaging $1.31 in the first half of 1930. To tighten compliance, the OCC replaced private sector umpires with officials to monitor production in the field. In June and July of 1931 national crude prices plunged to an average of $0.33 per barrel. The causes were high production, a weakened economy, and—we shall shortly see—a monster new oil strike in Texas.

Then on August 3, 1931, a federal court ruled against the OCC and suspended Oklahoma's quotas. The reaction from Oklahoma elected officials to the court's interference was immediate and severe. The day after the court's order, Oklahoma Governor William "Alfalfa Bill" Murray declared martial law, commissioned his cousin Cicero Murray (a lieutenant colonel in the National Guard), and ordered troops into the fields to shut down 3,106 active wells, exempting only small wells producing fewer than 25 barrels per day. A Texas newspaper reported, "Governor Murray asserted the right to impose quotas based on the need to maintain tax revenues that kept schools open, protected the property of independent producers, and conserved the state's energy resources. 'The state's natural resources must be preserved,' Alfalfa Bill roared, 'and the price of oil must go to $1 a barrel; now don't ask me any more damned questions.' "[12] He lashed out at what he called the "quill suckers" who questioned his legal authority and insisted state law expressly gave him power to prohibit production when the price of oil was less than its value.[13] Quotas would remain in place, Alfalfa Bill vowed, until "we get dollar oil."[14]

Although crude prices never reached the governor's $1 target (press reported the top price was $0.70), in early October 1931 Governor Murray reopened the fields but retained state oversight of state quotas.[15] In announcing the troop withdrawal Murray predicted oil prices would rise and warned if they fell, "I can always shutdown the wells again."[16] Prices continued weakening and he made good on this threat on May 6, 1932, declaring martial law once more to respond to drilling derricks

encroaching on Oklahoma City's limits.[17] On May 20, Oklahoma's lieutenant governor lifted martial law while Alfalfa Bill was out of state cam-
paigning to be the Democratic nominee for president.[18] After calling the
acting governor a "damn fool," an agitated Governor Murray returned
from the campaign trail in New York and on May 27 reimposed martial
law.[19] In September 1932, a newspaper reported that Oklahoma National
Guard troops resorted to "fists, pistol butts, and tear gas" in a melee with
oil workers employed at Wilcox Oil & Gas Company.[20]

After the U.S. Supreme Court reversed the lower court's injunction
against Oklahoma's quota order, Oklahoma passed a stronger bill on April
10, 1933, allowing production control. Now that the courts recognized the
state's authority to restrict production, the troops could be withdrawn.
"Six years after the first proration order," oil historian Bradley noted,
"political control over Oklahoma crude production was complete."[21]
(See figure 4.1.)

Then came Texas's turn.

The Lone Star State, which in 1927 accounted for 24 percent of national
production at 217 kb/d, was moving in parallel with its sister oil state
to the north.[22] While Texas gave the TRC authority to impose quotas to

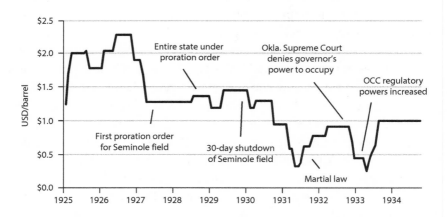

FIGURE 4.1

Oklahoma proration and midcontinent U.S. crude prices, 1925–1934. OCC: Oklahoma
Corporation Commission.

Source: API, *Petroleum Facts and Figures* (1959).

prevent physical waste in 1919 and updated that law in 1929, Texas legislators had been more squeamish than their Oklahoman counterparts. Texas officials were especially sensitive to the perception that their true aim was to influence prices and their statutes expressly prohibited regulations aimed at preventing economic waste. Texas officials insisted regulators could only limit *physical* waste. Until the late 1920s, the TRC had used its authority only to regulate well spacing in order to reduce fire hazards and prevent water infiltration into wells drilled too close to each other.[23]

But as in Oklahoma, large new discoveries in the late 1920s triggered price crashes which sent oil companies pleading to the TRC to impose quotas to stabilize prices. The 1926 discovery in west Texas of the giant Yates field—then the largest in the United States—prompted companies to do so. At first the TRC told the private companies to work out voluntary quotas. The TRC considered approving private voluntary quotas, but since the companies were explicitly proposing to restrict production to meet demand and thereby stabilize prices, the Commission decided to steer clear. As usual, private voluntary efforts to restrict production from the Yates field fell short.[24]

Failure of voluntary quotas at Yates prompted the TRC to issue its first field-level quota in late 1927. To buttress its insistence that physical and not economic waste (and certainly not price fixing) was the goal, the TRC argued that low oil prices caused by excess production would cause many very small, low-volume and higher-cost "stripper wells" to *permanently* cease operation. Stripper wells were less likely to be restarted than bigger, more efficient wells when oil prices recovered. The permanent loss of stripper well production amounted to "waste" in the TRC's view. As in Oklahoma, the TRC went on to impose quotas on other fields to prevent supply migration from regulated to unregulated areas.[25] These early mandatory quotas between 1927 and 1930 met with little resistance. Only a small number of oil companies operated in the regulated fields, and they accepted the TRC's legitimacy and authority.

Although the TRC steadily became more assertive, its authority rested on new, untested, and disputed legal grounds. When TRC extended quotas statewide, they sparked protests by companies who challenged the TRC's justification of quotas with "waste" and contended that the Commission was illegally trying to prevent "economic waste" by fixing prices.

In February 1931, the Texas Supreme Court upheld the TRC regulations, finding the Commission aimed to prevent physical waste and not to control prices.[26]

But Texas regulators would not enjoy peace for long, as the mother of all gushers was about to shake up the entire structure of oil regulation in Texas, transforming oil price formation in the United States and, eventually, the world.

THE BLACK GIANT

Dubbed the "Black Giant," the monster field was discovered in 1930 by a wildcatter named Columbus Marion "Dad" Joiner. Joiner was sixty-six years old when he arrived at Rusk County in East Texas in 1926 to pursue new opportunities. Deploying a rusty, pieced-together drilling rig, and a crew mostly made up of local farmers, Joiner drilled and then abandoned two wells before finally striking an enormous pool of oil on October 3, 1930.[27]

News of the strike spurred thousands of land deals in a matter of weeks. By April 1931 the field "was producing 340,000 barrels per day and a new well was being spudded every hour."[28] By July 1931, the 220-square mile field was producing 1 million b/d and enabled Texas, which had overtaken Oklahoma in 1928 as the nation's top-producing state by a small amount, to leap ahead. By 1932, Texas was producing twice as much as its neighbor, accounting for 40 percent of U.S. production.[29]

"A splendid gift of nature to the American people," oil historian Nordhauser observed, "[it] was a disaster for the petroleum industry."[30] In what was by now a familiar pattern, the spectacular new find caused oil prices to collapse. Crude prices in East Texas tanked from $1.00 per barrel in 1930 to as low as $0.10 per barrel by the end of July 1931. Black Giant's ripples threatened to weaken oil prices throughout the entire United States. An API official cautioned: "East Texas will bankrupt 95 percent of the independent operators of the United States and shake the majority of the major companies if allowed to produce at its present rate."[31]

Texas Governor Ross Sterling had watched events unfold to his north and grew increasingly worried about harmful oversupply in his state. Until early August 1931 he remained opposed to Oklahoma-style quotas with the goal of stabilizing prices and to deploying soldiers to shut off wells, but he was evidently beginning to soften. On August 7, he told reporters, "I doubt the wisdom of Governor Murray's move but sometimes drastic action is necessary."[32]

For the TRC, burgeoning East Texas production presented a new and difficult challenge. Unlike other fields where the TRC had imposed quotas—again only with the intention of preventing waste instead of stabilizing prices—on a small number of companies, thousands of producers drilled in East Texas. Normally placid TRC meetings turned into boisterous circuses. "Rather than a gathering of expert and industry leaders intent on finding the most effective policy through which to balance public and private interests," TRC historian Childs wrote, "hearings now became a Roman senate of numerous, competing self-interests."[33]

The TRC attempted to impose quotas on East Texas, beginning in April at 90,000 b/d. As in Oklahoma, the courts came into the picture and thwarted the quota order. Opponents of quotas won injunctions staying the TRC's hand and producers exceeded the limits with impunity. In an increasingly tense political atmosphere, quota opponents vehemently denounced the TRC's policies as price fixing. Professor David Prindle lucidly described how proponents of quotas were trying to have it both ways while not being forthright about it.

> Unrestrained production squandered natural resources. To try to conserve these resources was reasonable, legal, and even patriotic. But unrestrained production *also destabilized prices and encouraged competition.* To try to control the market was monopolistic, illegal, and wicked. Opponents of control argued that [quotas] would be a price-fixing scheme and therefore illegal, which was also true—the fact is that [quotas are] both a means of conservation *and a stratagem for price-fixing.*[34]

In July 1931 a federal district court surprisingly decided to side with the anti-quota producers—and against the TRC. In reversing the Texas Supreme Court, the federal court concluded that the TRC had indeed illegally regulated *economic* waste.

The federal court's decision forced Governor Sterling's hand. On August 17, 1931, he followed Oklahoma Governor Murray's example by

declaring martial law and ordering 1,200 national guard troops into East
Texas oil fields. Their mission, Governor Sterling declared, was to rein in
"an organized and entrenched group of crude petroleum oil and natural
gas producers . . . who are in a state of insurrection against the conservation laws of the State."[35] The troops were commanded by General Jacob F.
Wolters, who in civilian life was an attorney for Texaco, one of the state's
larger producers. This was not lost on small producers, who opposed quotas, regarding state-imposed supply limits as a form of subjugation to the
interests of larger companies.[36] During the predawn hours on Monday,
August 17, 1931, the residents of Kilgore, Overton, and other towns of East
Texas woke up to the tramping sound of eight hundred troopers of the
Fifty-sixth Cavalry Brigade of the Texas National Guard marching over
muddy ground, illuminated by the eerie light of countless gas flames at
producing wells.[37] (See figure 4.2.)

FIGURE 4.2

Martial law. Militia are deployed to shut wells in East Texas oil fields. The postcard
reads "Hoof Beats Drown Drilling Din as Cavalry Men Patrol East Texas
Oil Fields."

Source: From the postcard collection of Jeff Spencer; original postcard photo by Jack Nolan.

A Texas newspaper, the *Bryan Daily Eagle* reported, "It was hoped the action would bring higher prices for midcontinent crude and possibly stabilize the American petroleum industry."[38] Bayonets worked at first. Crude oil production in East Texas fell sharply and the price of crude in that part of the state, which had averaged $0.24 per barrel in August 1931, rose to $0.75 by March 1932.[39]

Reeling from the Black Giant and heartened by the U.S. Supreme Court's backing of Oklahoma's restrictions in 1932, the Texas legislature shed its aversion to regulating production for the purposes of price stability and enacted the Market Demand Act of 1932, which expressly authorized prevention of *economic* waste as well as physical waste.[40] Texas was now in the price-fixing business in all but name.

This implicit shift toward quotas for price-fixing deeply antagonized hold-out free-market proponents like Texas State Senator Joe L. Hill, who protested "[i]t is the rankest hypocrisy for a man to stand on this floor and say that the purpose of proration [quotas] is anything other than price-fixing. I sit here in utter amazement and see men get up and blandly talk about market demand as an abstract proposition, and contending that it has got no relation to price-fixing."[41]

As oil states established mandatory supply controls, illegal oil sales by drillers—called "hot oil"—remained a formidable problem that kept oil prices under downward pressure. Efforts by drillers to evade state production controls from 1931 through 1935 constituted "one of the most illustrative cases of civil disobedience and lawbreaking ingenuity in U.S. history." One violator encased his well in a cement blockhouse, dubbed the "Fortress of Gladewater."[42] In addition to greed, drillers were motivated by their need to pay back loans incurred to sink wells. Two experts explicated their economic predicament:

> The drilling cost of a well in a field like East Texas (a shallow and cheaply drilled pool) runs from $20,000 to $30,000. A large part of the original investment of the independent operator is usually borrowed—probably at a premium because of the speculative nature of the enterprise. Assuming that the principal sum draws interest of at least 6 percent and must be amortized in the first three or four years of operation and that one-eighth of the gross income is paid out as royalty, and that a further outlay for

production taxes, gathering, transportation and operating expenses is necessary before an operator can realize any income from his well, it is obvious that an insufficient volume of production, even at a "fair" price, tempts an operator, burdened with such unavoidable "costs," to increase his volume by illicit production.[43]

Enforcement and compliance with initial quotas in East Texas was weak. Even companies that supported mandatory quotas as a necessary evil were tempted to sell oil on the black market. Drillers drilled thousands of new wells, which authorities had trouble monitoring. Local enforcement authorities were often sympathetic to drillers exceeding limits, and bribes for lenient enforcement were common. The *Oil Weekly* reported it "would require an army to watch all of the 12,500 wells in the [East Texas] field and another army to watch the watchers." Some 10 percent of the field's wells were estimated to be defying quotas.[44] The TRC acted warily, as it enjoyed little support from other segments of government, and the state legislature, under pressure from small producers, frequently changed laws governing quotas.[45] Quotas greatly varied month to month, which aided bootlegging, and were eased before elections and tightened afterward.[46]

Massive flow from the Black Giant field in East Texas destabilized oil prices throughout the midcontinent states. Total production from the field was estimated to exceed total U.S. daily consumption by 700,000 barrels per day.[47] Production in East Texas hit an all-time high in April 1933 and pushed crude oil prices under $0.25 per barrel. By the summer of 1933, Bradley noted, allowable production combined with hot oil output "captured the national spotlight as single-handedly destabilizing the entire U.S. oil market."[48]

To a lesser extent, Oklahoma also suffered from excessive hot oil production. Much of this hot oil crossed state borders, and was therefore out of reach of state authorities. So state officials implored Washington's help mainly to help enforce state production limits by outlawing the interstate transport of hot oil.

In Washington, Franklin Delano Roosevelt's incoming administration championed aggressive federal intervention in the economy and had fewer qualms about price fixing than its Republican predecessors, who had showed only weak interest in helping states control production. Though FDR was no natural friend of the Texas- and Oklahoma-dominated oil industry and was wary of oil industry executives, his motivated and strong-willed secretary of the interior, Harold Ickes, took particular interest in finding solutions to oil's chronic instability, to the delight, initially, of the beleaguered industry. "Our task," Ickes declared in September 1933, "is to stabilize the oil industry upon a profitable basis."[49] Ickes enthusiastically sought direct *federal* control of oil production and prices.

With FDR and his crusading interventionist New Deal policies, the state regulators and oil industry's problem abruptly shifted to too much federal help, not too little. The oil industry welcomed Roosevelt's willingness to enforce state production controls, but feared overly broad federal regulation of the industry.[50] As part of sweeping measures to recover from the Great Depression, President Roosevelt signed the National Industrial Recovery Act (NIRA) into law in June 1933. NIRA suspended antitrust laws and required industries to devise codes for competition—essentially fixing wages and prices, formulating production quotas, and restricting entry by new firms.[51] NIRA included Section 9(c) outlawing interstate transportation of hot oil, as the states wanted.[52] Federal officials deployed to East Texas to help enforce production limits and within a week, rail shipments—the principal way interstate hot oil moved—all but stopped by the summer of 1933. "For the first time since the August 1931 shutdown," Bradley noted, "the great field was under control, although it would prove to be a lull, not dissolution and defeat, for the black marketeers."[53]

But now tension rose between the federal government and oil state regulators. NIRA had included a provision allowing a federal Petroleum Administration Board to make quota recommendations to the states. But state officials desired higher production limits than federal officials wanted. Interior Secretary Ickes threatened states with legal action for implementing quota limits above federal recommendations, and brought California to court for defiance in December 1933.[54]

As federal and state officials wrangled, the vast number of drillers, insufficient enforcement, and sheer human ingenuity caused production again to rise above legal limits. Illicit nighttime production, secret pipelines linking wells to refiners, and other ruses abounded. One female driller duped enforcement personnel by disguising her hot oil with converted bathroom faucets.[55] Another "devised a left-handed valve that appeared to be off when it was fully open."[56]

Efforts to enforce production limits by federal and state regulators haphazardly continued through 1934 but hit a wall in 1935 when the U.S. Supreme Court ruled Section 9(c) of NIRA to be unconstitutional. However, Congress then enacted a provision sponsored by Texas Senator Thomas Connally (D) that restored 9(c)'s provisions minus the legal flaws. The 1935 Connally Hot Oil Act outlawed the interstate transport of oil in contravention of state supply controls and included fines for noncompliance. The Hot Oil Act also provided for Washington to help regulators set limits by collecting and disseminating data on supply, demand, and inventory conditions in the oil market.

Officials gained further power from a tax Congress levied on oil production in 1934, not so much for revenue but to facilitate policing of hot oil. The tax authority gave officials new inspection powers over producers and refiners.[57] In the summer of 1935, Congress decided to shirk away from direct regulation of the oil industry (to drillers' relief) and instead passed legislation backing a new Interstate Compact to Conserve Oil and Gas and its associate commission, the Interstate Oil Compact Commission (IOCC), then composed of Texas, Oklahoma, Kansas, Colorado, Illinois, and New Mexico. Other states joined the IOCC in later years but not all implemented quotas. With the enactment of the Connally Act and the establishment of the IOCC, "virtually all the conservation pieces [in other words, mechanisms for production control] had been fitted together save for the uniform adoption of unitization schemes, a point at which the discussion [about mandatory controls] in the 1920's had begun."[58] States would enact unitization rules in subsequent years, though they existed alongside quotas. Whereas, in the 1920s drillers endlessly debated *between* unitization and quotas, starting in the 1930s officials imposed both.

Buttressed by clear state and federal authority, East Texas hot oil was under control by the eve of World War II (see figures 4.3 and 4.4).

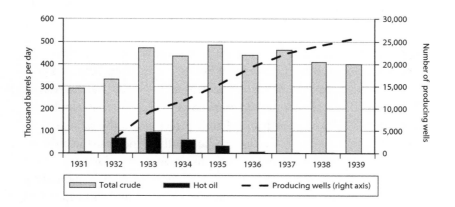

FIGURE 4.3

East Texas producing wells, total output, and hot oil.

Source: Williamson et al., *American Petroleum Industry*.

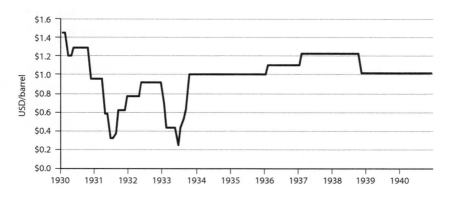

FIGURE 4.4

Midcontinent U.S. crude prices, 1930–1940.

Source: API, *Petroleum Facts and Figures* (1959).

HOW QUOTAS WORKED

By 1935 the core elements of oil stability machinery were in place and covered states amounting to 80 percent of U.S. production. The main purposes of this machinery, Williamson and Andreano noted, "were to restrict the flow of crude from new and old areas so as to keep current supply and demand more nearly balanced at profitable prices and at the same time to minimize the more flagrant 'wastes' and hopefully to increase the ultimate recovery of oil from a given pool."[59] State laws governing industry practices now allowed officials to order production changes—including mandatory reductions—to limit supply to estimates of demand and to keep prices stable and profitable for industry.

"The heart of state petroleum regulation," Bradley notes, was "the control of wellhead production."[60] There were three forms of state supply controls. The first and most drastic was ordering field shutdowns, such as the military actions of 1931 in Texas and Oklahoma. Kansas, New Mexico, and Texas also ordered field shutdowns in 1939, though they didn't need the military to enforce them.

The second form of supply controls was an upper ceiling on a field's maximum efficient rate (MER) of production, somewhat like a safety speed limit.[61] This was intended to protect reservoir pressure and maximize the amount of oil that could eventually be produced.

The third form of controls, called "market-demand proration," were production quotas set at levels intended to match oil supply to demand and thereby keep prices stable. "Of all state oil regulations," Bradley noted, "market-demand proration is the most complex, controversial, and consequential."[62] Whereas limiting production to a well's MER was clearly intended to promote physical conservation, market-demand prorationing was intended to stabilize prices. Let's look closer at how this system, which again we will call "quotas," worked.

State regulators set oil production quotas—called "allowables" back in the day—on a monthly basis.

The first step for regulators determining quotas involved collecting data on market supply, demand, and inventory conditions. State commissions charged with issuing quotas held monthly or bimonthly hearings to obtain estimates of demand, for which crude purchasers were required to submit "nominations" or intended amounts of purchases in the next period. While crude buyers were not legally required to purchase the amount nominated, there was pressure to do so.[63] Crucially, when making their nominations to regulators who used them to generate "market demand" estimates, crude purchasers were not allowed to assume or forecast any future prices, but instead were required to assume the most recent price. Thus, quota formulation was implicitly but clearly designed to promote price stability. "The fact that prices are not mentioned in nomination hearings," Bradley noted, "is not an escape from price fixing."[64]

Next, officials would estimate the supply available in the following period, taking into account inventory from in-state wells exempt from quota, supply in other states, and imports. Officials in Washington helped state regulators by collecting and furnishing data. State regulators then subtracted the available supply from the expected demand, and the result was a rough estimate of the need or "call" for that state's crude oil supply that month. Regulators calculated a statewide supply limit to meet the "call" on their state's crude oil with the overriding goal of avoiding price changes. They then imposed quotas on individual pools and wells in the state.[65]

While formulaic in appearance, in practice commissioners based their quota decisions as much on data as on their "feel" for market conditions.[66]

In pursuing its conservation and price stabilization objectives, the TRC also intended to protect the economic interests of small, independent oil producers most threatened by price busts and thereby support the state's economy.[67] For example, they exempted from quotas high-cost or "marginal" wells, such as low-volume so-called stripper wells or wells that required expensive secondary recovery (through stimulation techniques like forcing gas or water into the reservoir to increase pressure and lift oil to the surface).[68] Regulators imposed quotas on lower-cost, more productive wells operating under natural drive (most often where natural gas or water trapped in the reservoir creates higher pressure than at the bottom of the well, which naturally pushes the oil up to the surface). A well producing under natural drive is "known as a flow well. The natural lift stage of production is referred to as flush production."[69] Flowing wells could be more easily and cheaply dialed up and down, like adjusting the flow of water from a kitchen spigot.

Designed to help small, high-cost producers, TRC's quota system added to overall oil production costs and kept oil prices higher than they would have been under purely competitive conditions. Oil state and federal officials were primarily interested in price stability, but also in industry profitability to protect local economies and to serve the national interest by furnishing a large, secure store of vital energy.

Oklahoma's quota laws blazed the way in 1915, and during extreme oil price weakness in the late 1920s, Kansas, Texas, Louisiana, New Mexico, Mississippi, Arkansas, and Michigan followed suit. Quota states did not coordinate quota limits or collectively set them, though each informally adhered to federal estimates of their shares of national demand in a given year. Freezing market shares was good for Texas and Oklahoma, which made major finds in the early 1930s, and bad for Kansas, which increased its reserves tenfold in the mid-1930s but barely increased its market share, since quotas prevented drillers from offering oil on the market at cheaper prices.[70]

While each state implemented quotas somewhat differently, they shared basic elements. And the goal was the same—to limit supply of oil to estimated demand, thereby stabilizing prices.[71] Texas, as the largest producing state, played the most important role in determining national oil prices. The TRC would adjust the state's quotas partly based on increases and decreases in other states in order to keep the national supply total equal to national oil demand.[72]

Most officials continued to adamantly deny that price fixing or stabilization was the goal of quotas. TRC head Ernest O. Thompson, whose presence on of the TRC lasted from 1933 to 1965, insisted that "in Texas we do not permit price to even be discussed at our hearings."[73] But as political science professor David Prindle noted, the commissioners "were far too intelligent not to understand that the byproduct of market-demand prorationing must be price support."[74] Indeed Thompson wrote in 1935:

> Texas wants a good price for crude petroleum. . . I am convinced that the people of Texas do not want us so to administer the oil law in a manner that would lower the price of crude oil.[75]

SPARE PRODUCTION CAPACITY

Quotas on flowing wells restricted production below what it otherwise would have been and thereby resulted in "shut-in" supply. Wells shut in by quota could, if authorities ordered, be quickly restarted, within days or weeks.[76] The amount of shut-in but quickly producible oil supply became known as spare production capacity or just "spare capacity." Quota regulators did not target a certain volume of spare capacity per se. Spare capacity was the byproduct of tighter quotas imposed in response to excess production. Quotas also encouraged the buildup of spare production capacity. Regulators imposed quotas on individual wells in addition to fields, so producers wanting to produce more oil had to drill more wells. The continued drilling of new wells added to production capacity, which tended to be offset by lower quotas for all wells, which increased spare capacity.[77]

Mandatory quotas introduced supply flexibility where none had previously existed and became the "spigot" that Rockefeller wished he could have had to prevent the industry from shooting itself in the foot through overproducing. Officials could turn crude supply up and down, thereby offsetting the oil supply's usual "stickiness"—its inability to quickly change in response to new market conditions. Whereas it could take months to years to find, develop, and produce oil from a new field, new oil supply from spare capacity could flow in days to weeks. Quotas brought order to the chaos of crude oil production.[78]

Thus, the tumultuous 1931–1935 period gave way to an oil market utterly transformed, from barely restrained private sector drilling to heavily regulated production. Oil prices never bottomed below $1.00 per barrel again. After several price busts and one boom since Standard Oil's breakup in 1911, aggressive state control of production backed by the use of military force and new legal authority to regulate production to prevent *economic* waste (again code for price fixing, which authorities continued to deny was the true aim), crude oil prices found stability.

The new quota system was challenged by an old problem in the oil industry—new producing regions that did not agree to abide by limits. Only Texas and Oklahoma implemented the strictest form of quota, limiting output from individual wells and fields. California and Illinois had much weaker regulations; California wasn't even a member of the IOCC until 1974 and Illinois, although a member did not implement quotas.[79] Such holdouts saw strong production increases in the late 1930s, forcing Texas and Oklahoma to cut their production. Foreshadowing today's tensions between OPEC and non-OPEC countries, Texas and other quota states were annoyed at being forced to play the "swing supplier" role, cutting their states' production to offset increases elsewhere, while the "free-riders" benefitted from high and stable prices that resulted from their restricted output. "Illinois' share of national production increased from 0.4 percent to 10.9 percent" between 1936 and 1940 while California was able to hold on to its sizeable market share despite large new discoveries in the midcontinent region. In 1939 TRC chairman Thompson was angry enough at free-riding states to even suggest abandoning quotas.[80]

STABILIZING PRICES, FROM TEXAS TO THE WORLD

As U.S. industry and officials were fashioning supply controls at home in the late 1920s and early 1930s, the oil business was rapidly expanding abroad where the problem of excess production and pressure to control it followed. After Rockefeller's early (and unsuccessful) attempt to forge an alliance with the Nobels and Shell, the U.S. oil industry largely ignored overseas oil developments until the peak oil scare after World War I, which induced industry and officials to search abroad for new finds and to pay more attention to foreign competitors.[81] It became apparent that achieving stability would require restricting supply not just in the United States—the world's leading crude producer and exporter—but abroad as well.

Opinion on how to manage foreign oil supplies was divided. Larger integrated oil companies with stakes in foreign fields were more welcoming of imports, as were independent refiners who could use cheaper foreign supplies in their refineries. But domestic drillers clamored for import restrictions. With state authorities imposing quotas, the last thing they wanted was to attract imports (initially from Mexico and Venezuela, for the most part). As usual, the oil industry tried voluntary measures first. Voluntary import restraint attempted in 1931 failed to pacify the independents. Domestic oil firms had the ear of state and federal officials and an edge over major international oil firms because their domestic footprint in counties and states was greater and they employed more American workers. In the wake of the price collapse caused by the Black Giant, President Hoover signed a law in June 1932 that set a tariff of $0.21 per barrel on imported crude, equal to 23 percent of the domestic crude price.[82]

While quota and import tariffs kept oil prices high and stable at home, growing competition between American, British, and Dutch companies in foreign markets intensified. Just as huge new fields in Oklahoma and Texas prompted authorities to impose quotas, so too would the discovery of new oil fields in the Middle East and an episode of ruinous price competition spur multinational companies—with official backing—to cooperate to stabilize prices abroad.

Standard Oil and its successor companies started out as refiners. While they eventually acquired some crude oil fields, their main concentration was in pipelines, refining, and marketing. Until 1920 the leading "children" of the broken-up Standard Oil—large U.S. oil companies like Exxon and Mobil—were not interested in acquiring oil reserves abroad. The U.S. drillers had been finding plenty of oil, so the main problem was excess production. But a temporary slowdown in the pace of U.S. discoveries as well as shortages and price spikes after World War I changed all that. Peak oil fears abounded, and remaining U.S. wells were higher cost than those being found abroad. U.S. oil companies therefore saw themselves losing competitiveness vis-à-vis their UK and Dutch rivals who had access to massive, cheap deposits in Asia and the Middle East. U.S. companies only enjoyed easy entry to Latin America. While they actively developed reserves in Mexico, Venezuela, and Colombia, U.S. international oil companies desperately wanted access to reserves further afield.

As they began to search abroad for access to reserves, they encountered resistance from the British and Dutch, who jealously guarded their Middle East and Asian holdings and sought to keep them out of the hands of the U.S. "oil trust." On the eve of World War I, Britain established a direct ownership stake in Anglo-Persian Oil Company (later called and hereafter referred to as British Petroleum or BP), which was producing from Iran's prolific fields, and after World War I, Britain and France controlled former Turkish possessions in what is now called Syria and Iraq. The hunt for oil was on throughout the region. Iraq was expected to be promising; oil had gushed for centuries and discovery wells confirmed that oil was likely plentiful. The U.S. companies, with muscle from Washington, pressed their international rivals for access to any new Middle Eastern finds. After lengthy and difficult talks, BP, with a nudge from London (which did not want to offend Washington), consented to allow American oil companies into Iraq. In July 1928 BP, Royal Dutch/Shell, the Compagnie Française des Pétroles (CFP, later Total), and five U.S. companies belonging to the Near East Development Corporation (Exxon, Socony, Gulf, Arco, and Pan-American) struck an agreement to jointly exploit oil reserves in Iraq.[83] Partners initially named the venture the Turkish Petroleum Company but later changed to the Iraq Petroleum Company. They agreed to a "self-denying" clause, stipulating that none would independently develop oil resources in the former Turkish possessions (except Kuwait). While the full extent of the Middle East's oil resources was yet unknown, the partners agreed to produce them jointly. To demarcate the area where they committed to joint ownership, a red line was drawn around the Saudi peninsula, encompassing the Levant, Turkey, and Iraq.

Paradoxically, while U.S. majors began negotiating joint control of Middle Eastern fields during the shortage scare of the early 1920s, by the time they consummated a deal at the end of the decade the problem had shifted to excess production, not just in the United States but also abroad. A kerosene price war in India that quickly spread to global markets was one result of this, finally coming to an end in late 1928, when Mobil, Shell, and BP agreed to divide the Indian market.[84]

Oil industry executives were shocked that a local kerosene price war could so quickly threaten global oil markets. So in August 1928 Royal Dutch/Shell's Sir Henri Deterding invited Exxon president Walter C. Teagle and BP head Sir John Cadman to Achnacarry Castle in Scotland for a weekend of scotch tasting, grouse shooting, and negotiations to prevent disorder in global oil markets. Other oil executives, including those from Gulf and Standard Oil of Indiana, attended. Cadman's goal, with the backing of the British government, was to enlist Shell and Exxon into a network of alliances to enable stable marketing of BP's new oil supplies from Iran and Iraq. He had been negotiating with Deterding on an alliance to divide the African market and now wanted to expand the discussion to include his American rivals.

In talks lasting two weeks, the oil executives noted that widespread fear of peak oil ten years earlier had resulted in enormous investments in new fields and a buildup in inventories. Now, the problem was not shortages but "tremendous overproduction." They estimated "world shut-in production amounts to 60 percent of the production actually going into consumption" and that an adequate supply "for a long time" was ensured.[85] In such an environment, were each company to battle for market share by undercutting each other, the result would be "destructive competition," excessive investment in production, transportation, and refining capacity, and excessive operating costs that would harm the entire industry. The risk of overbuilding, price wars, and chaos was not theoretical; the oil industry was by now all too aware of oil's tendency toward volatility.

They realized no single producer could sweat the others and hope to dominate the global market as Rockefeller had done when most production and refining was confined to the U.S. northeast. "And so a concordat, rather than conquest, was now the objective of the oil men of Achnacarry."[86] The time had come, they concluded, for majors to unite to prevent overproduction from ruining them all. Deterding, Teagle, and Cadman drafted a memorandum that laid out the basic formula of a cartel system to manage Middle Eastern oil supplies.[87]

Now referred to as the Achnacarry agreement, the accord aimed to restrain crude production growth, to pool transportation facilities, and to avoid price wars in retail markets. Members agreed to freeze current market shares "as-is" or as they stood in 1928 (hence, the other familiar name for this accord: the "As-Is Agreement"); refrain from adding supply except as needed to meet incremental consumption and without threatening another member's share; and abstain from gaining share in any market except by acquiring assets of a company not party to the agreement. The agreement was revised in the course of arduous, subsequent meetings mainly focused on established local cartels in consuming countries in order to jointly administer sales and pricing. Each company was given a quota level for petroleum product sales and agreed not to transfer any part of the quota to a nonmember. Majors also agreed to operate cartels to set prices for refined products like gasoline and heating oil in European consuming markets. The overall objective was to prevent price wars and sustain large profits ("rents") arising from the difference between the low cost of production in concessions, particularly in the Middle East, and high refined product prices in consuming markets. The three agreed success required opening up the agreement to new members, and by 1932, Mobil, Gulf, Texaco, and Atlantic had joined the system.

When the As-Is Agreement was being negotiated, the heads of Exxon, BP, and Shell saw Middle Eastern oil supplies as promising and deemed their joint exploitation optimal, but the size of the supply was unknown. The enormity of the discoveries in the 1930s and 1940s, thus came as a surprise, and perhaps none more so than in Saudi Arabia. In 1926 a BP executive dismissed the possibility that oil would ever be found in Saudi Arabia (and suggested exploring instead in Albania, a conclusion he and Great Britain would deeply regret before long).[88] Two U.S. companies, Chevron and Gulf, had obtained leases in Bahrain, a small island sheikhdom adjacent to Saudi Arabia's Eastern Province, and in 1932 struck commercial quantities of oil.[89] This stimulated interest in Kuwait, other Gulf principalities, and the Arabian Peninsula. In 1933, Saudi King Ibn Saud signed a decree granting Chevron a sixty-year "concession" on the Eastern Province, which would become the world's largest source of crude oil.

"Concessions" were the means by which the majors typically produced oil in foreign countries. Whether alone or jointly, majors operated under a contractual framework—the concession—with a host government, thus intimately linking industry and ruling regimes. While they greatly differed, concessions entailed the following elements:

- The host government would grant a company or consortium of companies the exclusive right to explore and develop oil in a defined area for a defined period of time.
- The company or consortium owns any oil found and can dispose of it as it wished.
- The company or consortium bears all financial and commercial risks.
- The company makes certain payments to the host government such as signature bonus, surface taxes, and royalties.[90]

Seven integrated international oil companies established concession consortia throughout the Middle East. They included BP, Shell, Exxon, Mobil,

Texaco, Chevron, and Gulf and were dubbed the "Seven Sisters" in the 1950s by Enrico Mattei, the head of the Italian state-owned oil company Eni. Over the subsequent years and decades one or more of these companies controlled the bulk of production in Iraq, Saudi Arabia, Kuwait, Qatar, Iran, Venezuela, and Indonesia. By 1949, they held 82 percent of proved oil reserves outside the United States.[91] Through a complex network of jointly owned subsidiaries and affiliates they also controlled 57 percent of global refining capacity and the bulk of transportation and marketing facilities outside the United States and Soviet Union.[92]

As part of these concession arrangements, the Seven Sisters restrained output from major new finds in order to prevent price collapses, the industry's old demon. Called "production planning" and implemented via "offtake" agreements (both terms synonymous with quotas), the agreement provided for coordinated adjustment in a certain concession's production depending on developments in other concessions and global market conditions. As with domestic U.S. quotas in the oil states, the main goal of the Seven Sisters' production planning was to keep oil prices stable.[93] Former OPEC Secretary General Dr. Francisco Parra noted the similarity between production planning and offtake agreements and TRC quotas.

> The majors could, and did, jointly program offtake from other countries . . . and the major purpose behind the programming was, obviously, to avoid adverse price effects—otherwise why bother? It was not a vastly different system in principle from the Texas Railroad Commission, where a total production allowable for a forward period was determined by the nominations of offtakers, and the total then prorated to each producer.[94]

GETTING THE PRICE FORMULA RIGHT

An important feature of the Seven Sisters' system of international oil market control involved the pricing of crude oil and refined products in concessions and sales in consuming markets. To understand how crude oil prices were set after the 1920s and through the early 1970s, it is helpful to think of the world as two separate markets—U.S. and non–U.S.

In the United States, domestic crude oil prices were set in freely traded markets through arms-length transactions (where the buyer and seller are not affiliated). Each region in the United States tended to have one large buyer that acted as a price leader, making the first announcement of the price he was prepared to pay for oil from the wells. Smaller refiners would then set their offer prices in relation to the leader's. There was no cooperation or price fixing and transactions were closely policed by state and federal antitrust authorities. The leader could not impose a price out of line with levels justified by supply and demand. If he set prices too high he would overpay relative to his competitors and if too low he would not obtain the barrels needed during the given period. Therefore, the price leader had an incentive to lead with a price as close as possible to market conditions. (Of course, those market conditions were heavily influenced by state quota authorities.)

Outside the United States, price structures were very different, as there were no actively traded markets for crude oil. Most crude production outside the United States was handled by major integrated firms for use in their own refineries.[95] However, majors did trade some crude with one another and sold some of their supply to independent refineries. Participants in the As-Is Agreement needed a price formula that would prevent price wars, and established a "basing point" price formula. The final sales price would be linked to a price at a given location—the base point, usually a major source of supply or exports—and the transportation costs between the base point and final destination. Final sales prices would be quoted only in *receiving ports*.[96] Requiring prices to be quoted in receiving ports based on a base point and freight charge instead of at the wellhead boosted transparency and therefore trust, since operators could more easily see how much oil was being transacted at what prices in a relatively limited number of receiving terminals as opposed to thousands of wells.

The goal of the basing point price system was to discourage cheating through transparency and to prevent price wars. The cement and steel industries had operated similar systems. The bane of cartels, after all, had been cheating by members tempted to illicitly sell below the price established by the cartel but still high enough to earn the clandestine seller a juicy profit. Since the base price was published for all to see and freight charges were jointly agreed, all producers could be confident they weren't being undercut by a rival. Uniform pricing of their crude in all destinations reduced suspicion that any given sale may have been the result of unseen discounting by a competitor.[97] The formula was also easy to administer.

For sales the cartel made to nonmembers, Shell, Exxon, and BP selected as its base price the price of crude oil in the U.S. Gulf of Mexico (a West Coast basing point was also established for sales to Asia, but the Gulf handled most exports) and added to this base price the cost of freight from the U.S. Gulf of Mexico to the final destination. The rationale for selecting the U.S. Gulf Coast as the base point stemmed from the fact that the U.S. had been and was by far the world's largest producer and exporter, and was the source of marginal supply. If a refiner anywhere on the planet needed extra crude, the most likely source would be the United States and the price of that crude would be the cost at a Texas port plus transportation charges to the refiner.[98] Freight rates were set by cartel members and frozen for six months, then reset. The price formula, used for crude and refined product prices, became known as "Gulf-plus" or "Texas-plus."[99]

For example, assume Exxon wished to sell an Italian refiner a cargo of oil it produced from its concession in Iraq. The distance from the Al Basra loading terminal to Porto Marghera near Venice is roughly 4,700 nautical miles. But Exxon would charge the refiner a higher freight rate, as if the cargo had instead traveled from the U.S. Gulf Coast to Italy, a longer and therefore costly distance of 6,400 miles.[100] The extra profit cartel members earned by pricing all crude sales as if they had been delivered from the Texas Gulf Coast even when they had not was called "phantom freight."

In the case above, Exxon's cost of delivering oil from Iraq to Italy was well below the cost of transporting oil from the U.S. Gulf Coast to Italy, which was reflected in the price the Italian refiner had to pay. The ability to capture "phantom freight" profits was also enhanced by the pooling of transportation facilities, preventing overcapacity and excess cost (a goal of Rockefeller's Standard Oil as well). Instead of charging each other the cost of freight from the Gulf Coast to the destination port as they did for nonmembers, they would only charge each other freight costs between the shipping ports (which was often closer to the final destination than the U.S. Gulf Coast). The freight savings, along with cartel members' agreement to pool transportation facilities and vessels, further boosted their profit.

For the majors, one happy consequence of their decision to base international oil prices on prices in Texas was fat profits.[101] The U.S. quotas kept oil prices stable and high. By linking their sales to Texas-plus prices, cartel members would have even less reason to cheat by undercutting prices and starting a price war because they were guaranteed to receive top prices under the basing price system, courtesy of U.S. oil state regulators. Moreover, world crude prices based on high U.S. ones would dissuade independent competing refiners from entering the market.

WAR AGAIN BRINGS WASHINGTON
AND THE OIL INDUSTRY CLOSER

The approach and arrival of World War II restored pragmatic cooperation between industry and government, temporarily disrupted in 1938 when FDR's Justice Department opened a wide-ranging antitrust case against hundreds of oil companies. Now the aim was to maximize output and efficiency and quickly provide the enormous amounts of fuel needed for the war effort. The Justice Department's antitrust suit was resolved and industry received an exemption to allow pooling and coordination of activities. Harold Ickes was named Petroleum Coordinator for National Defense and eventually Petroleum Administrator for War. Ickes hired a seasoned oil executive as his deputy and presided over a 30 percent increase in crude production. The United States provided 6 of the 7 billion barrels used to achieve victory.[102]

During the latter stages of World War II the importance of spare capacity—having a supply of shut-in but readily available oil—became apparent. At the war's outbreak, the United States had plenty of extra production capacity. In addition to cutbacks from quotas in the mid-1930s, U.S. oil exports to Europe fell by almost 25 percent after the war broke out, obliging the TRC to cut quotas by about 20 percent. Additional curtailments in 1942 resulted in spare capacity of around 40 percent of potential in Texas.[103]

At first, wartime planners worried less about spare capacity and more about making disparate oil transportation, refining, and marketing systems work as efficiently and at as high volume as possible. Regulators sanctioned Rockefeller's old strategy of pooling railcars and other transportation facilities. As for the crude producing upstream, in 1940 the United States produced 3.7 million barrels per day, equal to three-quarters of its potential of 4.8 million barrels per day.[104] This surplus capacity, according to the official history of wartime oil planning, initially "nourished the delusion of plenty, and caused many to question the need for finding and developing new domestic reserves."[105]

But oil planners realized that the existing spare capacity would not be enough. Sustaining higher crude production for military purposes would require developing more reserves and launching an aggressive program of "wildcat" drilling, secondary recovery (injecting gas or water into fields to maintain pressure), and boosting stripper well production. The Petroleum Administration for War, which oversaw the oil sector during the war, pushed for price increases to stimulate production. While some local price increases were granted, such as to Pennsylvania producers in 1942, a proposed broad increase was rejected and instead subsidies for stripper wells were implemented in 1943.

After the war, officials credited sustaining spare capacity as one of the most important accomplishments of wartime oil policy.[106] Had no wartime drilling boom taken place to replace reserves consumed in the conflict, planners estimated that potential production would have fallen to 3.2 mb/d by war's end; but additional drilling kept it at 4.6 mb/d, close to the prewar level.[107] Despite increasing production by 1.0 mb/d (27 percent), the United States still maintained a surplus capacity until the second half of 1944, when enormous fuel requirements needed for the final push against Germany and Japan forced drillers to produce all-out, exceeding the MER by more than one hundred thousand barrels per day.[108]

While prosecuting the war, the United States and United Kingdom officials became preoccupied with how to manage what they expected would be a deluge of oil supply from the Middle East once hostilities ceased. Leaders were not confident that the Seven Sisters' system of controlling output and stabilizing prices would stand the strain of massive new supplies, but the wartime Allies had different opinions about the best way forward. American officials were concerned about exhaustion of domestic supplies and wanted to open up the Middle East to unrestricted output, one aim being to shift Europe's dependence from the United States to Middle East. The British, meanwhile, feared a postwar wave of drilling in the Middle East would crush prices and destabilize oil producing regimes (and, given the connection of contracts to regimes, jeopardize their oil concessions). The United States and United Kingdom officials' concerns were colored by decades of rivalry and distrust in the global oil market. The British suspected U.S. officials wanted to break into the Kingdom's Iran concession whereas the Americans suspected the British of wanting to move in on the U.S. companies' Saudi interests and holdings. Both were suspicious of the Seven Sisters operations, especially after the United Kingdom government discovered it was paying phantom freight charges for oil used by its navy in the war effort.

Suspicions of the Seven Sisters united the two nations and convinced U.S. and United Kingdom officials to negotiate terms for a bilateral oil market cartel composed of both governments. Negotiations between the wartime allies started in April 1944 and aimed at what the State Department called the "orderly distribution of abundance" of Middle Eastern oil.[109] On August 8 both sides signed the Anglo-American Petroleum Agreement that set up an eight-member International Petroleum Commission. The Commission would, among other things, estimate global demand and suggest production quotas to various countries. The agreement included assurances that both governments would implement commission recommendations.

The Anglo-American Petroleum Agreement met quick and stiff opposition from the oil industry, again wary of *federal* usurpation of control over quotas and price fixing that seemed to be lifted straight out of the playbook the TRC and Seven Sisters' As-Is Agreement. The oil industry sharply opposed Washington's attempt to enter the oil market management business. In the end the Anglo-American Petroleum Agreement was withdrawn so it could be watered down to suit the industry's concerns, but was ultimately abandoned.[110]

With the war won and an Anglo-American scheme to control the global oil market toppled, the TRC and multinational oil companies turned back to stabilizing oil markets. But their task was complicated by two interrelated challenges—how to handle massive new discoveries of oil that, confirming wartime planners fears, had been found and were starting to be produced in the Middle East, and how to adapt and modify the Texas-plus international price formula in light of this new center of gravity and in response to wartime scrutiny.

Both U.S. and British authorities had been immensely angry to discover that the basing point price formula included "phantom freight" charges; since the Seven Sisters' pricing formula was not published, officials only found out about it after the British government launched an investigation. Under government pressure, majors adjusted the Texas-plus system to reduce "phantom freight" by adding a second "basing point" in the Persian Gulf, closer to European markets.[111] After the war the U.S. Congress also investigated the majors' wartime pricing policies and discovered that the majors were making a tidy profit selling low-cost oil from the Middle East to the United States. Senate hearings after the war revealed that the cost of producing oil in Saudi Arabia was estimated to be about $0.40 per barrel (including a $0.21 per barrel royalty that went to the Saudi Arabian government) but that these barrels were then sold to the United States Navy at $1.05 per barrel or above. This arrangement led to sharp criticism of Chevron and Texaco, and brought further scrutiny to the pricing system.[112] The Texas-plus basing point system lost further economic rationale as the United States became a net importer of crude in 1948. Whereas before World War II the Caribbean and U.S. Gulf were the world's most important oil-producing and oil-exporting regions, afterward that role shifted to the Middle East.

The majors and their Texas-plus price system were not the only subjects of criticism from the United States and Europe; soon, they came under fire from the concession governments themselves. Since concession agreements typically included a royalty on every barrel produced, host governments cared more about maximizing the barrels produced than the price per barrel. But in 1948, a nationalist government in Venezuela won a fifty-fifty share of *profits* from oil production, and Saudi Arabia and other Middle East producers soon demanded the same fifty-fifty treatment.[113]

To fulfill this demand would amount to a sea change in how oil was priced worldwide. Under the old Texas-plus system, crude oil was rarely quoted or priced in a producing country; instead, majors quoted prices in delivery ports. But to effectuate the new fifty-fifty profit-sharing system, producers needed to establish a price in the host producing country as a basis on which to calculate income and profits. Thus, in 1949 the Texas-plus price system was replaced by oil prices quoted at ports of loading in Venezuela and the Persian Gulf. The Seven Sisters were obliged to establish the same "base point" for all their customers that they had initially set just for sales between themselves.

Through the early 1950s, the administered prices set in concession countries mirrored Texas prices. But the inundation of new Middle Eastern oil combined with the entry of new producers unaffiliated with majors—called "independents"—made it increasingly difficult for the majors to maintain price parity between the Middle East and the United States. Venezuela granted some independent producers access in the 1950s, followed by Libya, Saudi Arabia, and Iran;[114] these independents were able to undercut the Seven Sisters on price, threatening them with loss of market share. Meanwhile, host governments stepped up the pressure on majors to increase production from concessions. The majors' profits were getting hit from both sides—from pesky independent producers selling oil below Texas-based prices and host governments who now saw half the profits and clamored for still higher sales volumes, which further put downward pressure on prices.

The large Middle Eastern finds and the trend toward lower prices posed challenges not just for the majors but for the oil industry and regulators in Texas as well. For the U.S. industry, the threat was that large new supplies of cheap oil would flood the U.S. market and depress prices. Both independent refineries and major integrated companies with refineries in the States preferred to run low-cost Middle Eastern crude through their units to capture a higher profit on gasoline and heating oil. And once the Texas-plus price formula broke down, buying cheap Middle Eastern barrels became easier. Total U.S. crude imports nearly quadrupled from 203,000 b/d in 1945 to 781,000 b/d ten years later, while the Middle East's oil rose from zero to one-third of every barrel imported.[115] The U.S. regulators had a new challenge on their hands.

A POSTWAR BALANCING ACT FOR THE TRC

Despite the new oil gushing from the Middle East, the United States did not immediately experience the excess supply and price bust officials feared after the war ended. Instead, pent up demand and inflation (exacerbated by the lifting of wartime price controls) caused global crude oil prices to rise nearly threefold, from $1.05 per barrel at the end of the war to $2.75 in 1947.[116] Demand was strong enough that the TRC ordered full production in 1947 (the last time it would do so until 1972).

This first major oil price increase after World War II arose from tight supply and demand conditions, due in part—Robert Bradley argues—to government policies unrelated to quotas and oil companies' desire to keep prices high.[117] But the next two price increases were buttressed by state supply regulators. If not initially caused by state quotas, two price hikes in the 1950s were certainly sustained by them. The second price hike, in 1953, followed the lifting of another set of price controls toward the end of the Korean War and a TRC order to lower production. Crude prices jumped by 2.5 percent between January and February and 8.4 percent between May and June.[118] The 1953 price increase was controversial because the market had not tightened due to strong demand or insufficient supply—indeed, overall national production of crude and stocks were high and outpacing demand.[119] The price hike stemmed, at least in part, from lower TRC quotas.

The third price hike was precipitated by the 1956 Suez Crisis, and serves as a good illustration not just of the impact of TRC involvement but of the difficulty in managing a global market—and one centered in an increasingly fractious region.

In October 1956, mounting tensions between nationalist Egyptian leader Gamal Abdel Nasser and Britain, France, and Israel boiled over into military conflict. Disruption in traffic through the Suez Canal and of oil piped to the eastern Mediterranean from Middle Eastern fields pushed oil prices up, and shortages threatened Western Europe (which depended on Middle Eastern supplies). Europe clamored for more oil from the United States.

Washington acquiesced and began planning for the possibility of a prolonged disruption in Middle Eastern oil. In September the Interior Department convened officials from the four biggest producing states—Texas, Louisiana, New Mexico, and Oklahoma—to assess spare production capacity levels. Their host, Interior Department's Director of the Oil and Gas Division H. A. Stewart, told the press that U.S. states would have to increase shipments by between 0.5 mb/d and 1.1 mb/d to prevent "slow petroleum starvation" in Europe. Domestic producers estimated U.S. spare capacity to be 2.25 mb/d, more than enough to cover Suez flows to the United States and Western Europe (see figure 4.5). States had assured Stewart the oil was available, although a tanker shortage might impede rapid resupply of the East Coast or Europe if Middle Eastern barrels were lost.[120] Yet, Texas was in no hurry to increase production; in fact the TRC cut production quotas for October, although it promised to reverse policy if an emergency developed.[121]

The possibility turned to reality as fighting caused closure of the Suez Canal, which, along with the sabotage of an Iraqi pipeline to the Mediterranean, resulted in the loss of 1.5 mb/d or 10 percent of global supply in November.[122] Washington implemented emergency plans to pool oil supplies. The large oil companies, located primarily in western Texas with good transportation links to Gulf ports, immediately urged the TRC to sharply increase quotas to enable greater exports of oil. But smaller independent companies concentrated in eastern Texas and lacking good pipeline connections, staunchly opposed higher quotas. All they would see was lower prices with little opportunity to sell. Smaller companies

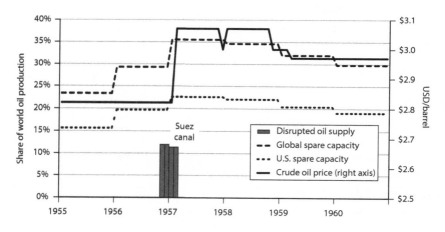

FIGURE 4.5

Spare capacity exceeds Suez shipments.

Source: API, *Petroleum Facts and Figures* (1959), as modified by the Rapidan Group. © The Rapidan Group.

Citation: Senate Committee on Foreign Relations. Subcommittee on Multinational Corporations. Multinational Petroleum Companies and Foreign Policy Hearings, 93rd Cong., 2nd sess., 1974, 335. http://babel.hathitrust.org/cgi/pt?id=mdp.39015078592071;view=1up;seq=345.

argued that there was no emergency and that the crisis could helpfully thin out excess crude stocks.[123] The TRC sided with the independents, ordering just a small increase in quotas, although it again promised to act quickly to increase quotas if an emergency arose.[124]

Louisiana was quicker to increase production: The state's conservation commissioner, John Hussey, ordered large allowable increases in November and December. Louisiana's allowable production hit a record 973,000 b/d for December from October's allowable level of 850,000 b/d.[125] Oklahoma increased quotas by 42,000 b/d from November to December. Texas finally followed as prices rose and U.S. inventory declined, but its relatively small increase—only 75,000 b/d in December—greatly complicated efforts by the majors and Western countries to organize an "Oil Lift" to supply Europe. Although states increased production, there had as yet been no request or order to hike production from Washington (in fact, a furious President Eisenhower suspended emergency plans to provide Europe with oil until United Kingdom, French, and Israeli forces began evacuating seized Egyptian territory)[126] and through January TRC only permitted production to slowly rise, well below levels requested by the large oil companies.

As oil prices jumped 6.7 percent in January, some in Britain charged the TRC with trying to gouge European consumers and demanded Texas increase production. "My back is as stiff as any Englishman's," TRC Commissioner Olin Culberson retorted, "I'm not meddling in their business and they haven't had much luck meddling in mine."[127] When a London newspaper reporter told Culberson that British industry would be ruined if the TRC did not allow higher production, the commissioner replied: "So what, buddy? I obey the sovereign laws of Texas, not England."[128]

By February 1957, the Oil Lift was a mess. "Official statements," Associated Press reported, "reflect disagreements, confusion, and much concern over missed objectives." President Eisenhower, though still furious over the invasion of Egypt, warned the oil industry that he might have to intervene to ensure sufficient crude oil was transported to Europe.[129] Texas's governor pushed back, insisting President Eisenhower first restrict crude oil imports and persuade refiners to reduce gasoline stocks before Texas increased production. But under persistent criticism (although still no federate mandate), in February the TRC ordered a 211,000 b/d production boost for March 1957.[130] A mild winter and the quick reopening of the Suez Canal also ameliorated the shortage. Soon after, the crisis passed. In April the TRC and other oil states shut in production to prevent price weakness.

Although the United States' high spare production capacity was a byproduct of quotas rather than a design, the Suez Crisis illustrated its benefit in times of supply disruption. Ample spare capacity prevented oil price shocks by offsetting lost supplies and denying foreign adversaries leverage over the United States and its allies. The United States saw this again eleven years later, during the Six-Day War between Israel and its Arab neighbors in June 1967. Not only was the Suez Canal closed but production in several Arab countries was curtailed, taking some 6 mb/d off the market initially. As Arab country exports resumed the maximum loss was closer to 1.5 mb/d, with another 500 kb/d going offline in late June and early July due to a conflict in Nigeria.[131] But Texas and Louisiana estimated each could increase production by 1.0 to 1.5 mb/d within 15 days and—facilitated by the TRC—total U.S. supply surged by almost one million b/d, nearly two thirds of the maximum loss from the Arab embargo. The availability of spare capacity, once again, proved to be a valuable national security asset.[132]

Unlike price increases in 1947, those in 1953 and 1957 were perpetuated by Texas ordering production cutbacks in response to competition from large amounts of cheap new oil from the Middle East (see figure 4.6).

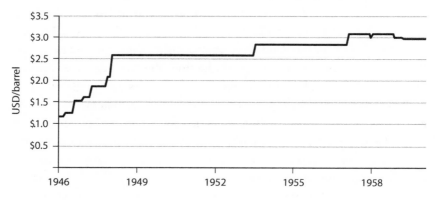

FIGURE 4.6

Monthly U.S. crude prices, 1947–1960.

Source: API, *Petroleum Facts and Figures* (1959); Dow Jones & Company, Spot Oil Price: West Texas Intermediate.

The higher prices caused by the Suez crisis were made to stick through lower quotas imposed by Texas and oil states[133]—but having to cut production to accommodate "foreign oil" of course made independent oil producers and their elected officials in producing states and Washington very unhappy, even if it did raise spare capacity that could be used in times of crisis. By the mid-1950s some 23 percent of total world supply was being held off the market in the United States but mainly in Texas. (Another 12 percent was being held off by the Seven Sisters in the Middle East.) The TRC hadn't liked being the swing producer to offset excessive California and Illinois production in the 1930s, and it didn't like doing so for foreign oil. Not just TRC but also the domestic oil industry and its congressional supporters clamored for protection from the tsunami of oil imports from the Middle East. While tariffs on imports had been imposed in the early 1930s, they had been reduced in 1939 and 1943 when the need for oil was high, and again after World War II in the context of the General Agreement on Tariffs and Trade in 1947.[134] But even as the United States shifted from being a crude exporter to importer, the flood of new cheap oil from the Middle East would revive the debate about import controls.

The TRC tried to shame and intimidate majors by demanding they make data about their imports public, hoping revelations of high imports would paint them in a negative public light.[135] In 1949 and 1950 Congress launched three investigations of allegedly nefarious actions of the "International Petroleum Cartel," as they called the Seven Sisters. They found no evidence of illegal collusion or consumer harm, but conveyed a thinly veiled threat of legislative restrictions on imports if the deluge continued. The majors got the message and in 1954 agreed to voluntarily limit imports to the United States, as they once had in 1931. Voluntary import quotas were assigned based on a company's past import share, similar to the As-Is Agreement which froze companies market shares at 1928 levels. But voluntary import quotas went unheeded, as nearly all prior voluntary restraints on supply had been.

As cheap Middle Eastern crude imports rose, the TRC was faced with the difficult decision of whether to slash production further. "There is a point beyond which this [TRC] cannot go in reducing the allowable for the state without seriously crippling a great many producers," TRC's Culberson said in June 1956, after a meeting where the Commission increased quotas despite company nominations for a cut. Culberson decried producers abroad as well as those in other states where quotas had been rising for stealing Texas's market share.[136]

As imports flooded the market, U.S. independent oil producers joined the chorus of complaints to the federal government, invoking the national security argument that cheap imports were killing a vital domestic energy sector. In 1955, the federal government oversaw voluntary import quotas that applied to all states east of the Rockies. The West Coast, relatively deficient in oil endowment, was not expected to adhere to limits as long as those imports were "reasonably competitive" with domestic oil.[137] The goal was to limit imports to 1954 levels. Venezuelan and Canadian imports were exempted, as the main worry was huge imports from the Middle East. Exxon and some other majors that imported Middle Eastern oil agreed to go along, given thinly veiled threats from Washington of mandatory controls. But other companies did not.

Actual imports continued to climb beyond 1954 levels, raising ire among domestic producers and pushing Washington toward mandatory controls. In 1957, a Cabinet-level Special Committee concluded that while cheap oil imports were "attractive," "excessive" reliance on them would jeopardize national security.[138] By 1959, President Eisenhower instituted compulsory oil quotas roughly equal to 9 percent of domestic consumption. Canada and Mexican imports were exempted. Byzantine in design and extraordinarily complex to implement, the Mandatory Oil Import Program (MOIP) lasted 14 years.[139]

The same forces roiling the U.S. market were also troubling the majors. Just as competition from new suppliers had aborted early attempts by Pennsylvania drillers to establish cartels in the 1800s, it began to weaken the hold of the most powerful and long-lived producer cartel ever seen. In Venezuela, independents accounted for some 15 percent of total production by 1966. Libya opened up to independent producers like Amerada Hess, Conoco, and Nelson Bunker Hunt, and saw its production rise from zero in 1960 to 2.6 mb/d in 1968.[140] In the late 1950s, Iran signed two exploration and development agreements for concessions in the Persian Gulf offshore with nonmajors. In 1957, Saudi Arabia entered into an agreement with another nonmajor, the Japan Petroleum Trading Company, to explore and develop fields in the Neutral Zone offshore area. Crude oil from the Soviet Union also began making its way into the market, as the discovery and development of large fields in the Soviet bloc led to a rapid growth in oil exports, from less than 100,000 b/d in 1956 to nearly 700,000 b/d in 1961. By the late 1950s, the Seven Sisters' decades of dominance of the international oil market was besieged by independent producers who had found their way into major producing countries outside their control.[141]

While irrepressible supply and demand pressures, driven in the United States in large part by quotas and import quotas, forced U.S. prices up and Middle Eastern ones down, host governments resisted any reduction in administered prices because, under the new system where royalties were paid on profits rather than barrels produced, that would lower their payments. Yet to sell their oil in an increasingly crowded and competitive market, majors found themselves compelled to offer discounts off of administered prices in the Persian Gulf, while still paying the royalties on unchanged administered prices. The Seven Sisters' profits were getting squeezed. By the late 1950s the frustrated majors concluded it was only reasonable that host countries should share the burden of lower real-world crude oil prices. Channeling the producer's viewpoint, Parra wrote, "Now was the time to in effect reaffirm the principle that profit sharing meant profit sharing, on the downside as on the upside."[142]

In September 1959, Exxon led a round of administered price cuts of about 5 percent, angering Venezuela and the Middle East countries. In August 1960 the majors cut administered prices another 10 percent, triggering a storm of indignation—and, unknown to them at the time, precipitating the creation of a group that would eventually inherit the role of stabilizing the global oil market.[143] Infuriated at the sudden loss of revenue, the host governments banded together to form a new organization uniting petroleum-producing countries to resist the majors' price cuts. It was called the Organization of the Petroleum Exporting Countries, better known by its acronym, OPEC.

TWILIGHT FOR TEXAS AND THE SEVEN SISTERS

The late 1950s marked the apogee of the TRC and the Seven Sisters' control over international oil supply and prices. The majors' control weakened and then collapsed in the 1970s as host governments took over control of pricing and nationalized concessions. And in the United States, the Texas era of price control was ending by the late 1960s as soaring domestic demand outpaced supply. With an import tariff, the United States had disconnected itself from the global oil market to some extent. Outside the United States oil prices fell during the decade, despite healthy demand, because of the surge in cheap oil supplies that were effectively barred from the U.S. market. In the United States, the TRC was able to keep crude prices stable for most of the 1960s, but had to increase quotas in order to do so, resulting in less U.S. spare capacity (see figure 4.7).

But soaring U.S. demand and slowing supply growth gradually eroded the TRC's market power: In August 1970 the *San Antonio Express* reported an "obviously reluctant" TRC ordered production up to 80 percent of potential, the highest level since October 1951. Commissioners were reluctant because they feared producing at such high levels would lead to pollution and would overly tax field equipment. But they felt they had no choice given a "statutory" duty to increase allowable production "when the market was there."[144]

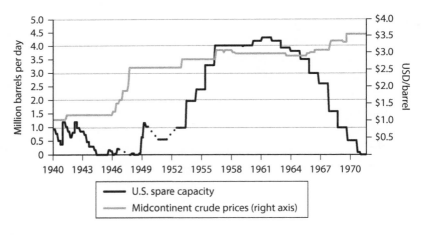

FIGURE 4.7

U.S. spare capacity and crude prices. The dotted lines denote areas where data are missing.

Sources: Frey and Ide, *Petroleum Administration for War*; U.S. Senate; BP, "Energy Outlook to 2035"; API, *Petroleum Facts and Figures* (1959); Dow Jones & Company, Spot Oil Price: West Texas Intermediate. © The Rapidan Group.

Obliged to continue ordering higher production to keep up with rising demand and thereby watch spare capacity shrink, the end of the road for the TRC's oil market management came on March 16, 1972, at their first-ever meeting in El Paso. Presiding over a rooftop ballroom packed with oil executives, a disappointed and worried Chairman Byron Tunnell ordered full production for the first time since 1947, calling the decision "a damn historic occasion and a sad occasion"—"sad" because there was plenty of oil to be found, Tunnell said, but Congress had impeded the search with tax increases and new environmental policies. As it was, Texas's 8,500 oil fields could no longer serve as "reliable old warriors," surging to meet emergency demand from other states and allies as they once did.[145] Because the state's fields had not been allowed to produce all-out in decades, and equipment was old and worn, Tunnell and the other commissioners were not sure how much more oil could be produced—perhaps, they thought, another 150,000 to 200,000 barrels per day.[146]

Thus, by the end of 1972 the last vestiges of the Texas era of oil market control disappeared. And on the back of increasing domestic demand, the rationale for import quotas also weakened: The United States now needed more oil from abroad. In 1973 President Nixon declared the MOIP unnecessary and counterproductive, and terminated it.

The Texas era of oil market management had lasted from roughly 1927 to 1972 and coincided with an astounding growth in the global supply and demand for oil. Just as massive expansion in oil production amid generally falling prices in the late nineteenth and early twentieth centuries enabled the growth of kerosene in illumination and eventually the transition to gasoline in transportation, so too did even bigger, low-cost new supplies from the Middle East, United States, and Russia in the 1950s and 1960s enable the consumption boom that ensconced oil as the lifeblood of modern civilization to this day. In the oil market, supply often created or facilitated demand. Both epochal transitions were associated with relative market stability arising from the firm hand of industry, governments, or both on the supply of oil.

The post–World War II boom in oil consumption came from both new and old uses. With the new cheap supplies available after World War II, oil started to displace coal for heating and electricity generation. During the late 1960s and early 1970s, "mass motorization" drove demand.

From 1950 to 1973 the worldwide number of automobiles and other passenger vehicles exploded from 53 million to nearly 250 million.[147] Europe
and Japan saw massive increase in oil use for motorized transport. Rapidly expanding civil aviation and the birth of the plastics industry also
boosted oil use. It was the dawn of the era, as preeminent oil market
scholar Daniel Yergin called it, of the "Hydrocarbon Man."[148]

> Whatever the twists and turns in global politics, whatever the ebb of
> imperial power and the flow of national pride, one trend in the decades
> following World War II progressed in a straight and rapidly ascending
> line—the consumption of oil. If it can be said, in the abstract, that the
> sun energized the planet, it was oil that now powered its human popula-
> tion, both in its familiar forms as fuel and in the proliferation of new
> petrochemical products. Oil emerged triumphant, the undisputed King,
> a monarch garbed in a dazzling array of plastics. He was generous to his
> loyal subjects, sharing his wealth to, and even beyond, the point of waste.
> His reign was a time of confidence, of growth, of expansion, of astonishing
> economic performance. His largesse transformed his kingdom, ushering
> in a new drive-in civilization.[149]

Between 1945 and 1970 U.S. oil demand tripled from 1.7 billion barrels
to 5.4 billion barrels while per-capita oil use doubled from thirteen to
twenty-six barrels.[150] World energy demand tripled between 1949 and 1972,
but oil demand more than quintupled (see figure 4.8). Europe's demand
rose thirteenfold as it recovered from war, and Japan's consumption rose
137-fold. In both regions this was largely due to the dramatic displacement
of coal with oil. This was part of a global trend. Worldwide, coal provided
two-thirds of energy demand in 1949. By 1971 positions had switched—oil
and gas provided two-thirds and coal one-third.[151] The post–World War
II oil boom was only possible due to the enormous amounts of low-cost
Persian Gulf oil that flowed to market, as well as substantial increases in
U.S. production during the period.

Born out of the boom and bust of the 1920s, the oil industry—with the
help of Texas and the officials of other states—had fashioned an expansive
system of "evening and adjusting." The TRC and sister agencies implemented quotas to force low-cost U.S. oil off the market, supporting higher

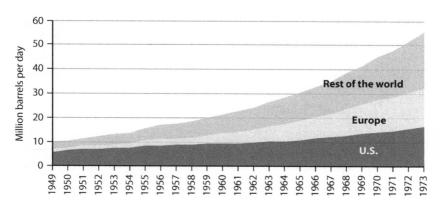

FIGURE 4.8

Global crude consumption, 1949–1973.

Source: BP, "Statistical Review of World Energy," 1959, 1960, 1961, 1962, 1963, 1964, 1965, 1966.

but stable prices. Majors haunted by the specter of familiar ruinous global price wars erected an extensive cartel system to maintain market shares, pool facilities, limit the flow of crude from massive new discoveries, and set high and stable prices for crude and refined products in consuming markets that generated large profits.

Whereas Rockefeller and Standard Oil had stabilized the early oil industry by monopolizing, refining, and integrating with transportation, the much larger and globalized oil market of the twentieth century required upstream wellhead control in the United States as well as cartelization of the bulk of foreign production, transportation, and refining.

The U.S. quotas and majors' cartelization never completely controlled all global oil production; competition particularly from the Soviet Union and independent producers was brisk. But the Texas era of supply management did vanquish boom-bust price cycles. From the super-low prices following the 1930 Black Giant discovery up until the early 1970s, industry-government regulation of supply and prices provided the world with remarkably stable oil prices as consumption skyrocketed in developed countries and supply boomed all over the world. After 1934 prices essentially only moved up (adjusted for inflation, see figure 4.9), despite massive new discoveries that in the uncontrolled period would likely

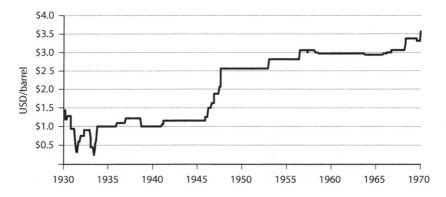

FIGURE 4.9

Monthly U.S. crude prices, 1930–1970.

Source: API, *Petroleum Facts and Figures* (1959); Dow Jones & Company, Spot Oil Price: West Texas Intermediate.

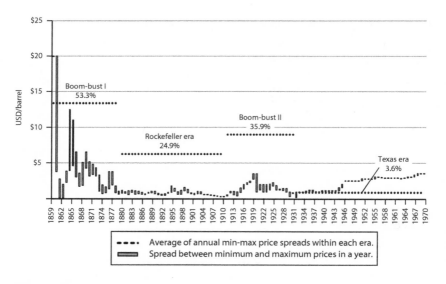

FIGURE 4.10

Annual ranges of monthly U.S. crude oil prices, 1859–1970.

Sources: *Derrick's*, vols. I–IV; API, *Petroleum Facts and Figures* (1959); Dow Jones & Company, Spot Oil Price: West Texas Intermediate.

have triggered collapses. Crude oil price volatility averaged 3.6 percent during the Texas era, compared with 36 percent in the preceding Boom-Bust II period between 1911 and 1934 (see figure 4.10). Texas and other quota states acted as the oil market's "swing producers," adjusting supply readily, substantially, and over a prolonged period of time (measuring years) to stabilize prices.

WERE MANDATORY QUOTAS AND CARTELIZATION NECESSARY TO STABILIZE THE OIL MARKET?

That extensive supply controls coincided with an explosion in oil use amid stable nominal and declining real prices is indisputable. Most historians and academics agree that the TRC and the Seven Sisters achieved price stability by exercising market power—the ability to affect and sustain prices above levels that they could obtain in purely competitive conditions—and that this stability allowed for an orderly and vast boom in global oil exploration, production, transportation, refining, and marketing. To exercise this power, suppliers needed a dominant position in the market. Between them, U.S. producers and concessions controlled by the Seven Sisters accounted for 95 percent of global crude production and 89 percent of proved reserves in 1948.[152] Moreover, the Seven Sisters controlled about 57 percent of global refining capacity.[153] While oilmen and oil states wanted to raise prices to support profits and investment, oil price stability was arguably a larger motivation.

If a dominant market position is a necessary condition for raising and stabilizing prices, producers must also be willing to cooperate. Here the TRC, other oil states, and the Seven Sisters were remarkably successful. Through formal and informal arrangements and linkages, they controlled supply and stabilized both near-term prices and long-term price expectations. Leading contemporary energy economist James Hamilton noted: "The remarkable stability of nominal crude oil prices in the periods between [spikes] . . . can be attributed to state regulatory commissions' policy of defending [administered] prices whenever discounts threatened to produce a break."[154] Former ENI senior executive Leonardo Maugeri described the TRC as the "backbone of U.S. oil control . . . that was born out of chaos . . . [and] turned out to be a very successful and enduring pillar of the oil world.[155] Even free-market advocate Morris Adelman conceded the TRC did its job very efficiently and smoothly, providing industry with what it craved most—stable prices.[156] Most importantly, quotas enabled massive new, rapidly expanding and low-cost Middle East supplies to enter the market without causing chaos and ruinous price collapses.[157]

The dominant view is that oil's intrinsic characteristics make it inherently unstable, and that without supply regulation or cartelization of some form prices will tend toward booms and busts. While people may be in agreement on this, they're not necessarily in agreement as to whether preventing booms and busts is a good reason for regulation or cartels. Paul Frankel argued on the side of regulation when he wrote that the oil industry is "not self-adjusting . . . make[s] for continuous crises . . . [h]ectic prosperity is followed all too swiftly by complete collapse, and redress can be hoped for only from the efforts of 'eveners,' adjusters, and organizers."[158] Economists Melvin De Chazeau and Alfred Kahn underscore that oil's "fluctuating and inelastic supply" combined with price-insensitive demand constitute an "explosive economic force" that without government intervention "could shake the industry to its foundations, and has done so from time to time in the past."[159]

Quota supporters credit supply regulation with eliminating "feast-and-famine" investment practices and thereby preventing new finds from flooding the market and wiping out incumbent producers while maximizing long-term output.[160] While supporters acknowledge the industry could have achieved some measure of stability without intervention as it matured,[161] they deem that the combination of state quotas and the majors' cartelization were necessary and effective at imposing the stability necessary to the orderly expansion of oil in the global economy during the twentieth century. Some quota proponents have also drawn the link between stability and broader positive impacts, especially in oil states. TRC Chair Ernest Thompson underscored in a 1936 speech that "the price of crude oil . . . was restored to a dollar a barrel and has existed steadily at that point for three years. Oil producers and refiners are prosperous and contented. Into the treasury of the state flows a constant cash revenue—a revenue that wipes out deficits, that balances budgets, that builds highways, and that affords the funds necessary for public education."[162]

Perhaps the most unapologetic supporter of government quotas was resource economist Erich Zimmermann, whose 1957 book *Conservation in the Production of Petroleum* unabashedly concluded mandatory quotas imposed by "state police power" were necessary given the oil industry's unique characteristics. "As the facts are, the [oil] industry faces the alternatives of practicing effective voluntary self-restraint, an impossibility, or submitting to the police power of the state."[163] Zimmermann swept away fierce condemnation of quotas as a price fixing scheme that was camouflaged as a conservation measure, concluding price stability helped the cause of conservation and that "the elimination of violent short-run fluctuations of prices is socially desirable."[164]

Nevertheless, both oil state quotas and Seven Sisters cartelization have been fiercely criticized. The main objection is that quotas and cartels force high prices on consumers. A quota, John Blair wrote in 1976, is "doubly objectionable in that it inflates both prices and costs. Prices are inflated by restricting production to (or below) demand; costs are inflated by reducing the output of more efficient, low-cost wells and keeping in operation inefficient, high-cost wells."[165] The TRC, Professor David Prindle noted in 1981, encouraged widespread drilling, resulting in not only "hundreds of thousands of economically unnecessary" wells but also associated "drillers, work-over services, pipelines, and all the other industrial paraphernalia of the oil fields . . . economists have expended much ink demonstrating that this policy was irrational."[166]

Free-market oil historians and analysts Robert Bradley and Morris Adelman, while they acknowledge that early rule-of-capture laws created excessive drilling and waste, contend that the industry, left alone, would have eventually resolved this through unitization of fields and integration. Instead of adjusting laws to permit more sensible drilling and industry organization, domestic drillers appealed to the government for help, resulting in "misguided government intervention and special interest politics."[167] "The United States," Adelman wrote, "did for the producing industry what it could not do for itself: restrain output to keep up the price."[168] Another camp, reflecting primarily antitrust sentiments, levelled criticism at the major international oil companies for running a cartel and imposing what to many appeared an arbitrary price regime designed to stifle competition and extract rents. Fodder for this group came from a FTC report entitled "The International Petroleum Cartel," issued in 1952 at the request of the Senate Monopoly Subcommittee of the Small Business Committee that was investigating the effects of cartels on small business. Prodded by the domestic oil industry, the committee wanted to understand if the majors were running a series of monopolies, imposing excessively burdensome prices on the United States and friendly economies, and—"most important of all"—dumping cheap Middle Eastern oil in the United States, thereby "causing injury to independent American oil producers." The FTC report, though not polemical in tone,[169] was perceived as a damning portrait of the Seven Sisters' operations and stoked much controversy in the 1950s.[170]

The FTC noted that the Seven Sisters "clung tenaciously" to their basing point price system, even after making modifications under government pressure, and that the system had proved "highly profitable to the small number of major international companies that dominate world production."[171] The report detailed that the majors continued to base global prices on Texas ones "notwithstanding the fact that this country has become a net importer of petroleum," employed "freight charges that may not have any real relationship to transportation costs actually incurred," and relied on efforts by international companies to "adjust production to world demand." On the latter point, the FTC acknowledged that supply restraint was also practiced by "the conservation movement in the United States"—i.e., quotas by Texas and other oil state regulators.[172]

Regardless of where you stand on the effectiveness of regulation, what's beyond doubt is that the Texas era from 1934 to 1972 saw the TRC and the Seven Sisters bring unprecedented stability to a chronically volatile oil industry, stabilizing prices as massive new oil supplies were unlocked from the Middle East and other areas, thus enabling a postwar hydrocarbon boom, and giving the United States valuable geopolitical leverage. This would all end abruptly with the Arab Oil embargo of 1973 that ushered in conditions more familiar to modern minds with oil: instability and crisis.

2

THE OPEC ERA:
1973–2008

5

THE BIRTH OF OPEC: 1960–1969

As the 1960s dawned, titanic shifts in the global oil market had begun to erode the foundations of the Texas era of price stability. Texas era regulators and major oil company executives had used every tool in the supply manager's toolkit to stabilize prices at high levels—quotas, market share agreements, pooling arrangements, and price formulas. While oil state regulators and major oil companies did not formally cooperate, both had the same overriding goals: Calibrate the flow of oil to the market to roughly equal demand. Prevent excess production and investment in infrastructure. Avoid price busts. But with sweeping changes in the patterns of oil supply and demand as well as increasingly assertive anticolonial movements in the Middle East steadily gathering force, the stage was set for chaos in the oil world.

PRODUCING COUNTRIES PUSH BACK AGAINST THE SEVEN SISTERS

After World War II, the Seven Sisters not only started losing revenue from their concessions (as noted earlier, in 1948 Venezuela imposed a formula requiring majors to share profits from oil concessions on a fifty–fifty basis and other producing countries in the Middle East soon followed suit)—in some cases, they began to lose control altogether. Iran provides a good illustration of how the majors as well as various governments in the volatile region, at least initially, were able to react to shifts in the global oil market without disturbing price structure in a big way.

Hoping to replicate Mexico's nationalization of its oil industry thirteen years earlier, in April 1951 the newly elected and fiercely nationalist prime minister of Iran, Mohammad Mossadegh, signed a law nationalizing the country's oil assets. The ejection of BP—Iran's sole southern concessionaire, then called the Anglo-Iranian Oil Company—prompted threats and reprisals from London. BP and her six other Sisters promptly boycotted Iranian oil exports, forcing the country's production to fall to near zero. The sudden loss of Iran's oil spurred U.S. officials to activate some of the procedures and policies used during World War II to encourage maximum oil output and efficient transportation, and the majors increased production from their concessions in Saudi Arabia, Kuwait, and Iraq. Although world production rose by three times more than the amount of Iran's lost supplies by 1952,[1] the United States and the United Kingdom were concerned enough about permanently losing Iran's oil and about possible communist encroachment that in early 1953 they began preparing and executing steps to undermine Mossadegh and replace him with a friendlier premier. Mossadegh was overthrown in a coup in August 1953, the Shah was reinstated, and the door to the West reopened (wider than before, as Washington insisted that BP share its Iranian concession with other companies, including U.S. independent producers).[2]

Once the embargo was lifted, the new participants in Iran's production had to find a way to integrate Iran's exports without flooding the market. It was a tricky endeavor, not helped by the Shah's determination to make up for lost export revenue from 1952–1954 by raising output. The majors turned to Saudi Arabia. Exxon, present in Saudi Arabia and about to enter Iran, appealed to Saudi King Ibn Saud's anticommunist feelings to ask that he reduce Saudi production to accommodate Iranian oil's return to the market. The king grudgingly agreed, but insisted that Iran's production be limited to only the amount needed to keep the communists at bay.[3] By first increasing sales from concessions outside Iran and then reducing them to accommodate Iran's return, the majors were able to handle the political and market disruption without much swing in oil prices.

But while nationalization was reversed in Iran and the majors were able to minimize market disruption, the dynamics were indicative of a larger

trend that was not in the majors' favor. Anticolonial, nationalistic senti-
ment swept away regimes in other major oil-producing countries where
the Seven Sisters operated. The intensely anti-Western feeling stemmed
mostly from Egypt's Arab nationalist leader, Gamal Abdel Nasser, who
was idolized by revolutionaries in the Middle East. Nasser regarded Western oil concessions as an intolerable affront and a humiliating legacy of
colonialism. He promoted Pan-Arab solidarity and political unification,
instilling a will throughout the Arab world to singly and collectively confront the West. Since Egypt did not have much oil, Nasser's Pan-Arabism
did not translate into collective attacks on the Seven Sisters' concessions.

But nationalist, anti-Western uprisings in 1958 in two major oil-
producing countries—Iraq and Venezuela—resulted in new regimes eager
to confront the Seven Sisters, and triggered a series of events that would
lead to oil-producing countries wresting control of the oil market and price
structure from oil state regulators and major international oil companies.

In January 1958, a revolution in Venezuela overthrew military dictator
General Marcos Pérez Jiménez. The interim government in Caracas was
hostile to foreign oil companies, which revolutionaries blamed for supporting the dictatorship. Before the interim government ceded power to
a democratically elected one at the end of the year, and with the incoming
government's blessing, it increased Venezuela's share of oil profits from 50
to 70 percent and threw the president of Exxon's Venezuela subsidiary out
of the country. In February 1959, new president Rómulo Betancourt asked
Pérez Alfonzo, an idealistic lawyer and elected official, to be his mines and
hydrocarbons minister. Pérez Alfonzo had been responsible for Venezuela's
oil affairs in 1948 when he held the post of minister of development, and it
was he who oversaw the enactment of the fifty–fifty profit split on oil producers, just before a military coup forced him into a ten-year exile in the United
States and later Mexico. Back at his post, Pérez Alfonzo quickly established a
national oil company and strengthened regulation on oil production.

While Pérez Alfonzo had been in exile in the United States, he had
closely studied the Texas Railroad Commission (TRC) and other quota-
setting states. Deeply impressed, he concluded that Venezuela and other
producers needed the same thing—a strong cartel to ensure fair and stable prices for oil producers.[4] Pérez Alfonzo retained a TRC consultant to
advise him on how quotas operated.[5]

The main reason Pérez Alfonzo favored an international cartel was that Venezuela's production costs were about four times higher than those in the Middle East (about $0.80 per barrel versus $0.20, respectively). As a high-cost producer, Venezuela stood to benefit if lower-cost Middle Eastern producers restrained their production. Just as TRC quotas benefitted higher-cost wells at the expense of lower-cost ones forced to curtail production, Pérez Alfonzo hoped that high-cost Venezuela could shift and share the burden of cuts by including low-cost Middle East producers in collective production restraint agreements. Moreover, Pérez Alfonzo was an ardent physical conservationist and believed Texas-style quotas would prevent excessive production and depletion of reserves.[6]

But Pérez Alfonzo would have to deal with more immediate problems before he could realize the dream of creating a cartel. Just as Pérez Alfonzo assumed office, President Eisenhower announced new oil import quotas, stemming from domestic U.S. political opposition to rising imports. Quotas were a special threat to Venezuela; 40 percent of its exports went to the United States.[7] Venezuela's close proximity to the United States had offset higher costs relative to its competitors in the Middle East, but Eisenhower's new quotas swept that away.

Shocked at the import quotas and offended by special exemptions Washington granted only to Canada and Mexico, Pérez Alfonzo at first tried to cut a special deal with the United States. He flew to Washington to propose a hemispheric oil system in which Venezuela would be assured a slice of the U.S. market. U.S. officials showed no interest in Pérez Alfonzo's proposal and offered no response.[8] Insulted, Pérez Alfonzo turned his attention to Middle Eastern producers, and to propose his plan for an international cartel modeled on the TRC. He hoped and expected nationalism coursing through Middle Eastern countries would prime them to join in his plan.

In July 1958, Iraqi army officers overthrew Iraqi King Faisal II, murdering him and his strongly pro-Western prime minister, Nuri es-Said. Before the coup, Iraq and the majors operating the Iraq Petroleum Company had been amicably negotiating the terms of their relationship, but relations with foreign oil companies soon soured under the new and shaky military regime.

In the meantime, the Seven Sisters' profits were being squeezed as they were forced to sell their oil at lower actual market prices but were at the same time obligated to calculate profits, tax payments, and royalties on higher, administered prices that existed on paper but did not reflect supply and demand realities.[9] For the majors, it was only fair that producer governments share the burden of lower oil price by receiving less revenue. So the majors reduced administered prices in 1959. The majors' move to reduce these administered prices turned out to be just the spark Pérez Alfonzo needed to ignite producer anger against majors—and to convince them of the need for a cartel. Incensed, Egypt's Nasser convened the First Arab Petroleum Conference in Cairo in April 1959. Pérez Alfonzo saw his chance to implement his Texas-style producer cartel plan and led a delegation to the conference, one of two non-Arabs to attend. (Another non-Arab, Iranian Manucher Farmanfarmaian, director at the National Iranian Oil Company, attended the conference as an observer, though not in an official capacity.) Delegates noisily railed against foreign oil companies and decried the concession system as a humiliating relic of an outdated colonialist era, but the conference produced little. However, Pérez Alfonzo worked assiduously and quietly on the sidelines to sell his plan to create a collective organization of producers that would confront the majors.

The pivotal meeting was between Pérez Alfonzo and Saudi oil minister Abdullah Tariki, who was quickly won over and became a strong proponent of Pérez Alfonzo's plan. While Venezuela and Saudi Arabia were vastly different in terms of production costs and experiences as oil producers (Venezuela old, Saudi Arabia new), they shared a common connection to the United States, as the same American companies (Exxon, Mobil, Texaco, and Chevron) operated concessions in both countries.[10] Pérez Alfonzo and his new friend and collaborator Tariki convinced Farmanfarmaian and delegates from Iraq, the United Arab Republic (UAR, Egypt and Syria's short-lived union), and Kuwait to sign a secret gentlemen's agreement referred to as the Maadi Pact that called for annual consultations to discuss, among other things, the coordination of oil production.[11]

While the Maadi Pact was the first step toward creating a producer organization, it was fairly inconclusive. But the majors soon gave producing countries the push they needed to unite. Pressure on the majors' profits had continued with soaring production of cheap Soviet production, and Exxon—desperate to stanch the losses—initiated a second round of cuts in administered prices in August 1960, this time by 7 percent.[12]

The move was controversial even within Exxon, with CEO Jack Rathbone insisting on the cut over the objections of colleagues and advisors who warned of a potentially vicious blowback from host governments. Exxon's unilateral move, made without consultation with producer governments, was followed by other majors. Rathbone's nervous colleagues were proved right; later, they would dub him the "Father of OPEC."[13]

With the second round of administered price cuts, a senior Exxon executive in Iraq who had opposed the cut, noted, "all hell broke loose"— he was lucky to get out of Baghdad alive.[14] The Seven Sisters' collective, if disjointed, imposition of administered price cuts spurred producer governments toward a collective response. "OPEC couldn't have happened without the oil cartel [Seven Sisters]," one Kuwaiti said, "We just took a leaf from the oil companies' book. The victim had learned the lesson."[15]

Following Exxon's administered price cut, Pérez Alfonzo—OPEC's real father—sprang into action. Joined by Tariki, his immediate goal was to transform the Maadi Pact from a gentlemen's agreement into a firm alliance able to confront the majors. Iraq's new revolutionary government was happy to host a meeting of aggrieved producers.[16] Iran, Iraq, Kuwait, Venezuela, and Saudi Arabia met in September 1960 in Baghdad and formed the Organization of the Petroleum Exporting Countries, OPEC. Collectively, OPEC producers accounted for "over 80 percent of the world's oil exports."[17]

OPEC's immediate focus was on preventing any further erosion in its share of income from the concessions. At the heart of the struggle between OPEC members and Seven Sisters was a disagreement on how to share what industry called the "rent"—the margin between relatively low costs of production and the high prices of petroleum products sold in consuming countries. The rent was big and flowed in two directions—to company profits and to government tax revenues. The implementation of fifty–fifty profit share by the producers ten years earlier was an attempt to claw more rent from the Seven Sisters. The Seven Sisters' cuts in administered prices in 1959 and 1960 were an attempt to recapture rent from the producers. But the tide was turning toward host governments and away from large Western oil companies operating colonial-era concessions.

Thus, OPEC's first significant decision (and, as it turned out, the only significant decision it would make in its first ten years) was to collectively oppose any further cut in administrative prices. While the majors did not perceive OPEC as much of a threat, they stopped cutting administrative prices for good, both to avoid angering the new producer group and because supply and demand fundamentals started to firm up in the 1960s, making further cuts unnecessary.

While presenting a united front against administered price cuts, OPEC members bickered about everything else. Differences were exacerbated by tensions stemming from historical rivalries. Baghdad at first did not even recognized Kuwait's sovereignty, considering it a province of Iraq. Arab Saudi Arabia and Persian Iran vied for regional dominance and led competing sects within Islam. On oil strategy, Iran and Venezuela differed strongly over OPEC policy: Whereas Caracas wanted OPEC to cut supplies to prop up prices, Iran wanted to increase supply as much as possible while resisting administered price cuts and negotiating for higher royalties and taxes. Quotas were too aggressive for the Shah, whose memories of Western embargo and intervention were fresh; he was not eager to overly antagonize Western oil companies and their governments, and directly seizing control of supply would violate the concession agreements. (Saudi Arabia was likewise wary of antagonizing the United States, which they looked to as a partner and protector from the Soviet Union.) Legal contracts were still considered sacrosanct in OPEC's early years, and breaching them was a step too far. Generally, other OPEC members sided with Iran and opposed quotas and collective supply cuts to raise and stabilize prices. OPEC governments depended on the majors for access to global markets and with supply growth exceeding demand, the members of OPEC regarded each other as competitors. Moreover, burgeoning production from countries that were initially outside OPEC, such as UAE, Libya, Algeria, and Nigeria, could offset cuts from the original five OPEC members.[18]

So while Pérez Alfonzo pushed for TRC-style supply cuts, OPEC initially chose just to study rather than implement this strategy. Pérez Alfonzo's leverage within OPEC—his main ally, Tariki—had only weak influence in Riyadh, where the Saudi royal family was distracted by a prolonged power struggle between factions led by King Saud and Crown Prince Faisal that would drag on until 1964. OPEC's priority, most members agreed, would be to bargain collectively with the majors for higher administrative prices and tax takes—i.e., higher rent.

The five OPEC members set up a secretariat and agreed to meet twice a year, but policy divisions, rivalries, and turnovers in leadership slowed progress. Iraq stopped attending meetings from 1961 to 1963 over its territorial claims on Kuwait. In April 1965, Venezuela made another push within OPEC (by then expanded to include Indonesia, Qatar, and Libya) to set quotas. OPEC's economic staff prepared demand forecasts for OPEC crude oil from mid-1965 to mid-1966, as counterparts at the TRC did for Texas crude oil. In July, OPEC members met to discuss how to share this output. But support within OPEC remained anemic, especially since the two biggest proponents of quotas within the organization—Pérez Alfonzo and Tariki—had by then left the scene. Tariki had been replaced by Sheikh Ahmed Zaki Yamani in 1962 and Pérez Alfonzo, who grew steadily disenchanted and then disgusted with the course Venezuela and OPEC adopted in the 1960s, resigned in 1963. (In the 1970s Pérez Alfonzo famously declared "[oil] brings trouble . . . Look at this *locura*—waste, corruption, consumption, our public services falling apart. And debt, debt we shall have for years."[19]) So ultimately this first attempt by OPEC to agree on Texas-style quotas was "a farce," according to former OPEC Secretary General Francisco Parra, who participated in OPEC's early meetings.[20] Iran insisted on a high quota and was widely viewed by other members as unlikely to ever make cuts. Saudi Arabia refused to abide by any quota and Libya said it would not consider its quota binding. The agreement was not implemented and each member pursued its own separate production policy.[21]

By the late 1960s, OPEC did not have much to show for itself other than fostering a bit more solidarity among member governments and winning some price and tax achievements. OPEC had failed to unify members into a strong organization, much less to implement Pérez Alfonzo's dream of setting quotas. While the Seven Sisters later regretted their 1960 administered price cut and never repeated it, neither they nor Western countries were overly concerned about OPEC as a threat to oil market stability. The oil companies largely ignored OPEC and continued dealing with individual concession governments.

OPEC may well have withered and died by the 1970s. But powerful undercurrents in global supply and demand were developing in the 1960s that would soon rejuvenate and reshape OPEC's potency and role as the world's dominant force in the oil market.

6

OPEC TAKES CONTROL FROM TEXAS AND THE SEVEN SISTERS: 1970–1980

I n the 1870s, the oil market was transformed by Rockefeller from chaos to stability. The 1970s were equally transformative but in the other direction: from stability to chaos. In the early 1970s, OPEC destroyed the old order, just as the U.S. Supreme Court had terminated the Rockefeller era in 1911. The result was much higher and more volatile prices than seen during the Texas era.

For the first one hundred years in the oil market's history, with a few exceptions and a few peak oil scares, the main problem for the oil industry was managing excess supply. To prevent gluts from crashing prices, regulators and cartelized oil companies were obligated to hold back or "shut in" production from flowing wells. But starting in the 1960s trends in global oil supply and demand began shifting the other way. World oil demand rose sharply in the late 1960s, growing by 8 percent per year on average in the second half of the decade and by nearly 9 percent in 1969 alone.[1] Many analysts expected demand to keep booming. In 1971 the U.S. National Petroleum Council estimated demand outside the communist world would increase from 37 mb/d in 1970 to 92 mb/d by 1985.[2] And while the amount of new oil being produced continued to outpace the amount consumed, the gap between the two began to close. U.S. foreign policy officials grew concerned that most of the oil needed to meet the massive projected oil demand would come from OPEC producers, and the bulk of that from the Middle East.

As domestic demand raced ahead of supply, the United States increasingly turned to crude imports. The United States' spare capacity as a percentage of global demand fell from over 15 percent at the beginning of the

1960s to around 5 percent at the decade's end, making the United States vulnerable to an oil supply disruption. Washington's anxiety about a supply cutoff was well-founded, given the disruptions they had seen already from Middle East conflicts in 1956 and 1967. The ongoing Arab-Israeli acrimony posed a constant threat of another.

Until the 1970s, Washington's attention to broad oil industry practices and oil prices had waxed and waned depending on the price of oil and whether the nation was at war. Generally, the federal government adopted a standoff attitude, sometimes policing against collusion and anticompetitive behavior, but leaving it up to the states and industry to run the domestic market. But all this changed during wartime, when officials prioritized and oversaw maximum output, in part by relaxing antitrust rules on oil companies.

During the Cold War, Washington's top foreign policy concern with regard to oil was to prevent Soviet encroachment on the Gulf's huge oil reserves, as well as its processing and export facilities—hence the CIA's help in overthrowing Mossadegh in 1953 to prevent Iran from entering the Soviet orbit. Looking to backstop U.S. Cold War interests and support allies in the Gulf, the State Department shielded majors from harsh anti-competition probes and Washington also granted majors fiscal incentives to operate in the region, so as to keep large producers friendly to the United States and ensure access to the regions, mammoth reserves.[3] Although its interest also fluctuated, in general, Congress was responsive to the interests of domestic oil companies, which had a bigger political footprint in states than their international counterparts. Congress often pushed on behalf of domestic production for protection from cheap foreign imports.

But with soaring demand and rising dependence on the Middle East, OPEC countries became increasingly assertive in their long-running battle to claw more rent and reassert control (if not at first ownership) from Western majors, and U.S. officials found themselves in the unpleasant position of having to choose between their own oil companies—both majors like Exxon and Chevron but also many independent oil companies that had entered foreign concessions, particularly in Libya—and the governments of OPEC producing countries. While it may be going too far to say Western officials sided with OPEC, the reality was that the majors received little to no support from their capitals in the late 1960s and early 1970s. While Washington kept an eye on oil for Cold War considerations, it was not a top priority in the United States. Inflation, civil rights, the Vietnam War, and Watergate dominated the news. The United States and Great Britain relied on Iran and Saudi Arabia to step up and play the regional policeman role, and were selling them lots of weapons.[4] Leaders were unwilling to challenge Gulf producers.

To the extent that federal officials thought about international oil markets and policy, they tended to lean toward OPEC because they regarded higher U.S. import dependence as inevitable and feared a supply cutoff above all. U.S. officials were resigned to OPEC's increased leverage; some officials even welcomed higher oil prices, which would slow galloping demand growth (one of the causes of rising import dependence).[5] Former OPEC Secretary General Parra related that U.S. State Department officials quietly urged OPEC countries to raise taxes on production, knowing they would feed through to higher prices.[6] On the supply side, industry officials welcomed higher oil prices, partly to underpin investment in large but costly oil discoveries in Alaska (Prudhoe Bay, discovered in 1968) and the North Sea (giant Ekofisk and Forties discoveries in 1969 and 1970, respectively).

With the market tightening, exports growing, and Washington distracted and sympathetic to OPEC, power was shifting fast to OPEC producers, who promptly used it against foreign operators, majors and independents alike.

OPEC MEMBERS MAKE THEIR MOVES

Libya was the first to capitalize on its growing leverage. The country got a late start as an oil producer, inviting foreign companies to search for oil in 1955. In 1959 Exxon made the first big strike and investment soon intensified. Oil companies prized Libya for its location outside the volatile Middle East and proximity to European consuming markets. Moreover, Libya produced a blend of crude oil that yielded valuable "lighter" products such as gasoline and jet fuel. Libyan production rose briskly from 1.2 mb/d in 1965 to 3.4 mb/d in 1970.[7] And with little domestic demand, most of Libya's production was exported. By the mid-1960s Libya was the world's sixth-largest exporter, and by the end of the decade it supplied about 30 percent of Europe's crude.[8] Libya's oil output surged just as the Soviet Union's began to wane, sustaining and even increasing downward pressure on oil prices.

Unlike other producing countries, Libya did not restrict oil concessions to one producer or consortium. Libya came late to the game, but was open to all. It had invited many majors and independent firms like Amerada Hess and Occidental to operate as well as the Seven Sisters. About half of Libya's production was in the hands of independent oil companies that were not integrated with refineries and had no reason to restrain supply to support prices. Blocked by import quotas from selling to the United States and unconstrained by the Seven Sisters' cartelized production, transportation, and marketing rules, independent operators producing in Libya dumped their oil in nearby Europe.

As production expanded, Libya's monarch King Idris I pressured producing companies for fiscal concessions. King Idris's strategy involved targeting one company intensely and, when it complied, demanding the same from others. On September 1, 1969, a military coup overthrew King Idris I and installed 27-year-old Muammar Qaddafi as leader. Qaddafi followed King Idris's strategy of singling out the weakest first to then squeeze all oil companies much harder.[9] Targeting Occidental because it had little production outside the country, by September 1970 Libya extracted an increase of $0.30 per barrel in administered prices and higher income taxes.[10] Qaddafi then turned on the other twenty independent and majors, demanding the same concessions won from Occidental.

As small independent operators in Libya buckled and conceded, pressure grew on the majors—Exxon, Texaco, and Chevron—to meet Qaddafi's terms. Exxon resisted, so Libya turned the screws by ordering production cuts from the company's fields. The majors discussed approaching Qaddafi *en bloc* and turned to Washington and London for support. London did not bite, and a top State Department oil official in Washington told Congress that he thought Libya's initial demand for a $0.40 per barrel hike was fair enough. By mid-October 1970, all producers in Libya had agreed to higher administered prices and income tax rates.[11]

The defeat of foreign companies in Libya marked a turning point in the balance of power between international oil companies and host governments. A game of follow the leader started. Other producers, marveling at Qaddafi's unheard-of victory at wringing a substantive increase in both taxes and administered prices, now clamored for the same. Jealous that Qaddafi had in a few months achieved more than OPEC had in five years, Gulf producers—particularly the Shah of Iran—insisted on a 55 percent income tax rate. Then OPEC governments started leapfrogging each other, demanding bigger concessions from operators. For example, after Iran won a 55 percent income tax from majors, Venezuela demanded 60 percent.[12]

Fearful of being picked off one by one, the seven majors, Total, and eight independents banded together in a united front to bargain with OPEC. Companies obtained clearance from the U.S. Justice Department to avoid antitrust risk, and prepared to compensate any producer forced to cut production as a pressure tactic, as Libya had done to Occidental. But OPEC rejected the oil companies' proposal for one all-encompassing negotiation and insisted on two separate tracks, one with producers on the Mediterranean such as Libya and another with Persian Gulf producers. The Shah played on Western officials' and companies' fears, warning the former that if oil companies resisted, "the entire Gulf would be shut down and no oil would flow,"[13] and admonishing that the "all-powerful Six or Seven Sisters have got to open their eyes, and see they they're living in 1971, and not in 1948 or 1949."[14] Washington—terrified above all of a supply cutoff it no longer had ample spare capacity to offset—sided with the Shah and against oil companies, supporting OPEC's demand for two regional negotiations. Talks began in Tehran to cover the Gulf and in Tripoli to address the Mediterranean market.[15]

Their bargaining power extremely low, Western oil companies capitulated on February 14, 1971, to Gulf producers, signing a Tehran agreement that buried for good the two-decade-old fifty–fifty profit-sharing deal Venezuela first won in 1948 and raised the minimum host country take to 55 percent (which the Gulf countries, spurred by Qaddafi, had already won). The Tehran agreement also raised concession-administered prices by $0.30 immediately and to $0.35 in 1975. When the Mediterranean producers concluded the Tripoli Agreement in April 1971 the oil companies had agreed to even bigger price increases—enraging the Shah of Iran, who felt he had been leapfrogged.[16]

The OPEC producers' efforts to wrest money from foreign operators were greatly aided by supply and demand dynamics that continued to work in their favor. In the early 1970s, oil demand was raging and large new discoveries outside OPEC had yet to come online. The U.S. production peaked in 1971 and then started to decline. Huge new oil discoveries in Alaska, Mexico, and the North Sea were still in their early development phases and would not result in new barrels on the market for another five years or so. Any incremental barrels had to come mainly from OPEC, which was now raising prices consumers had no choice but to accept. The sudden shattering of decades-old relationships between oil companies and host governments disrupted relationships between buyers and sellers, adding to buyers' panic, confusion, and willingness to pay a fear premium for any barrels they could find. Security of supply was the watchword; price was no option.

Frantic inventory building also helped drive oil prices higher. During the Texas era, private crude oil inventories tended to vary within a small range. When refiners are confident about supply availability and stable future prices, they have no reason to hoard. But OPEC's price hikes created perceptions of future price hikes, which made oil companies want to store. The rush to buy was fueled when President Nixon abolished import quotas in April 1973, unleashing a new wave of Middle Eastern oil sales to U.S. traders and refiners.[17] Refined product prices followed crude upward. Between 1970 and 1974 U.S. gasoline prices increased by nearly 50 percent, from $0.36 per gallon to $0.53 per gallon—sharp, but not sharp enough to significantly reverse demand.[18]

With prices rising and demand strong, OPEC producers held leverage and knew it.[19] The majors were disunited and weakly supported by their governments, encouraging further forays by OPEC countries. The Tehran and Tripoli Agreements were supposed to last for five years, until 1976, but by 1973 they were already starting to fall apart. Dependence on OPEC for additional supplies was growing. But most significant in pushing OPEC countries to demand new terms was the fallout from President Nixon's decision on August 15, 1971, to devalue the U.S. dollar.

Many OPEC producers, including Saudi Arabia, had U.S. dollar-based oil contracts, which lost significant value when the greenback was delinked from gold. An oil exporter receiving dollars saw the number of barrels needed to purchase one ounce of gold rise by 200 percent between 1971 and 1973, from 12 to 34 barrels of oil per ounce of gold.[20] Producers insisted that, to compensate for the weaker dollar, it was necessary to set higher prices than they had originally agreed on in Tehran and in Tripoli.

In January 1972, OPEC met with majors in Geneva and obtained agreement to link administered prices to a basket of currencies instead of the dollar, resulting in an immediate 8.5 percent price increase.[21] In June 1973, OPEC met in Geneva and decided to press for another hike in administered prices. In early August Saudi Oil Minister Yamani "warned Aramco that the Tehran agreement would have to be renegotiated" altogether.[22]

A new development in global oil price history fueled OPEC's assertiveness toward the fall of 1973. The price of oil set in small, "spot" markets started to rise above administered prices.[23] "Spot transactions" refers to arm's-length, often one-off or single-cargo deals between two autonomous parties, usually between an independent producer and a seller (private- or state-owned oil producer) and unconnected to a long-term contract. Relatively rare in the post–World War II decade when intracompany transfers between subsidiaries of the Seven Sisters dominated most internationally traded oil, spot transactions proliferated after the late 1950s as smaller independent countries began to produce and sell oil. Even though such spot market transactions amounted to only about 3 percent of internationally traded oil, they had a psychologically important effect as they soared above administered prices. Rising spot prices convinced OPEC, Maugeri wrote, "that consumers were so oil crazy that they were ready to pay well above official [administered] prices, which they consequently raised in a rush to catch up with spot values."[24] While spot transactions and their prices were not widely reported in the press, they would come to be seen as the most authentic indicator of the real market price of crude oil—and they were on the move.

Emboldened, OPEC summoned oil companies to a meeting in Vienna on October 8, 1973, to reopen the 1971 Tehran and Tripoli Agreements. Beleaguered U.S. oil companies again sought and were grudgingly granted an antitrust waiver from the Justice Department to negotiate.[25]

The majors offered OPEC a 15 percent increase in administered prices; OPEC demanded a 100 percent hike, a doubling from $3 to $6 per barrel. Western companies sought guidance from their capitals and were told to resist as such a price shock would harm economic growth. Talks ended inconclusively on October 14, with participants distracted by the outbreak of another war between Israel and its Arab neighbors two days before the conference began. Unlike the prior conflicts, this one would mark an epochal change in the history of the oil market.

THE 1973 ARAB OIL EMBARGO

Since refounding in 1948, Israel had been at odds with its neighbors—to put it mildly. War erupted immediately after Israel declared independence and again in 1956 and 1967, the latter resulting in a humiliating loss of territory by Egypt, Jordan, and Syria. Eager to reclaim it, Egypt and Syria mounted a surprise attack on Israel on October 6, 1973, while Israelis were observing Yom Kippur (Day of Atonement). Soon supported by Iraq and Jordan, Arab armies made large territorial gains. After absorbing initial blows, Israeli planes struck Syrian exports terminals at Banias and Tartus. That damage, combined with Saudi cutbacks through the Tapline[26] to the Mediterranean Sea, immediately took 1 mb/d off the eastern Mediterranean crude market. Arab producers had long seethed at Western support for Israel and decided to use its newfound oil weapon to intimidate Israel's supporters by cutting supply and raising administered prices.

Administered price hikes came first. On October 16, 1973, a group of five Arab OPEC representatives and Iran met in Kuwait City and announced a unilateral price increase of the benchmark Arabian Light from $3.01 to $5.11 per barrel, a 70 percent bump that lifted administered prices higher than prevailing market ones (see figure 6.1).[27] From then on, OPEC would no longer go through the pretense of negotiating with foreign oil companies. Administered price changes would be imposed unilaterally by OPEC members.

Arab oil producers believed production cuts were necessary to make enforcement of higher administered oil prices credible. On October 17, after Iran's representative had departed the Kuwait meeting,[28] remaining

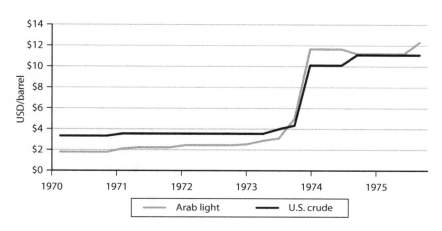

FIGURE 6.1

Administered (Arab Light) and market (U.S.) prices.

Source: Bloomberg, "Arabian Gulf Arab Light Crude Oil Spot Price to Asia"; API, *Petroleum Facts and Figures* (1959); Dow Jones & Company, Spot Oil Price: West Texas Intermediate.

Arab producers agreed to cut production by 5 percent per month relative to September's level until Israeli forces left territory seized after the 1967 war. The next day Saudi Arabia announced a 10 percent production cut. After the U.S. announcement of a major aid program for Israel on October 19, Riyadh retaliated by announcing a total ban on exports to the United States, and other Arab producers soon followed suit. A ceasefire between Israel and its Arab enemies was implemented on October 25, but Arab producers kept up the pressure; meeting again on November 4, they decided to reduce supply to 25 percent below September's level.[29]

The Arab oil embargo failed to pressure Israel or the United States to change policy. But its impact on oil prices and psychology were significant. The war, embargo, and production cutbacks triggered widespread confusion in markets already preoccupied with fears of supply shortages. In December, OPEC raised the administered price of the informal benchmark crude, Arabian Light, to $11.65 per barrel (around $60 in 2016 prices), four times what it had been four months prior and six times 1970 levels. Iran had encouraged the $11.65 per barrel price, justifying it with a study the Shah had commissioned that set that as the cost of alternative fuel to oil.[30] Market-based prices raced ahead of administered ones; Iran was reportedly able to sell oil at auction for $17.40 per barrel.[31] "It is hard to find in history," Maugeri wrote, "a comparable revolution in the price of a strategic resource."[32]

Israel and Arab countries held disengagement talks that lasted until May 1974, during which time the oil supply situation gradually returned to normal. The Arab oil embargo failed to achieve its aim of forcing an Israeli withdrawal and was formally ended in March 1974.[33] The embargo had only caused a small and short physical supply disruption; traders diverted non-embargoed crude to embargoed countries,[34] and inventory draws and increased supply from outside OPEC offset the temporary loss of OPEC crude. So while the OPEC embargo was purely a symbolic move—as Saudi Oil Minister Yamani would admit[35]—it was an incredibly effective one. It amped up feelings of insecurity in the U.S. and other consuming countries while goading OPEC members to further accelerate price increases and nationalize foreign–owned oil assets.[36]

It is difficult to overstate the depth of the gloom that descended on Western officials and business people in the 1970s at the prospect of massive future dependence on Middle Eastern oil imports. Over the four preceding decades, the United States and its allies had enjoyed stable oil prices and felt secure about supply security, though the 1967 and especially 1956 disruptions did cause a fright, particularly in Europe. But shifts that began after World War II and gathered force in the 1960s—soaring oil demand and replacement of the U.S. with the Middle East as key supply region— triggered a convulsion and reshaped the global oil market, shattering prior complacency about energy security and energy policy. Western governments and majors had ignored OPEC after it was created in 1960. "But now, in the middle 1970s, all that had changed," Daniel Yergin wrote. "The international order had been turned upside down. OPEC's members were courted, flattered, railed against, and denounced. There was good reason. Oil prices were at the heart of world commerce, and those who seemed to control oil prices were regarded as the new masters of the global economy."[37]

Western shock and dismay was compounded by lack of unity between the United States and Europe, which struggled to formulate a common policy. France sought to appease Saudi Arabia; the United States tried to rally Europe against OPEC; other European countries and Japan fell somewhere in the middle. Every country tried to get the best deal it could from Arab producers—*chacun pour soi.*[38]

Unable to agree on a unified way forward, Western countries were left to their own national responses—and in the United States, that response was "energy independence." In a major speech on November 7, 1973, devoted to reassuring and mobilizing an American public traumatized over the energy crisis, President Nixon alluded to the "Manhattan Project" and the spirit of the "Apollo Project," and called for making the U.S. energy self-sufficient by 1980 through conservation, increased domestic production, and alternative fuels. He called his plan Project Independence. His top energy advisor told him seven years was impractical (and indeed oil import dependence rose from 34 to 44 percent by 1979)[39]and Nixon's pledge soon became a joke as energy dependence continued rising.[40]

If President Nixon's promises about energy independence did little to alleviate the energy crisis, wage and price controls he imposed made it worse. Economy-wide wage and price controls first went into effect in August 1971 with a 90-day price freeze, including on refined products. They were followed in November 1971 by a second phase, which allowed non-oil firms to pass along higher import costs but kept prices frozen for crude oil or products like gasoline, heating oil, and heavy fuel oil. With oil import prices rising, domestic importers were starting to lose money. Problems developed particularly in the heating oil market, and shortages appeared during the winter of 1972–1973. In January 1973 price controls were made voluntary for smaller oil importers and refiners amounting to about 5 percent of the market, but heavy public pressure was placed on them to restrain increases, including the threat of reimposition of mandatory price controls. Meanwhile, prices on crude and refined products remained frozen for the big oil producers and importers accounting for 95 percent of the market, constrained in their ability to expand production.[41]

Customers of the big companies—independent marketers, fuel oil distributors, and other large fuel purchasers—found themselves unable to get the supply they needed at controlled prices. This is not surprising, since basic economics tells us when prices are held below market-clearing level, producers suffer losses if they produce or expand. Physical shortages result. Rising prices and shortages thrust the oil industry into the public's crosshairs. Claims that the big firms were "holding back" supplies began to surface. Political pressure rose for the federal government to expand regulation beyond prices onto supply via the direct allocation (in other words, rationing) of supplies of crude and refined products. In response, Congress passed the Emergency Petroleum Allocation Act of 1973, spawning what oil historian Daniel Yergin described as an "awesome Rube Goldberg system of price controls, entitlements, and allocations" that made Eisenhower's oil import quotas (also complex but which Nixon ended in 1973) appear by comparison "to have the simplicity of haiku."[42]

Under the byzantine system,[43] the Federal Energy Administration (the precursor to the Energy Department established under President Carter in 1977) decreed that "old oil" produced from domestic wells and not exceeding the rate of output in 1972 could sell for no more than $5.25 per barrel. "New oil"—oil from domestic wells in excess of 1972's production rate, or from wells drilled after 1972—sold for $11.47 per barrel. Imported crude sold for $13.28. The policy was intended to spur domestic production while holding domestic prices below those being imposed by OPEC. In March 1975 U.S. refiners processed approximately 41 percent "old" oil, 27 percent "new" oil, and 32 percent imported oil, and the effective blended price was $9.49.[44]

Price controls succeeded in their aim of insulating the United States from rising global oil prices. But they created at least two unintended, negative consequences. First, producers were effectively encouraged to stop producing "old" oil because they expected price controls to end eventually. Rather than produce for $5.25, they preferred to keep the oil in the ground and sell later at a higher price. Domestic production fell, which increased dependence on imports.[45]

Second, the price controls increased incentives to import oil which in turn emboldened OPEC and made the U.S. more likely to see higher prices.[46]

The famous gas lines and shortages of the mid-1970s originated partly from price controls[47] (to the extent controls held prices below market-clearing levels, they stimulated consumption), but mainly from allocation programs, state regulations, and consumer panic. Allocation programs, which stipulated the geographic allotment of fuel and were based on historical consumption patterns, denied oil companies the flexibility to move supplies from ample to lacking parts of the country. State regulations limited how long stations could remain open (previously they were open around the clock) and allocated purchases based on an odd or even license plate number. Finally, consumers used to stable pump prices got socked with a 40 percent increase after the Arab oil embargo and watched pump prices rise during the day. In the past drivers would let the fuel gauge go down to near-empty before filling up, but now—fearing higher prices or worse, not being able to get gas at all—they topped up frequently, even by small amounts, and got in lines to do so. Gas lines themselves resulted in higher fuel consumption due to idling.[48]

Price controls lasted until 1979 and allocations until 1981. Most public and private sector experts concluded that price and allocation systems made dislocations in the 1970s worse and that relying on market forces would have been less disruptive.[49] The cost of these price controls, as estimated by Harvard economist Joseph Kalt in 1981, included 0.3 to 1.4 mb/d of forgone domestic production and a $1–6 billion annual "deadweight loss" to the economy. This didn't include costs of regulatory administration, enforcement, compliance, and lobbying, nor does it include difficult to quantify economic distortions or the environmental costs of extra oil consumed.[50]

While the United States had been able to impose unified restrictions (if of questionable efficacy), European countries had different national interests and were unable to form a united response to the oil crisis.[51] Opportunities for quick savings in oil consumption were also more limited in Europe than in the United States because European oil use was concentrated in the industrial sector whereas, in the United States oil was primarily used in transportation.[52] It is cheaper and easier to drive less than to shut down a factory. Nonetheless, concerned with the impact of fuel oil shortages in the industrial sectors, European countries pursued a policy of restricting oil use in transportation through a combination of fuel taxes, rationing of gasoline, restrictions on heating and lightening, limited driving bans, speed limits, and fuel price increases.[53] Similar conservation policies were also adopted in Japan during the crisis.[54]

By the end of 1974 shaken oil-importing countries began to realize their go-it-alone policies were counterproductive and started to appreciate the potential benefits of collective action. That year U.S. Secretary of State Henry Kissinger convinced thirteen Western European countries (France joined in 1992), Japan, and Canada to form the International Energy

Agency, whose main mission would be to prepare for another disruption by encouraging the building of strategic stocks (oil inventories held or controlled by governments for use in a major disruption) and sharing oil with each other in an emergency. Members initially agreed to hold strategic stocks equal to 60 days of imports, but in 1976 IEA members decided to gradually raise the import cover commitment to 90 days by 1980.[55] Strategic stock releases following a severe supply interruption were "expected to help calm markets, mitigate sharp price spikes, and reduce the economic damage that had accompanied the 1973 disruption." Strategic Petroleum Reserve releases would also "buy time" for a geopolitical crisis "to sort itself out" or for diplomacy to resolve before the oil disruption itself caused it to metastasize beyond ability of diplomacy to resolve.[56]

The establishment of the U.S. Strategic Petroleum Reserve became the centerpiece a comprehensive national energy law signed in December 1975 by Nixon's successor President Ford to address the ongoing "energy crisis." Called the Energy Policy and Conservation Act, the law also included a ban on crude oil and refined product exports, conservation standards for appliances, and vehicle fuel limits called Corporate Average Fuel Economy (CAFE) regulations. While CAFE was initially intended to promote energy security by lowering oil imports and to save consumers money at the pump, in recent years the federal government has added reducing greenhouse gas emissions to CAFE's objectives. Oil began pouring into underground salt caverns chiseled under the Texas and Louisiana coasts in July 1977, and the SPR came to life.

Other IEA countries also established crude and in some cases petroleum product reserves. But persistent divisions between the allies limited the IEA's effectiveness. Whereas the United States saw the IEA as a weapon against OPEC, more docile EU and Asian members preferred to keep it a low-key forum to collect data and share technical perspectives.

OPEC'S TURN TO ADMINISTER PRICES

While the short-lived Arab Oil Embargo enjoyed most of the notoriety, a more important and enduring change took place at the same time: OPEC assumed control of administering prices. The process of administering prices in producing countries had swung from unilateral imposition by majors after World War II, to an informal freeze in the early 1960s, to unilateral imposition by producer countries in the 1970s. OPEC members suddenly found themselves—to their utter surprise and delight—fully in charge of their own production and pricing for crude oil.

At first OPEC shunned the spot market and attempted to implement their own version of the defunct majors' administered price system. They agreed to designate Saudi Arabia's Arabian Light crude blend as a reference or marker crude; other producers would price their blends in relation to it, adjusting for quality and freight differences.

But OPEC settled into its new price setting role with some difficulty. OPEC members bickered over the appropriate price for the Arab Light benchmark and differentials between it and other members' crude sales. Riyadh—at least publicly—opposed aggressive proposals for additional price increases and even sought decreases for fear of harming consuming economies and further angering the United States.

Meanwhile OPEC confronted another tricky problem: How to market oil as they nationalized foreign concessions. Under traditional concessions, foreign oil companies were obligated to pay host governments taxes and royalties, but majors owned the oil and sold or refined it as they saw fit. However, starting in the early 1970s OPEC countries demanded and received partial and eventually full ownership of the oil. As OPEC members came to own more of their crude, they had to figure out how and where to sell it. At first OPEC countries just forced majors to buy back their equity crude at inflated prices. But rising prices in small spot markets started to look more attractive to OPEC governments which began to sidestep their concession companies and sell their equity crude in spot transactions directly with third-party brokers or other intermediaries.[57]

During most of the 1970s, except in a brief spell during economic weakness in 1974, OPEC did not need to grapple with the tough work of imposing quotas and production cutbacks, as cartels usually do and the TRC and Seven Sisters did. There was no need for OPEC to play the TRC role its founder Pérez Alfonzo had hoped for it. Amid widespread fears of shortages, prices stayed high without the need for OPEC to consider formally restricting supply.

However, individual OPEC members did decide to cut back oil supply for their own reasons. Many producers held production back out of fear of premature depletion of reserves—that old concern about "physical waste" from the earlier days in Oklahoma and Texas. Anxiety about endless voracious demand and shortages did not just swirl in Western consuming countries, but also in producing ones. OPEC countries feared consuming countries would pressure them—even force them—to produce all out and to the point of exhaustion, then discard them. When Kuwait decided to limit its oil production to 3 mb/d to preserve resources in 1972, it exacerbated fears of a shortage.[58]

Moreover, though Western oil companies were no longer setting prices after 1973, they did retain—until nationalizations were completed later that decade—some leeway in terms of how much to produce. While host governments would badger, punish, or reward majors for keeping production below desired levels, Western companies preferred to keep substantial amounts in reserve in case of seasonal fluctuations and contingencies.[59]

In addition, some OPEC countries refused to discount their oil at times of demand weakness, such as during 1974 and 1975, instead holding oil back until prices went up. While OPEC members squabbled about large spare capacity and the need to "share losses" during this period, they shied away from attempting to set formal market share agreements. Producers were on their own and lived with the consequences of their own actions. The unwillingness of producers to discount caused Libya's spare capacity to rise to over half of its production capacity, 1.6 mb/d of 3 mb/d by August 1974.[60]

When supply surpluses appeared in mid-1974 and oil prices weakened toward the end of the year, OPEC staff recommended production cutbacks. OPEC rejected formal quotas, although the question of sharing losses began to dominate their discussions. Saudi Arabia informally agreed to act as the shock absorber, cutting production from 8.8 mb/d in October 1974 to 5.7 mb/d in March 1975.[61] This was the first instance of Saudi Arabia acting as a swing producer.

The period from 1974 through 1978 was relatively calm. OPEC kept administered benchmark prices generally stable, implementing only two increases. In inflation-adjusted terms, crude oil prices actually fell about 10 percent in value from immediately after the Arab oil embargo of 1973.[62]

It appeared the world had reached a new, higher, but stable, normal level for oil prices. But that normality was about to be dashed by a revolution in Iran.

1979 CRISIS

In 1977 widespread public dissatisfaction by Islamist and secular Iranians at the authoritarian monarchy of Mohammad Reza Shah Pahlavi resulted in regime-rattling demonstrations that intensified in early 1978. Oil worker strikes the next year reduced Iran's oil exports from 4.5 mb/d to less than 1.0 mb/d. A military government installed by the Shah restored production, but by the end of 1978 violence and strikes had intensified, expatriate oil workers had begun evacuating, and oil exports had come to a complete halt. In 1979 protests snowballed into a full-blown revolution. The Shah fled Iran in January 1979 and an Islamic Republic was proclaimed that year, headed by returned exile and now Supreme Leader Ruhollah Khomeini.

The Iranian revolution caused a severe disruption in oil supplies—much more so than had been seen during the Arab oil embargo of 1973 (see figure 6.2). Iran was then the world's second-largest oil exporter after Saudi Arabia. While Saudi Arabia and other OPEC producers were able to partially offset Iran's loss and global oil production actually increased in 1978, the swiftness of Iran's decline startled the market.[63] Actual world production rose in 1979, but the loss of Iran's 2 mb/d (about 3 percent of the prior year's supply) triggered a 126 percent price increase for oil[64]— even though inventories and spare capacity were still ample. One explanation of the outsized price spike was a desire by importers to build *even higher* inventories as a precaution.[65]

Japan was particularly hurt by the sudden loss in supply. Tokyo had prioritized making Iran a niche supplier and received 20 percent of its supplies from the country. After two decades of astounding growth, Japan's leaders suddenly confronted their country's core vulnerability—the near-total absence of oil resources. Shocked by the sudden cancellation of their long-term contracts, Japanese refiners embarked on a frantic spree in the spot market, buying all the crude they could, wherever they could, becoming increasingly resourceful along the way.[66] Spot

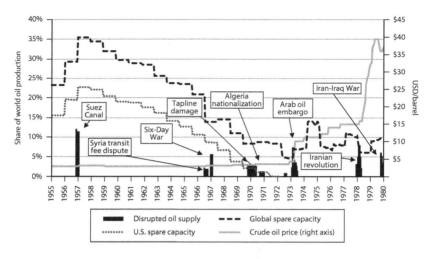

FIGURE 6.2

Oil disruptions, spare capacity, and crude prices.

Sources: The Rapidan Group; BP, "Energy Outlook to 2035"; U.S. Senate; API, *Petroleum Facts and Figures* (1959); Dow Jones & Company, Spot Oil Price: West Texas Intermediate, as modified by the Rapidan Group.

markets—which had been growing but were still largely used as a balancing mechanism, enabling buyers to obtain an extra cargo here and there if due to logistical or other factors they found themselves short—started to see even more trading. The Japanese were joined by independent oil companies and a host of new buyers scrambling to procure crude in the increasingly liquid spot market, including "Wall Street refiners, state oil companies, trading houses, and oil traders."[67] Havoc ensued, as buyers scurried into the spot markets looking for immediately available cargoes to replace lost Iranian volumes. Spot prices were increasingly monitored closely by OPEC as an indicator of the "real" market price of oil—and this real price was rising.

Under long-term contracts, OPEC producers were obliged to sell oil to customers based on administered prices. But by February 1979, spot market prices were twice as high as administered ones.[68] Thus, traders who could buy OPEC oil at lower administered prices and sell it on the higher spot market made large profits. This had two consequences.

First, some OPEC producers began selling more oil directly to third parties at higher spot prices. Second, OPEC raised administered prices toward higher spot levels, which in turn fueled more panic and hoarding that translated into higher spot prices. The self-reinforcing cycle continued.

Saudi Arabia fueled the panic by cutting production by around 600 kb/d in January 1979.[69] Spot oil prices rose from $12.80 per barrel before the first Iranian oil worker's strike in October 1978 to $21.80 in February 1979 just after the Shah left, and hit a high of nearly $40 in November of that year.[70] One oil executive recoiled at the "ratchet" strategy that appeared to be similar to the TRC's strategy following disruptions in Iran and Suez and the Middle East in the 1950s of holding back supply to ensure price increases stuck. "When Iranian oil went off the market," he said, "OPEC tacitly agreed to limit production. It is much simpler to limit production so that price increases are automatic. The OPEC nations are acting the same way the TRC did for 30 years."[71] If not yet a functioning cartel, OPEC producers were starting to experiment with exercising supply cutbacks to make oil price increases stick.

In March 1979 Iranian oil began trickling back onto the market, but fear and panic enabled the OPEC producers to demand large surcharges on their oil sales. Saudi Oil Minister Yamani called it a "free-for-all." Publicly Saudi Arabia continued to maintain an opposition to exorbitant oil prices. Yamani insisted Saudi Arabia wanted to avoid recessions and incentives to invest in substitutes for oil.

In Washington, the sudden loss of a top Middle East ally and attendant oil price spikes whipped smoldering expectations of an imminent oil shortage into a full-blown panic. Gasoline lines reappeared in 1979 after Iran's exports were cut off. Iran tended to produce a type of crude oil that yielded a lot of gasoline; refiners were forced to replace Iranian barrels with heavier crudes that did not yield as much. Once again, rising prices, federal allocation rules, and local regulations created local shortages and fueled panic buying. Gasoline stocks in California ran low and as rumors of shortages circulated "all 12 million vehicles in the state seemed to show up at once at gasoline stations to fill up." Some states limited purchases to a small dollar amount, which had the perverse consequence of forcing motorists to tank up more than once, worsening gasoline lines.[72]

The new energy disaster sent Washington into crisis mode. In 1979 the CIA warned that gas lines and oil price increases signaled an "underlying oil supply problem . . . the world can no longer count on increases in oil production to meet its energy needs."[73] In June 1979 Energy Secretary James Schlesinger reminded people that he had been warning of an inevitable supply shortfall since 1977 and, upon leaving office in August of that year, warned that oil was tapped out and "unless we achieve the greater use of coal and nuclear power over the next decade, this society may just not make it."[74] In 1980 the CIA warned "[w]e believe that world oil production is probably at or near its peak . . . [p]olitically, the cardinal issue is how vicious the struggle for energy supplies will become."[75]

The public erupted in anger at oil companies and at President Jimmy Carter, whose approval ratings nosedived to about Nixon's during the worst of Watergate. Carter excoriated oil companies but, recognizing (in what had become consensus view) that 1970s price controls failed, began decontrolling oil prices.[76]

Congress also banned construction of fuel-oil-fired power plants, promoted switching from oil to coal for industrial fuel, and enacted subsidies for renewable energy sources like solar, wind, and ethanol, and tax credits for home insulation. A 55-mile-per-hour speed limit was introduced.[77] (Many of these policies, such as fuel economy regulations and renewable subsidies, remain in effect today, although in changed forms.)

Carter also famously launched the federal Synthetic Fuels Corporation (SFC) to use chemical engineering to produce liquid fuels, mainly from coal—coming full circle, as 110 years before, petroleum was first commercialized to replace oil refined from coal. The SFC also intended to develop liquid fuels from oil shale (not today's famous "shale oil" but instead kerogen-laden rocks), oil sands, and heavy oils. (The SFC failed to commercialize alternatives to oil, and was terminated in 1986.[78])

None of Carter's measures brought immediate relief and the country spiraled deeper into crisis. During the first weekend of summer—June 23 and 24, 1979—58 percent of the nation's gasoline stations were closed on Saturday and 70 percent were closed on Sunday.[79]

To address the immediate problem of soaring oil prices, President Carter also quietly implored Saudi Arabia to increase production. With the overthrow of the Shah, Tehran was no longer the linchpin U.S. ally in the region, and that included on oil matters. From now on, when an American president needed more oil, he would call Riyadh. And Saudi Arabia's substantial production and excess capacity enhanced the kingdom's role in stabilizing price. Riyadh obliged, increasing supply from 8.8 mb/d in June 1979 to 9.8 mb/d by November of that year.[80] Prices eased a bit but other OPEC countries reduced output, causing prices to resume their climb—particularly after Iran seized U.S. hostages in November.

As the Iran revolution and the oil disruption and price shock brought the United States and Saudi Arabia closer together, it also intensified ancient Saudi-Iranian ethnic, religious, and geopolitical rivalries, making them a permanent feature of geopolitics—and as we shall see, OPEC oil policy—in the decades since. Saudi Arabia is the center of Islam's Sunni sect and home to its two most revered sites, Mecca and Medina. The majority of Iran's citizens adhere to the Shiite sect of Islam; while Shiites also dominate Iraq and Bahrain, they comprise only 15 percent of the world's 1.6 billion Muslims.[81] Tehran and Riyadh compete for leadership within Islam, although before the nineteenth century, their rivalry had been suppressed by distance, lack of direct economic and political linkages, and intervention by foreign powers. In the 1950s, when both became major oil powerhouses, their vital interests became closely intertwined. Until 1979 both monarchies kept tensions low. But the 1979 Iranian revolution established a revolutionary Islamic state scathingly critical of the Sunni sect and especially of the Saudi monarchy and unleashed a succession of mostly indirect conflict and proxy wars.[82]

UTTER CHAOS

Supply disruptions arising from upheaval in Iran and Iraq in the late 1970s dwarfed those earlier in the decade. "[I]n the summer and early fall of 1979," Daniel Yergin noted, "the world oil market was in a state of anarchy whose global effects far exceeded those of the early 1930s, in the wake of Dad Joiner's discovery in East Texas, and those of the very earliest days of the industry in western Pennsylvania."[83] Saudi Arabia, which prized itself as the guarantor of stability, was embarrassed by the chaos. "We feel so unhappy," said Saudi Oil Minister Yamani at the time. "We don't like to see it happening like this."[84]

Just when circumstances in the oil market seemed impossibly dire, they got worse. In September 1980 Iraq attacked Iran, severing oil exports from both. World oil production slumped by 5 percent from 1979 to 1980.[85] Crude oil prices briefly exceeded $40 per barrel and averaged another 17 percent higher than 1979. Combined, world crude prices had risen by $23 per barrel—163 percent—between 1978 and 1980.[86]

The United States had already formally declared its commitment to stability in the region, and deepened its links to the region. After the Soviet Union's invasion of Afghanistan in late December 1979, President Carter—reflecting increased worries from U.S. defense planners about a threat to the Gulf's energy resources—stated the United States would not allow the Persian Gulf to be dominated by a hostile outside power, and established a new military command (the Rapid Deployment Joint Task Force, forerunner to CENTCOM) to back it up. It quickly was dubbed the Carter Doctrine. President Reagan added a corollary to the Carter Doctrine with a policy that would "guarantee the territorial integrity and internal stability of Saudi Arabia." Under the Reagan Corollary, the United States supported Iraq against Saudi Arabia's chief regional rival Iran while ordering reflagging and escorts of oil tankers in the 1980s.[87]

The traumatic price spikes in 1973 and 1979–1980 are often twinned, but are very different. In 1973, OPEC deliberately imposed price increases while taking control of pricing from majors. The process was hardly elegant, but it was deliberate. There was no significant disruption of crude oil, and shortages in consuming countries were largely due to domestic price controls and rationing. In the case of the 1979 Iranian revolution and the 1980 Iran-Iraq War, there *was* a major supply disruption, especially the latter, although commercial inventories were quite ample. The disruption and panic sent market prices up, and OPEC simply followed along by raising prices. By 1981 OPEC's administered prices reached $34 per barrel, roughly three times their level three years before.

7

OPEC'S RUDE AWAKENING: 1981-1990

As the 1980s dawned, the consensus held that oil prices were headed unceasingly upward. Oil experts believed that the recent quintupling in oil prices would not hurt demand and that new oil supplies from investment prompted by higher prices would be slow in arriving. Actually OPEC hoped (and consuming countries feared) that the group could enjoy a sustained large market share and high prices.[1]

But those widespread expectations and fears were about to be dashed by another mammoth changeover in global oil supply and demand trends. Suddenly and unexpectedly, OPEC was hit by a triple whammy—collapsing demand, soaring competition from new producers, and weakening in the role of administered prices versus market—determined ones. It was OPEC's turn to be shaken to its core by an unexpected upheaval in the global oil market.

Contrary to expectations, global oil demand plummeted by 9 percent from 65.3 mb/d in 1979 to 59.8 mb/d in 1984. Oil demand in the Organisation for Economic Co-operation and Development (OECD) member nations was hit the hardest, plunging 15 percent from 44.7 mb/d to 38.0 mb/d during the period (see figure 7.1).[2] Demand slumped due to a deep global recession, consumer and government responses to earlier high oil prices, conservation, improved efficiency spurred by past price increases, and fuel switching. The final factor—fuel switching or "demand destruction"—was structural. In 1971, residual fuel oil accounted for 20 percent of total OECD oil use. By 1984, it had fallen to 10 percent, having been replaced by coal, natural gas, and nuclear power.[3]

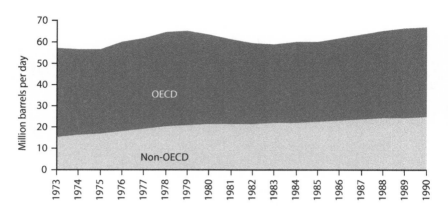

FIGURE 7.1

Global crude consumption, 1973–1990. OECD, Organisation for Economic Co-operation and Development.

Source: EIA, "Monthly Energy Review," July 2015.

While demand fell, supply piled up. Prior investments in massive new fields outside OPEC finally began to yield new supply. The largest increases came from Mexico, Norway, and the United States. By 1983 Alaska was producing 1.7 mb/d (20 percent of the U.S. total) as production from Prudhoe Bay ramped up (after environmental opposition to building a pipeline had caused years of delay).[4] Mexico's production rose from an average of 0.8 mb/d in the 1970s to 2.9 mb/d in 1983 after the massive Cantarell came online in 1981.[5] New supplies from Soviet fields also became available. But most important—and worryingly from OPEC's standpoint—were large new fields in the British (Forties) and Norwegian (Ekofisk) North Sea. Production from these fields, located close to European markets, competed directly with OPEC exporters. Plummeting demand and soaring non-OPEC supply cut savagely into the cartel's market share, which fell from over 50 percent in the early 1970s to less than 30 percent by 1985 (see figure 7.2).

OPEC was fast losing control over setting the price of oil. Since the 1950s, administered prices had served as benchmarks for calculating tax and royalty payments to host governments under the concessions. OPEC continued to set administered prices after wresting control from the

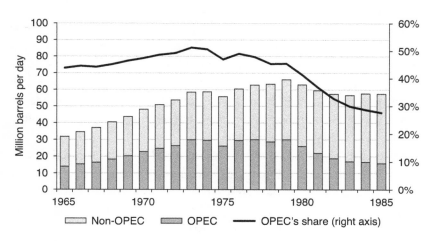

FIGURE 7.2

OPEC's share of global oil production.

Source: BP, "Statistical Review."

Seven Sisters in the early 1970s. But by the end of that decade concessions were more or less extinct as producers had nationalized them. Now shorn of links to old concessions, crude refiners and traders bought crude on spot markets, where prices were not determined by OPEC but instead determined by arms-length trading between parties with no link other than a desire to exchange crude oil for cash. Administered prices were fast becoming a relic.

As a seller's market turned into a buyer's market, OPEC producers found they were not able to sell as much crude as they wanted at administered prices. Spot prices began falling below administered ones for the first time since OPEC had seized the reins from concession operators ten years earlier. OPEC publicly expressed annoyance with spot markets and some, like Saudi Arabia and Kuwait, refused to sell any oil on a spot basis. But privately, most OPEC producers—particularly Nigeria and Venezuela—unloaded barrels on spot markets in their desperation to raise revenue.

The combination in the early 1980s of weakening demand and expansion of market-based spot crude trading prompted a transformation in how both producers and consumers viewed oil. Whereas in the 1970s oil was considered a special commodity whose price would inexorably rise as voracious consumption devoured limited remaining resources, in the 1980s people started to consider oil just another commodity, no longer impervious to market forces, but instead subject to them, albeit with a multiyear lag. Soaring prices had eventually—with a multiyear lag— helped break consumption growth and triggered massive new supplies, turning perceived dearth into a glut.

The turnabout forced OPEC to become a real cartel by restricting supply, as founder Pérez Alfonzo had envisaged. The easy days of simply announcing price increases were over. Now, OPEC had to follow in the footsteps of Rockefeller, the TRC, and Seven Sisters by allocating market shares to members, and holding up prices.

A tipping point came in early 1982 when the United Kingdom government under Prime Minister Margaret Thatcher cut oil prices, following a buildup in inventories. (The United Kingdom had nationalized North Sea fields in 1975, administered them via a state-owned British National Oil Corporation [BNOC, also called Britoil], and sold oil under administered prices as OPEC countries did.) British price cuts particularly threatened Nigeria, whose barrels competed directly with the North Sea oil but whose price was linked to a competitively high Arab Light marker.[6] Meanwhile, Iran cut prices unilaterally, eager to maximize revenues during its war with Iraq and determined to undermine Saudi Arabia's leadership role in OPEC. Saudi Arabia was busy trying to defend a $34 price that buyers refused to pay as cheaper barrels came on the market.[7]

As in 1926, when Exxon and Shell started slashing prices for Indian kerosene, a global price war loomed. OPEC had been setting prices since 1973, but now falling demand for its crude required that the cartel cut production to defend those prices. Riyadh came to realize it could either aim for a $34 per barrel price or a relatively high 8.5 mb/d production level, but not both.[8] In March 1982 OPEC, for the first time, adopted country level quotas and an overall target of 18.5 mb/d. Saudi Arabia was not given a formal production quota though it was assumed that it would be 7.5 mb/d, equal to the total OPEC quota less the other members' shares. It said it would adjust its production if necessary, so long as other OPEC producers respected their quotas.[9] "After twenty-two years of existence,"

OPEC historian Ian Skeet notes, "OPEC had finally agreed to turn itself into the cartel that Pérez Alfonzo had originally planned it should be and which many critics had mistakenly claimed it already was."[10]

Like their TRC forbears, OPEC members became preoccupied with trying to match supply increases with demand increases to keep prices stable. OPEC analysts would assess the pace of global demand, the likely changes in oil production outside their organization, and the amount of oil in inventories as well as expected or desired change in inventory levels. From these they would derive an estimated demand or "call" for their crude (hence the ubiquitous term "call on OPEC") and try to link quotas to that level.[11]

Oil cartels, as the earliest attempts in the western Pennsylvania Oil Regions proved over 100 years earlier, are susceptible to disintegration because individual members have a strong incentive to cheat, especially if they believe other members will adhere to limits. So it was with OPEC, which never achieved the durable discipline and cohesiveness the Seven Sisters did—hardly surprising, as OPEC never controlled as much traded oil and was composed of economically and politically rivalrous members. The OPEC member cohesion soon fell apart as most producers ignored quotas and produced as much as they could. Iran, then at war with fellow member Iraq, did not even pretend to abide by quotas, and most of the other members continued to sell oil on the spot market.

Meanwhile, competitive pressure from outside OPEC rose, and they came together again to attempt cooperative action. In February 1983, Britain once again announced price cuts from soaring North Sea production, putting more pressure on Atlantic Basin crude prices (and turning the screws on Nigeria in particular). In March 1983, OPEC met and agreed to its first-ever cut in official selling prices (OSPs, as their administered prices were called), lowering the Arab Light benchmark to $29 per barrel. OPEC now stated *formally* that Saudi Arabia would act as the swing producer. Riyadh dutifully cut production in the face of strong supply growth from the North Sea and Mexico. But OPEC producers continued to cheat, worsening the glut, and prices dove. Despite the cheating, Saudi Arabia continued to cut production in 1984 into 1985. By August 1985 Saudi production had hit 2.3 mb/d, down 6 mb/d or 72 percent since OPEC began collective cuts in March 1982.[12]

The Saudi decision to act as a swing producer between 1982 and 1985 prevented a collapse in spot market prices, which drifted slowly down from $33 to $28 dollars per barrel between 1982 and the end of 1985. While trending lower, oil prices were relatively stable when measured on the basis of the range of monthly price swings. From April 1983 until November 1985 monthly oil price swings averaged 4 percent, the lowest period since the OPEC era began.

But Saudi Arabia bore tremendous cost as the only OPEC member cutting supply to hold up prices for everyone else. The kingdom was hemorrhaging financial reserves, losing international standing, and incurring domestic discontent with a policy that seemed to support other members' interests over its own.[13] As Saudi Arabia lowered its production, it repeatedly warned it would not tolerate bearing the brunt of the adjustment. Veteran Saudi Oil Minister Zaki Yamani warned in a speech in September 1985 that Saudi Arabia was fed up:

> Most of the OPEC member countries depend on Saudi Arabia to carry the burden and protect the price of oil. Now the situation has changed. Saudi Arabia is no longer willing or able to take that heavy burden and duty, and therefore it cannot be taken for granted. And therefore I do not think that OPEC as a whole will be able to protect the price of oil.[14]

Saudi warnings were largely ignored. At the October 1985 OPEC meeting, the Saudi Oil Minister Yamani said, "Saudi Arabia would no longer play the swing-producer role," but other producers both inside and outside OPEC considered Yamani's warning another bluff. That same month, the United Kingdom told the head of OPEC that it would not force North Sea production cuts, while Norway announced it planned to increase production by 40 percent.[15] Rampant cheating by other OPEC producers and defiance from non-OPEC producers tipped Saudi Arabia over the edge. It was time to teach other producers a lesson by deploying the most powerful economic weapon in the kingdom's arsenal—quickly producible oil held off the market in spare capacity.

In late October 1985, Saudi Arabia opened the taps and flooded the market. It did so by formulating a new pricing policy designed to push out as much oil as customers could handle. Instead of selling oil to refiners based on an administered price, the kingdom would sell on a "netback" basis. Under netbacks, Saudi Arabia guaranteed its refinery customers a fixed refining margin.[16]

This was a dream come true for refiners. Under the previous system, the refiners' margin was uncertain. Refiners paid up front (ex-ante) for the crude, but they bore the risk of losing money if refined product prices fell in the two months or so that it took to transport that barrel to a refinery, process it into gasoline and fuel oil, and sell it (ex-post). Let's say a refiner bought Saudi crude at $20 per barrel in the expectation he could refine and sell it, earning a $2 per barrel margin based on prevailing prices of refined products.[17] But during the time it took for those barrels for which he had sunk $20 each to arrive, product prices in the refiner's home market might have fallen by $3 per barrel, leaving the refiner with a loss. Prices could and often did move sharply even while tankers were plying their way to destination ports, slicing into the margin the buyer had expected when they purchased the Saudi crude. The fear of loss induces the refiner to shop around for the cheapest crude available.

But under netback pricing, Saudi Arabia promised customers a guaranteed margin ex-post regardless of how crude and product prices behaved beforehand. So the crude producer bears the risk of price fluctuations instead of the refiner. Say the Saudis guaranteed refiners a $2 margin. Whereas in the case above the refiner lost $1 per barrel (paid $20 but sold for $19), under netback pricing the Saudis would accept a lower crude price of $17 so that refiner would still make $2 per barrel. Adelman called netback pricing a "costless hedge against price changes."[18] Freed from having to worry about whether they could earn a profit, refiners had incentive to buy all the Saudi oil they could—and they did. At first, Saudi Arabia shrewdly targeted its netback sales at the Atlantic market where it had a particular advantage as a nearby producer and would therefore force prices down faster.[19] But Japanese traders grew angry they were not allowed in on the bonanza offered to Europeans, so in November Saudi Arabia extended netback pricing terms to all customers.[20] As demand rose, Saudi Arabia's production doubled from 2.2 mb/d in August 1985, escalating to 4.5 by December.[21]

The effect on the market was immediate. To avoid losing sales to Saudi Arabia, other OPEC producers had to implement a netback price and soon a full-blown (if undeclared) price war was on—among OPEC and non-OPEC producers alike. Refiners gorged on Saudi and OPEC crude, creating a glut of refined products that lowered product prices, which in turn fed back to weaker crude oil prices. Arab Light crashed from $28 in the fourth quarter of 1985 to $11 by the summer of 1986.

OPEC members demanded an emergency meeting, but Saudi Arabia and its ally Kuwait brushed them off. Riyadh insisted that non-OPEC producers such as the United Kingdom cooperate with OPEC in cutting, if not join the cartel. That was a nonstarter in Margaret Thatcher's London. So Riyadh applied more pain, continuing to inundate the already glutted market. In May 1986 a new socialist Norwegian government offered to cut if OPEC would, but OPEC could not agree. In July, sales of Saudi light grade were rumored to hit $6.08, and Riyadh raised production again to 6.0 mb/d.[22]

The spectacular breakdown in cartel discipline led some to conclude that the oil market was reentering a period of ungoverned prices, as had been seen following the breakup of Standard Oil in 1911.[23] While the price collapse helped extend U.S. economic recovery (oil consumers, especially airlines, were thrilled at the low prices) and hurt the Soviet Union's economy by slashing its oil revenue, the speed of the price collapse and the prospect of a return of oil price instability also triggered concern in Washington among oil experts and officials. Oil producers and their bankers were terrified by the negative impacts for the oil industry and oil-producing countries, especially heavily indebted Mexico and Nigeria. One expert testified to Congress in 1986 that by undermining producing countries, it could hurt U.S. exports and defaults could "threaten the stability of our financial system with deleterious implications for the real economy as well."[24] Domestic oil industry executives warned of higher import dependence and another boom cycle as investment cuts thinned supply. The sudden and sustained price crash led to other industry changes: private investment in new fields slowed, and there was a wave of mergers and acquisitions among oil companies.[25]

The Reagan administration's Interior Department warned that the country had better prepare for a long period of boom-bust prices. "Unfortunately there is no evidence of stability on oil prices," a 1988 Interior Department report noted. "On the contrary, there is evidence that the natural tendency of the crude oil market is to move through boom and bust phases."[26] The Interior Department went on to warn "the Federal government should be concerned about the boom and bust cycle of world oil prices because this cycle affects the U.S. economy in several ways." The cyclical pattern of oil prices can increase inflation, unemployment and business risk associated with currency fluctuations. The pattern also reduces labor productivity, the security of U.S. financial institutions, and the competitiveness of U.S. industry as it is affected by currency fluctuations.[27]

One idea that cropped up at this time was to help domestic producers through a variable tariff on oil imports. This would entail establishing a floor price in the domestic U.S. market for imported crude oil. If prices fell below the floor, a tax would kick in by the amount of the difference between the market price and floor. So if the floor was $60 per barrel and prices fell to $40, a tax of $20 per barrel would automatically go into effect. If market prices subsequently rose, the tax would decline and when market prices rose above the floor, in this example $60, the tax would disappear. The goal was to guarantee (or threaten, depending on your perspective) that oil prices would never go below a chosen level.

Proponents of a variable import tariff asserted that it would serve national security interests in protecting domestic energy producers by insulating them from price bust, and that it would promote investment in and the purchase of new energy technologies and more efficient equipment by guaranteeing prices would not fall below a certain level. Opponents argued that a variable import tax would harm the economy and U.S. competiveness by raising costs, would require complex and inefficient rules to prevent domestic producers from incurring a windfall (as by possibly invoking the "old" versus "new" oil designations of the 1970s), and would violate trade rules.[28] The opponents' argument won out and the tariff was never enacted.[29]

While unwilling to reimpose oil tariffs, the Reagan administration was concerned enough about the negative national security implications arising from the harmful impact of collapsing oil prices (and their harmful effect on domestic producers) that it tried to talk Saudi Arabia into cutting production and propping up prices.[30] Cheap oil was a "two-edged sword for America," Vice President George H.W. Bush said, "and one of them has got to be the fact that this country—our country, the United States of America—has always felt that a viable domestic oil industry is in the national security interests of the United States. We recognize that, as we talk about national security interests, that that comes in conflict at some point—and I don't know where that is—with the totally free-market concept that we basically favor. . . . I feel that, and I know the president of the United States feels that." In April 1986, Vice President Bush departed for Riyadh to "tell Saudi Arabia that the protection of American security interests require action to stabilize the falling price of oil."[31] Bush met with senior Saudi oil officials and had a three-hour late-night audience with King Fahd. Although they agreed the world needed stable oil prices, they did not agree on how to achieve them or what price to target. Bush's visit had no immediate impact on Saudi oil policy: Saudi production actually rose from 4.0 mb/d in March 1986 to 6.2 mb/d by August 1986.[32]

Saudi Arabia's strategy of flooding the market succeeded, at least temporarily, in winning production cuts from other producers. In August 1986 OPEC reached a fragile agreement to cut production to 16.8 mb/d, down from 20.5 mb/d. Saudi Arabia and Iran tamped back to their quota levels and others cut a bit as well. Norway announced it would reduce exports by 10 percent, to "help stabilize oil prices at a higher level." Similar pledges were made by China, the Soviet Union, Mexico, Egypt, Malaysia, Oman, and Angola (though these promises were not kept).[33] OPEC spent the rest of 1986 bickering over whether and how to apportion further cuts in order to boost the price of their new benchmark, a basket of OPEC export grade crudes.

In October 1986 King Fahd fired Oil Minister Yamani, who had refused to obey the king's order to achieve an agreement that would target $18 per barrel while guaranteeing Saudi Arabia a higher quota, which the minister considered to be an impossible contradiction.[34] Yamani argued in vain that Saudi Arabia could not have its desired price and more supply; if it wanted a higher price the kingdom would have to cut production. Nevertheless, at a meeting in Geneva in December 1986, new Saudi Minister Hisham Nazer and his OPEC colleagues agreed to an $18 per barrel price target (the $18 pricing being a "reference price"[35] based on a basket of six OPEC and one non-OPEC, Mexican, administered crude prices) and accepted a new, more flexible quota system that would be revised every three months.[36] (This pricing system, albeit somewhat modified, endures today.)

The price plunge, and the recognition of the control that OPEC (and especially Saudi Arabia) had over oil prices, led to a shift in the United

States' attitude toward a group that it had routinely denounced since its founding. For example, in May 1987 U.S. Secretary of Energy John Herrington—who had once called OPEC's control over the market "unacceptable"—indicated that the United States was supporting Saudi efforts to achieve stability for oil prices. "I don't look for $9 a barrel oil again," he stated. "We realize we have all been through a wrenching experience internationally and within the U.S. Everybody sees the downside and we all agree it is not beneficial to go through radical surging in prices."[37]

OPEC RELINQUISHES PRICE SETTING TO THE MARKET

The $18 per barrel price target represented an attempt by OPEC to return to some semblance of normality. Saudi Arabia ended netback pricing and resumed setting administered prices. But as Yamani predicted, Saudi Arabia was obliged to cut its production into early 1987 to support prices. And more to the kingdom's chagrin, the days of administered prices were fast dying out. Oil trading was increasingly done in arms-length transactions and in spot markets and the forward market, where oil was bought for the future instead of for immediate delivery. Mexico was the first producer to adopt market-based pricing, in 1986. Within a couple of years all other producers followed, dropping administered prices for market-based ones.[38] Moreover, the expansion of spot market transactions and associated, rapid penetration of market-based futures contracts for crude and refined products rendered a return to administered prices impractical.[39] By 1988 Saudi Arabia and other OPEC producers conceded that henceforth prices would be set in free markets, with their crude oil sales priced against market-determined benchmarks depending on the destination of their exports.[40]

The implication of market-based pricing was that producers would no longer set—and haggle over—administered prices. Instead, OPEC would leave the prices to the market and instead use supply agreements or quotas as the main policy tool to reach or maintain a target price. In a sense, this shifted the nature of OPEC's control away from the Seven Sisters and more toward the TRC, which directly controlled supply to achieve a price target but did not administer prices per se.

Henceforth, OPEC's primary goal would be to monitor global supply, demand, and inventories in order to determine how much oil it should supply to the market to achieve its price target.[41] But OPEC differed markedly from the TRC in that it was not a single governmental body with the power to compel producers within its jurisdiction to limit supply to regulated amounts.[42] Nor did the thirteen OPEC countries resemble the Seven Sisters who, while competitive rivals, succeeded in jointly cooperating in an elaborate, rules-based framework to manage supply. OPEC's thirteen members varied significantly by size, revenue needs, and geographic location—not to mention having deep-seated geopolitical rivalries, often laced with ancient animosity and distrust.

While often referred to as a "cartel," analysts of OPEC structure and behavior are divided over the right word for it. Terms include "classic cartel," "clumsy cartel," "dominant firm," "loosely cooperating oligopoly," "residual firm monopolists" and "bureaucratic cartel."[43] Precise classifications aside, by 1986 it became clear that any real power OPEC enjoyed over prices depended largely on the policies of its largest producer and main spare capacity holder, Saudi Arabia.

Between the crude price bottom in 1986 and Iraq's invasion of Kuwait in August 1990, OPEC tried to manage the market by setting and adhering to individual quotas. Compliance was poor. Most OPEC countries cheated, producing at their maximum level. Generally, only Saudi Arabia withheld producible oil from the market. But OPEC got lucky as supply outside the organization—in Mexico, the Soviet Union, and the United Kingdom—slipped in the late 1980s.[44] But for these fortuitous supply cuts, low oil prices due to weak OPEC discipline may well have continued through the decade and the organization could have disintegrated. Instead, the misfortune of other producers enabled OPEC to increase its market share from 29 percent in 1985 to 37 percent in 1990.[45] Arab Light prices ranged between $13 and $19 per barrel from the first quarter of 1986 through the second quarter of 1990.[46]

Relatively stable prices below $20 were far from OPEC's glory days of $30 plus, but it could have been much worse. OPEC, Parra wrote, "had escaped by the skin of the teeth."[47] But just as a new normal set in at the end of the decade, another Persian Gulf conflict upended the oil market.

THE GULF WAR

The Iran-Iraq War, raging since September 1980, ended in 1988 with no victors. Iraq was saddled with $100 billion in debts, principally owed to Saudi Arabia, Kuwait, and the UAE. The lower oil prices after the 1986 collapse cut Iraqi revenues, deepening dictator Saddam Hussein's misery and desperation. To Saddam Hussein's indignation, Kuwait and the UAE were egregiously overproducing relative to their quotas at the end of the decade. Total OPEC production was running about 2 mb/d above its combined quota ceiling, and in the first half of 1990 prices of Mediterranean crudes (where Iraq then sold most of its barrels) fell by a third, vaporizing $500 million per month of Saddam's direly needed revenues.[48] Saddam Hussein was also enraged that Kuwait was reportedly drilling under the border and tapping Iraqi fields.[49] Iraq had historic and geographical reasons for coveting Kuwait; Baghdad considered Kuwait its province and by absorbing the smaller neighbor could increase its meager 36-mile coastline nearly tenfold.

Plunging oil prices and financial distress tipped Iraq from bellicosity into belligerence toward Gulf Sunni powers that had supported Saddam in its war with Iran. During last-ditch meetings in July 1990, Kuwait and the UAE promised to cut production but promptly reneged. Saddam invaded Kuwait on August 2, 1990, opening the world's first oil war.[50]

Kuwaiti oil disappeared and Iraqi oil was promptly embargoed. Prices initially doubled from $17 to $36 in September as both producers abruptly disappeared from the market. Once again, it became clear how useful spare capacity was during a large geopolitical disruption. Saudi Arabia ramped up production; its output rose from 5.4 mb/d in July to nearly 8 mb/d in September and held that level for more than a year. Despite the loss of Iraqi and Kuwaiti oil, total OPEC supply was back to pre-invasion levels by November 1990. That extra supply from OPEC, plus inventories, more than covered the supply shortfall from Iraq and Kuwait.[51]

Meanwhile, the United States acted both abroad and at home. U.S. military forces streamed into the Saudi Eastern Province to protect the fields and facilities from Iraq as an international military coalition was assembled to eject Iraqi forces from Kuwait. Washington readied the Strategic

Petroleum Reserve (SPR), established for emergencies precisely like this. On September 27, 1990, the Department of Energy conducted a test sale from the SPR and on the eve of air operations on January 16, 1991, the United States and other IEA countries ordered the first release from strategic stocks. Crude oil prices fell sharply soon afterward, reflecting the market's confidence in quick military victory by allied forces. The IEA strategic stock draw also reassured market participants, but in the end, only 17.3 mb of the total 33.75 mb offered were taken from the strategic stocks. Knowing it was available seemed to reduce panic buying.[52] However, analysts argued that the SPR should have been used earlier, at the outset of the crisis in August 1990, which could have prevented a doubling in oil prices in the second half of 1990—a price spike that triggered a U.S. recession.[53]

Spiking oil prices reversed much more quickly after the Gulf War than they had after the outbreak of the Iran-Iraq War. In both cases, crude oil prices at first doubled as two major producers were suddenly removed from the market. But unlike the early 1980s, during and after the first Gulf War oil prices quickly declined. In addition to the rapid Saudi supply increases and the availability and use of strategic reserves, two other factors helped stabilize prices: the absence of price controls in consuming countries, which dampened speculative buying and storing, and the new futures markets, which could absorb buying pressure, dampening though not displacing impact on physical prices.

However, the price shock sufficed to induce France and Venezuela to attempt corralling major producers and consumers into what became known as a "producer-consumer dialogue" on oil. Since the upheavals in the 1970s, oil producing and consuming countries have occasionally tried to hold multilateral talks on ways to promote price stability. But interest ebbed and flowed, depending on which side enjoyed more leverage. In the 1970s, despondent consuming countries like France were eager to talk, but high-riding producers showed little interest. When markets were glutted in the early 1980s, roles reversed: OPEC wanted to talk but consumers were less interested. Veteran oil market expert Robert Mabro, a strong proponent of the consumer dialogue, described the rationale for producer-consumer cooperation as grounded in a need to stabilize inherently volatile long-term oil prices.[54] The solution, Mabro advised, was that firms should share information about their investment plans while officials agreed to share the burden of holding and using spare production capacity and strategic stocks to defend a long-term price level. The main concern was less stabilizing day-to-day oil price fluctuations, but *long-run prices* that industry and governments can base investment and revenue plans. However, talks in 1991 led nowhere. The United States was hostile and preferred to conduct global oil policy bilaterally, usually in direct talks with Saudi Arabia.

ANOTHER TUMULTUOUS DECADE

The 1980s were as tumultuous and transformative as the 1970s for the oil market and oil prices. The decade started and ended with major conflicts in the Persian Gulf that triggered wild price instability and hastened transformations in the oil market. OPEC transitioned from a loose association of producers wielding newly acquired power to set administered prices for their crude exports to a cantankerous supply-regulating cartel attempting to influence market prices.

But OPEC's initial success in replicating the TRC's role as supply regulator was not terribly promising. It depended on Saudi Arabia playing the swing producer role—which it abandoned spectacularly in 1985 and 1986, triggering a price collapse. Fortuitous supply cuts outside OPEC and stronger demand later in the decade enabled OPEC to enjoy relative price stability. The Gulf War further cemented Saudi Arabia's primacy within OPEC. But the 1980s demonstrated that if the OPEC era was to achieve the goal of oil price stability that producers and consumers craved, it would require either Saudi leadership or luck—or both.

8

OPEC MUDDLES THROUGH: 1991-2003

T he first two decades of the OPEC era were extraordinarily tumultuous and marked by price upheavals instead of stability. But the third
decade would be different. Things were settling down into a less volatile "new normal" for OPEC and the oil market.

Oil demand was in flux during the 1990s, but on the whole rose at a
more moderate rate than in the 1970s. The breakup of the Soviet Union
triggered a staggering 4.7 mb/d—a 56 percent drop in former Soviet
Union countries during the decade, but China's demand doubled, rising
by 2.1 mb/d. While not growing at the torrid 5–9 percent rates of the late
1960s and early 1970s, consumption had recovered from the miserable
near-flat growth in the 1980s (0.3 percent on average) to grow in the 1990s
by 1.5 percent on average or 1.1 mb/d per year.[1]

Like demand, the supply side of the oil market was also in flux, but net
supply increases were moderate. Supply from the former Soviet Union
imploded from 11.5 mb/d to 7.1 mb/d by 1996, but then began inching back
up, hitting 7.5 mb/d by the end of the decade. United Kingdom production slumped from 2.7 mb/d to 1.9 mb/d in the late 1980s and early 1990s
but roared back by the end of the decade to almost 3.0 mb/d. Norwegian
production nearly doubled, from 1.7 mb/d in 1990 to 3.3 mb/d in 1997.

OPEC producers were able to increase production and restore market
share while also restoring a comfortable spare capacity cushion, mostly
held in Saudi Arabia, of between 4 and 5 percent of global demand.
Kuwaiti production quickly recovered from wartime devastation, rising
from zero in May 1991 to 1.6 mb/d in December 1992.[2] Sanctions kept

Iraqi supply largely off the market until 1996, but ramped up quickly to 2.6 mb/d by 1999, when limits on oil sales were removed under the U.N. oil-for-food program.[3]

For OPEC as a whole, spare capacity (excluding sanctioned Iraq) rose from below 1.3 percent of global production in December 1991, during the First Gulf War, to over 5 percent by the spring of 2003.[4] During the ten-year period from summer 1991 to summer 2001, Saudi crude production oscillated between 8.0 mb/d and 8.9 mb/d, with only rare departures from this range (including a small dip below 8.0 mb/d in the summer of 1999 in reaction to the Asian crisis). Saudi Arabia was able and willing to cut supply by a relatively small amount for a brief time, along with other producer cuts, and the kingdom's share of OPEC production remained above 25 percent.[5]

One of the biggest challenges OPEC faced during the 1990s was contending with Venezuela, which adopted an all-out production increase while openly flaunting both quotas and OPEC itself (ironic, given that Venezuela was one of OPEC's leading founders and the first champions of collective quotas). In 1990, Andrés Sosa Pietri—the new president of Venezuela's state-owned oil company, PDVSA—pushed for a looser link both between the state-owned oil company and government in Caracas and between Venezuela and OPEC, which he regarded as a "relic of the past."[6] Venezuela's production rose steadily to 1 mb/d above its OPEC quota by mid-decade. This maverick approach, later dubbed "The Opening" or "La Apertura" was advanced by his successor, Luis Giusti, who in 1996 opened Venezuela to outside investment in exploration and production under a ten-year plan to double production from 3.3 to over 6 mb/d. Venezuela's brash approach triggered protests and warnings from OPEC, to which Giusti retorted that the organization had to "change or disappear."[7]

Immediate crisis was averted as oil prices unexpectedly increased in 1996 and briefly in the first week of 1997 to nearly $27. The cause of the oil price spike remains uncertain; some have attributed it to data published by the international oil watchdog International Energy Agency indicating a large gap between global demand and supply, others to vigorous U.S. growth and explosive trade-generated demand from developed, free market

Asian "Tigers" (Hong Kong, Singapore, South Korea, and Taiwan) as well as countries like Malaysia, Indonesia, the Philippines, Thailand, and the Chinese province of Guangdong, collectively known as "the new tigers."[8] Another factor may have been that many U.S. refiners expected Iraqi supply to return in late 1995 and 1996. Anticipating lower prices, those refiners ran down inventories ahead of a cold winter. Other factors included simmering tensions in Iraq and a potential shortage of heating oil in the United States.

THE GHOST OF JAKARTA

The unexpected price increase in 1996 and 1997 averted a full clash between Venezuela and other OPEC members.[9] But later in 1997 the Asian financial crisis hit, abruptly hurting oil demand, and threw OPEC and other oil producers back into crisis mode. The Asian financial crisis had its origins in the aforementioned strong growth, which had attracted massive capital inflow that was channeled into a real estate bubble. In July 1997 the Thai currency (baht) collapsed, triggering other Asian currency and banking collapses that mushroomed by year-end into widespread economic downturn and bankruptcies.[10] But as OPEC prepared to meet in Jakarta in November 1997, producers' minds were less focused on the gathering Asian crisis than on the oil price spike that had preceded it. On November 27, OPEC ministers approved a 2.5 mb/d or 10 percent quota hike, confident that demand was robust enough to keep prices stable.[11]

OPEC producers soon regretted the decision.

The mismatch between slowing demand and rising supply caused oil inventories to swell rapidly in consuming countries in early 1998. After an IEA report, in an about-face from a few years before, estimated global supply would *exceed* demand by an unusually large 3.5 mb/d in the second quarter of 1998, oil prices tanked. By early 1999, prices for some grades of crude oil fell as low as $8 per barrel. In a March 1999 cover, *The Economist* blared that the world was "drowning in oil." OPEC producers quickly realized they had made a mistake, and thereafter would be haunted by the "Ghost of Jakarta"—the folly of loosening quotas without accurately assessing if oil demand was strong enough to keep the prices steady.

OPEC TURNS LEMONS INTO LEMONADE

The shocking collapse in oil prices spooked OPEC and other oil producers, and OPEC members responded with an unusually strong show of discipline. While the price crash was the main reason for higher cooperation, other circumstances played a part. First, relations between regional geopolitical archrivals Iran and Saudi Arabia had entered a temporary warm phase. President Khatami of Iran was relatively moderate and his oil minister, Bijan Zangeneh, was a technocratic pragmatist willing to strike deals.[12] Second, Venezuela's defiant attitude softened due to plummeting oil prices and after Hugo Chávez was elected president in December 1998, Caracas reversed the La Apertura policy and became a stronger supporter of production restraint. And third, other producers likely did not wish to test Saudi resolve, fearing that Saudi Arabia could reprise its 1986 actions and unleash its spare capacity on the glutted market, crushing prices further.[13]

Despite the tail winds, corralling OPEC and non-OPEC producers into agreeing to share the burden of cuts was arduous and took time. While some OPEC producers acted within a few months by cutting production, it took about a year of low prices (crude oil prices fell 36 percent between the first cuts in March 1998 and the lowest level in December that year)[14] to compel recalcitrant producers inside OPEC (like Venezuela and Iran) and outside (like Norway) to cut production. Russia promised cuts but did not follow through. On March 22, 1998, Saudi Arabia secretly met with Venezuela and Mexico (while not an OPEC member, Mexico's oil supply was perking up after flatlining in the 1980s, and Saudi Arabia wanted to rein it in) to coordinate production restraint. The three countries announced a "Riyadh Pact" to restore order by calling for a round of cuts targeting 1.7 mb/d.[15]

Under the Riyadh Pact, Saudi Arabia agreed to match combined cuts by Venezuela and Mexico.[16] Oil prices briefly rebounded at the surprising show of resolve, especially the patch-up between Venezuela and Saudi Arabia. At a meeting on March 30, 1998, OPEC reversed the Jakarta decision, announcing 1.612 mb/d in production cuts, excluding Iraq.[17] Crude prices briefly rallied to over $15 but subsequently resumed falling due to trader skepticism that the producer cuts would be sufficient.[18] Deeply dismayed, Saudi Arabia, Venezuela, and Mexico met again in early June, conceded past cuts were inadequate, and pledged to reduce output by another 450 kb/d (225 kb/d for Saudi Arabia, 125 kb/d for Venezuela, and 100 kb/d for Mexico).[19] During another meeting on June 24, 1998, OPEC implemented another round of major cuts and, notably, Iran agreed to contribute real production cuts instead of imaginary ones (Iran was infamous for offering cuts from its own inflated estimates of its production rather than lower actual production).[20] Nevertheless crude prices kept tumbling, shedding another third and bottoming just above $10 at the end of 1998.

It was not until 1999 that OPEC cuts started to eat into the glut. OPEC crude production fell from 29 mb/d in March 1998 to 26.4 mb/d by June 1999 and fell again to just below 26.0 mb/d in December 1999.[21] Non-OPEC producers Norway, Oman, and Mexico also made significant cuts and prices rose smartly, more than doubling from $10 at the end of 1998 to $25 one year later.

The 1998 price collapse prompted protests from domestic U.S. producers who pushed a bill that came to be known as the "No Oil Producing and Exporting Cartels Act" (NOPEC) that would amend the Sherman Act to make it illegal for governments to try to limit oil and gas production to control oil prices; the bill failed to pass. (The bill resurfaced in the subsequent decade in response to rising oil prices, but was opposed by President George W. Bush and never signed into law.)[22]

The 1998 price drop prompted panic among producers but elicited little more than a shrug from the Clinton administration. After the tumultuous 1970s and early 1980s, during the long period of relatively stable oil prices from 1986 to early 2000s (with the exception of the 1990–1991 Gulf War), Washington reverted to aloofness and complacency with regard to the oil industry and energy security. In 1986, the Reagan administration decided to ease fuel economy standards for model years 1987 and 1988.[23] During the 1990s the Clinton administration and Congress looked the other way when the auto industry and motorists exploited a loophole in fuel economy standards for gas-guzzling sport-utility vehicles. SUVs and minivans are also exempt from a federal "gas-guzzler tax" enacted in 1978.[24]

Public and official concern about energy security abated during the 1990s. Despite a doubling in dependence on imported oil after 1985, from about 25 percent to over 50 percent, in 1996, a Republican Congress and Democratic White House agreed to sell off some of the strategic reserves in 1996 to plug holes in the federal budget. The 1996 SPR release also coincided with a rise to over $25 per barrel crude prices, a relatively high level for that period.[25] It would not be the first time Washington responded to rising fuel prices by releasing strategic stocks intended for use in supply emergencies.

Washington's nonchalance likely stemmed from two factors. First and foremost, gasoline prices were stable during the 1990s. Second, while U.S. dependence on crude imports continued to increase, the share of imports from OPEC and the unstable Persian Gulf remained steady to low compared with previous decades, with a greater share coming from more stable hemispheric neighbors Canada and Mexico.[26] So domestic U.S. oil producers found little help from Washington in 1998. Energy Secretary Bill Richardson floated the idea of helping producers by buying oil for the Strategic Petroleum Reserve (ironically, given that Congress had sold SPR oil two years before), but the idea went nowhere. The Clinton administration did not see the 1998 price drop as a deliberate move by Saudi Arabia or OPEC, and was in general less friendly toward the oil industry than the Reagan administration. And in any event, unlike 1986, the collapse in 1998 quickly reversed.

While U.S. producers looked on helplessly, a reinvigorated OPEC tried to establish a more formal system to stabilize prices, buoyed by its success at raising oil prices and reinvigorated by a new Saudi oil minister, Ali Bin Ibrahim Al-Naimi, as well as a more compliant Venezuela. Minister Naimi, who had begun working for Saudi Aramco as an office boy in 1947 and went on to earn degrees in geology at Lehigh and Stanford universities, rose steadily through the ranks at Aramco. He was appointed oil minister in 1995 and served until 2016, and became the most important voice on Saudi oil policy, known for leading journalists who would flock around him at OPEC meetings on morning fast-walks around Vienna.[27]

At its March 2000 meeting OPEC announced a new price band mechanism. Under it, a target range for the OPEC basket price was set at $22 to $28, and members agreed to a quota adjustment factor whereby quotas would rise by a total of 500 kb/d if prices exceeded $28 for twenty con-secutive days, and would be reduced by the same amount of if prices fell below $22 for ten consecutive days. OPEC did not intend for this adjustment factor to work wholly on an "automatic" basis, however. It was meant as a general framework for members while signaling in advance OPEC's intention in the event prices moved outside the range.

Later in the year, prices started to move outside the band. By September 2000, crude prices rose above $30, raising alarm in Washington, which was holding a presidential election that fall. Energy Secretary Richardson intensively lobbied OPEC for higher production and lower prices. There was no supply disruption, but market forces were pushing heating oil prices up and, for many elected officials, that counted as an emergency. In September 2000, under election pressure, presidential candidate Al Gore reversed his earlier opposition to tapping the SPR to counteract rising heating oil prices ("All [oil-producing nations] would have to do is cut back a little bit on supply and they'd wipe out any impact from releasing oil from the reserve," Gore had said in February that year[28]) and called for a release. OPEC increased production in October but then cut it in November and December, when supply fell below September's level.[29] Prices remained stubbornly high. In November 2000 Secretary Richard-son and other IEA officials flew to Riyadh and agreed they could live with oil prices in the low-to-mid $20s. Prices thereafter fell back to the high $20 range until just after September 11, 2001, when they fell sharply on economic weakness following the terrorist attacks on Washington, D.C., and New York.[30]

Seeing oil demand weaken, Riyadh pressured other producers to show discipline. In January 2001 OPEC agreed to decrease overall produc-tion by 1.4 mb/d;[31] Saudi Arabia implemented 0.5 mb/d of cuts between December 2000 and February 2001, while Iran, UAE, and Venezuela con-tributed about 0.1 mb/d each. The global economy continued to deterio-rate throughout 2001, prompting OPEC to cut another 1 mb/d in March and again in July. OPEC's 3.3 mb/d in quota cuts[32] from September 2000 to July 2001 stabilized prices around $25, but sagging demand sent the OPEC basket price down to $17 in November 2001.

In response, OPEC effectively suspended the price band mechanism and went into emergency mode. With memories of the 1998–1999 price collapse fresh, in November 2001 OPEC cut quotas another 1.4 mb/d[33] and enlisted nonmembers Angola, Mexico, Norway, Oman, and Russia to contribute a combined 462.5 kb/d in either production or export cuts.[34] In terms of actual production (which quota changes did not always correspond to) EIA data show that OPEC producers slashed output by 3 mb/d in production between January 2001 and January 2002, with Saudi Arabia cutting 1.4 mb/d. In February 2002 Saudi production had fallen to 7.2 mb/d, the lowest level since just prior to the First Gulf War in 1990.[35] By April, 2002 total OPEC production had fallen to nearly 25.2 mb/d, a six-year low.[36] While some non-OPEC producers like Norway cut production as promised, Russia did not. Moscow's failure to comply earned it a widespread reputation for untrustworthiness among producers, which Riyadh has neither forgiven nor forgotten to this day.

With rising oil prices and electricity disruptions (primarily in California), the new President George W. Bush administration made energy policy a priority, tasking Vice President Cheney with overseeing a broad overhaul of domestic and international energy policies. The energy task force recommended dozens of policies aimed at increasing supply and promoting conservation and alternative fuels, such as reforming and raising fuel economy standards. Al-Qaeda's terrorist attacks and the prospect of military conflict in Middle East dispelled the complacency about energy security that had set in during the 1990s. After the attacks the United States began refilling the SPR, not only by replacing barrels that had been sold seven years before but for the first time filling the stockpile to its capacity.

Then in late 2002 and early 2003, geopolitical turmoil helped OPEC put a floor under oil prices. First, a Venezuelan oil workers' strike against Hugo Chávez in December 2002 resulted in a collapse in Venezuelan production and exports that lasted over three months. Then in March 2003, another U.S.-led coalition invaded Iraq. These two major disruptions, combined with election violence in Nigeria, suddenly removed almost 3 mb/d of supply between November 2002 and April 2003. Unlike the Gulf War in 1990, the International Energy Agency decided not to release strategic stocks immediately upon commencement of the major military offensive against Iraq. Instead, the IEA signaled willingness to release if a disruption materialized. Oil prices, which had risen from $23 to $34 (for Brent) over the four months prior to the March 2003 invasion, fell to $24 days after military operations began, likely due to Saudi Arabia's increased production and the U.S.-led coalition's swift success at securing oil facilities before they could be damaged.

OPEC'S GOLDILOCKS PERIOD

While oil prices were steadiest in the early 1980s (when Saudi Arabia was still willing to play the swing producer role), OPEC market management in the 1990s and early 2000s was fairly impressive (see figure 8.1). With a few brief exceptions, crude prices oscillated in a $15–$22 range for most of the nineties, and OPEC reacted with unusual discipline to the price crash after its unfortunate decision to increase production in 1997. OPEC was able to recapture market share, which rose from 37 percent in 1990 to over 40 percent by the end of the decade (see figure 8.2).

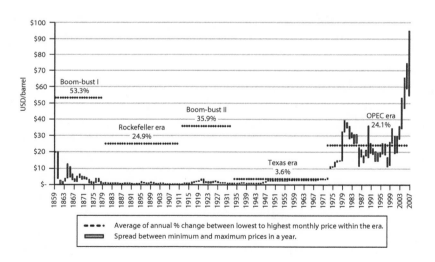

FIGURE 8.1

Annual ranges of monthly U.S. crude oil prices, 1859–2007.

Sources: Derrick's, vols. I–IV; API, *Petroleum Facts and Figures* (1959); Dow Jones & Company, Spot Oil Price: West Texas Intermediate; and U.S. Energy Information Administration, Cushing, OK WTI Spot Price (FOB); the Rapidan Group. © The Rapidan Group.

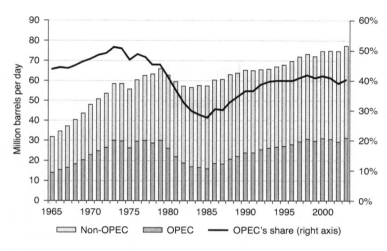

FIGURE 8.2

OPEC's share of global oil production.

Source: BP, "Statistical Review."

As the new decade and century dawned, there even seemed to be a consensus between OPEC and consuming countries that a range between \$20 and \$30 was acceptable and durable. Writing in 2003, former OPEC Secretary General Francisco Parra expressed confidence that OPEC producers could achieve a stable price range of \$22–\$28, but with one qualification. Success, Parra cautioned, depended "in large measure on a dangerous reliance on essentially one country—Saudi Arabia, and its continued good will—as sole guardian of the world's spare producing capacity."[37]

9

TWILIGHT

OPEC's Power to Prevent Price Spikes Ebbs and Vanishes: 2004–2008

For OPEC and the oil industry, the 1990s and early 2000s were relatively stable and orderly compared with the preceding periods. But once again, starting soon after the turn of the twenty-first century, tectonic shifts in global oil demand and supply began to reshape the oil market, subjecting oil producers, consumers, and governments to massive oil price volatility not seen since the 1920s and 1930s and shattering perceptions that OPEC could maintain oil price stability.

On the demand side, global GDP growth picked up strongly between 2003 and 2007, averaging a healthy 5 percent per year. Strong economic activity caused oil consumption to grow by 6.5 mb/d (8 percent) over the period.[1] Whereas consumption of oil had been rising by an average of 1.0 mb/d during 2000 through 2003, from 2004 to 2007 consumption rose by 1.6 mb/d, 60 percent faster.[2] In China, demand exploded stemming from faster economic growth and rapid industrialization and urbanization. Electricity shortages played a big role, too. To keep the lights on, China was forced to fall back on older power plants burning distillate and heavy fuel oil. Many businesses, facing periodic compulsory shutdowns to save energy, also invested in diesel power generators.[3] The confluence of these factors more than doubled China's oil demand growth, from 0.4 mb/d in 2003 to 0.9 mb/d in 2004.[4]

Demand patterns also started to shift, and in doing so somewhat exaggerated the tightness in the market. European countries tightened regulations on distillate fuel by lowering the amount of sulfur it could contain, sending refiners scrambling to make the cleaner fuel. Doing so required "light" crude oils that came from producers like Nigeria—which was prone to unrest and disruptions—and were in relatively low supply.[5] Since benchmark oil prices are set on such lighter grades like Brent and WTI, the acute tightness of "light crude" registered heavily in the market.

On the supply side, production growth outside OPEC was unexpectedly weak while the costs of production soared due to increases in the cost of steel pipe, drilling rigs, oil field services, and cement. IEA forecasts continually overestimated the increase in supply from outside OPEC from 2004 through 2007 (see figure 9.1).

Russia was largely responsible for the disappointments in non-OPEC supply. Between 2000 and 2004 Russia succeeded in reversing its decline of the 1990s, squeezing 500–700 kb/d out of old fields each year during that period. But this trend unexpectedly reversed in 2005 as President Putin became less friendly to the independent oil companies, foreign capital, and technology that had generated the supply boom and that was needed to opening up new, difficult fields.[6] Putin cared less about how much oil was produced and more about who benefited financially and politically

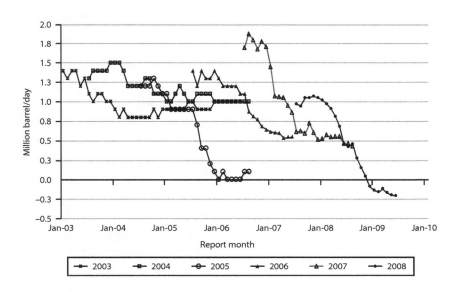

FIGURE 9.1

Annual non-OPEC production growth, 2003–2009, IEA projections.

Source: IEA oil market reports, January 2003–June 2009.

from the production. He persecuted the oil barons and effectively national-ized oil production. Investment waned, and Russia's production plateaued.

In addition to Russia's big slowdown, giant workhorse fields like those in the North Sea and Mexico's Cantarell, which made life so difficult for OPEC when they began large-scale production in the late 1970s and early 1980s, were in decline. Delays to the startup of new complex, mostly off-shore projects in Brazil, Canada, U.S. Gulf of Mexico, North Sea, and elsewhere also plagued the industry and compounded the issue. The 1990s had featured mergers and acquisitions, but relatively little investment in new production.

Unexpectedly strong demand and weak supply resulted in steadily ris-ing crude prices. But OPEC remained wary of increasing supply. Min-isters were still haunted by the "Ghost of Jakarta" (pumping too much oil into the market while demand is unknowingly weakening, producing a price crash). By December 2003 oil prices had risen beyond OPEC's $22–$28 price band and kept ascending. All eyes in the market turned to OPEC to see if it could fill the gap between roaring demand and tepid non-OPEC supply. The oil market was "calling on" Saudi Arabia and other OPEC producers to increase production—but there was not a lot of shut-in or spare capacity for them to use.

At the end of 2003, OPEC only held around 1.7 mb/d or about 2 percent of total world demand in spare, less than half of the level a year earlier. As usual, most of that capacity was in Saudi Arabia, which had already increased production due to the Iraq invasion, Venezuela labor strikes, and disruption in Nigeria. Moreover, some OPEC producers were unable to increase production. Supply was falling in Indonesia, an early member of OPEC (it would leave the cartel in 2009 but reenter in 2015 as an importer) and Iraq's production would not bounce back for five years.

To add to the challenge, Saudi Arabia was reluctant to use what little spare capacity it had. With fears of the 1997 Jakarta debacle still fresh, Saudi Arabia wanted to avoid oversupplying the market. After all, the oil market is notoriously uncertain and supply and demand could turn suddenly loose as fast as it could tighten. As a producer dependent on oil revenues, Saudi Arabia and other OPEC countries fretted about lower prices more than higher ones. After the 2003 invasion many hoped Iraq's pro-duction would quickly resume, a concern producers had to take seriously.

Saudi Arabia had even *cut* production when the March 2003 military invasion phase of the Iraq conflict ended without a major disruption to Kuwaiti or Saudi facilities.

But with soaring Chinese demand, weak supply growth outside OPEC, and Iraq's failure to bounce back (its monthly output would not exceed prewar highs until July 2008),[7] Saudi Arabia became more willing to increase production. Its output rose from 8.5 mb/d in the fourth quarter of 2003 to new highs of 9.5 mb/d by the middle of 2004. At 9.5 mb/d, Saudi production was approaching its maximum capacity, which EIA estimated to be between 10.0 and 10.5 mb/d. Thus, the world's spare capacity cushion had fallen to between 0.5 mb/d and 1.0 mb/d—less than 1 percent of global oil production.[8] Compared with about 4 percent to 5 percent of production in the 1990s or almost 35 percent in the 1950s, the oil market was running on a thin cushion of spare capacity.

But even with this higher Saudi supply, annual average crude oil prices rose by 35 percent from 2003 to 2004 (from $31 to $42 per barrel),[9] and then by another 36 percent in 2005 (to $57). In February of that year, OPEC suspended its $22–$28 target band since the OPEC basket price had remained above the range ceiling for a year and had become superfluous (see figure 9.2).[10]

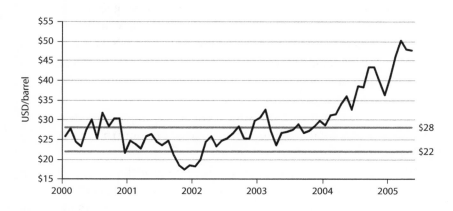

FIGURE 9.2

OPEC basket price.

Source: Bloomberg, *OPEC Secretariat Crude Oil Basket Daily Price.*

Market participants and analysts began to notice the unusually low spare production capacity, and to regard it as a factor that contributed to higher oil prices.[11] "Surging global demand caught out most forecasters and pushed prices higher as the market responded to the thin availability of spare capacity," noted *Middle East Economic Survey* reporter Bill Farren-Price in January 2005. "The narrowing buffer of spare production capacity for OPEC oil producers in 2004 refocused interest on oil capacity expansion plans for 2005."[12] This was a complete change from the depressed 1998 to 1999 period, when leading analysts said chronic *excess* OPEC production capacity would cap oil prices around $20 into the future.[13]

By early 2005, structurally tightening markets dispelled fears of another Jakarta and convinced Saudi Arabia to increase oil production capacity. But spending billions to boost production capacity was not a decision Saudi Arabia took lightly. And like a city's investment in a fire department, the new equipment was going to spend a lot of time sitting idle. Despite the costs and reservations, in January 2005 Saudi Arabia Oil Minister Naimi told the press that the kingdom planned to increase its maximum production capacity to 12.5 mb/d from the then-prevailing level of around 11 mb/d. Saudi Arabia's goal, Minister Naimi said, was to maintain at least 1.5 mb/d of spare production capacity. Saudi Arabia began taking some older fields, including a 500 kb/d producer named Khursaniyah, out of mothballs and expanding export facilities.[14] And in 2006, the kingdom announced a mammoth $10 billion program to develop three new fields—Khurais, Abu Jifan, and Mazalij.[15] Collectively named the Khurais Megaproject, it would be the kingdom's most complex oil development, spanning half the size of Connecticut and requiring enormous infrastructure investments, including a sprawling network of pipes, water injection systems, and deep wells. These new upstream investments in crude oil production capacity intended to raise total Saudi production capacity from 11.3 to 12.5 mb/d,[16] but would not be available until 2009.

Meanwhile, super tight supply and demand propelled oil prices up to historic highs. Without ample surplus capacity, oil experts noted at the time, OPEC's ability to stabilize oil prices declined, resulting in higher oil price volatility.[17] Combined with logistical bottlenecks in the oil industry's "downstream" transportation and refining segments, low spare reduced the oil market's ability to respond to shocks such as geopolitical disruptions, natural disasters, refinery accidents, or waves of speculative buying.[18] Low spare capacity also put the onus on the price of crude to balance the market. And because the inelasticity of oil supply and demand means that only big price increases stimulate lower demand and higher supply, big price increases were exactly what happened.

In the 1970s, oil prices spiked partly due to the *perception* of tighter oil markets if not the looming exhaustion of supplies. This was especially true earlier in the decade, when actual disruptions were small. Even when the Iranian revolution and Iran-Iraq War disrupted supply, it is questionable whether physical oil tightness adequately explained the price spikes, given substantial unused OPEC production capacity and ample if not brimming inventories.[19] But after 2005, it was much clearer that the oil market was structurally tightening. The implication was faster price increases, more volatile prices generally, and spikes when disruptions or disruption risks occurred.

Compounding tightening demand and supply trends, supply disruptions returned after the relatively placid 1990s. Between December 2002 and March 2003, a labor strike at Petroleos de Venezuela disrupted an average of 1.6 mb/d.[20] Just as Venezuela was coming back on the market, unrest in the Niger Delta and the war in Iraq further disrupted global supplies. In the run-up to Nigerian elections, militant groups attacked oil facilities, forcing oil companies to evacuate all nonessential personnel and disrupting an average of 0.25 mb/d between March and August of 2003. Nigerian militant groups funded themselves through "bunkering"—stealing fuel from pipelines and siphoning it off to barges, an increasingly profitable business at a time of rising oil prices. These armed factions became the basis of a new group that emerged in 2006, the Movement for the Emancipation of the Niger Delta, and significantly disrupted Nigerian production between 2006 and 2009 by an average of 0.6 mb/d. In Iraq, the invasion by the "coalition of the willing" on March 20 brought the country's oil production to a halt, disrupting 2.4 mb/d at its peak and 1.4 mb/d on average in 2003. Three wars and decades of neglect took a heavy toll on the Iraqi oil industry, leaving significant amounts of disrupted supplies until early 2008.

Demand stickiness meant that consumption did not fall swiftly in response to higher prices. China needed to keep the lights on and would pay any price to keep importing oil. In the United States, drivers had adjusted their behavior by buying more efficient cars after the huge price increases in the 1970s—but after the big price drop in 1986 and with relatively low and stable gasoline prices in the 1990s, drivers reverted to bigger, less fuel-efficient cars and got in the habit of driving more. The census data indicates commutes lasting more than an hour rose by 50 percent during the 1990s. "I drive 55 miles each way to work every day," one sport-utility vehicle owner told an Associated Press reporter in May 2007. "So I really don't have a choice, unfortunately."[21]

Stubbornly strong demand and weak supply growth sent crude price hurtling above $70 in 2006.[22] Moreover, prices of oil for future delivery were beginning to rise to new, unprecedented levels. The advent of crude oil futures trading in the 1980s enabled analysts and industry to monitor a transparent indicator of longer-term expected oil prices.[23] In the 1990s, longer-term crude oil prices tended to be uncorrelated with shorter-term ones, implying traders and investors "looked through" near-term influences on oil and assumed longer-term prices would be relatively stable in a range between $18 and $26 per barrel. But after 2000, longer-dated futures prices rose along with spot ones, implying market participants believed tightening in supply and demand conditions were not just a short-term but longer-term, structural phenomenon.[24]

These sustained and large oil price increases took most completely by surprise. Market participants were familiar with price spikes due to wars and upheaval, but not to spikes caused by the normal workings of supply and demand. Oil industry and traders had grown accustomed to the notion that OPEC held spare production capacity precisely to prevent such extreme price moves from taking place.[25] Understanding these supply and demand dynamics was complicated by the problem of poor data on oil consumption, production, and inventories. The industry has always prized data. In the first days of oil in the 1860s, producer associations in western Pennsylvania prioritized collection of data on the market as a whole, and data collection and analysis were also central to the Standard Oil operations, state quotas, and Seven Sisters' administration of their joint production and marketing operations. But OPEC was trying to manage a global market, which was especially challenging because data are notoriously incomplete and patchy, especially in the emerging markets.

THE PEAK IS NIGH!

As they had in the past, shock and uncertainty caused by unexpected price increases after 2003 rekindled perennial fears of an imminent limit in global oil production growth.[26] Peak oil fears resurfaced. Despite their checkered history at predicting past peaks, peak oil disciples emerged from the woodwork as oil prices soared.[27] In 2005, the late veteran energy investment banker Matt Simmons published *Twilight in the Desert*, warning that Saudi Arabia was overstating its production potential and was closer to tapped out than widely believed. "Eighty-five million barrels of oil a day is all the world can produce, and the demand is 87 million," prominent oil investor and hedge fund trader T. Boone Pickens said in May 2008. "It is just that simple."[28] On the other side of the debate, prominent oil historian Daniel Yergin, among others,[29] argued that current peak oil fears would prove just as unfounded as others had been given technology's tendency to surprise by unlocking new oil resources.[30]

The peak oil theory stems from an older debate about whether limits to the amount of finite resources like land or energy may jeopardize society's ability to grow, and how peak production of a given resource affects the economy. Peak production occurs when half of the underground endowment is extracted, after which production can continue but will necessarily slow. Peak production should not be confused with "running out." Peak refers to maximum production rates, after which production continues but at a slower and terminally declining rate than the peak. Technological progress combined with consumer responses to price signals (when prices go up, consumers use less of something or substitute for it) make it difficult to predict when production of a commodity like oil will peak. And with the discovery of new technologies and resources, the peak production of an older commodity does not spell an end to economic growth.

Peak production debates typically center on commodities that are critical for human survival: food, water, and energy. In the case of peak oil, the timing and pace of peak production is not just an academic matter. While economists believe people could adjust to steadily rising prices, and abrupt spike caused by unexpected peaking would be catastrophic, economically and politically. Modern transportation, agriculture, defense, and other core systems depend on oil, and there is no near term alternative to oil in these vital sectors. Peak oil adherents warn against assuming that past smooth energy transitions, such as the transition from wood to coal in the 1800s or the transition from coal to oil in the 1900s, are a model for peak oil, which will be "abrupt and revolutionary." In 2005 a report by three researchers sponsored by the U.S. Department of Energy (though not reflecting government views) titled "Peaking of World Oil Production: Impacts, Mitigation, & Risk Management" concluded:

> The peaking of world oil production presents the U.S. and the world with an unprecedented risk management problem. As peaking is approached, liquid fuel prices and price volatility will increase dramatically, and, without timely mitigation, the economic, social, and political costs will be unprecedented. Viable mitigation options exist on both the supply and demand sides, but to have substantial impact, they must be initiated more than a decade in advance of peaking.[31]

Modern-day peak oil adherents such as Colin Campbell and Jean Leherrère trace their lineage to Marion King Hubbert, a U.S. geologist who in 1956 correctly predicted U.S. oil production would peak and start falling in the late 1960s to early 1970s. But Hubbert erroneously predicted U.S. production would keep on falling and approach exhaustion by 2018.[32] Instead, as we shall see later, since 2010 the shale oil boom caused U.S. production to rebound and rise to nearly 1970s peak (see figure 9.3).

One of the challenges involved in trying to predict when oil production will peak and start to decline is measuring the amount of "proved reserves" (oil that can be drilled profitably given prevailing prices and technology) in the earth's crust. Estimates of proved reserves depend on current and future price and prices and technological innovation, both of which are constantly changing and unpredictable.

In the 1950s Hubbert was able to correctly predict the U.S. peak partly because he had good data on proved reserves from the well-drilled and analyzed U.S. fields. And yet Hubbert was very off on his prediction of where production would go from there because he did not foresee the U.S. shale revolution, which led to a 90 percent increase in proved reserves

FIGURE 9.3

U.S. crude production, 1920–2015.

Source: EIA, U.S. Field Production of Crude Oil (Thousand Barrels per Day).

between 2008 and 2014. At 36.4 billion barrels, proved reserves are less than 4 billion barrels shy of the 1970 high (see figure 9.4).[33] Oil industry ingenuity has repeatedly wrong-footed those who have tried to predict the timing of peak oil production.

At the global level, our knowledge of subsurface oil resources globally remains especially foggy. Poor data about global reserves made Hubbert's

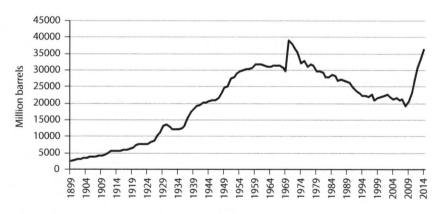

FIGURE 9.4

U.S. proved crude reserves, 1899–2014.

Source: EIA, Crude Oil Proved Reserves, Reserves Changes, and Production.

prediction of a 34 mb/d peak in world supply around the year 2000 miss by a wide margin. Oil production in 2014 was over twice that amount.[34]

There is an old industry shibboleth that one only knows how much oil a reservoir contains when it stops producing. That said, the oil industry has been able to defy frequent peak predictions in the past and increase reserves while also increasing production. In 1980 world reserves equaled 28 years of production. Existing proved reserves are currently estimated to be around 1.7 trillion barrels, equal to 58 years of production. Reserves amounted to 58 years of production in 2014, although this measure fails to account for the role technology and new discoveries can play in increasing reserves and therefore should be taken with a grain of salt.[35] The IEA estimates another 6 trillion barrels of technically recoverable resources (that is, not necessarily economical to produce today but still present) remain buried in the earth's crust.[36] While those technically recoverable resources are by definition not producible at present given prevailing prices but could be produced with existing technology, the history of the oil market shows that price and technology changes and the acumen of oil explorers and producers should not be underestimated. The consensus among geologists and oil supply experts is that between reserves in the ground and likely new reserves that will be discovered and developed there is enough oil to last until the middle of the century.[37]

BURN THE SPECULATORS!

Sharply rising oil prices also rekindled suspicion about and anger toward speculators. "Speculator" is a loaded term, and often misunderstood—in the case of oil, it refers simply to a person who buys or sells oil for some purpose other than immediate use (usually, in anticipation of a future price change).[38] Speculators have been around as long as markets have existed and often been blamed for causing shortages and price spikes for critical commodities, especially food. Also called profiteers and hoarders, speculators are seen as making shortages worse—with a supply shortfall coming, they hoard supplies and hold them off the market, only charging exorbitant prices to desperate consumers when the shortage hits.[39] In the sixth century BCE, Athens established complex laws in an attempt to prohibit speculation in grains like corn, including restrictions on storage, and the penalty for violation was death.[40]

Oil exchanges flourished in the industry's early decades but largely died out during most of the twentieth century as the TRC and Seven Sisters managed supply and stabilized process. Exchanges made a return in the 1980s. In today's oil industry, speculation is accomplished by buying and selling oil futures and derivatives contracts on organized exchanges such as the Chicago Mercantile Exchange and the Intercontinental Exchange in London. Exchanges and trading exist because oil market participants want to hedge or insure against adverse oil price moves. A fuel purchaser for an airline company goes to an exchange to lock in forward prices for jet fuel. A refinery wants to lock in prices for gasoline it will sell in four months. A shale oil producer may seek protection on the price of output from the company's wells in the next year—and its lending bank may insist on it.

The oil industry also values exchanges because they provide transparent, publicly available, and unbiased price information. It is logistically impractical to record and publish the prices and quantities of every individual physical oil transaction. So to aid in "price discovery," exchanges standardized contracts that dictate both the size (1,000 42-gallon barrels) and grade (of which there are many to choose from) of each transaction. For prices to reflect broad market conditions, the more buyers and sellers in the exchange the better.

Speculators are necessary for well-functioning exchanges because they provide "liquidity"—a deep pool of ready buyers or sellers. Excluding speculators would have drastically limited the number of sellers and buyers and therefore the number of transactions, reducing the value of the exchanges and providing a transparent price signal to everyone. Speculators are needed to take the price risk that hedgers want to shed. Speculators are happy to take a bet on where prices are going, whereas many oil market participants prefer to focus on what they do best: fly planes, produce gasoline, drill for oil.

While not punishable by death as in ancient Athens, oil speculation has remained unpopular in the modern oil industry. Refiners like Rockefeller and western Pennsylvania drillers disdained speculators for having no real attachment to the oil business and instead trafficking only in oil and

later pipeline certificates (often frantically and based on rumors and senti-
ment). Manic buying and selling by uninformed speculators, those in the
oil industry believed (and many still do), just adds volatility to a market
already all too prone to it. Today, the line between speculating and hedging gets blurred. For example, some oil producers may decide to "hedge"
or lock in prices by buying futures contracts when they believe prices are
going to fall. But a producer who decides not to lock in prices when they
are expected to rise is in effect speculating on rising prices.[41]

Since the widespread return of exchange-traded oil futures in the 1980s,
OPEC as well as many Western politicians and oil executives have frequently denounced speculators for causing oil price volatility. They argue
that speculators distort oil prices because they are ignorant about the oil
industry and market, often exhibiting a herd behavior seen in equity markets and causing oil prices to become unhinged from supply realities.

The price run-up during 2004–2008 spawned accusations against
speculators once again, especially against a new type of speculator: the
"massive passives."[42] Unlike old-style speculators perfectly happy to either
buy or sell oil contracts depending on which way they saw prices heading
in the future, new "passive" or "long-only" investors only bought. Retail
investors, pension funds, and sovereign wealth funds became interested
in "long-only" holdings in oil and other commodities during the post-
2000 commodity price boom. They sought oil and other commodity
exposure because of weak returns on other asset classes like equities or
bonds. In addition, commodities offered diversity and returns that were
uncorrelated to the usual equities and bonds holdings. Banks and brokers
met demand from these new financial investors by creating investment
vehicles or so-called commodity index funds that gave their clients "long"
exposure to the commodity markets without their having to actually own
any physical commodities.[43]

Some commentators and market participants concluded that massive
passive buying itself was causing the mammoth oil price spike, insisting that rising prices could not be explained by underlying supply and
demand factors in the global oil market.[44] The most prominent proponent
of this view was investor Michael Masters, who gave that idea considerable traction when he was featured in testimony before the Senate Homeland Security Committee in May 2008.[45]

Those who disagree with the view that speculators, whether traditional buy-or-sell or passive buy-only, distort oil prices make several counterpoints. First, they assert, oil market participants are not better informed than anyone else about the "true" supply and demand—partly because of enormous gaps in data. As the wildly inaccurate forecasts by OPEC and oil companies from the late 1960s through early 1980s show, oil companies have hardly demonstrated superior clairvoyance about future oil prices. Academic studies on the subject have shown that speculators contribute to stability and reduce volatility by providing liquidity and information to the market.[46] And although speculative buying and selling of futures contracts can have impacts on the price of oil, that is not necessarily a bad thing from society's perspective, academics and officials (including Ben Bernanke, who was then chair of the Federal Reserve) noted in 2004. To the degree that speculators are informed and their buying or selling brings new information to the market, their actions can enhance social welfare by making oil available when it is needed. They can also signal a tightening market, and the resulting price increase stimulates more production and less consumption, thus making more oil available in the future.[47]

Second, to "distort" or "manipulate" prices, speculators would have to hoard physical supply and take advantage of weak or broken convergence between paper and physical markets. That is because under exchange trading rules, anyone who holds a "long" futures contract when it expires in a given month must take physical delivery, and whoever is "short" must deliver the oil. Futures and physical prices converge primarily because any discrepancy creates a profitable arbitrage opportunity. Traders would jump on the price discrepancy, finding a way to take delivery in the futures market and then offset the position in the spot market until the discrepancy was no longer profitable. This mandatory convergence between paper and physical barrels at monthly settlements keeps oil futures linked to physical reality in the oil market.[48] There is no evidence that this convergence, which is closely watched by market participants, is broken. Furthermore, the size of the futures market when combined with its strict regulatory environment, makes it near impossible for one or more individuals to corner the oil market by accumulating and removing enough oil supply to manipulate prices. In fact, oil inventories had fallen significantly below normal in 2007 and 2008, suggesting that as high and fast as oil price had risen, they were still not rising enough to bring demand down to available supply.[49]

Third, critics of Masters' thesis that long-only investors were behind the increase in prices point out that the price of commodities not actively traded on futures exchanges (thus, out of reach of speculators, including massive passives) were rising as much or even more (in the case of rice and iron ore) than those traded on exchanges like oil.[50] This suggests the cause of co-movement among commodities, including oil, was economic, not rooted in financial flows.[51] In October 2008 the IMF noted the broad commodity boom was similar in magnitude to the commodity price boom of the early 1970s,[52] when there were no major futures trading in oil, much less "massive passives."

While massive-passive purchasing of oil futures correlated with moves in crude oil prices, correlation is not causality. Because a rooster's crow correlates with the sunrise does not mean that the rooster causes the sun to rise. Writing in June 2009, the IEA noted the correlation of financial flows with rising oil prices, but concluded that tight OPEC spare capacity provided a "plausible account of how the fundamentals have changed and provide a clue as to why oil was priced so high in the first half of 2008, fell some 75 percent in the following six months, and is now hovering around $70 per barrel."[53]

Energy economist James Hamilton concluded that although the oil price run-up from 2004 to 2008 was influenced by the inflow of investment dollars into commodity futures contracts, oil's low price elasticity of demand and the failure of production to increase sufficiently prior to the peak explained the phenomenon. Supply and demand, instead of speculation per se, was the cause of oil's dramatic price moves.[54]

Officials agree with Hamilton. An interagency task force led by the U.S. Commodity Futures Trading Commission and composed of several federal departments as well as the Federal Reserve, the Federal Trade Commission, and the U.S. Securities and Exchange Commission conducted an in-depth study and concluded

> that current oil prices and the increase in oil prices between January 2003 and June 2008 are largely due to fundamental supply and demand factors. During this same period, activity on the crude oil futures market—as

measured by the number of contracts outstanding, trading activity, and the number of traders—has increased significantly. While these increases broadly coincided with the run-up in crude oil prices, the task force's preliminary analysis to date does not support the proposition that speculative activity has systematically driven changes in oil prices.[55]

THROW IN THE (STRATEGIC) RESERVES!

Political heat generated by soaring gasoline prices in and after 2000 led not just to scrutiny of speculators but also to demands to use strategic oil stockpiles to dampen oil price volatility. As a rule, when oil prices are rising, even in the absence of a disruption, calls to release strategic stocks go out. During the 1996 price run-up, many analysts called for SPR releases due to rising oil prices stemming from relatively low commercial stocks.[56] (When oil prices are falling, one rarely hears calls to stabilize prices filling the SPR. Decisions to refill the SPR usually proceed an emergency that rekindles energy security concerns, such as President George W. Bush's decision to fill the SPR to capacity in the wake of the September 11 terrorist attacks.)

The IEA had coordinated IEA strategic stock releases twice before: the first at the outset of Operation Desert Storm during the Gulf War in January 1991, and the second in 2005 in conjunction with Hurricane Katrina in the Gulf of Mexico. The U.S. Congress or presidents have also ordered a number of other unilateral releases, including three instances in 1996 when Congress mandated releases to raise cash for the budget.[57]

But releasing oil from U.S. reserves in response to rising prices was controversial. In September 2000, President Bill Clinton ordered a release of 30 million barrels from the SPR amid rising oil prices. Vice President Al Gore, then two months away from a neck-and-neck race with George W. Bush for the presidency, had publicly called for a release, reversing his earlier opposition.[58] Clinton justified the release due to concerns about low commercial heating oil inventories and the associated risk of higher prices. But President Clinton's claim and the timing of the release were widely criticized as a thin excuse for politically motivated intervention in the market. Even President Clinton's treasury secretary, Lawrence Summers, perceived the release as interference in the market who warned of setting a "dangerous precedent."[59] And indeed, the 2004–2008 price booms led policymakers to call on President Bush to release strategic stocks, even though there had been no disruption.[60] He refused on grounds the SPR should be reserved for severe supply interruptions.

Assuming strategic stock release and fill capabilities of several million barrels per day or more, it is theoretically conceivable that officials could direct SPR sales and purchases with an aim toward offsetting not only geopolitical disruptions but also supply-demand imbalances of equal amount. "For example," the International Energy Agency (IEA) noted, "at a drawdown rate of 2 million barrels per day, public stocks could flow for 24 months." At a rate of 4 million barrels per day, strategic stocks would cover one year.[61] And in theory policymakers could buy oil during periods of depressed prices with the aim of imposing a floor.

However, there are many problems with the notion of using strategic stocks to stabilize oil prices, even if policymakers were willing to buy and sell depending on tightness or surplus in the market.[62] The main problem is that buy and sell decisions would doubtless be influenced by political or budgetary considerations, not just for market stabilization. Moreover, to be effective, strategic stock releases would need to be coordinated among IEA members. Some IEA members could find themselves squabbling about burden sharing just like OPEC members do, as some would argue it makes no sense for one country to release stocks while others hold on to or increase theirs.[63]

Another problem with using strategic stocks to stabilize prices is operational. The SPR was designed for large-scale, infrequent withdrawals in anticipation of major supply emergencies, not frequent withdrawals and fills. Frequent, small uses of the SPR caused the underground salt caverns holding crude to deteriorate, because to release oil freshwater is injected into the salt caverns. Injecting freshwater in small volumes at low rates results in uneven salt leaching that misshapes the caverns, reducing their integrity. (One solution would be to invest in infrastructure to inject fully saturated brine instead of freshwater, although this would require expensive capital expenditures.[64])

Officials may not have sufficient information to inform decisions on when and how to add or subtract from the global market to keep prices stable, and could well run out of supplies before they managed to flatten prices. Moreover, even assuming political interference could be excluded, officials could try to defend price levels or ranges that are inconsistent with actual market fundamentals. If they tried to hold prices below levels justified by fundamentals, they would expend all of the reserves, giving them away at cheap prices to market participants. If SPR use failed to stabilize prices, it would reduce or eliminate whatever psychological impact having the untapped option conferred.[65] Conversely, if officials were really willing to gut against the grain and attempt to prop up prices above levels justified by market supply and demand, they would have to buy and fill until capacity was reached, at which point prices would collapse below the official target levels.

Two final risks are that private companies would reduce their inventories held to address price volatility—both from regular interaction of supply and demand and due to disruptions—or that OPEC producers could offset SPR releases intended to cap prices by withdrawing production.[66]

These risks, however, did not stop calls for the government to do something—anything it could—to arrest the upward climb of oil prices.

PEAK OF THE BOOM

Amid dire warnings about peak oil and demands to crack down on speculators and release strategic stocks, oil prices kept rising into 2008. A series of sabotage attacks, strikes, and commercial disputes in Venezuela, Iraq, Nigeria, and the North Sea hit the market and contributed to the rapid increase in crude prices.[67] For the first time ever, in February 2008, crude prices breached $100. As the summer of 2008 approached, they were hurtling over $140.[68]

The crude oil price shock between the fourth quarter of 2007 and the second quarter of 2008—37 percent in real terms, 41 percent nominal, for U.S. imported crude oil prices—was "by any measure . . . one of the biggest oil shocks on record."[69] In the United States pump prices tracked those of crude to astounding new highs. In real terms, average national pump prices for regular grade gasoline exceeded their prior high, which had been set in March 1981 ($3.80 per gallon), in April of 2008 ($3.84) and then jumped up to peak at $4.43 in June.[70] In nominal terms, pump prices peaked in July 2008 at $4.06 per gallon.

The shock walloped consumers. About 71 percent of Americans surveyed told Gallup gasoline prices were causing financial hardship.[71] The CEO of Northwest Airlines, Doug Steenland, testified to Congress in June 2008 that U.S. airlines were "on track to spend $61.2 billion on jet fuel [that] year, $20 billion more than in 2007, and [were] projected to incur losses totaling close to $10 billion." Between December 2007 and June 2008, the soaring price of oil and jet fuel forced eight airlines out of business and two more into bankruptcy, while the surviving carriers trimmed capacity and reduced services.[72] Truckers and other fuel-intensive workers conducted strikes and protests in the United States and Europe. A Gallup poll in May 2008 found majorities favored releasing oil from the strategic petroleum reserve, opening U.S. coastal and wilderness areas to drilling, and even imposing price controls.[73]

Politicians and industry executives continued blaming speculators. Senator Susan Collins (R–ME) said "[c]onstituents get it . . . [t]hey don't see the reason for it. They don't see (supply) shortages. They don't see [the Organization of the Petroleum Exporting Countries] greatly reducing production or other reasons prices are going up so much."[74] In his plea to Congress, the CEO of Northwest Airlines said: "I cannot overstate the importance to my company and the entire U.S. airline industry of immediate congressional action to halt excessive speculation in oil futures markets."[75] Despite the academic consensus that speculation was not behind the price increase, deep and widespread anger and protest at stratospheric oil prices triggered a wave of official investigations, studies, and hearings. In June 2008 the House of Representatives directed the Commodity Futures Trading Commission to "curb immediately" what it perceived to be excessive speculation in energy futures markets.[76] Officials and regulators probed aggressively but sided nearly unanimously with the academics, finding little to no causality between commodity index inflows and rising commodity prices and saying instead that supply and demand fundamentals explained the dramatic moves.[77] Officials found neither evidence of such hoarding nor weak or broken convergence between futures and physical markets. The IEA did its own probe and found no evidence that speculation caused unusual inventory building while oil prices were ascending.[78]

The press was littered with forecasts for continued—apparently unstoppable—price increases. Goldman Sachs forecasted oil prices would exceed $140 in the summer of 2008 and could average $200 in 2009.[79] An OPEC minister predicted $200 oil; Gazprom's CEO saw $250 in 2009.[80] Driving these dire predictions were warnings from the IEA that OPEC spare capacity would dwindle to "minimal levels by 2012" and that by 2015 the world oil supply could come up short by as much as 12.5 mb/d.[81] Warnings about low capacity from IEA hit hard, especially because most private experts believed IEA's estimates of spare capacity were generous from the start.[82] By anyone's standard, OPEC's spare capacity was unusually low between the Second Gulf War and 2007. And in the first half of 2008 it was starting to shrink again.

In January, President Bush told reporters: "I hope OPEC nations put more supply on the market. It would be helpful." But Saudi Oil Minister Naimi insisted oil inventories were normal and that Saudi Arabia would only add more supply if the market justified it.[83] When Bush visited Saudi Arabia to ask for more oil in person, he was reportedly rebuffed. He traveled again to Riyadh in May, and this time Saudi Arabia announced a 300,000 barrel per day supply boost.[84] But prices continued to rise, drawing new wails of complaint from U.N. Secretary-General Ban Ki-moon and other leaders.

No one was sure exactly how much spare capacity was left, but as crude prices lurched higher, pleas from the United States, most of the other G8 (not including exporter Russia), and other oil-importing countries grew more insistent that it be used, and fast. WTI crude began May 2008 trading around $113; before the month was over it had almost reached $133 before falling back. June trading opened at $127 and ended the month just under $140 per barrel.[85] Saudi and other OPEC officials continued to insist that supply was adequate and that speculators were driving up prices. U.S. Energy Secretary Samuel Bodman would hear none of that, tartly telling reporters on the eve of a June 22 emergency summit of oil-producing and oil-consuming countries in Jeddah, Saudi Arabia: "Market fundamentals show us that production has not kept pace with growing demand for oil, resulting in increasing prices and increasingly volatile prices. There is no evidence that we can find that speculators are driving futures prices" for oil.[86] And United Kingdom Prime Minister Gordon Brown joined U.S.

officials in calling for Saudi Arabia to increase production so that "instead of uncertainty and unpredictability, there is greater certainty, and instead of instability, there is greater stability."[87]

Under tremendous international pressure, Saudi Arabia announced another production hike at the June 22 emergency summit.[88] Saudi production was headed up to 9.7 mb/d, the highest level since 1981. Naimi told visiting officials that the kingdom was willing to boost its production capacity above the 9.7 mb/d level planned for July in 2009, but only if—in Saudi Arabia's view—the market required it.[89] "After months of blaming the spike in oil prices on speculators," the *Washington Post* editorialized, "the Saudis have finally admitted, tacitly to be sure, that the root cause is insufficient supply."[90] Crude oil prices peaked on July 11 at an intraday high of $147.27.[91]

BUST

Unbeknownst to oil market participants gawking at oil's towering spike in the middle of 2008, a collapsing real estate bubble was about to drop the floor out from under crude oil prices, triggering a price bust as sudden and spectacular as the boom.

In 2006, a U.S. real estate bubble began deflating, spilling over into foreclosures, delinquencies, and financial institution failures. Credit tightened, transmitting distress to the real economy and slowing real estate investment and household spending. By the end of 2007, the U.S. economy was in a full recession. The collapse of the U.S. securities firm Bear Stearns in March 2008 intensified concerns about a financial crisis, and September brought more foreboding signs as Washington was forced to seize the government-sponsored housing lenders Fannie Mae and Freddie Mac.[92] On September 14, 2008, the U.S. subprime mortgage crisis erupted into a global financial emergency when Lehman Brothers—the fourth-largest investment bank in the country—declared bankruptcy. Like many other financial institutions, Lehman held enormous amounts of low quality household debt securities. Its failure prompted contagion risk and a widespread collapse in market confidence. In October some $10 trillion of global equity value vaporized, in the largest monthly loss ever recorded.[93]

The world was quickly engulfed in a global credit crunch and economic growth screeched to a halt.

We know that consumers don't quickly adjust their consumption of gasoline when oil *prices* change—but they do when their *income* changes. An employed worker has little choice but to pay whatever the pump price is to drive to work, but after losing his job, an unemployed person's need to drive drops quickly. In 2008 incomes were collapsing and oil demand along with them, falling by 0.7 mb/d in 2008 and by 1.1 mb/d in 2009.[94]

As it became clear that the world was entering a massive recession, oil prices plummeted. In October of 2008, prices fell to almost $60 per barrel—half their level just two months earlier. By December prices had tumbled to $33, an astounding crash of 78 percent in just six months. Looking back on the year, the energy publication *MEES* noted that "traders went from imagining crude oil prices reaching $200 per barrel to contemplating 'demand destruction.'"[95]

The price volatility whipsawed oil consumers, from truck drivers to home heating oil merchants to automakers and airlines. In January 2009 the *New York Times* reported:

> The volatility is showing up at the retail level. Drivers who only a few weeks ago were finding relief from the summer's $4-a-gallon gasoline are now shaking their heads as the average national price for unleaded regular gasoline has surged to $1.79, from $1.62, since Dec. 30. Oil volatility has complicated the efforts of automobile companies to figure out future strategies. Toyota had to suspend production at one plant that builds the Tundra pickup truck for several months when gasoline prices soared last summer. Toyota then delayed completion of a second plant meant to build the Prius hybrid when falling gasoline prices led to weakening demand for that fuel-efficient model. The gyrations in prices affect shipping and other businesses around the world. Cathay Pacific, one of many airlines that use fuel hedging strategies, recently acknowledged that it had hedging losses of hundreds of millions of dollars as a result of the collapse in fuel prices.[96]

US Airways Group reported a third-quarter loss of $865 million, citing the recession and volatility of oil prices. At the time, several airline companies were hedging against the risk of high jet fuel prices using derivatives called swaps. Had oil prices continued to rise to $200 per barrel in 2008, an airline that had locked in a lower price through this kind of transaction would have been very happy because the earnings on their swaps contracts would have offset the higher costs of physical jet fuel. But these trades lost money when oil prices ripped through the lower end of the range they were designed work within.

While the credit crisis was the root of the Great Recession, soaring oil prices had helped weaken the economies of oil-importing industrialized countries by disrupting trade balances, putting upward pressure on inflation and interest rates, and hurting consumer and business income (in the United States, household spending on energy more than doubled from 2003 to 2008, to about 8 percent of income[97])—and ultimately making them more vulnerable to financial contagion.

10

OIL'S THIRD BOOM-BUST ERA: 2009-?

As OPEC members sat down at their regular ministerial meeting on September 9, 2008, crude oil prices had tumbled precipitously from $147 to $106 per barrel but were by no means low. Producers were unsure where prices were headed, and opinions about what to do were divided. Traditional "hawks" (producers who favored higher oil prices, especially Venezuela and Iran) wanted OPEC to cut quotas, but "doves" (led by Saudi Arabia, who favors relatively lower prices) preferred to stand pat and see how things developed. After haggling into the wee hours of the morning, OPEC ministers announced a return to quotas they had fixed a year earlier totaling 28.8 mb/d.

"With the exception of Saudi Arabia, all other members were unable to greatly exceed their quotas," as Rafiq Latta noted in *MEES*. Saudi Arabia was producing well above, and even Riyadh's traditional ally Kuwait joined the chorus of ministers clamoring for Saudi Arabia to cut back. Returning to quotas, OPEC said, would lower actual OPEC output by 520 kb/d.[1] Riyadh remained steadfastly opposed to cutting production unilaterally. Although Riyadh could have vetoed the OPEC decision, it did not do so, but Saudi officials told the press on the sidelines it intended to ignore the wishes of other producers and keep up healthy supply to the market.[2]

By October, things were much worse. As crude prices tumbled another third to just below $70, OPEC held an emergency meeting on October 24, 2008. In response to what rattled ministers called "a dramatic [price] collapse—unprecedented in speed and magnitude," OPEC agreed to cut crude supplies by 1.5 mb/d effective November 1. Saudi Arabia agreed to shoulder the brunt of the initial cuts, slashing output from 9.4 in October to 8.5 mb/d in December 2008. Other producers cut 500 kb/d.[3] But prices kept falling as data showed demand skidding and inventories rapidly accumulating. OPEC convened another emergency meeting in Oran on December 17, when crude had plummeted to $45. Now panicked, ministers ordered the largest production cuts in the organization's history: another 2.2 mb/d effective January 1, 2009. "No one expected the organization to take such a decisive action," OPEC President and Algerian Energy Minister Chakib Kehlil told the press. "We hope we surprised you."[4]

As with OPEC's emergency cuts in 1998 and 1999, the late 2008 shut-ins had less to do with managing the market and more with responding to an emergency. A successful cartel manages supply to avoid booms and busts. Having failed to prevent a boom from 2005 to 2008, OPEC was at least able to muster enough discipline to collectively cut in the bust that followed. One OPEC official told a journalist after the Oran meeting: "This is no joke. Everyone recognizes that . . . when the chips are down, people do act."[5] But by acting only when the chips are down OPEC resembled more ad hoc reactions of Pennsylvania drillers than the steady, firm management implemented by the TRC or Seven Sisters.

In Iran's case, cutting production was painful for reasons beyond the loss of revenue. Because of the advanced age of Iran's fields, ramping production down and up presented logistical and operational problems. Moreover, Iran produced a lot of natural gas as a byproduct of oil production, which it used for domestic heating; cutting oil and therefore, gas production before winter could create gas shortages that would be politically unpopular.[6] Yet even Tehran acted, and although it did not fully comply with its lower quota, it showed unusual if partial compliance by cutting production by about half its mandated amount, according to OPEC data.[7] Total OPEC production fell by 3.6 mb/d between September 2008 and January 2009. Saudi output fell by 1.3 mb/d, about 37 percent of the total OPEC cut.[8]

Brent crude oil prices bottomed in late December 2008 at $33.73—down 76 percent in just over five months[9]—but with lower supply to meet lower demand, prices began a steady ascent and were back above $90 by early 2011. An uprising against Libyan strongman Muammar Qaddafi in February 2011 drove 1.5 mb/d of Libyan supply off the market, and crude prices surged above $100 per barrel. While other Arab Spring revolts did not impact supplies as in Libya, they triggered fear about possible disruptions and therefore triggered precautionary buying of oil. From 2011 through the first half of 2014 crude ranged between $100 and $125 with brief departures above and below (see figure 10.1).[10] After the 2005–2008 boom-bust, stability had returned to the oil market. But the calm was precarious.

The period following the tumultuous 2008 bust was a happy one for OPEC producers. Most were able to enjoy maximum output, and all enjoyed stable prices around the $100 level. OPEC oil revenues, which were about $326 billion, in real terms in 1982, soared to over $950 billion in 2012.[11] Thanks to production cuts—most but not all by Saudi Arabia—and opening of the Khurais Megaproject—which increased Saudi Arabia's production capacity by 1.2 mb/d—OPEC's spare production capacity rose back to around 5 percent of the market by 2010, which corresponded to the relatively calm 1990s.[12] Saudi Arabia held nearly all this spare production capacity, and could therefore look forward to exercising leverage over other producers. However, this carefree environment masked underlying dynamics that belied the idea of OPEC's return to market manager, and whitewashed the tensions building inside OPEC.

The first ominous trend was that spare capacity immediately began to dwindle again after its recovery in 2010, falling to an average of 2.9 percent

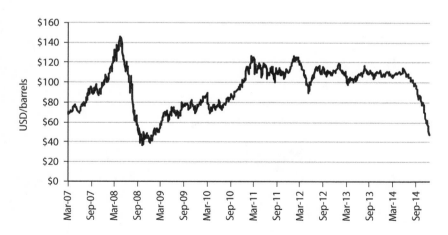

FIGURE 10.1

Brent: First month future contract price.

Source: Bloomberg, ICE Brent Futures (CO1).

of global production between 2011 and the middle of 2014. In the mid-1990s spare capacity had trended up—an indication that OPEC producers were showing restraint by not producing every barrel they could. But in 2011, spare capacity began trending down as producers able to do so increased their production. Oil demand was moderate, well below the breakneck rates prior to 2008 (it averaged 1 mb/d per year from 2011–2014 compared with the 1.6 mb/d between 2003 and 2007).[13] As oil disruptions unexpectedly lowered supply (Iraq was struggling to recover from the 2003 invasion, Libya saw its supply disrupted during the revolution, and after 2012 about 1.0 mb/d of Iran's exports were cut due to international sanctions), Saudi Arabia increased its production and its spare capacity fell. By July 2011, Saudi Arabia's production had risen to 9.8 mb/d, the highest monthly level in thirty years.[14] Gradually eroding Saudi spare capacity meant that the latent risk of price volatility grew. If demand picked up or another disruption occurred, Saudi Arabia's ability to increase production swiftly and prevent a price spike was lower. The market was again running on a thin cushion (see figure 10.2).

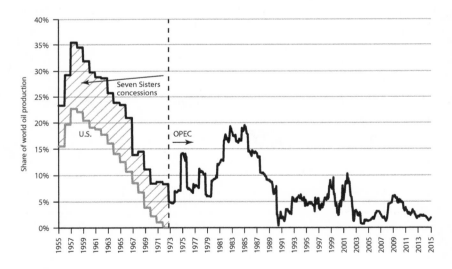

FIGURE 10.2

Global crude oil spare capacity.

Source: The Rapidan Group; EIA; BP, "Energy Outlook to 2035"; U.S. Senate. © The Rapidan Group.

Meanwhile, there was the risk of another price bust. Saudi Arabia remained adamantly opposed to replaying the swing producer role that it had in the early 1980s. This implied that if the oil market became over-supplied, there was no swing producer willing to cut production to keep prices stable. Thus, the stable—but high—prices after 2010 precariously rested on an unstable structure. Any disruption or demand pick up could trigger a boom and the emergence of new oil supply, a bust.

Dwindling spare capacity from Saudi Arabia had further repercussions on the balance of power within OPEC. Since the 1970s, Saudi Arabia's possession of substantial spare capacity had given it enormous clout within OPEC, conferring on Riyadh the power to wield and if necessary enforce the threat of flooding the market over other producers. Saudi Arabia had used its leverage with devastating effect in late 1985 and 1986, and the threat of a repeat helped producers muster the will to contribute cuts in the late 1990s and early 2002. But with the oil market firm and Saudi spare capacity low, its clout ebbed, and its traditional rivals within OPEC—and geopolitically, in the case of Iran—were emboldened to challenge the Saudis in setting OPEC policy.

Saudi Arabia's diminished sway within OPEC became apparent at the group's meeting on June 8, 2011. Overall crude prices were headed toward $110 per barrel and Libyan supply was off the market, triggering clamor from the West for OPEC to offset the loss. Saudi Arabia had been hesitant to increase production. One reason had to do with crude quality: Libya exported a lighter, higher-quality type of crude than the denser variety of oil Saudi Arabia had in spare. Saudi Arabia's hesitation alarmed Washington and other consuming countries, which were actively considering using strategic stocks during the spring of 2011. By the time OPEC met, Saudi output was at 9.6 mb/d and spare capacity below 3.0 mb/d. Saudi Arabia had decided more supply was indeed needed, and wanted OPEC to ratify its forthcoming production increase in the form of a 1.5 mb/d quota hike. But hawks Venezuela and Algeria were assertive and the meeting, chaired by hardliner Iran, denied Saudi Arabia a quota increase. Formal changes in OPEC policy require a consensus. Whereas in the past Saudi Arabia's heft enabled it to obtain acquiescence from other producers, it was now clear that its authority had declined.

The standoff led to an unusual "shock failure."[15] The OPEC meeting ended in disarray without issuing a formal communique. Saudi Arabia did not take the rebuke well: An exasperated Saudi Oil Minister Ali Naimi exclaimed "I think this is one of the worst meetings we have ever had in the OPEC," adding, "[i]n my sixteen years as a minister, I have not seen [such] an obstinate position."[16] Then, for good measure, the Obama administration persuaded reluctant IEA countries to implement a coordinated strategic stock release on June 23. Ultimately, Saudi Arabia increased production anyway, by another 300 kb/d in November 2011.

OPEC convened again amid improved relations on December 14, 2011, and scrapped country level quotas established at Oran in December 2008, replacing them with an OPEC-wide target of 30 mb/d. This target replaced the old 24.8 mb/d collective target and was intended to ratify then-prevailing production. Setting the target at 30 mb/d also represented an admission that setting individual country quotas was impractical. While they did succeed in coming to an agreement—unlike in the summer—these events reinforced trends that sustained animosity inside OPEC. Gulf Sunni producers Saudi Arabia, UAE, and Kuwait were enjoying flush production well above old quotas, whereas several other producers were unable to increase or experiencing disruptions. Summing it up, Venezuelan Oil Minister Rafael Ramirez told the press attending the December 14, 2011, meeting, "Some countries especially from the Gulf have an overproduction. They have to reduce."[17] But Riyadh had grown weary of setting quotas. "We have learned our lesson," a very senior but anonymous Saudi official later told *MEES* in 2013. "Every time we go to quotas, who bears the brunt? Us. We have learned the lesson. We are no longer the swing producer," the official said. "Who needs quotas?"[18]

Increased production from OPEC, as well as releases from strategic stocks, helped to push oil prices back down to near $100 in 2012. But with OPEC openly dysfunctional, and Saudi spare production capacity uncomfortably low, Washington was paying sustained, close attention to oil markets. If not panicked, officials were apprehensive and attentive. Having concluded, after the 2005–2008 price surge, that speculators were not driving prices, official consensus was that good old supply and demand fundamentals were at work. Western officials would likely have been happy if OPEC could keep oil prices bound to a set range; consumers, budget planners, central bankers, and industry crave stability above all, so could acclimate to even a high price level, as long as it was stable. But stability could not be assumed. It was painfully obvious that Saudi Arabia could not be relied upon to keep prices from soaring. From the administration's perspective, the biggest threat was an economically damaging oil price spike.

The White House grew especially nervous when prices breached $115 and either threatened or on occasion surpassed $120—the threshold where prices were believed to harm consumer confidence and economic growth. When officials feared oil prices were likely to surpass $120, pleas for more oil would go out to Saudi Arabia[19] and strategic stocks would be readied (and in the case of June 2011, used). High and carefully watched by officials and market participants, oil prices appeared to have settled into a "new normal" range of $100–120 between 2011 and the middle of 2014.[20]

WASHINGTON KEEPS A FINGER ON THE SPR TRIGGER

While oil prices were relatively stable from 2010 to 2013, they were also high—around $100. And policymakers were acutely aware that spare capacity was relatively low, creating a risk of economically damaging price spikes in the event of disruptions or any tightening in supply-demand fundamentals. The only tool the United States and other strategic stock-holding countries had to counter short-term price spikes was the use of strategic stocks. In June 2011 Representative Edward Markey (D-MA), former ranking member on the House Natural Resources Committee and a prominent proponent of using the SPR, called releases "the one tool America has at her disposal to immediately help drive down prices at the pump."[21]

The law requires the president to find a "severe energy supply interruption" before ordering a major (unlimited amount) SPR release, but the definition of a severe supply interruption is controversial.[22] Debates about the SPR's utility or about more flexible definitions of emergencies requiring a release lies outside the scope of this discussion. For our purposes, the question of whether to use SPR to stabilize oil prices in general—not when or how to respond to emergencies—is pertinent.

The objective of SPR is to release a lot of oil quickly in response to an emergency supply interruption, thereby dampening any economically harmful price impact. The maximum speed and rate of SPR releases is untried and therefore unknown. The Department of Energy, which manages the SPR, publicly states the initial drawdown rate is 4.4 mb/d for delivery within 13 days of a presidential decision,[23] though in 2015 noted the SPR requires "significant maintenance and upgrades to enhance its distribution capability."[24]

The first two drawdowns were relatively uncontroversial as they preceded major supply emergencies.[25] The June 23, 2011, IEA release of 60 million barrels was unique and more controversial.[26] The administration justified the release on "the disruption of global supplies caused by unrest in Libya and other countries"[27] but it took place four months after the Libya disruption and two months after oil prices had peaked.[28] While OPEC refused to sanction production hikes on June 8, Saudi Arabia, UAE, and Kuwait indicated they would increase production anyway. Less than half of IEA countries contributed releases, as many apparently felt it was unwarranted.[29]

The June 23, 2011, SPR release took many in the market by surprise and raised questions about whether the SPR would be used more flexibly as a market-stabilizing tool instead of an immediate offset to major disruptions.[30] "This looks like a thinly veiled stimulus. The big question weighing on the market is why now?" one senior market strategist at an investment bank said.[31] Independent oil expert Ken Koyama, the chief economist at Japan's prestigious Institute of Energy Economics, Japan, wrote in a report, "I suspect that oil market participants might have taken the IEA decision as designed not only to respond to the physical supply disruptions but also to stabilize oil-market prices."[32] Many analysts, industry participants, as well as the president's political opponents sharply criticized the release as intended for political convenience.[33]

These concerns about political release of the SPR resurfaced in 2012 when oil prices had climbed above $120 per barrel, prompting President Obama to lobby other advanced countries in the G8 for another coordinated stock release. Other countries were opposed however and no release took place. The head of the IEA, Maria van der Hoeven, said the market was well supplied and there was no emergency disruption requiring a release.[34]

ENTER THE SHALE REVOLUTION

Since the TRC and Seven Sisters lost control in the early 1970s, it seemed that every five years or so something dramatic and unexpected came along to transform the oil market. Between 2010 and 2015, small and independent U.S. oil producers—whose forebearers ignited the modern oil market and subsequently discovered giant gushers like Spindletop and the Black Giant—once again sprang a surprise on the world oil market: U.S. shale.

If the shale boom has a father, it is veteran oilman George Mitchell—one of Houston's largest oil and gas producers. In the 1980s, geologists employed by Mitchell noticed that when sinking deep wells through shale rock, geological instruments registered large amounts of natural gas. Shale—"a fine-grained sedimentary rock formed by the compaction of silt and clay-size mineral particles"[35]—was long known to hold oil and gas, but no one knew how to get it out. Mitchell came up with the idea of trying to get at the gas using hydraulic fracturing or "fracking." Fracking essentially entailed shattering rock to liberate gas or oil molecule trapped inside, and had been used widely since the earliest days of the oil industry. A rudimentary form of fracking was used after the Civil War by drillers who dropped explosive "torpedoes" into wells to shatter rock and accelerate oil flow, and the technology was further developed with the support of the federal government amid fears of shortages during the oil and gas boom in the early 1970s. By then, a common oilman saying was "when everything else fails, frack it."[36]

Mitchell's innovation was to try to frack in much deeper wells *extending into shale rock*. In 1982 he sunk his first well into the Barnett shale, a vast geological formation that runs under and mostly westward from Dallas. While successful, the endeavor was expensive. Throughout the 1980s and 1990s Mitchell and his colleagues doggedly tinkered and experimented with various fracking methods, and in 1997 eventually came up with the method of blasting water mixed with small amounts of proppants (sand or other solid particulate material strong enough to prop open fractures and liberate oil and gas) down into the wellbore where it would shoot out laterally into the rock, creating fissures through which the liberated gas molecules would flow.[37] So-called "slick water fracks" were much cheaper than prevailing methods. As technology improved, several factors came together after 2000 to enable oil drillers to produce large amounts of shale gas profitably, including "government policy private entrepreneurship, private land and mineral rights ownership, high natural gas prices, market structure, favorable geology, water availability, and natural gas pipeline infrastructure."[38]

Commercial shale gas production began in the Barnett shale in north-central Texas in 2000. More companies started drilling wells in the Barnett shale and soon it was producing "almost half-a-trillion cubic feet of natural gas per year." Soon development moved on to other shale formations, including "the Haynesville in eastern Texas and north Louisiana, the Woodford in Oklahoma, the Eagle Ford in southern Texas, and the Marcellus and Utica shales in northern Appalachia."[39]

Shale gas drillers were successful; they helped crush the price of natural gas, which ranged from a $6.00 to $14.00 per mmBtu between 2005 and 2008 but has fallen to a range of $1.70 to $6.00 since.[40]

As the shale gas boom triggered a natural gas price bust, drillers shifted fracking from natural gas to oil wells. As a result, U.S. shale oil (also called "light tight oil," LTO) soared from less than 0.5 mb/d to over 4.5 mb/d in 2015.[41]

Shale oil wells ramp up and then fall fast, adding a totally new dynamic to the oil industry, which was used to wells that can continue to produce for decades. In the case of conventional wells, oil flows naturally out of a reservoir and up through a wellbore as long as the pressure in the well is lower than the pressure in the reservoir. At first, oil is naturally pushed out by pressure caused by gas or water in the reservoir. But as this natural drive depletes, oil then has to be pumped or otherwise artificially lifted from a well (those familiar nodding donkey arm wells are pumps lifting oil out of wells). Natural and artificial lifts normally only obtain about 30–35 percent of the oil in place in a reservoir. To get to the rest, drillers employ improved oil recovery or well stimulation techniques such as injecting water or gas into the reservoir to boost well pressure, pushing the oil up. When stimulation is exhausted, it's time for the final step, called enhanced oil recovery or EOR. The EOR techniques include pumping acids into the reservoir to create fissures in the rock through which oil can flow or heating up the oil by injecting hot water or steam into the rock. Another related EOR technique is hydraulic fracturing. By pulling oil out of a well

with artificial means; pushing it out through stimulation; and finally blasting, heating, or acidifying the reservoir, producers can sustain oil flow
from a field for many years or decades, extending the plateau and allowing
for a gradual decline.[42]

But in the case of shale oil wells, drillers go right to the EOR stage.
Shale oil is not produced from a reservoir, but instead out of the source
rock many thousand feet below it. As shown in figure 10.3, shale oil production both rises and falls much faster than oil from a conventional
well. A typical shale well in the Bakken region of North Dakota declines
65 percent in the first year, 35 percent in the second year, 15 percent in the
third and 10 percent per year afterward. As indicated in figure 10.3, within
four years a shale well's production has fallen to below 20 percent of the
initial level, whereas a conventional oil well is still producing at between
70 and 80 percent of its initial rate.[43]

Such steep decline rates mean that for overall shale production to grow—or
even remain constant—many new wells must be continually drilled or fracked.
If shale drilling or fracking in a given region were to slow or stop, the legacy

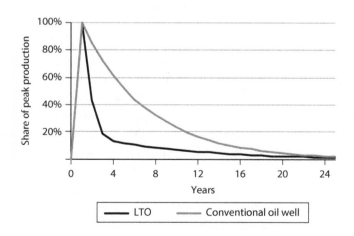

FIGURE 10.3

Typical production curve for a light tight oil (LTO) well compared with a conventional
oil well.

Source: Based on IEA data from *World Energy Outlook 2013* (license: www.iea.org/t&c), as modified
by the Rapidan Group.

decline rates from already-producing wells would cause overall production from the area to decline relatively swiftly. If conventional oil production is like sticking a straw in the ground and letting natural pressure
push oil out steadily for a long period of time, shale oil production is like
wringing a wet sponge: You get a lot of liquid right away, but it dries up
fast. To keep shale fields flowing, one must continually wring the sponge,
in this case by drilling and fracking wells, which requires continuous and
copious capital spending.

Shale wells also differ from conventional wells in that they have higher
operating costs and require more sustained capital investment. Fracking
(and disposing of frack water) is more like a manufacturing process than
drilling. Operating costs are higher because shale production requires
not just drilling but then fracking and often refracking the same wells,
requiring crews and infrastructure to be continually employed. And to
keep production up in a field, more wells must be continually drilled
and fracked.

Because of its relatively high operating costs, capital intensity, financing
needs, and steep decline rates, shale oil is much more responsive or "elas-
tic" to prices. Overall shale oil production was expected to react to price
changes within months instead of the years associated with traditional oil
drilling projects. As IEA's *World Energy Outlook 2013* noted, "large initial
natural decline rates make [shale oil] production potentially much more
responsive to fluctuations in oil prices than conventional fields: a decision
to stop drilling translates into a rapid fall in output." The IEA estimated
shale production would fall by 30 percent per year for the first three years
if investment in new drilling halted.[44] Shale's unique flexibility led OPEC
to regard shale oil as a possible swing producer in a way that conventional
wells are not.

The surprising shale oil boom made for heady times in the United
States and other oil-importing countries. "North America has set off a
supply shock that is sending ripples throughout the world," IEA Executive Director Maria van der Hoeven said on May 14, 2013.[45] Shale, some
asserted, would overthrow OPEC. "It is hard to overstate the degree to
which the North American supply boom has, since its onset, consistently
defied expectations," the IEA exclaimed in 2014.[46] While OPEC officials tended to publicly express skepticism, as time went on their views

ranged from extreme anxiety on the part of OPEC members that competed directly with lighter shale oil, like Algeria and Nigeria, to a more nuanced view by Saudi Arabia, who saw the upside of another potential swing producer.

HOW SAUDI ARABIA'S REFUSAL TO SWING WRONG-FOOTED OIL PRICE PREDICTIONS

By 2014, the shale oil boom was a major factor in the predictions of future oil supply and prices. Leading oil forecasts that year assumed crude oil prices would fall gently by 2019, from about $111 in 2013 to $95,[47] while OPEC forecasters expected prices would remain around $110 per barrel through the end of the decade. Forecasters saw oversupply building in coming years, mainly because of new production from outside OPEC—not just the U.S. shale oil boom but also new Canadian Oil Sands projects. The IEA also saw supply coming from new projects in Argentina, Brazil, Mexico, and Kazakhstan.[48] Many of these projects were high-cost, started when oil prices were rising toward or at $100 per barrel in recent years, and were predicated on high prices continuing.

The consensus was that fast-rising new supply from OPEC's competitors, mainly in North America, would start outpacing global demand growth. In total, IEA projected global demand would increase by 7.6 mb/d between 2013 and 2019 while supply outside OPEC would rise by 6.2 mb/d.[49] In other words, OPEC's competitors were going to gobble up 82 percent of projected demand growth, leaving OPEC with crumbs. The big question, as IEA put it, was "will OPEC producers need to 'make room' for this new supply?"[50] Conventional wisdom in industrialized countries and official forecasting bodies for the better part of thirty years held that non-OPEC producers would produce all they could while OPEC cheerfully restrained production in the interest of stable prices.[51] In other words, oil companies outside OPEC had all the fun while OPEC did all the hard work.

It got worse. The IEA also projected OPEC producers would increase their production capacity by a total of 2.1 mb/d by 2019, with Iraq responsible for most of the production increase and Saudi Arabia only a very

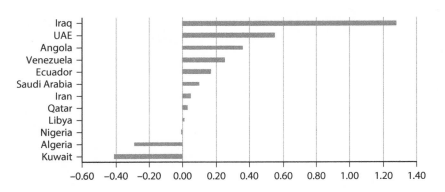

FIGURE 10.4

Forecasted incremental OPEC crude production capacity 2013–2019 (mb/d).

Source: IEA, *Medium Term Oil Market Report* 2014.

small amount. In other words, OPEC's market share was expected to grow by only around 1.0 mb/d but members were going to add two times that much in new capacity (see figure 10.4). OPEC needed to make room not only for shale and oil sands, but also for new production capacity within its ranks. Therefore by forecasting *total* OPEC production would fall, IEA effectively assumed one or more OPEC members would have to be willing to cut their own supply by around 1.5 mb/d, while others like Iraq and UAE increased, to avoid excessive overall production, which would lead to inventory builds and a price collapse.

In line with what IEA's forecast implied, analysts at the OPEC Secretariat in Vienna forecasted OPEC crude production would fall by 1.5 mb/d between 2013 and 2019, though they did not identify which members would cut nor did they estimate new production capacity among members.[52]

Similarly, BP's 2014 *World Energy Outlook* forecasted OPEC spare capacity would rise from 3.4 mb/d in 2013 to 6.6 mb/d in 2019, implying some OPEC producers needed to cut *over 3 mb/d*, that is, over two times the amount implied by IEA and OPEC. While cautioning that OPEC cohesion was a risk, BP said it assumed OPEC members would cut production, but did not specify which ones.[53]

OPEC's decision on whether to make room for new supply inside and outside OPEC carried enormous repercussions for oil prices. If one or more OPEC producers agreed to cut production, they could fend off a price collapse and the IEA's predictions about prices falling gradually from $111 to $95 would hold. But if OPEC countries refused to cut production and decided to fully produce from new fields, prices would precipitously drop. None of these forecasts envisaged oversupply and a price collapse; all assumed stable prices through the end of the decade. Thus IEA, OPEC, and BP—and most market participants and industry— assumed OPEC would cut to keep prices stable.

But while IEA, BP, and OPEC forecasters clearly assumed OPEC producers would cut or forego new supply to stabilize prices, none of forecasters identified which OPEC members would be willing to cut. A reasonable guess would be: Saudi Arabia. Only Saudi Arabia has shut in its own flowing wells (as in the early 1980s) or invested in costly new production capacity with the intention of keeping it idle (as in 2006 with the Khurais Megaproject). All other OPEC members produced all-out, and there was little indication that they would suddenly step up to the swing producer role. Iraq hardly has a sterling record of compliance with OPEC quotas, making Baghdad unlikely to hold back any production. Iran's oil was sanctioned, and Tehran would doubtless be chomping at the bit to increase production and recover lost market share once sanctions were lifted. Angola, Venezuela, and Ecuador were planning to increase production, and were very unlikely to hold any back. Of the OPEC producers expected to add to capacity, only UAE might have contributed modest cuts to its Gulf Sunni ally Saudi Arabia.

Highlighting the assumptions baked into these forecasts, a clear narrative emerges: Since Saudi Arabia wasn't expected to significantly add to its total production capacity, the only way OPEC spare capacity would go up was because Saudi production would go down. Thus consensus oil price forecasts were crucially predicated on Saudi Arabia effectively replaying the swing producer role it had abandoned in 1985 (and had deeply and loudly regretted since) and agreeing to cut its production by as much as 2.3 mb/d.

To fulfill expectations embedded in the oil forecast, the kingdom would have had to consent to a decline in its market share within OPEC from around 30 percent to the mid-20 percent range, low levels not seen since the last time Saudi Arabia swung in the early 1980s (see figure 10.5).[54]

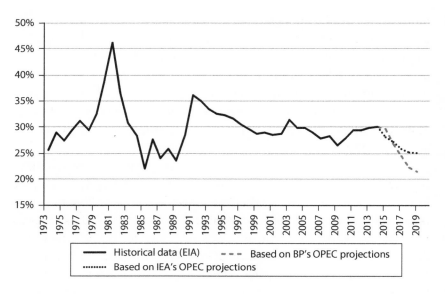

FIGURE 10.5

Saudi Arabia's share of OPEC crude production.

Source: EIA, "Monthly Energy Review" January 2016; IEA, *Medium Term Oil Market Report*, 2014; BP, *Energy Outlook 2035*; Rapidan Group. Rapidan Group estimates are based on EIA historical data. Projections are made by the author and assume that BP and IEA projections of higher OPEC spare capacity are realized by production cuts from Saudi Arabia.

Consensus assumptions that OPEC (read: Saudi Arabia) would cut production to make room for shale and other competitors yielded two comforting conclusions. Oil prices would remain stable around $90–$100 and spare capacity would rise 50–100 percent to a more comfortable 4–6 mb/d range—a vital shock absorber that was desperately needed given ongoing tumult and geopolitical disruptions or disruption risk in the Persian Gulf, North and West Africa, and Latin America. But the assumption that Saudi Arabia would play the swing producer role was deeply flawed. Cutting production in a healthy market, handing over market share to Iraq (and likely Iran, when its oil was back on the market), and supporting high oil prices so shale and oil sands projects could flourish was not in the cards for Riyadh. Whereas consensus forecasts might have assumed that a declining call on OPEC crude would be offset by Saudi Arabia cutting production, what these forecasts were really but unrecognizedly signaling was a supply glut and price collapse.[55]

NIRVANA INTERRUPTED: THE GREAT OPEC PRICE WAR OF 2014

The oversupply embedded in consensus five-year outlooks appeared in the middle of 2014. In July, the IMF revised global GDP projections for 2014 sharply downward to 3.4 percent, after weak U.S. and emerging market data for the first quarter of the year. That IMF growth downgrade as well as unexpected weak oil demand data for the second quarter of the year caused IEA analysts to sharply cut projected global oil demand growth between July and August.[56] In September the agency was reporting "further signs of a clear slowdown in global [oil] demand growth."[57] EU economic growth was "petering-out, while U.S. petrochemical usage fell alongside pronounced declines in Japanese power-sector demand." Weak Chinese growth also contributed to the lower outlook for oil demand, the IEA said. The slowdown, IEA said, was "nothing short of remarkable."[58]

On the supply side, U.S. shale oil production increased faster than most analysts expected as producers were able to access plentiful capital to unlock vast shale oil deposits. The U.S. shale industry continued to surprise officials and analysts alike by exceeding production growth outlooks and by the middle of 2014 was expected to add over 1.0 mb/d to the global oil market (see figure 10.6).

In addition, by the summer, rebels in eastern Libya lifted a months-long blockade of the Ras Lanuf and Es Sider terminals, enabling production to rise toward 1.0 mb/d in the third quarter of 2014 despite an ongoing civil war. Combined, unexpected demand and supply changes shifted the market balance from tight to loose. OECD commercial inventories, which had been trending steadily downward, were suddenly on the way back up.[59]

On September 5, 2014, oil prices fell below $100.[60] This started to make some producers uneasy; IMF and bank estimates showed that Russia, Venezuela, and other producers needed a $100 oil price to keep their budget balanced (the so-called "fiscal breakeven price").[61] Saudi Oil Minister Ali Naimi dismissed jitters, saying on September 11 that "oil prices 'always go up and down' and that he didn't understand 'the big fuss about it this time.'"[62] But on September 16, after meeting with Russia's energy minister, OPEC Secretary General Abdalla Salem El-Badri said

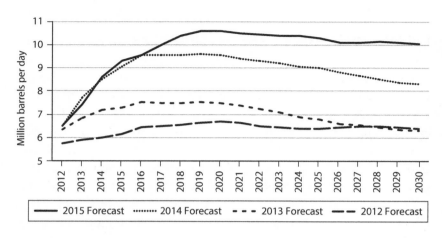

FIGURE 10.6

EIA annual energy outlook, U.S. crude production forecast.

Source: EIA, "Annual Energy Outlook," 2012, 2013, 2014, 2015.

he expected OPEC would lower its output target by 0.5 mb/d when it met on November 27. Market analysts took El-Badri's comments to mean that OPEC was starting to get worried.[63]

Saudi Arabia held fast to its message that action was not yet justified. On September 23, UAE Oil Minister Suhail Al Mazrouei (a close ally of Saudi Arabia on oil matters) countered al-Badri's comment, saying it was premature to make a decision.[64] And on September 29, Ibrahim al-Muhanna (senior advisor to Saudi Oil Minister Naimi) waved off concerns that recent years of stability were at risk. "What we have seen over the last five years will likely continue for another five years, and maybe beyond," Muhanna said. Based on the expensive nature and higher responsiveness of shale well drilling to prices of shale oil production, he predicted that crude prices would stay above $90. Further, should the price fall below $90 it "would be for a short time before going back to the level of around $100."[65]

But by October, crude prices had dropped to $89.[66] Calls for an OPEC response grew louder. As Libyan supply unexpectedly rose to a post-revolution high of around 900 kb/d, the perceived "need" for someone to cut supply grew. The question became less whether OPEC should cut and instead which OPEC producer would do it. At the end of the month OPEC Secretary General El-Badri kept mum on what OPEC would do at its meeting on November 27, but told journalists on the sidelines of an energy conference that if oil prices remained where they were, half of U.S. shale oil production would be lost. (ConocoPhillips's chief economist, Marianne Kah, disagreed with El-Badri, contending that $80 would not threaten the bulk of U.S. shale oil production.[67])

Ministers took their seats at OPEC's Vienna headquarters on November 27, 2014, which fell on Thanksgiving Day in the United States. Oil Minister Naimi understood that the clamor for "OPEC cuts" really meant "Saudi" cuts, and firmly repeated his refusal to cut unless other producers, including Russia, did so. Naimi also made clear he would not stand for the usual Russian tactic of promising cuts and not delivering. Russian officials claimed that unlike in Saudi and other OPEC producers, oil companies were private and could not take orders from Moscow. Saudi Arabia was not swayed by any of these arguments. Also lurking in the background was Moscow's support for Syrian dictator Bashar al-Assad, which Riyadh bitterly resented.

The UAE and Kuwait supported Saudi Arabia's position at the meeting, but Iran, Venezuela, Nigeria, and Algeria were strongly opposed. In June 2011, consensus rule deprived Saudi Arabia of its request for a 1.5 mb/d quota hike. Now, OPEC's consensus rule worked in Riyadh's favor. The prevailing target was 30 mb/d, set in December 2011. OPEC policy could not change if one producer objected. Thus, Saudi and UAE objection to any change meant the output target would stay at 30 mb/d. No cuts.

The day the decision not to cut was announced prices tanked $5.17, from $77.75 to $72.58, suggesting it came as a surprise to many people.[68] Prices kept falling, crashing through $60 at the end of December and then lurching down to $46.59 on January 13, 2015—a 60 percent plunge from the June high of $115.06.[69] Prices recovered briefly during the first half of the year, only to collapse again, bottoming at $26.68 on January 20, 2016. The nineteen-month collapse was the second-largest price drop in thirty years, after the 2008 collapse following the "supercycle" price peak that summer (see figure 10.7).

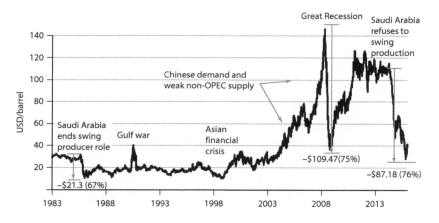

FIGURE 10.7

Crude price busts (Brent): 1983–2016.

Source: Bloomberg NYMEX WTI Futures (CL1), Accessed through Bloomberg Terminal March 30, 2016.

SAUDI ARABIA NOT KIDDING ABOUT NOT SWINGING

OPEC watchers and market participants can be forgiven for expecting Saudi Arabia to cut production despite public statements implying they would not. But circumstances in 2014 were very different in one key respect: Saudi Arabia wasn't being asked just to cut once, instead to embark on a multiyear series of cuts to offset relentless year-after-year supply growth from U.S. shale producers, as well as new supply from Canada, Brazil, and others including Iraq and Iran. Three years of $100 oil prices had resulted in a lot of new investment and that new oil was headed to the market in coming years. In the case of shale oil, the new oil arrived much faster than conventional or standard oil projects, a point we will explore shortly. Thus, Saudi Arabia was not being asked to make a one-time cut to address temporary oversupply or lead in emergency cuts (since prices had not yet collapsed), but instead embark on years of sustained cuts to balance the market—in other words play the swing production role as it did in the early 1980s and the Texas Railroad Commission and Seven Sisters did in the decades prior to the 1970s.

Market observers—with very rare exception[70]—were shocked by Saudi Arabia's refusal to play the swing producer role and cut production in late 2014. The decision was seen by many as a major inflection point in Saudi policy. After all, Riyadh had on occasion cut production by small amounts (up to around 1.0 mb/d) for seasonal and logistical reasons, and had borne the brunt of collective cuts when more serious oversupply developed, such as in 2009. It would not have been out of the ordinary for Saudi Arabia to cut production by about 0.5 mb/d, eliminating at least half of the near-term oversupply. But this narrative misses the fact that on November 27, Saudi Arabia was not being asked to make temporary and relatively minor adjustments, or to lead producers in emergency cuts after a price collapse had occurred. It was being asked to embark on possibly years of playing the swing producer by cutting substantially and long term.

That is, in 2014, Saudi Arabia was being asked to do the same thing it had sworn in 1985 never to repeat. In the early 1980s, the kingdom had steadily cut supply over a period of several years while others continued to increase production. And that is exactly the scenario the Saudis were facing again—supply cuts over five years to hold prices up. As Saudi Oil Minister Naimi explained in an April 2015 speech:

> The experience of the first half of the 1980s was still in our minds. At the time, we cut our production several times. Some OPEC countries followed our lead, and the aim was to reach a specific price that we thought was achievable. It didn't work. In the end, we lost our customers and the price. The kingdom's production dwindled from over 10 MMBD in 1980 to less than 3 MMBD in 1985. The price fell from over $40 per barrel to less than $10. We are not willing to make the same mistake again.[71]

Ever since, Saudi Arabia had repeatedly signaled it "would go *along* [with collective cuts] but not go *alone*."[72] In 1987, Saudi Minister Yamani's successor Hisham Nazer stated that he could "firmly and definitively rule out any prospect that Saudi Arabia might be ready to resume the role of swing producer under any circumstances." Nazer said: "We will conscientiously support OPEC and support the work of the committee, but we will not appoint ourselves custodians of the policies of OPEC; nor will we be willing to play the role of swing producer at all."[73] In 2000, Oil Minister Naimi reaffirmed that

"Saudi Arabia is willing to use its capacity to moderate the price. Not as a swing producer—and I want to clarify and emphasize that. We are not in the business of being swing producer."[74] Again in 2013, Minister Naimi made it clear that Saudi Arabia was prepared to swing one way—up:

> Saudi Arabia fulfills any demands when the oil supply decreases anywhere. This is different from taking any production step when the price decreases. When this happens, OPEC countries must be serious and reach a real collective agreement regarding the decrease. History stands witness that whenever it is agreed to reduce production, the only countries which abide are Saudi Arabia, Kuwait, Qatar, and the UAE. Why, then, are we holding them responsible for maintaining the price, while the other countries are not willing to participate?[75]

This was not just talk; the kingdom's upstream investment policy revealed a diminished appetite for holding sufficient spare capacity to act as a swing producer. In 2006 Saudi Arabia had launched the massive Khurais Megaproject with the stated goal of ensuring it had sufficient spare production capacity in the future (after nearly running out in 2004 and seeing markets tighten in 2005). But since running out of spare capacity again in 2008, Saudi Arabia has not announced any plans to increase production capacity. In November 2011, Saudi Aramco CEO Khalid Al-Falih (who succeeded Naimi as oil minister in May 2016) announced that the kingdom would no longer invest in production capacity and would instead, prioritize "downstream" refining and natural gas.[76] Going forward, Al-Falih said, Saudi Arabia would keep total capacity around 12 mb/d, thereby retaining 1.5 to 2.0 mb/d of spare capacity.

It is unclear exactly why the kingdom decided to stop investing in crude production capacity. It may have decided that it could play the swing producer role even with just 1.5 mb/d in spare capacity, or (relatedly) concluded that the circumstances that produced the 2008 supply demand tightness—strong Chinese demand, weak growth in supply, high industry costs, and (in Riyadh's view) excessive speculation—were a unique confluence that was unlikely to be repeated. Or the kingdom may have been thinking ahead to the return of disrupted supply; Saudi officials noted Iraq was making progress in attracting foreign investment in its fields, and could substantially increase its production.[77] Iran's production could also ramp back up after sanctions. Thus, the kingdom was cautious about spending billions of dollars to develop new production capacity that may not be needed.

Saudi Arabia may also have decided that investing "downstream" and in natural gas was a better use of resources than expanding production capacity. Downstream oil investments—in refining, petrochemicals, and energy services capacity—would enable Saudi Arabia to diversify its economy, capture more of the energy value chain (that is, process crude and gas into high-value products instead of just exporting the raw material), and create jobs for Saudi workers.[78] Investing in natural gas was crucial for the kingdom to reduce the large amount of oil it burns to generate electricity as well as to feed its new petrochemical facilities.

Whatever the constellation of reasons for it, Saudi Arabia was clearly sticking by its longstanding refusal to play the swing supplier role.

Financial, commercial, and geopolitical circumstances reinforced the kingdom's refusal to cut production unilaterally in 2014. The kingdom had accumulated over $700 billion in foreign exchange reserves and had extremely low domestic debt, putting it in a much stronger financial position to withstand a bout of low oil prices than other oil exporters with bigger debt burdens and smaller foreign exchange war chests. Commercially, were Saudi Arabia to cut unilaterally it would have handed market share to rivals Russia, Iran, and Iraq. These producers sold the same type of heavier oil and were targeting the same markets in growing Asia.

Geopolitical tensions also influenced oil policy. Relations between Tehran and Riyadh were much worse in 2014 than they had been under relatively moderate Iranian president Khatami in the late 1990s when both last cooperated in cutting supply. Russia was inserting itself in the region more aggressively and on the side of Iran and of another archenemy, Syrian dictator Assad. And while relations between Saudi Arabia and Iraq had improved since Saddam Hussein's ouster in 2003, Riyadh and other Gulf Sunni powers considered now-Shia-dominated Iraq to be sympathetic to Iran. While geopolitical motives were probably exaggerated in the Western media, they certainly played some role.

Finally, Riyadh declined to swing because it believed U.S. shale oil producers could do most or all of the swinging for them. If oil prices fell enough to make investing in new shale wells unprofitable—initially expected to be

$80–$90 per barrel, although this proved too high—then enough supply would exit to balance the market. This did not amount to a "war on shale" for two reasons. First, Saudi Arabia does not regard shale oil, a light and low-sulfur crude grade, as a direct competitor for the bulk of its crude grades, which are heavier and contain more sulfur. Second and more importantly, Saudi Arabia *likes* shale because it is more responsive to oil prices and therefore contributes to price stability. In March 2015 Saudi Oil Minister Naimi said, "some speak of OPEC's 'war on shale' . . . they are all wrong," adding, "new oil supply growth—much of it coming from the U.S.—is a welcome development for world oil markets.[79] Saudi officials genuinely wanted shale oil to survive and thrive, in large part because it could adjust relatively quickly—up *and* down.[80] For instance, when shale oil suddenly rose by over 3 m/bd after 2010, it helped to offset disruptions from Libya and Iran and prevent another calamitous oil price spike. In fact, Saudi Oil Minister Naimi mused that the potential for shale oil development worldwide was so encouraging that perhaps the kingdom didn't need so much capacity. "It is not a question whether Saudi Arabia has spare capacity. It is a question of whether we need to spend billions maintaining it at all," Naimi said.[81]

Thus, OPEC's refusal to cut production on November 27 opened a great experiment to see if U.S. shale oil could replace Saudi Arabia as the price-stabilizing swing supplier of oil to the global market. Saudi officials remained confident shale would protect a floor, although they lowered that level by $10–$20 per barrel between September and November. On November 28, 2014, *MEES* reported: "The Saudis seem to believe that most of the marginal [shale] barrels will disappear at a price of $70–$80 per barrel, if not immediately then possibly during the second half of next year." No one had been thinking much about a potential price collapse or shale's need to swing down before 2014; Saudi Arabia's refusal to cut forced oil industry and market participants to confront this question for the first time.

SHALE TO OPEC: GO SWING YOURSELF

With Saudi Arabia's refusal to cut, oil traders suddenly understood that prices would have to fall to levels that drove higher cost production out of the market. Because traditional wells are relatively inexpensive to run once they are built, prices would have to fall to below operating costs of between $5–$30 per barrel for wells to stop running. But since shale production required constant and expensive drilling and fracking of new wells to sustain overall output, a slowdown or halt in new drilling would cause supply to fall off much faster than conventional wells. Shale wells declined quickly after first being drilled, so the idea was that supply would decrease soon after prices fell below shale oil investment breakeven levels—the level needed to support drilling of *new* shale wells. The Saudis believed this breakeven level to be about $70–$80 per barrel. Private-sector estimates of shale breakeven costs tended to lower. For example, in December 2014 Scotiabank estimated investment breakeven prices for new shale wells drilled in Texas and North Dakota were around $68–$69 per barrel.[82]

The big question was: Would slowdown in new shale wells lead to a fast-enough production decline to balance the oil market, before inventories swelled too high and triggered a price collapse? With OPEC and other analysts assuming that investment in new shale wells would become uneconomic below $70, would Texas be forced back into the swing producer role it had abandoned in 1972, this time joined by North Dakota? This was *terra incognita* for the oil market; no one knew how shale would react to low oil prices, or how quickly.

The question was immediately tested when WTI oil prices crashed to $44 in late January, well below the assumed shale investment breakeven prices.[83] Prices quickly rebounded as shale oil company executives began to announce that they were in fact slashing cuts to spending on drilling wells. In February EIA forecasted that oil production out of the continental United States at the end of 2015 would be 120 kb/d less than what the agency had forecasted just two months before.[84] With evidence of carnage in the shale sector, investors and traders assumed that oil prices had bottomed.

Brent crude prices began to rise smartly, rising 50 percent from the mid $40s in January 2015 to nearly $60 by mid-April.[85] Shale was replacing the Seven Sisters and OPEC and had become the new swing producer—or so it appeared.[86] "With OPEC ceding control for the first time since the 1980s," Bloomberg reported in April 2015, "U.S. shale oil has been anointed the world's new 'swing producer' by everyone from ConocoPhillips and Goldman Sachs Group Inc. to former Federal Reserve Chairman Alan Greenspan."[87] Share prices of shale oil companies, which had plunged in value by 25 percent in the weeks following the November 27 OPEC meeting, recouped over half its losses by mid-April.[88] All eyes turned to shale: "We have seen that shale oil works very well at $100 per barrel," EIA head Adam Sieminski said in March 2015, "[n]ow we are going to find out if it works at $50 to $75."[89]

It was shale's turn to surprise the market. While shale companies began idling drilling rigs, actual production rose by far more than projected. By March 2015 oil production in the lower forty-eight states (excluding off-shore Gulf of Mexico) had risen to 7.7 mb/d, some 400 kb/d higher than the DOE had projected in December 2014.[90] Shale was still working at falling oil prices. Many shale companies had hedged some of their future production in derivatives markets, thus locking in higher prices.[91] Furthermore, the costs of producing shale (including hiring service companies to frack wells, disposing of the briny "flowback water," and transportation) fell rapidly with prices. This was bad news for the profits of service companies (and bad news for workers too, with over 93,000 jobs lost in the sector between January and November 2015),[92] but good news for drillers who were realizing savings. And finally, shale oil producers were employing new methods and technologies to improve their efficiency and further lower the cost of producing. For example, producers were able to drill more wells from a single well site and improved productivity by adding thousands of pounds of sand to frack fluids.

Shale producers—like the traditional drillers before them—had other reasons besides profits to keep operations going despite falling costs. Many shale oil companies were required to continue drilling to keep their lease. If they stopped drilling, they could lose the lease and the opportunity to produce in the future. And many were heavily indebted, so in order to make interest payments and adjust to stricter credit conditions, they needed to maintain or even increase output,[93] which they could do by shifting their best rigs and crews to the more productive fields. So all in all, while total spending on drilling sharply fell and the number of drilling rigs collapsed, the actual production of shale oil proved more resilient than expected.[94]

By the middle of 2015, it was becoming clear that shale oil would not swing, at least not fast enough to remove excess supply and avert another short-term price bust. Exacerbating the problem, Saudi Arabia and Iraq were both ramping up production: Saudi Arabia increased production by 300 kb/d between January and March, and by another 350 kb/d between

April and July,[95] while Iraq increased production by an astounding 1.1 mb/d between February and September.[96] With increased Iraq and Saudi production and with shale producers proving more resilient than expected, global oversupply grew. In July OPEC was producing 33.8 mb/d—nearly 4 mb/d above its 30 mb/d target. Excess oil supplies flowed into bulging inventories. Crude oil prices crashed again, from $60 at the end of June to $42 on August 24. They recovered in autumn to around $50 but resumed falling in November. After OPEC again failed to signal any production cut at its December 7, 2015 meeting, crude oil prices resumed their plunge. On January 20, 2016 Brent crude prices hit a new low: $26.01. Crude had now fallen by $89 (77 percent) from its June 2014 daily peak of $115 and by 66 percent since the November 27, 2014, OPEC meeting.[97]

As prices careened below $30 in early 2016, panic spread from inside OPEC to the world. All eyes turned to oil prices, as equity analysts began to look at oil prices as a barometer of the health of the global economy and financial markets. Falling oil prices were thought to be coupling with stock markets, dragging equities down at the highest rate in 26 years. In other words, wherever oil prices went, stocks followed, in this case down. As a result of falling oil prices in January, global equity markets "recorded one of the worst ever starts for a new year."[98] Some analysts believed plummeting oil prices and equity markets reflected slowing economic growth, such as in China. The Bank for International Settlements noted an "intense debate" about how falling oil prices would impact economies, flagging in particular the high debt burden of the oil and gas sector, which had grown by 250 percent from 2006 to 2015 and stood at roughly $2.5 trillion.[99] Some worried that crashing oil prices could trigger a banking crisis and downturn as the Lehman crisis had spectacularly done six years earlier. "Oil credit crunch could be worse than the housing crisis," blared one commentary headline on CNBC.[100] Others noted that while the oil crisis was leading to losses at Wall Street banks that had lent producers sizable sums, comparisons with the mortgage crisis were overblown as the scale, complexity, and direct economic impacts were less severe in the case of shale oil debt.[101]

Whatever the true extent of the risk, crashing oil prices in January and early February 2016 exhibited a reminder that there is a downside to price busts, even for economies that ought to benefit from cheaper oil prices. Crashing oil prices can be both a symptom and a potential cause of financial and economic damage.

Since oil's earliest days in 1861, price busts spurred producers to words and actions in order to put a floor under prices. Saudi Arabia remained firmly opposed to cutting production. But with alarm bells clanging in the White House, the Treasury Department, finance ministries, and private board rooms around the world, Saudi Arabia felt compelled to *say* something to affect market psychology for a short period of time. Saudi Arabia and other producers feared oil prices would keep falling through the spring and summer, and wanted to impose at least a temporary floor under prices until the second half of the year, when they hoped and expected a tightening supply and demand balance would firm up oil prices on their own. So on February 15, Saudi Oil Minister Naimi dropped his "let the market set prices" stance since November 2014 and the next day joined with Russia, Qatar, and Venezuela in calling for a collective production "freeze" at levels prevailing in January 2016. Iran refused to go along, vowing to increase its production after just having been freed from sanctions, including on its oil exports.

At first, oil analysts reacted with caution and skepticism to the concept of a production "freeze" at January 2016 levels that excluded Iran. Saudi Arabia, Russia, and other producers were at or near record high levels in January 2016. Moreover, Iran was expected to increased production by around 500,000 b/d. Analysts knew if producers kept producing at January's levels while Iran increased production, already record high global oil inventories would keep filling, keeping prices under downward pressure.

At best, a production *freeze* was a very poor cousin to earlier emergency *cuts* that producers have occasionally resorted to since 1861 and most recently in 1998–1999 and 2008 to stabilize prices. So to fortify the message to the market Saudi Oil Minister Naimi laced the "freeze" signal with a threat oil traders would remember and respect—collective supply cuts. In comments to the press on February 16, Naimi called the freeze idea the "beginning of a process" that may require "other steps to stabilize and improve the market."[102] Traders got the message and aggressively reversed their bets on falling oil prices while others bought into the rally (see figure 10.8).

Jawboning worked. By the close of February, oil prices had begun to rebound—eventually rising by some 40 percent, to over $40 per barrel by mid-April. Producers met in Doha on April 17, 2016, intending to formalize a production freeze but failed to agree at the last minute after Saudi

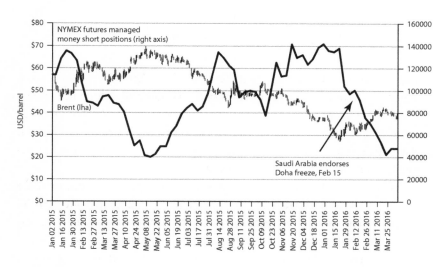

FIGURE 10.8

Brent and NYMEX futures managed money short positions.

Source: Bloomberg, ICE Brent Futures (CO1); NYMEX Futures Managed Money Short Position. Accessed through Bloomberg Terminal April 6, 2016.

Arabia refused its support unless Iran also joined. Oil prices held steady despite producers' failure to clinch a freeze deal, partly because of unrelated major disruptions in Nigeria, Iraq, Libya, and Kuwait preceding or coinciding with the April meeting.

At this juncture, it is difficult to predict if producers will just talk the market up or take the harder step of supply cuts. Significant supply cuts are unlikely unless oil prices collapse once again. Were prolonged oversupply or another price collapse to spark renewed producer meetings and cuts, it would not equate to OPEC restoring control over price stability. Any ad hoc, temporary emergency measures would be just that—an emergency response to a price bust that has already occurred, not coordinated supply control to prevent price busts in the first place. The time to prevent a price bust came and went in the fall and winter of 2014.[103] The only thing that seems certain is that oil prices have remained much lower for much longer than OPEC expected in the fall of 2014, and that the oil market is operating without the stabilizing force of a swing producer.

CALLING IT AN ERA

An epic transition took place in the global oil market from 2008 to 2014, as it became clear there was no swing producer able and willing to regulate production with the goal of stabilizing oil prices. Saudi Arabia failed to prevent prices spikes in 2008 and refused to prevent a price bust in 2014. These twin episodes amount to a clear demonstration that no swing producer is able and willing to adjust production to stabilize prices.

In reality, the oil market has not had a true swing producer since 1986, but this was masked by the absence of a need for one. OPEC had responded to episodic emergency disruptions and price collapses, and no chronic oversupply had developed. Saudi Arabia and OPEC acted proactively after the 1998–1999 price collapse, attempting to stabilize prices within a price band and with Saudi attempts to anticipate shifts in global supply and demand by adjusting production. Though insignificant, compared with Saudi Arabia's drastic supply cuts in the early 1980s to prop up prices, these relatively minor actions prior to 2008 created the impression that OPEC, or Saudi Arabia, were in charge of the oil market.

Indeed, oil market events over the last ten years have demonstrated that the market is operating without a safety net. Any semblance of a price ceiling imposed by Saudi Arabia was shattered when crude prices soared to $145 in summer of 2008, a price peak that coincided with Saudi Arabia essentially running out of spare capacity.[104] Saudi Arabia's loss of spare production capacity resembles 1972, when the TRC ran out of spare capacity and therefore lost control of the oil market for good. Whereas after 2004 Saudi Arabia embarked on new investments to raise spare production capacity, in 2008 it did not. Saudi Arabia does retain a small amount of spare capacity—about 1.5 mb/d according to the latest EIA data, though estimates by private sector analysts tend to be lower.

If we learned in 2008 that Saudi Arabia was no longer able to defend a price ceiling, since 2014 we've learned it is unwilling to put a floor under oil prices. Riyadh's refusal to swing along should not have been surprising; Saudi policy was set against it after 1986 and constantly restated. But it also was not tested until after 2009, when three years of $100 oil prices unleashed investment in new production—including fast-rising shale.

For the first time since the early 1980s, Saudi Arabia was being asked to step into the role of a genuine swing producer. It declined.

While Saudi oil policymaking is famously enigmatic, the kingdom's leaders seem to have concluded that the oil market had become too big to manage successfully on its own, and that OPEC as a cartel had not been and never would be cohesive enough to do the job. Given this, it seems to have decided that the optimal strategy is to hunker down and prepare to live with more volatile prices instead of vainly trying to prevent them. In February 2016, Saudi Oil Minister Naimi addressed a major energy conference in Houston and explained to the oil industry why OPEC did not cut on November 27, 2014: "[T]here was no appetite for sharing the burden. So we left it to the market as the most efficient way to rebalance supply and demand. It was—it is—a simple case of letting the market work."[105]

Since the beginning of the oil industry, letting the market work has meant boom and bust oil prices. Ten years into the boom-bust era, crude oil price changes so far have averaged 33 percent, on par with the last boom-bust era one hundred years ago (see figure 10.9).

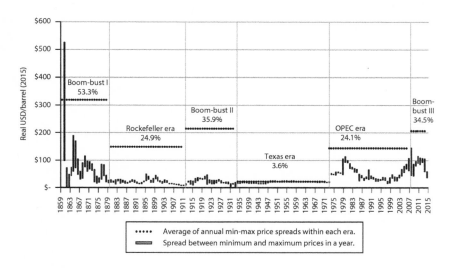

FIGURE 10.9

Annual ranges of real monthly U.S. crude oil prices, 1859–2016.

Sources: Derrick's, vols. I–IV; API, *Petroleum Facts and Figures* (1959); Dow Jones & Company, Spot Oil Price: West Texas Intermediate; and U. S. Energy Information Administration, Cushing, OK WTI Spot Price (FOB). © The Rapidan Group.

Oil's price stickiness on the supply and demand sides means extreme price movements may be with us for a while. While the days of monopolists, soldiers, cartels, and regulators stabilizing the oil market may be over, we may conclude before long that the only thing worse than someone controlling the global oil market is no one doing so. Coping with the economic and foreign policy repercussions of extreme oil price movements will demand new and sustained attention and innovative thinking from our academic, corporate, and government innovators. Our economic vitality and international stability depend on their success.

EPILOGUE

A CHALLENGE WITH NO EASY SOLUTION

If the study of oil market history teaches anything, it is humility about predicting future trends and events. In oil markets, it can be also challenging to understand *what just happened*, let alone to predict what will. Yet oil's paramount role in our economic, foreign, and environmental affairs compels us to analyze, probe, and speculate about the future and for that, a clear picture of *what just happened* is vital.

I have attempted to put recent oil market developments in the context of oil's history and the broad forces that shape oil price stability and volatility. I've explored oil price's natural proneness to volatility, why industry and governments loathed it, and the great lengths to which they went to suppress it. For the better part of the last hundred years, to protect a vital industry, economic growth, and national security, the oil industry and governments in major producing countries felt compelled to regulate supply with the primary goal of stabilizing oil prices. Major oil companies, later joined or instructed by government officials, imposed supply control, which usually involved a small number of companies or officials able and willing to act as the "swing producer," adjusting supply to balance demand with the goal of stabilizing prices. Standard Oil played that role in oil's early decades. The TRC and Seven Sisters took charge in the early 1930s and were succeeded, albeit less successfully, by OPEC in the early 1970s. Being the swing producer was not always fun and at times required substantial supply cuts to avoid a glut and price bust, as we saw particularly in the 1950s and early 1980s. Acting as the swing producer also required adding supply in the case of a geopolitical disruption—as seen during the 1956–1957 Suez Crisis, the 1967 Six-Day War, and the Gulf Wars—and also when supply and demand conditions tightened.

Around 2008 we exited over seven consecutive decades of public-private production control and entered a third era of market-driven oil prices. The implication is we should expect more frequent, wider oil price gyrations. The boom-bust cycles we saw from 2004 to 2008 and the bust since 2014 (with a boom likely to follow in coming years) is the new normal; the relative stability between 2010 and 2013 may recur from time to time—previous boom-bust eras also saw temporary periods of relatively stable prices before the next boom or bust—but will be an anomaly.

When oil supply and demand are unbalanced and no supply regulator is present, oil prices should range between a floor defined by the cost of production and a ceiling defined by economic pain. In current circumstances, this suggests a likely oscillation in a range well below $30 and above $100. When supply and demand are balanced or imbalances are small, price range may be smaller. But when imbalances are more pronounced, the range will grow. And price swings reinforce themselves. Price busts like the one since 2014 cancels or delays multiyear investment programs and slowly but surely stokes demand that in a few years contributes to the next price boom, which in turn attracts new investment and can slow economic growth, contributing to the next bust. "The problem of oil . . . is there is always too much or too little," Myron Watkins wrote in 1937, and that remains true today and will be tomorrow.[1]

If the return of oil price volatility is going to be a big problem, one obvious solution is to "get off oil" fast. But as I noted at the outset, that won't happen any time soon given the pervasiveness of oil in our economy and the unwillingness of political leaders to impose the type of draconian policies—heavy taxation, and rationing, which may result in slower economic growth and lost elections, if not political instability—that a quick shift from oil would require. For the foreseeable future, likely many decades, our economy will run on oil and its price will remain a top public concern.

Recognizing full well the danger of predictions, let me conclude with a look to the future, and to some of the questions I think we'll need to consider (and try to answer, as best we can) as we come, once again, into a period of boom-bust oil prices. In doing so I'm reminded of a briefing I attended while serving on the White House National Economic Council some thirteen years ago. The briefer, a senior official from the Department of Energy, had come to explain a thorny and complex issue without easy or obvious policy prescriptions (as most energy challenges are) and opened his remarks with "I hate to raise a problem without a solution but . . ."

WILL OIL PRICES STABILIZE THEMSELVES WITHOUT AN OPEC OR OTHER SUPPLY MANAGER?

Maybe, for short periods of time. After all, oil prices after the boom and bust collapse in 2008 ranged close to around $100 between 2010 and the next bust in 2014. But for prices to remain naturally stable, supply and demand would need to remain in rough balance. Future patterns of supply and demand are more likely to feature imbalances, sometimes large ones. Moreover, booming and busting oil prices will themselves contribute to future supply and demand imbalances.

Demand for oil is likely to remain strong barring a recession, and periods of low oil prices will encourage higher demand, albeit with a lag (as discussed in chapter 4). The big question for the coming years is whether the oil industry will invest enough—and in time enough—to produce the oil a growing world will require. The current price bust is delaying or canceling investment in new oil supply that the market may need in a few years but will not have. Bloomberg reported that "oil companies have canceled more than $100 billion in investments, laid off tens of thousands of workers, slashed dividends, and sold assets."[2] In January 2016 the energy consultancy Wood Mackenzie, Ltd., said project delays and cancellations since the 2014 oil price bust will impact 1.5 mb/d in 2021, "rising sharply to 2.9 mb/d by 2025."[3] In July 2016 they warned that "most major conventional oil projects risk being delayed or cancelled if global prices remain at or below $50 a barrel."[4]

In addition to this is the financial burden the oil industry bears (the IEA estimates about $300 billion) just to keep supply from declining.[5]

This is a particular concern in countries such as Russia, Mexico, and China that rely mainly on older, aging fields and need to spend a lot to keep pressure up, water out, and oil flowing.[6] IEA estimates an average decline of about 9 percent of annual production from mature fields if the industry does not invest to sustain output.[7] Collapsing investment will translate into less oil supply in the coming five years or so. IEA sees 4.1 mb/d being added to global oil supply between 2015 and 2021, down sharply from the total growth of 11 mb/d between 2009 and 2015. Worldwide, capital outlays for exploration and production fell by almost 25 percent in 2015, and are expected to be down another 17 percent in 2016. Upstream investment hasn't fallen for two consecutive years since 1986.[8]

It is possible that the growth in demand and growth in supply will balance out, and the world oil market will settle into a steady price range, as seen between 2010 and 2013. But it is more likely the future will resemble the past, with large and unexpected shifts in supply and demand amidst disruptions and upheaval. In this scenario, no swing producer will mean boom-bust oil price cycles. Because of oil's central importance in the economy, extreme oil price fluctuations will unsettle oil industry and officials and will have jarring impacts on household budgets, the cost of doing business, and geopolitical stability. If history is any guide, mayhem will drive officials to attempt to intervene for the sake of oil price stability.[9]

WILL SAUDI ARABIA OR OPEC REGAIN CONTROL?

OPEC as a group almost certainly will not regain control of the market; it would require members to achieve a level of cohesion and discipline it has never shown. OPEC's role as a cartel, as this book and other research has shown, is vastly overstated.[10] There is little evidence OPEC quotas affected members' production; one researcher found OPEC produced in excess of official quotas 96 percent of the time between 1982 and 2009.[11] Exceptions, we have seen, have been the occasional and temporary emergency cuts after price busts.

OPEC's influence and impact will continue to rest largely on the actions of Saudi Arabia. It is possible OPEC and other producers may continue to agree from time to time on emergency cuts after price busts. We saw temporary, emergency collective cuts with the Oil Creek Association in 1861 and among OPEC producers in 1998–1999 and at the end of 2008. Indeed, the present, post-2014 price bust phase could lead to a production freeze or even an emergency cut. But ad hoc, temporary, emergency cuts after a price bust differ entirely from proactive supply cuts to prevent price busts in the first place.

Genuine market management requires that one or more producers stand ready and able—over a sustained period perhaps lasting years—to proactively swing supply up or down, at times substantially, to prevent extreme oil price moves. On this measure, OPEC played the swing producer role just once, from 1982 to 1985, and it was Saudi Arabia that did all the swinging. Riyadh detested that experience and has vowed never to repeat it. Speaking at the World Economic Forum in Davos in January 2016, Saudi Arabia's current oil minister (but at the time Chairman of Saudi Aramco) Khalid Al-Falih said "if there are short-term adjustments that need to be made, and if other producers will coordinate, then we will be happy to cooperate . . . Saudi Arabia will not alone balance the market."[12] In other words, Saudi Arabia will go along, but not alone, with supply cuts to stabilize prices.

Saudi Arabia's reluctance to cut unilaterally is understandable. It only makes sense for a swing supplier to cut when it enjoys *market power*— the ability to raise and maintain price above levels that would obtain in free market conditions and even then only if the costs were bearable and its post-cut revenues went up. Otherwise, Saudi Arabia will not cut to bolster competitors' revenues. To have market power, a producer needs to dominate supply and face little competition. Texas held just under half of the U.S. oil reserves from the mid-1930s to 1970s giving it decisive control over the national oil supply.[13] Combined, the U.S. and Seven Sisters' market power stemmed from control of 89 percent of global reserves, 95 percent of production, and 57 percent of refining.[14] The kingdom accounts for 16 percent of proved reserves, 13 percent of production, and only 3 percent of refining capacity (although refining capacity is set to increase).[15]

Shale oil has further weakened Saudi Arabia's market power, at least for the time being. But even if down the road Saudi Arabia regained market power, its rising domestic demand for crude oil limits its scope to cut production. Domestic demand has been rising by 5–6 percent in recent years, averaging 3.3 mb/d last year (although low oil prices and the associated cuts in Saudi spending and subsidies could crimp growth in coming years).[16] Meanwhile, Saudi Arabia is rapidly expanding its domestic refining capacity, which it will presumably feed with its crude. The kingdom recently built two large 400,000 b/d refineries and a third of the same size is due in 2018.[17] By the end of the decade, Saudi Arabia's refining capacity should exceed 3 mb/d.[18] With Saudi domestic demand over 3 mb/d,[19] refining capacity heading toward 3 mb/d by end of the decade (as part of an ambitious plan to hold 8–10 mb/d of refinery capacity at home and abroad),[20] and a desire to sustain crude exports above 7 mb/d, it is difficult to see how Saudi Arabia can cut production below 10 mb/d for a sustained period of time.

Riyadh also shows no sign it intends to prevent future price spikes by retaining a sufficient amount of spare capacity. Currently Saudi Arabia claims its maximum production capacity is 12.0 mb/d; with production around 10 mb/d, that implies just 2.0 mb/d of spare capacity. Historically, 5 percent of global production is a generally recognized threshold for adequate spare capacity; in a crude oil market of roughly 91 mb/d, this implies at least 4.6 mb/d.[21]

Saudi Arabia may well dust off plans to increase its total production capacity from 12.5 mb/d to 15 mb/d, or even higher. Since 2011 Aramco (the state-owned oil company) has prioritized investment to expand refining, petrochemical output, petroleum products trading, and natural gas production.[22] But in April 2016, Deputy Crown Prince Mohammed bin Salman—the kingdom's top oil official, reformist economic policy czar, defense minister, and potential heir to the throne—said that with more investment the kingdom could produce 15 mb/d and as much as 20 mb/d.[23] I interpret this statement to indicate the kingdom may increase production to meet projected demand while competing with archrival Iran and other lower-cost Gulf producers for new investment.

Would a Saudi decision to increase production capacity lead to a rebuilding of sufficient spare capacity to cap future oil prices and thereby signal a return to market management? Probably not. In all likelihood, whether to meet demand at home or abroad while preserving a desired

1.5–2.0 mb/d level of spare capacity, Saudi Arabia will have to increase crude production capacity above its current 12.5 mb/d level in the coming years and decades. Saudi oil demand has been rising by 5 percent per year since 2010 and if it continues growing at that rate will rise by another 2.0 mb/d by 2025.[24] The kingdom hopes to reduce future oil consumption by removing subsidies and by replacing oil with natural gas in electricity generation, but the success of these efforts are uncertain. Assuming Saudi Arabia is successful at sharply slowing its consumption growth at home, new Saudi oil capacity may well be needed abroad, where production will be slowing due to the present price bust.

Whether the kingdom increases total production capacity, preventing price busts still requires that a swing producer hold enough spare capacity to swing up to cap prices and be willing to swing production *down* to prevent busts. Of that, there is no sign.

Even if Saudi Arabia can hold about 1.5 to 2 mb/d of spare capacity, history suggests this is unlikely to be sufficient to cap prices. Demand surges (like those after 2004) and supply disruptions (like those after 2011) are likely and could quickly overwhelm a 1–2 mb/d spare capacity margin. As I write, my colleagues at the Rapidan Group estimate geopolitical instability has disrupted some 2.2 mb/d and another 1.9 mb/d are at risk of disruption.[25] Saudi Arabia does not need to go back to the model of the 1950s when the TRC and Seven Sisters held up to one-third of world production in spare. But a 5 percent of production or 4–5 mb/d spare capacity level would be more comfortable than the current 1–2 percent.

For decades, analysts and observers have analyzed and debated the motivations for Saudi oil policy. There is no consensus or model that fits nicely, although most observers agree that Riyadh's oil policy balances revenue maximization with market share, and that the priority between the two can change depending on market circumstances. What is clear is that Saudi officials believe the price of oil should be set in the free market, and that the kingdom will not be a swing producer or make emergency cuts without others.

In April 2016, Deputy Crown Prince Mohammed bin Salman announced what would amount to an epochal change in Saudi oil strategy: the kingdom, he said, planned to float a small percent of Aramco in the open market. With this, Saudi Arabia intends to shift from being just a major crude producer toward becoming an economically integrated powerhouse. If these plans go through, Saudi Arabia will become more like a normal, if big, oil producer and may act less like the "central banker" of the oil market. Floating shares in Aramco would cut against holding and using spare production capacity to balance the oil market; investors in future Aramco shares would not be pleased and would want to be compensated.[26] Prince Mohammed is clear that Riyadh has no intention of resuming the production management model OPEC tried to enforce for three decades. "For us it's a free market that is governed by supply and demand and this is how we deal with the market," he told one interviewer.[27] "We don't care about oil prices—$30 or $70, they are all the same to us," Prince Mohammed told an another.[28]

CAN U.S. SHALE OR ANOTHER CARTEL REPLACE OPEC?

Since the shock OPEC decision not to cut in November 2014, one of the biggest questions in the oil market is: Can shale replace OPEC? We have a partial answer so far: No, at least not in terms of cutting enough to quickly put a floor under prices and preventing a massive inventory buildup.

Looking forward, another major question is how quickly shale will recover as prices rise. Will shale prove slower to react on the upside than it did on the downside? Some say shale will spring back quickly. Optimists point in particular to the large amount of "drilled but uncompleted" wells, or DUCs, drilled wells that haven't yet been fracked to start producing oil. Some estimate DUCs could add several hundred thousand barrels per day of production, with as much as over half a million barrels per day in North Dakota alone.[29] Indeed, some regard potential oil from DUCs as akin to spare capacity: a lot of oil that can start up quickly. If DUCs do end up serving this role, they will make OPEC even less relevant.

In my view, although DUCs in theory could certainly help cushion upward price moves, some caution is warranted. First, understanding of the number of DUCs and how much potential production they represent is limited. There are always wells left uncompleted for certain periods of time for various technical or logistical reasons; differentiating between

these wells and wells that firms intentionally leave uncompleted in anticipation of higher prices is difficult with available data. Second, DUCs are
more akin to inventory that can be released into the market when prices
are favorable than a sustained source of production over a period of several or more years. If, for example, two hundred DUCs in a shale basin
are gradually brought online once oil surpasses $60, that slight boost in
supply will increase for the months the DUC inventory is whittled down
and will inexorably decline after the last DUC is cleared.[30] Finally, no one
can be confident in how DUCs will perform, making production estimates elusive.

Beyond the question of DUCs, shale oil is likely too decentralized
and expensive to play the role of market balancer and price stabilizer,
even if production could adjust quickly enough. Shale oil production
results from thousands of independent firms all responding to their
own evaluations of market conditions and the highly varied economics of the acreage they control. As we have seen throughout history, it
is nearly impossible to organize many individual producers in collective efforts to restrain production. And given the variability of shale
formations, and the fact that break-even costs in one county can be
markedly different from the next county down the road, coordinating
supply would be extra difficult. Finally, even if producers could find
some way to agree on collective supply restraint, it would be illegal due
to antitrust rules.

The future role of shale oil in shaping oil price stability is one of the
biggest open questions for the near future, and one that has begun to
preoccupy energy economists and academics. Shale oil may prove to be a
much more flexible (or shorter cycle) form of oil production that, although
not replacing OPEC or the TRC, can react fast enough and in sufficient
size to provide the oil industry with natural self-adjusting features it has
lacked. In this scenario, shale becomes the new swing supplier, especially
if global shale oil production expands. Shale oil supply may not swing
as fast as wells controlled by the TRC or OPEC, but it could swing fast
enough to keep oil prices reasonably stable through the course of multiyear cycles.

On the other hand, shale could be destabilizing for prices if it proves
big and fast enough to contribute to gluts and price crashes—deterring

investment in other non–shale oil projects—but not big and fast enough to prevent booms.

The question of shale's longer-term impact on price stability is far from settled, although recent price crashes and resulting collapses in upstream investment suggest we will have to endure at least one cycle of the latter scenario before hopefully settling into the former.

Regulation of shale is another huge uncertainty. If shale oil production loses its "social license to operate" and is sharply curtailed or banned in the United States while prevented from expanding globally, the question of whether shale can replace OPEC will be moot, making price booms and busts more severe.

What about U.S. state and federal officials? Could they get back into the game of regulating supply? The TRC and other state regulatory bodies exist, and legal provisions could be enacted to return to quotas. It is tempting to reject such a notion out of hand, on the view that such heavy-handed government intervention is unthinkable. Yet we've seen in oil's history the extreme lengths to which industry and officials will go for the sake of oil price stability. Texas and Oklahoma sent in troops to shut wells and then imposed a quota system so strict it would later make OPEC envious. The federal government intervened heavily during the 1970s energy crises, mostly under Republican presidents. In 1988 an Interior Department report noted: "Over the last fifteen years, popular support for government involvement in energy markets has varied in direct proportion to the price of oil."[31] The economic, financial, and security stakes remain high today.

But even if the United States legalized cooperation among shale oil producers, it's not clear they could regulate supply as in 1932. Back then, the TRC held *cheap oil* off the market to help high-cost production flourish. To play the swing producer now, the TRC (and regulators in other shale states such as North Dakota) could order a halt to new shale drilling. But shale oil supply, unlike the old flowing wells in East Texas the TRC used to regulate, is relatively *expensive*. "Turning off" shale oil is more like shutting down a manufacturing plant than turning a spigot. Thus quotas on new shale drilling could quickly lead to no shale drilling at all; investors will not invest in expensive capacity that can be held off the market by government fiat.

COULD CONSUMING AND PRODUCING COUNTRIES
COLLABORATE TO STABILIZE OIL PRICES?

Episodes of price instability in the 1970s, early 1990s, and 2008 prompted consuming and producing countries to talk about possible collaborative approaches to stabilizing prices. Those talks tended to peter out as the crisis passed. Sustained oil price volatility, however, is likely to lead to more regular talks. Indeed, the International Energy Forum has been hosting regular working-level talks among importing and exporting country officials, oil company executives, consultants, and academics for several years. They could dust off old plans that call for some importing countries to fill strategic stocks to support prices while some producers maintain enough spare capacity to offset disruptions or prevent tight supply–demand balances from triggering price spikes. In theory such a system sounds feasible, but in practice it is likely an unworkable approach to price stabilization.

As we've seen, effective regulation or cartels work best when a small number of like-minded entities with a high degree of cohesion or trust dominate production. Rockefeller's sprawling network of affiliated companies, oil state regulators led by Texas, and the Seven Sisters fit this description to a much greater extent than does OPEC. Looking forward, it is difficult to imagine that the world's leading oil producers and consumers—including China, the United States, OPEC countries, and Russia—will succeed in creating and successfully stabilizing prices by regulating oil flow from strategic stocks and spare capacity. However, history shows that high enough oil price volatility can result in unexpectedly robust regulation and unexpected cooperation between unlikely parties.

We therefore cannot rule out a scenario in which future oil price gyrations rekindle efforts by producing and consumer countries to stabilize oil prices by coordinating production and stock purchases, respectively. Any producer–consumer system to stabilize prices by managing crude oil supply would likely require agreement between the United States and Saudi Arabia as the leading strategic stock and spare capacity holders, respectively. But each is headed in the opposite direction: Strategic stocks and spare capacity appear to be headed *down* in both countries, as broader bilateral relations have frayed. With regard to strategic stocks, the recent collapse of oil prices has sparked a vibrant debate among oil experts about the continued need and proper use of the Strategic Petroleum Reserve (SPR). Some say the SPR is no longer needed because of high commercial inventories and reduced oil import dependence.[32] Others argue that tight spare production capacity and the threat of geopolitical disruption constitutes an enduring major risk that strategic stock use can address. Those who agree on the need for an SPR debate whether it should be used more proactively, aggressively, and flexibly,[33] even for minor disruptions, noting that low OPEC spare production capacity results in higher oil price spikes when even small disruptions occur or threaten to occur. While experts debate the proper size and use of the SPR, in 2015 Congress ordered the SPR to be reduced by more than 20 percent (159 million barrels) over the next ten years, mainly to fund government spending unrelated to energy.[34]

HOW CAN WE COPE WITH HIGHER VOLATILITY?

Absent a supply manager or naturally balanced global oil market to ward off volatile oil prices, we may have to get used to them. "Do we simply have to live with the large swings in oil prices and their high volatility?" an IMF official asked in 2009. "To some extent, the answer probably is 'yes.'"[35]

As history shows, oil price gyrations are likely to trigger policy responses. The bigger the shock, the more aggressive the policy intervention. Yet history also teaches that unless policymakers and companies can control the bulk of crude production, few policy options can help and many are counterproductive. In general, policymakers and executives should realize that absent wellhead control of the bulk of low-cost oil production, boom-bust oil prices are unavoidable. Thus policies and corporate practices should aim to mitigate the resulting uncertainty and volatility in costs and revenues while adapting to new, larger price cycles and avoid panicky or mistaken reactions that may do more harm than good. That will mean avoiding some traps we've fallen into before, and learning from what's worked.

Resist the Temptation to Crack Down on Speculators

Extensive investigations and academic research indicates speculation is a good thing and even helps to reduce volatility. The active participation of financial investors in oil futures and derivatives markets is legal and desirable because it enables energy consumers and producers to transfer risk and protect against price swings. Investors also bring information to the market and smooth excessive price swings. Like all market participants, their activities should be well policed for manipulation and fraud. The Commodity Futures Trading Commission and other regulators police actively against instances of fraud or manipulation in financial markets. Overly hasty or incautious regulations could drive financial market activity to other, less transparent and less regulated venues.[36] Boom-bust prices are going to make consumers and producers desperate to hedge against volatility; policymakers should ensure they have a safe and orderly place to seek shelter. For example, in March 2015 the World Bank began helping countries arrange oil hedges and in 2016 helped Uruguay arrange a "milestone" deal that the World Bank "expects others to follow."[37]

A Variable Import Tariff Has Big Downsides and Likely Would Not Stick

The variable import tariff—a tax that kicks in when prices go below a certain level—was floated in 1986. It didn't go into effect; opponents argued that it would violate trade rules and be too costly and complex to implement without harming the economy. In addition to these potential downsides are two other problems with the variable import tariff from a price stability standpoint. First, Congress would have to be willing to stick with it, which would mean having the stomach to watch regressive fuel taxes levied on motorists and U.S. industry as oil prices fell below the policy floor. The history of energy policy regulation overwhelmingly suggests elected officials are unlikely to stomach taxes or burdensome regulations on motorists, especially when prices are falling in a weak economy.[38] The notion that future Congresses and presidents would allow a potentially massive tax to automatically hit motorists is fanciful. Any such tariff would most likely be suspended or abandoned once it began to bite, in which case industry and consumers would not regard it as credible, and any benefit from a price stability standpoint would be lost. Second, even if the tariff went into effect, it would insulate the U.S. producers only from low oil prices, not the global oil market. Indeed, a variable import tariff would make global crude oil price instability worse to the extent that it would shield domestic high-cost production from responding to the lower price signal by shutting in.

Don't Try Price Controls and Rationing Again

The historical experience with price controls and rationing was so negative it is likely (although not certain) that policymakers will not wish to repeat them. However, as memories of the 1970s fade and oil price volatility continues, it is possible policymakers will reach for them again, in which case hard lessons will have to be relearned. Summarizing our predicament and mistakes to avoid, energy expert Daniel Ahn wrote in 2012, "Oil markets will inevitably feature large and unavoidable price swings. Attempts to forcibly manage prices in a knee-jerk response to every shock, such as through manual price controls, trading bans or limits, or ad hoc government stockpile releases will only be counterproductive."[39]

Improve Data

One sensible public policy step is improving data quality to reduce uncertainty and therefore volatility. The oil market is turbulent enough; patchy and incomplete data make the problem worse. In the United States, the Energy Information Administration—the data and analysis arm of the Department of Energy—collects the timeliest and most comprehensive energy data of any country but suffers from severe funding and personnel shortfalls. Outside the United States, the quality and quantity of energy data are generally worse. European oil inventory and refinery data are collected on a monthly basis by a voluntary industry association. (One notable exception is the North Sea's field-by-field production data, which should be the global standard.)

As they get their own houses in order, IEA countries should encourage better data from non–OECD countries, especially emerging Asian consumers and major producers. The multinational Joint Oil Data Initiative, comprising data from more than one hundred countries,[40] is a good start, but its timeliness, completeness, sustainability, and comparability must be greatly improved. Most importantly, on the consumption side, China's fundamental oil data are incomplete because commercial inventory data are not reported.

Energy data reporting should be lawfully compelled, timely, and comprehensive. Upstream, governments should require industry to disclose and validate field-by-field production and reserve data. Doing so would reduce surprises, manic hoarding, and price volatility. Downstream, figures for production, storage, net trade, and refining stocks and flows should be comprehensively reported, enabling much better implied demand estimates.

Build Up Strategic Stocks and Coordinate Their Use in Emergencies

Given continued tight OPEC spare production capacity and the many geopolitical risks in key oil producing countries and regions, oil importing countries should bolster defenses against price shocks that could be transmitted by severe supply interruptions. They can do so by increasing strategic stocks and coordinating their use with others in cases of disruption. Congress may wish to reconsider selling off strategic stocks and instead bolster them. The psychological benefit of having strategic reserves in a crisis is difficult to measure but should not be overlooked.

Major importers China and India should be welcomed into the IEA and urged to cooperate with other IEA countries on the coordinated use of strategic petroleum reserves, emergency response, improved data, and sound energy policies.

Private Sector Responses to Price Stability

Grappling with boom-bust oil prices may require building more storage capacity and holding higher inventories. More storage capacity will be required as more of the supply adjusting happens above ground (in and out of storage tanks) than below ground (in and out of spare capacity). Oil is costly to store, but price booms exacerbate fears of running out,

so producers and consumers will pay the price of storage. And entre-
preneurial storage owners may see profit opportunities in filling storage
tanks up during price busts, holding, and then selling into the subsequent
price booms. For the market as a whole, flows into and out of storage can
temporarily moderate large imbalances in supply and demand. Oil storage
capacity has greatly increased in recent years, although this has mainly
been due to rising consumption and the shale oil boom, not necessarily
to contend with boom and bust oil prices.[41]

Another likely response to boom-bust oil prices will be more hedging
by firms exposed to oil price fluctuations. Oil producers and consumers from airline companies to truck fleets and perhaps one day motorists
will want to seek shelter from gyrating oil prices by "locking in" pump
prices. Hedging is no panacea, however. Although it can help a single
company protect against oil price volatility, it may not be practical or
available for oil companies investing in big projects with five-year horizons, when hedging is more difficult and costly.[42] Thus, hedging is a good
coping mechanism for consumers and producers with shorter investment
cycles—such as U.S. shale oil companies—but not as relevant for producers considering whether, for example to sink billions into high-cost,
risky investments in the Arctic or ultra-deep water. Moreover, although
hedging can protect individual firms exposed to price volatility, it cannot
abolish the reasons oil prices are volatile in the first place: inflexible supply
and demand for oil in the short run.

If refiners and producers come to expect recurring volatility, they may
seek shelter through integration. Recently, refiners have been able to profit
from wider margins while upstream producers have suffered in the glut.
(Of course, when crude oil prices next boom, the trend may reverse.)
Integrated companies fared better than pure-play producers during the
price bust that started in 2014. For an upstream producer, owning a refiner
can allow it to offset losses during crude oil price swoons while providing
a reliable supply source during booms. Saudi Arabia is already making
this adjustment to a higher volatility work by accelerating plans to build
and buy refineries at home and in Asia and North America.[43]

Oil exploration and production companies, especially shorter-cycle
shale companies and their investors, may have to adjust their business practices by husbanding capital at the high end of price cycles in

anticipation of price swoons. Companies and their lenders will adjust by resisting the urge to take on more debt and embark on high-cost projects at price peaks, conserving resources to ride out the next bust.

BUCKLE UP

For the first time in over eighty years we appear to have what many have craved and clamored for: a genuinely free, unmanaged market for crude oil, the world's most strategic commodity. No longer do we have a Standard Oil Trust, quota-setting state regulators, a Seven Sisters cartel, or a Saudi-dominated OPEC to interfere with the free interplay of supply and demand. The history of oil markets and oil's enduring features suggest a free market price is likely to be a volatile one. It is possible the unmanaged interplay global supply and demand will automatically yield stable prices, but it is more likely future oil trends will resemble those in the past and feature vast shifts, sustained imbalances, upheaval, and surprises. In the short term, oil is likely to range between shut-in costs—well below $30— and prices that induce demand slowdowns if not recessions—well above $100. Price gyrations through this range would destabilize not only our oil industry, but broader economic and financial sectors as well as geopolitics. Investors, officials, and thinkers will need to innovate and implement coping strategies to deal with the mixed blessing of an unmanaged oil market. Welcome back to boom-bust.

NOTES

INTRODUCTION: THE TEXAS PARADOX

1. WTI spot prices, EIA data.
2. Mabro, "Introduction," 4.
3. Guo and Kliesen, "Oil Price Volatility."
4. Tordo, Tracy, and Arfaa, "National Oil Companies and Value Creation."
5. Presentation to the CFTC, February 2016, 2015. http://www.cftc.gov/idc/groups/public/@ newsroom/documents/generic/eemaco22615_sieminski.pdf. Adam Sieminski, head of the U.S. Energy Information Administration (EIA) warned about the realistic possibility that Venezuela could see a supply interruption similar in scale to the national oil company strike of 2002–2003. Comment made at international Energy Forum, February 16, 2016; quote used with permission.
6. "Energy intensity has decreased over the last 22 years for the vast majority of countries. The drop has been larger for China, Russia and India than for the United States (US), the European Union (EU) or Japan. Several reasons explain this decline: faster growth of GDP than energy demand, the services sector having a growing share of the economy, energy efficiency programmes, etc." (IEA, "Energy Snapshot of the Week"). "From 1950 to 2011, energy intensity in the United States decreased by 58 percent per real dollar of GDP. Until the 1970s, energy intensity was falling relatively slowly, less than 1 percent per year" (EIA, "Today in Energy").
7. Smil, "Moore's Curse."
8. The magnitude of the rebound effect is in debate (Chan and Gillingham, "Microeconomic Theory of the Rebound Effect").
9. IEA, *World Energy Outlook 2015*, Table 3.3.
10. IEA, *World Energy Outlook 2011*, Table 3.3.
11. Smil, "Moore's Curse and the Great Energy Delusion."
12. Carrington, "Fossil Fuel Industry Must 'Implode.' "
13. Harvey, "World's Climate Pledges Not Yet Enough"; McKibben, "Falling Short on Climate in Paris."
14. IEA, "Global Energy Outlook."

1. AND THEN THERE WAS LIGHT: FROM CHAOS TO ORDER
IN THE KEROSENE ERA (1859-1911)

1. Bradley, *Oil, Gas, and Government*, vol. *II*, 1289–90.
2. Williamson and Daum, *American Petroleum Industry* 33–60. For more color on the early oil industry along Oil Creek, see McElwee, *Oil Creek*.
3. Nevins, *Rockefeller, vol. I*, 156–57. The first commercial refiner, Samuel M. Kier, set up shop in the late 1840s selling "carbon oil" to be used in lamps he designed. Based at first in Pittsburgh, city officials required him to move to a suburb for fear of an explosion.
4. Nevins, *Rockefeller, vol. I*, 153.
5. Ibid., 159–60.
6. Williamson and Daum, *American Petroleum Industry*, 72.
7. Ibid., 72–74.
8. Kuhn, "Ancient Chinese Drilling."
9. Williamson and Daum, *American Petroleum Industry*, 14–17.
10. Ibid., 74.
11. Nevins, *Rockefeller, vol. I*, 162.
12. This figure from Nevins, *Rockefeller, vol. I*, 147.
13. Nevins, *Rockefeller, vol. I.*, 165.
14. Nevins, *Rockefeller, vol. I*, 166–68. Speculators traded in drilling leases, equities of joint-stock companies formed to hold leases, and eventually forerunners of today's oil futures price contracts (Williamson and Daum, *American Petroleum Industry*, 121–27).
15. The first catastrophic explosion and fire at an oil well, in Rouseville, Pennsylvania, which claimed more than twenty drillers and onlookers, burned for three days before being extinguished (*Derrick's, vol. I*, 21). One especially unpleasant risk early oil drillers faced stemmed from the use of explosive "torpedoes" used to remove waxy paraffin that accumulated in the borehole and well bottom. Blasting the wax out of the well proved effective at stimulating more oil flow. One claimant to the idea of dropping explosive torpedoes was a Union officer during the 1862 battle of Fredericksburg, who witnessed cannon fire clear liquid out of a canal (Bradley, *Oil, Gas, and Government, vol. I*, 585). American historian and Rockefeller biographer Allan Nevins describes: "These cylindrical tubes, filled with fluid nitroglycerine, were carefully lowered into stubborn or partly exhausted well, and exploded by dropping a cast-iron weight upon them. The explosion shattered the rock walls at the bottom, and often brought a gush of oil and gas. The 'torpedo man,' travelling about the [Oil] Regions in a cart with his tubes and cans of nitroglycerine, was long a famous figure, usually given a wide berth. Occasionally a heavy jolt of his vehicle or slip of his foot set free the terrible explosive, and man, horse and cart disappeared in a blinding flash, with only a burst of smoke and a gaping hole to show what had occurred" (Nevins, *Rockefeller, vol. I*, 201).
16. See Williamson and Daum, *American Petroleum Industry*, Appendix E.

17. Pettengill, *Hot Oil*, 72.
18. Bradley, *Oil, Gas, and Government*, vol. I, 67.
19. Williamson and Daum, *American Petroleum Industry*, 161.
20. A barrel contained between forty and fifty gallons until 1872, when the forty-two–gallon barrel was standardized and remains in use today (*Derrick's, vol. I*, 704).
21. *Derrick's, vol. I*, 7.
22. Ibid., 711.
23. Hamilton, "Historical Oil Shocks," 3–45; Nevins, *Rockefeller, vol. I*, 181.
24. Chernow, *Titan*, 102.
25. Williamson and Daum, *American Petroleum Industry*, 344.
26. Maugeri, *The Age of Oil*, 6.
27. *Derrick's Hand-Book*, 15.
28. Nevins, *Rockefeller, vol. I*, 207.
29. Nevins, *Rockefeller, vol. I*, 309. Chernow, *Titan*, 149–150.
30. Kleinwächter, *Die Kartelle*, 245, cited in Schröter, "Cartels Revisited," 992.
31. Frankel, *Essentials of Petroleum*, 82–83. As the distinguished oil consultant Paul Frankel noted, their efforts to restrain supply "were not, in the first instance, designed with the deliberate purpose of charging customers extortionate prices, indeed, when things took a turn for the better they swiftly disappeared. They were nothing but emergency measures, applied only when the bottom had fallen out of the market."
32. *Pittsburgh Gazette*, "The Oil Trade—The Price and Supply to Be Regulated." November 28, 1861, 3.
33. *Derrick's, vol. I*, 24.
34. *Pittsburgh Gazette*, "The Oil Trade," 3.
35. *Derrick's, vol. I*, 711.
36. Ibid., 25.
37. Nevins, *Rockefeller, vol. I*, 173; Dolson, *The Great Oildorado*, 80.
38. Nevins, *Rockefeller, vol. I*, 278.
39. *Derrick's vol. I*, 132.
40. Frankel, *Essentials of Petroleum*, 70.
41. Nevins, *Rockefeller, vol. I*, 132.
42. *Derrick's, vol. I*, 19–20.
43. Chernow, *Titan*, 81.
44. The marketing segment of the oil industry included the bulk and retail storage, distribution, and selling of refined petroleum products like kerosene and later gasoline and diesel fuel.
45. Maugeri, *The Age of Oil*, 6.
46. Although capital was available for small-scale drillers, obtaining vast amounts to expand his extensive network of refineries, barrel-making shops, warehouses, shipping facilities, tank cars, and eventually pipelines bedeviled Rockefeller (Chernow, *Titan*, 104–5, 131–32).
47. Chernow, *Titan*, 130.
48. de Chazeau and Kahn, *Integration and Competition*, 76.

49. Chernow, *Titan*, 111, 114.

50. Emory and Van Metre, *Principles of Railroad Transportation*, 292. Pooling agreements between railroads were prohibited with the enactment of the Interstate Commerce Act of 1887.

51. Chernow, *Titan*, 114.

52. Ibid., 112–14.

53. Ibid., 116.

54. Williamson and Daum, *American Petroleum Industry* 303–8.

55. Chernow, *Titan*, 114–16. Railroad rebates were outlawed in 1887, but the practice did not cease until 1903.

56. Nevins, *Rockefeller, vol. I*, 311.

57. Ibid., 270.

58. Williamson and Daum, *American Petroleum Industry*, 353.

59. Scott's Pennsylvania Railroad would receive 45 percent of oil shipped by SIC members and the Erie and New York Central Railroads would receive 27.5 percent each (Chernow, *Titan*, 136).

60. Nevins, *Rockefeller, vol. I*, 321–22; Chernow, *Titan*, 135–36.

61. Nevins, *Rockefeller, vol. I*, 328.

62. Chernow, *Titan*, 135–36.

63. Ibid., 142.

64. Ibid., 138–39.

65. According to Williamson and Daum (*American Petroleum Industry*), the rejuvenated Petroleum Producers Association was renamed the Petroleum Producers' Union (351). Later in 1872, the name of the producers' cartel switched back to Petroleum Producers Association (358). To avoid confusion, this detail was omitted on purpose from the main text.

66. Nevins, *Rockefeller, vol. I*, 332–33; Williamson and Daum, *American Petroleum Industry*, 350.

67. Williamson and Daum, *American Petroleum Industry*, 351.

68. Chernow, *Titan*, 140–41.

69. Williamson and Daum, *American Petroleum Industry*, 356.

70. *Petroleum Centre Daily Record*, May 11, 1872, 2.

71. We've relied on Nevins's account of this episode.

72. Nevins, *Rockefeller, vol. I*, 415.

73. Ibid., 416.

74. Ibid., 415.

75. Ibid., 418.

76. Ibid., 421.

77. Ibid., 418–19.

78. *Petroleum Centre Daily Record*, October 26, 1872, 2.

79. *Petroleum Centre Daily Record,* "One Million Dollars Subscribed to the Petroleum Producers' Agency," November 6, 1872, 2.

80. Nevins, *Rockefeller, vol. I*, 423.

81. Typically, pipeline companies owned storage and would give drillers certificates for each 1,000 barrels of oil delivered. These certificates were then actively sold and traded,

becoming a proxy for spot and futures price contracts more common today. There were three types of certificates sold in early days: "On the spot" or just "spot" referred to oil for immediate delivery. "Regular" certificates were for delivery in ten days. And "Future" were for longer term delivery. There were many more speculators or traders who did not own or operate oil facilities than oil companies in the market. These "speculators" played a much bigger role in pegging oil prices than did Standard Oil. (Chernow, *Titan*, 259; Dolson, *The Great Oildorado*, 262.)

82. Nevins, *Rockefeller, vol. I*, 422.

83. Described in Nevins, *Rockefeller, vol. I*, 426.

84. Nevins, *Rockefeller, vol. I*, 427.

85. Ibid., 420–29.

86. *Titusville Herald*, "The Last and Only Alternative," January 14, 1873, 2.

87. Nevins, *Rockefeller, vol. I*, 429.

88. Ibid., 419.

89. Cited in Frankel, *Essentials of Petroleum*, 75.

90. Williamson and Daum, *American Petroleum Industry*, 384–85.

91. Ibid., 562–68.

92. Ibid., 564.

93. The ultimate disposition of inventories set aside by Standard Oil for the benefit of producers and workers is difficult to determine and obscure (Williamson and Daum, *American Petroleum Industry*, 567). Prices based on *The Derrick* and the Rapidan Group.

94. Williamson and Daum, *American Petroleum Industry*, 568.

95. Ibid., 549.

96. de Chazeau and Kahn, *Integration and Competition*, 429–30.

97. Author's calculation based on *The Derrick's Hand-Book of Petroleum*.

98. *The Derrick's, vol. II*, 825–26, and API, *Petroleum Facts and Figures*, 41.

99. Yergin, *The Prize*, 58–61.

100. Ibid., 71–72.

101. Maugeri, *The Age of Oil*, 12.

102. Yergin, *The Prize*, 124.

103. Standard Oil's headquarters was transferred from Cleveland to New York City in 1885.

104. Williamson and Daum, *American Petroleum Industry*, 466–70.

105. Nevins, *Rockefeller* (Abridgement), 301. The Abridgement of Nevins was published in 1959 and compiled by William Greenleaf.

106. Nevins, *Rockefeller, vol. II*, 708. Nevins credits Rockefeller with accomplishments that outweigh his bareknuckle but commonplace tactics: "[Standard's] elimination of waste and introduction of manifold economies; its application of the Frasch process [of desulfurizing oil], the Burton [refinery] cracking process, and the Van Dyke patents [for stimulating heavy crude production]; its standardization of products on a high level of quality; its development of valuable byproducts; its ready assistance to other industries, particularly in improving lubricants; its efficiency in home distribution, and its bold vigor in conquering world markets."

107. Nevins, *Rockefeller* (Abridgement), 301–4.
108. Chernow, *Titan*, 438.
109. Nevins, *Rockefeller* (Abridgement), 319; Nevins, *Rockefeller, vol. II*, 520.
110. Nevins, *Rockefeller* (Abridgement), 317.
111. Nevins, *Rockefeller* (Abridgement), 321. Several states also launched investigations of Standard Oil.
112. Nevins, *Rockefeller* (Abridgement), 323.
113. Chernow, *Titan*, 556.
114. Williamson and Daum, *American Petroleum Industry*, 429; de Chazeau and Kahn, *Integration and Competition*, 429–30; Bradley, *Oil, Gas, and Government*, 1089–94; Yergin, *The Prize*, 53–54.
115. Chernow, *Titan*, 259.
116. Tarbell, *History of Standard Oil, vol. 1*, 236.
117. Chernow, *Titan*, 259.
118. Williamson and Daum, *American Petroleum Industry*, 728.
119. Writing in 1959, Williamson and Daum (*American Petroleum Industry*) noted "few products associated with America have had so extensive an influence as kerosene on the daily living habits of so large a proportion of the world's population" (725).
120. Chernow, *Titan*, 258.
121. Ibid., 258.
122. Ibid., 257.
123. Ibid., 258.

2. NO ROCKEFELLER, NO PEACE: BOOM-BUST RETURNS

1. Williamson and Daum, *American Petroleum Industry*, 682.
2. Mexico's production more than quadrupled from 1911 to 1919, when it equaled 14 percent of U.S. production (Williamson et al., *American Petroleum Industry*, Table 2:6, 29).
3. Williamson et al., *American Petroleum Industry*, 182.
4. Maugeri, *The Age of Oil*, 22
5. Williamson et al., *American Petroleum Industry*, 183.
6. American Petroleum Institute, *Petroleum Facts and Figures* (1928), 171. U.S. railroads converted from coal to fuel oil between 1899 and 1920, attracted to oil's lower labor costs and more complete combustion (Nash, *United States Oil Policy*, 5).
7. Rotary drilling operated on the principle of boring, used in water wells. A drill bit was attached to the end of a pipe through which water or drilling fluids were forced under pressure. The fluids passed through the drill bit, forcing disturbed soil back up the well between the pipe and wall of the shaft to the surface. Pressure strengthened the well walls, preventing caving. The technique conferred large operational benefits on drillers, including the ability to reach greater depths and increasing speed (Williamson et al., *American Petroleum Industry*, 29–30).

8. API. *Petroleum Facts and Figures* (1959), 40; Williamson et al., *American Petroleum Industry*, Table 2:6, 29.

9. de Chazeau and Kahn, *Integration and Competition*, 102.

10. Logan, *Stabilization of the Oil Industry*, 1.

11. Williamson and Daum, *American Petroleum Industry*, 163.

12. Bradley, *Oil, Gas, and Government*, vol. II, 1290.

13. Nash, *United States Oil Policy*, 17.

14. Logan, *Stabilization of the Oil Industry*, 3.

15. Williamson and Daum, *American Petroleum Industry*, 376.

16. *Derrick's*, vol. I, 1898, reprinted 2006, 14.

17. Bradley, *Oil, Gas, and Government*, vol. I, 82. The exception of rules aimed at preventing flaring of natural gas that emerged from oil wells as a byproduct, called "casinghead gas." Such regulation was intended to prevent the inferior use of a scarce natural resource and to promote the use of natural gas in industrial growth.

18. Nash, *United States Oil Policy*, 8–9.

19. Ibid., 15–16.

20. Bradley, *Oil, Gas, and Government*, vol. I, 85.

21. Marshall and Meyers, *Legal Planning*.

22. Nash, *United States Oil Policy*, 16.

23. Bradley, *Oil, Gas, and Government*, vol. I, 86.

24. Bradley, *Oil, Gas and Government*, vol. I, 85, 87, 89–90.

25. Williamson et al., *The American Petroleum Industry*, 326.

26. Childs, *The Texas Railroad Commission*, 152.

27. History of the Railroad Commission 1866–1939. Also, Bradley, *Oil, Gas, and Government*, vol. I, 86.

28. Ibid., 157.

29. Ibid.

30. History of the Railroad Commission 1866–1939. Also, Bradley, *Oil, Gas, and Government*, vol. I, 86.

31. Childs, *Texas Railroad Commission*, 158.

32. Ibid., 159.

33. Frankel, *Essentials of Petroleum*, 3.

34. Frey and Ide, eds. *History of the Petroleum Administration for War 1941–1945*, 8.

35. Nash, *United States Oil Policy*, 29–38.

36. Ibid., 26.

37. Williamson et al., *American Petroleum Industry*, 183.

38. Nordhauser, "Origins of Federal Oil Regulation," 6; see also de Chazeau and Kahn, *Integration and Competition*, 127.

39. *Pittsburgh Press*, January 2, 1917, 28.

40. *Independence (Kans.) Daily Reporter*, January 2, 1917, 4.

41. *Pittsburgh Post-Gazette*, January 1, 1918, 19.

42. *Wall Street Journal,* August 13, 1919, 2, nominal prices.

43. *Call Leader* (Elwood, Ind.), March 21, 1916, 3.

44. The FTC reported gasoline demand rose 38 percent over the prior year whereas production rose by 31 percent.

45. Federal Trade Commission, *Price of Gasoline in 1915,* 159.

46. *Asheville (N.C.) Citizen-Times*, March 5, 1916, 5.

47. *Alexandria (Ind.) Times-Tribune,* July 18, 1918, 1; *Oshkosh (Wisc.) Daily Northwestern,* January 21, 1918, 7.

48. *Oregon Daily Journal,* July 29, 1920, 1.

49. *Wellington (Kans.) Daily News,* August 26, 1920, 3.

50. *Morning Tulsa (Okla.) Daily World,* June 2, 1920, 1.

51. *The Oregon Daily Journal,* August 8, 1920, 27.

52. Olmstead and Rhode, "Rationing without Government."

53. *Sandusky (Ohio) Star-Journal,* April 10, 1920, 14.

54. Federal Trade Commission, *International Petroleum Cartel,* 37–45; "Conservation Is Keynote of Oil Industry Today," *Wall Street Journal,* February 21, 1920, 3.

55. Ibid.

56. Nash, *United States Oil Policy,* 18.

57. Nash, *United States Oil Policy,* 44–45; *New York Times.* "Destroyers Get Oil Supply after Threat to Commandeer It." July 27, 1920.

58. de Chazeau and Kahn, *Integration and Competition,* 137. de Chazeau and Kahn cite Bureau of Mines data showing net national production increased from 301 mb (825 kb/d) in 1916 to 443 mb in 1920 (1.2 mb/d), an increase of 45 percent.

59. Nordhauser "Origins of Federal Oil Regulation," 8–9.

60. Rapidan Group price series.

61. Bradley, *Oil, Gas, and Government, vol. I,* 88. "A great movement often originates largely through accident. It is evident that the enforcement of conservation statutes were originally urged by most oil men, and attempted by most public officials, as a smoke screen for achieving stabilization, but with the result that the industry finally awoke to the realization that the conservation policies were, for themselves alone, highly desired ends." Robert Hardwicke, "Legal History of Proration of Oil in Texas," Proceedings, Texas Bar Association (October 1937): 99, cited in Bradley, *Oil, Gas, and Government, vol. I,* 88.

62. Bradley, *Oil, Gas, and Government, vol. I,* 89.

63. "State laws should require . . . production to be supervised by oil districts staffed by the various land owners in the area. Doherty's plan would have allowed no drilling in a newly discovered field until an oil district had been formed by the majority acreage . . . oil districts would have scientifically planned the location of wells so as to develop a field as a unit with the greatest economy. Under this procedure, royalties from the oil produced in the whole area would have been paid to the land owner(s) and apportioned . . . on the basis of probable amount of oil under his land before the reservoir was disturbed. . . ." Nordhauser, "Origins of Federal Oil Regulation," 12. See also Blair, *The Control of Oil,* 155–56.

64. Nordhauser, *The Quest for Stability*, 10–11.

65. de Chazeau and Kahn, *Integration and Competition*, 134.

66. "The small producer, with a lucky strike, can always hope to improve his market share; it may be in the interests of all to stabilize, but there will always be a maverick to start the competitive snowball. But the big firm, and especially the big vertically integrated firm, has heavy investments elsewhere which cry out for the assurance of continued supplies over time, investments which make it certain that he cannot hope to drive his rivals, similarly circumstanced, from the market. The big firm has more at stake and that larger stake makes it more conscious of the need and more willing to shoulder the burden of doing something to stabilize crude oil markets. . . . There was no other alternative than to seek the cooperation of the state, when conditions in the free market become intolerable." De Chazeau and Kahn, *Integration and Competition*, 145.

67. de Chazeau and Kahn, *Integration and Competition*, 145. Nordhauser, *The Quest for Stability*, 10.

68. Federal Oil Conservation Board, *Report to the President*, 1–2

69. Cited in Nordhauser, "Origins of Federal Oil Regulation," 19.

70. Report of the Federal Oil Conservation Board, September 1926, 2.

71. Watkins, *Oil: Stabilization or Conservation?*, 42.

3. WHY ARE OIL PRICES PRONE TO BOOM-BUST CYCLES?

1. Excluding other options to consumption, storage, and waste.

2. We will discuss ethanol, the closest rival to oil, later.

3. Frankel, *Essentials of Petroleum*, 55.

4. Comment to an energy roundtable in Washington, D.C., on September 9, 2014; used with permission.

5. Hamilton, "Understanding Crude Oil Prices"; see also Hamilton, "Causes and Consequences of the Oil Shock of 2007–2008," National Bureau of Economic Research Working Paper 15002 (2009), in which he notes that while price elasticities are difficult to measure and debatable, −0.06 appeared to be consistent with the run-up before the peak in 2008 (13–14). For a discussion of estimates of short-term estimates of crude oil demand, see also Difiglio, "Oil, Economic Growth," 49.

6. Crude demand excludes other inputs such as natural gas liquids and biofuels.

7. Anderson et al., *Universal Tuition Tax Credit*, 60.

8. Price elasticity of demand = change in quantity demanded divided by change in price. If a 1 percent increase in price causes oil consumption to fall by 0.06 percent, then to cut consumption by 5 percent prices must rise by 83 percent (0.05/0.83=0.06), whereas for fresh tomatoes with a price elasticity of −4.6, prices would rise by 1 percent (0.05/0.01=0.046).

9. Hamilton, " Understanding Crude Oil Prices," 15–16. Also, in Table 3 Hamilton cites Dahl (1993) and Cooper (2003) for short- and long-run crude oil demand price elasticities.

10. Hamilton, "Understanding Crude Oil Prices," 17. Hamilton cited Hughes, Knittel, and Sperling (2008) for the lower-demand elasticity findings relative to the early 1980s.

11. Demands for goods that account for a lower percentage of consumer income tend to be inelastic with regard to price. See Hughes, Knittel, and Sperling (2008), Section 4.

12. Hamilton, *Causes and Consequences*, 1.

13. Hamilton, "Understanding Crude Oil Prices," 18. See also Table 3 for other academic estimates.

14. Gately and Huntington, "Asymmetric Effects."

15. Tim Reid and Alister Bull, "Obama 2012 Team Fears Voter Backlash on Gas Prices." Reuters, April 5, 2011.

16. Yanagisawa, *Impact of Rising Oil Prices*, 2. Yanagisawa cites estimates made in 2011 by Deutsche Bank, Morgan Stanley, and others. In addition, a report in 2012 found "Analysts generally see the $120–130 level as a price that would prompt consumer and corporate to cut back on spending sharply, and hurt the recovery and growth of key economic sectors. A recent Reuters survey of 20 equity strategists put $125 a barrel as the point economy and stock markets could start to suffer" (EconMatters, "Another Oil Price Shock?").

17. IEA, *Impact of High Oil Prices*.

18. Smith, "World Oil," 150. This estimate is from the Organisation for Economic Co-operation and Development. Smith noted that IEA and System Sciences Inc. use an even more inelastic estimate—0.02 in the short run and 0.10 in the long run.

19. Frankel, *Essentials of Petroleum*, 33.

20. Ibid., 17, 37, and de Chazeau and Kahn, *Integration and Competition*, 67, 71. As production techniques have expanded beyond primary drive (when oil is pushed to the surface naturally by underground pressure) to secondary recovery (stimulating oil flow by injecting water and gas after natural pressure has dissipated), variable costs have increased, making output somewhat more sensitive to price. But even so, secondary recovery often requires new fixed capital investment in equipment that leaves fixed, sunk costs dominant.

    High fixed, low-variable costs are not unique to oil. Steel exhibits the same characteristics, although it has no comparison to the cheap and quick sources of new supply coming from new oil wells.

21. Another factor requiring all-out drilling of successful finds was the need to cover costs of dry holes. As noted above, finding commercially viable sources of oil is not cheap or easy. Unlike coal or wheat, the location of oil was uncertain. Although the industry's technological ability to find oil in the crust has vastly improved, throughout most of the history many more dry wells were found than gushers. Those dry wells cost money and had to be covered by the successful producing ones.

22. Cookenboo, "Crude Oil Pipelines," 30, cited in de Chazeau and Kahn, *Integration and Competition*, 69.

23. Crude oil varies considerably in terms of weight, sulfur content, and other characteristics that determine what types of refined products it yields when run through refinery equipment.

24. In a personal communication, former senior IEA official David Fyfe, Head of Market Research and Analysis for Gunvor, noted that builders, or full-cost buyers, of refineries are constrained to operate close to maximum throughput, whereas those purchasing assets at distressed prices can operate in a more flexible manner.

25. Smith, "World Oil," 154–55.

26. Petroff and Yellin, "What It Costs To Produce Oil," CNN Money. Petroff and Yellin cite figures from Rystad Energy Cubicle as of November 23, 2015.

27. Nysveen and Wei, "Offshore vs. Shale." Nysveen and Wei are a senior partner and head of analysis and an analyst at Rystad Energy, respectively.

28. Barden, "United Kingdom Increases Oil Production."

29. Penrose, *The Large International Firm*, 46–47.

30. de Chazeau and Kahn, *Integration and Competition*, 75. See also a statement by W. S. Farish, past president of Standard Oil Company (New Jersey) cited in Frankel, *Essentials of Petroleum*, 76. "Integration is the uniting into one business of several of the stages through which a material passes before it reaches the ultimate consumer. The conditions under which integration is desirable are: (1) large volume of business in a single commodity group; (2) highly specialized production, manufacturing, transportation and distribution techniques; and (3) substantial advantages (at some stages) in large-scale operation. These conditions characterize the petroleum industry, and it follows therefore that the relations between any one of the stages of the industry and the other next to it are peculiarly close. The refiner needs to be assured of his market. The marketer needs to be assured of his supply. Both need a steady flow of products for efficient operation. Neither is interested in another than the one major product and its related group of byproducts. Neither can transfer his specialized equipment to the handling of some different product. There is a high degree of mutual interdependence imposed by the facts." There is a healthy debate over whether integration was intrinsically inevitable or superior to nonintegration as a means to manage uncertainty, security of supply, and risks to sector and industry-wide instability; see Penrose, *The Large International Firm*, 47–50.

4. THE TEXAS ERA OF PRICE STABILITY: U.S. SUPPLY CONTROLS AND INTERNATIONAL CARTELIZATION (1934–1972)

1. Then called Standard Oil of New York and also known as Socony, which renamed itself Mobil in 1966 and in 1999 was taken over by Exxon, the successor of Standard Oil of New Jersey.

2. API, *Petroleum Facts and Figures* (1959), 4.

3. Nordhauser, *The Quest for Stability*, 28.

4. API, *Petroleum Facts and Figures* (1959), 41.

5. Weaver, Bobby D. "Greater Seminole Field," Encyclopedia of Oklahoma History and Culture, www.okhistory.org (accessed August 6, 2016).

6. Nordhauser, *The Quest for Stability*, 27.

7. Nordhauser, "Origins of Federal Oil Regulation," 68.

8. Nordhauser, *The Quest for Stability*, 27.

9. For this paragraph, including the "drastic step" quote, I relied on Williamson et al., *The American Petroleum Industry*, 322–26, and on Bradley, *Oil, Gas, and Government*, vol. I, 88. The OCC had issued minor, isolated quotas for smaller fields in 1915, 1921, and 1923, but the 1927 Seminole order was the first major one and expected to be "continuous." W. P. Z. German, "Legal History of Conservation of Oil and Gas in Oklahoma," 149–51, cited in Bradley, *Oil, Gas, and Government*, vol. I, 88.

10. Bradley, *Oil, Gas, and Government*, vol. I, 89. For the 2.75 to 40 percent estimate Bradley cited W. P. Z. German, "Legal History of Conservation of Oil and Gas in Oklahoma," 158, 184.

11. This paragraph relies on Bradley, *Oil, Gas, and Government*, vol. I, 89–90.

12. Roscoe, "Oklahoma Oil Fields Under Martial Law."

13. "Says Oil Fields Will Stay Shut," *Indianapolis Star*, August 6, 1931, 19.

14. Ruth Knowles, *The Greatest Gamblers* (New York: McGraw-Hill, 1959), 265. Cited in Bradley, *Oil, Gas, and Government*, vol. I. Texas producers cheekily offered to supply shuttered Oklahoma refineries with cheap oil, though they were practically hampered by lack of pipelines.

15. "Oklahoma Oil Fields Reopen Sunday Morning," *Middletown Times Herald*, October 9, 1931; "'Alfalfa Bill' Murray Withdraws His Soldiers, *Harrisonburg Telegraph*, October 10, 1931, 13.

16. "'Alfalfa Bill' Murray Withdraws His Soldiers," *Harrisonburg Telegraph*, October 10, 1931, 13.

17. Associated Press, "Murray Employs Soldiers to Halt Capital Drilling." *Denton Record Chronicle*, May 6, 1932.

18. Associated Press, "Murray Away; Burns Lifts Martial Law." *Hutchinson News*, May 20, 1932, 1.

19. Associated Press, "Martial Law Resumed in the Oklahoma Oil Field." *Hutchinson News*, May 27, 1932.

20. Associated Press, "Oil Conflict Flares Anew in Oklahoma." *Bend (Ore.) Bulletin*, September 22, 1932.

21. Bradley, *Oil, Gas, and Government*, vol. I, 87–91.

22. API, *Petroleum Facts and Figures* (1959).

23. *History of the Railroad Commission 1866–1939*.

24. There are three instances of private voluntary output restraints that had been widely described as successes. There were Salt Creek in Wyoming, Yates in Texas, and Dominguez in California. However, as Watkins noted, they were too small to affect the national oil market and were explained by the exceptionally small number of closely knit producers or the presence of the federal government as the principal lessor in certain districts (Watkins, *Oil: Stabilization or Conservation?* 43–44, footnote 10).

25. Childs, *Texas Railroad Commission*, 166.

26. Bradley, *Oil, Gas, and Government, vol. I*, 92. An exchange at a March 1931 TRC hearing illustrated the widespread view that public pretensions that quotas were aimed at physical and not economic waste (i.e., fixing prices). The following comes from a colloquy at the hearing between a pro-quota official from the Oil States Advisory Committee (established by oil states in February 1931 to coordinate efforts to control production, including lobbying the federal government for cooperation in combating "over-production, distress prices, and uneconomical uses" of oil) named Robert Penn and Dan Moody, a former Texas governor and attorney representing parties opposed to quota:

   Mr. Penn testified that conservation was the object of the Oil States Advisory Committee and "price was not mentioned and was not the actuating influence."

   Mr. Moody asked, "Why was price not discussed?"

   And Mr. Penn replied, "Because our attorneys told us we could be concerned only with conservation."

   "Are you not interested in prices?" asked Mr. Moody.

   "Yes," answered Mr. Penn, "all oil men are. We discussed prices as individuals. Unfortunately, we cannot consider price in fixing proration [quotas]."

   (Marshall and Meyers, *Legal Planning*, 710–11).

27. White, Joe L. White "Columbus Marion "Dad" Joiner and the East Texas Oil Boom," 1968, 27.

28. Yergin, *The Prize*, 247.

29. API, *Petroleum Facts and Figures* (1959), 41.

30. Nordhauser, *The Quest for Stability*, 69.

31. "Plans to Shut in West Texas Wells Dropped," *El Paso Herald-Post*, July 20, 1931; ten cent per barrel price also mentioned by Governor Ross Sterling in "Texas Governor Called in Senate Committee Probe, Says Oil Industry in Woeful Condition due to Overproduction," *Corsicana Semi-Weekly Light*, Corsicana, Texas, July 24, 1931, 13. Associated Press, "Oklahoma Oil Price Soar."

32. *Taylor* (Tex.) *Daily Press*, July 2, 1931.

33. Childs, *Texas Railroad Commission*, 204.

34. Prindle, *Petroleum Politics*, 29–30, emphasis added.

35. Texas Office of the Governor, *Proclamation of Martial Law*, 1931.

36. Rundell, *Early Texas Oil*, 227. Governor Sterling and another high-ranking military officer also had worked for major Texas oil firms (Childs, *Texas Railroad Commission*, 210).

37. "East Texas Flush Field Wells Close," *Daily Independent* (Murphysboro, Ill.), August 17, 1931. See also *Brownsfield Herald*, August 17, 1931, p. 16.

38. "Troops Guard Texas Oil Fields," *Bryan Daily Eagle*, August 22, 1931, 2.

39. Childs, *The Texas Railroad Commission*, 211. Childs cites the governor's office for the prices.

40. Bradley, *Oil, Gas, and Government, vol. I*, 91–94.

41. Blair, *Control of Oil*, 161.

42. Bradley, *Oil, Gas, and Government, vol. I*, 638.

43. Marshall and Meyers, *Legal Planning*, 704.

44. Bradley, *Oil, Gas, and Government, vol. I*, 638, 643–44.

45. Rundell, *Early Texas Oil*, 226.

46. Bradley, *Oil, Gas, and Government, vol. I*, 639, asterisk footnote; Williamson and Adreano, *American Petroleum Industry*, 549.

47. Bradley, *Oil, Gas, and Government, vol. I*, 640.

48. Ibid., 640–641.

49. Ibid., 101.

50. Williamson and Daum, *American Petroleum Industry*, 549.

51. Our Documents Initiative, "National Industrial Recovery Act."

52. Section 9(c). Bradley, *Oil, Gas, and Government, vol. I*, 98, 641.

53. Bradley, *Oil, Gas, and Government, vol. I*, 642.

54. Ibid., 642–43.

55. Ibid., 643; cites OGJ, December 14, 1933, R-10 in footnote 77. The OGJ mention is based on Ruth Sheldon Knowles, *The Greatest Gamblers* (New York: McGraw-Hill, 1959), 265.

56. Rundell, *Early Texas Oil*, 228.

57. Bradley, *Oil, Gas, and Government, vol. I*, 321.

58. Williamson and Daum, *American Petroleum Industry*, 550.

59. Ibid., 554.

60. Bradley, *Oil, Gas, and Government, vol. I*, 147.

61. Ibid., 148–57. The MER stood for the Maximum Efficient Rate, based on engineering and geological determinations that oil flow could reach without losing recoverable reserves. The MER was not a maximum capacity but instead the highest rate possible without causing damage to fields and thereby reducing total recovery of oil underground. MER was sort of a "safe operating speed" that could be and was exceeded.

    A third type of maximum limit was a restriction on the amount of natural gas that could be produced with oil, called the Gas-Oil Ratio.

62. Bradley, *Oil, Gas, and Government, vol. I*, 162.

63. Lovejoy and Homan, *Economic Aspects*, 37. For an overview of how state quotas were implemented, see chapter 6, 127–84.

64. Bradley, *Oil, Gas, and Government, vol. I*, 171. Writing in 1948, Eugene Rostow dismissed the notion that quotas contributed to conservation. "In the first place," Rostow noted, "the basic and dominant purpose of our present methods of production control is to limit production to what the Bureau of Mines estimate will be market demand, *at a price*." Rostow, *A National Policy*, 34–35.

65. Lovejoy and Homan, *Economic Aspects*, 140–41. Texas typically set quotas 12 percent above the target production rate due to historical experience indicating production interruptions and failure of some wells to meet their quotas caused actual supply to fall below scheduled production (Lovejoy and Homan. *Economic Aspects*, 138–39).

66. Lovejoy and Homan, *Economic Aspects*, 139.

67. Prindle, *Petroleum Politics*, 7.

68. The Commission also helped small producers by pressuring pipeline companies to connect to remote wells and allowing narrow well spacing (Prindle, *Petroleum Politics*, 41, 132).

69. Downey, *Oil 101*, 128–34.

70. Bradley, *Oil, Gas, and Government, vol. I*, 166.

71. Ibid., 162–91.

72. Prindle, *Petroleum Politics*, 73.

73. Quoted in Bradley, *Oil, Gas, and Government, vol. I*, 170.

74. Prindle, *Petroleum Politics*, 132.

75. Bradley, *Oil, Gas, and Government, vol. I*, 171.

76. In addition to compliance with quotas, drillers may shut in a well's production due to lack of equipment or economic reasons.

77. Bradley, *Oil, Gas, and Government, vol. I*, 175–76.

78. de Chazeau and Kahn, *Integration and Competition*, 124.

79. Williamson and Daum, *American Petroleum Industry*, 558–59; Bradley, *Oil, Gas, and Government, vol. II*, 1948.

80. Bradley, *Oil, Gas, and Government, vol. I*, 167–68. Direct quotes from Bradley on 167.

81. Initially, U.S. producers were mainly preoccupied with the threat of large imports from nearby Mexico, where major discoveries in 1910 established the country as a large producer and exporter, and Venezuela, where production rose from zero in 1916 to 290,000 b/d by 1928 (API, *Petroleum Facts and Figures* [1959], 433).

82. Bradley, *Oil, Gas, and Government, vol. I*, 718–19.

83. Federal Trade Commission, *International Petroleum Cartel*, 54.

84. Ibid., 197–98.

85. Ibid., 200.

86. Yergin, *The Prize*, 261.

87. Federal Trade Commission, *International Petroleum Cartel*, 199–200.

88. Yergin, *The Prize*, 281.

89. Gulf had to surrender its lease in Bahrain when it became subject to the Red Line Agreement and part of the Iraq Petroleum Company. Socal took it over from Gulf in 1934.

90. Parra, *Oil Politics*, 9.

91. Federal Trade Commission, *International Petroleum Cartel*, 23. Proved oil reserves are reserves that are economical to produce at prevailing prices and with technology.

92. Federal Trade Commission, *International Petroleum Cartel*, 25–28.

93. Skeet, OPEC, 5; Parra, *Oil Politics*, 69–73.

94. Parra, *Oil Politics*, 72.

95. These intra-company transfer prices did not reflect a market price and were used to calculate taxes. Companies shifted profits from higher to lower tax jurisdictions (Fattouh, "Origins and Evolution," 43).

96. In the industry's parlance, prices quoted in receiving ports are called "CIF," which stands for cost, insurance, freight. Prices quoted at shipping terminals are called "FOB," which stands for free on board.

97. Adelman, *World Petroleum Market*, 172.

98. "The United States was the early supplier of crude oil and oil products to Europe and to the world; it is not at all surprising that in those days prices in this country should govern those in foreign lands. Gulf Coast ports were the natural centers for bulk transfers to ocean-going

tankers from pipelines tapping dominant fields in Texas and the midcontinent. It was here too that growth of large refineries, drawing on a vast oil hinterland and serving worldwide markets, was favored" (de Chazeau and Kahn, *Integration and Competition*, 211).

99. "Gulf-plus" is most commonly used in the literature to describe the majors' price formula. However, I will use "Texas-plus" to avoid confusing with prices later "posted" in the Persian Gulf. For detail on how the Seven Sisters' basing price system worked, also referred to as Gulf-Plus or Texas-Plus, I relied on an unpublished dissertation by Ramón Espinasa as well as the Federal Trade Commission's *International Petroleum Cartel*, 349–75, and Parra's *Oil Politics*, 57–58.

100. *Sea-Distances.*

101. An important feature of pricing structure, although not central to our discussion here, is that majors' profits stemmed largely on the sale of refined products instead of crude. The bulk of internationally traded crude oil was moved between functionally distinct but closely affiliated if not directly controlled affiliate companies. Profitability of the integrated companies as a whole depended mainly on refined product sales to consumers (Federal Trade Commission, *International Petroleum Cartel*, 370).

102. Yergin, *The Prize*, 371–79.

103. Texas State Historical Association, "Oil and Gas Industry."

104. See note 61 on the definition of potential production, the Maximum Efficient Rate or MER.

105. Frey and Ide, *Petroleum Administration for War*, 173.

106. "The bringing about of a million-barrel-a-day increase in output *and maintaining the productive capacity* was the number one victory in the field of crude-oil production" (Frey and Ide, *Petroleum Administration for War*, 169); emphasis added.

107. Frey and Ide, *Petroleum Administration for War*, 444.

108. Ibid., 444–45.

109. Yergin, *The Prize*, 401.

110. Yergin, *The Prize*, 399–409; Frey and Ide, *Petroleum Administration for War*, 281.

111. In 1943 the British Navy insisted the majors establish a second "basing point" in the Persian Gulf for refined products, and the U.S. Navy did the same for crude and products in 1945. Under the dual basing point system, Persian Gulf base prices were the same as those in Texas and the point of "equalization" where supplies from the United States and Persian Gulf were delivered at equal prices became the mid-Mediterranean. Shipments originating from Texas or Persian Gulf beyond that point would incur "phantom freight" charges. In 1947, the "equalization point" shifted to London and in 1949 to New York, effectively eliminating "phantom freight" charges on Persian Gulf crude moving to Western Europe and the United States (Federal Trade Commission. *International Petroleum Cartel*, 374–75).

112. Federal Trade Commission, *International Petroleum Cartel*, 356–57.

113. BP refused to grant fifty-fifty to Iran. Refusal sparked nationalization of BP's assets in 1951 followed by the imposition of sanctions and a Western embargo that caused Iran's production to plummet from 650,000 b/d in 1950 to 20,000 b/d in 1953, and to slash Tehran's oil

revenues from $400 million to less than $2 million. Fearing communist encroachment, the United States agreed to help the United Kingdom, and backed a coup against Iranian Prime Minister Mohammed Mossadegh in August 1953. Ultimately, BP lost its monopoly over the concession as U.S. companies entered the country (Maugeri, *The Age of Oil*, 63–70).

114. Fattouh, "Origins and Evolution," 44.

115. DeGolyer and MacNaughton, *Twentieth Century Petroleum Statistics*, 61.

116. Frank, *Crude Oil Prices*, 29.

117. Bradley, *Oil, Gas, and Government*, vol. II, 1436–39.

118. Blair, *Control of Oil*, 166.

119. Frank, *Crude Oil Prices*, 64–65; de Chazeau and Kahn, *Integration and Competition*, 192–93.

120. United Press, "Boost in Production of Oil," *Medford Mail Tribune*, September 18, 1956, 1.

121. "Oil Allowable Cut Despite Suez Crisis," *Valley Morning Star* (Harlingen, Tex.: September 21, 1956, 15.

122. Hamilton, "Historical Oil Shocks," 11.

123. Associated Press, "16-Day Allowable Set for December," *Abilene Reporter-News*, November 15, 1956, 1; Associated Press, "Oil Output Reaches New Record Level,"*Odessa American*, February 24, 1957, 30.

124. *Waco* (Tex.) *Tribune-Herald*, November 25, 1956, 10.

125. *Albuquerque Journal*, "Oil and Gas Mining in New Mexico," Sunday, December 2, 1956, 38.

126. Yergin, *The Prize*, 492.

127. "Culberson 'Not Meddling' in England's Oil Affairs," *Abilene Reporter-News*, February 15, 1957, 30.

128. "Culberson Tells Britons to Quit Meddling in Oil," *Corsicana (Tex.) Daily Sun*, February 15, 1957, 1.

129. "Govt. May Act on Oil," *Oil City (Pa.) Derrick*, February 7, 1957, 1.

130. "Texas OKs Boost in Oil Output," *Circleville (Ohio) Herald*, February 20, 1957, 1.

131. Yergin, *The Prize*, 555–57.

132. Ibid., 557.

133. Blair, *Control of Oil*, 166.

134. Bradley, *Oil, Gas, and Government*, vol. I, 724.

135. Adelman, *Genie*, 47.

136. "Oil Production," *Corpus Christi Times*, June 21, 1956, 16.

137. Bradley, *Oil, Gas, and Government*, vol. I, 728–35.

138. Ibid., 731.

139. Ibid., 736–50. In addition to the exemption on Mexican and Canadian imports underwent other exemptions and revisions. For example, the West Coast had more lenient import quotas, likely due to its relative isolation from network of refineries, fields, pipelines, and ports in the rest of the country. As a result of exemptions and other factors, actual imports exceeded official targets.

140. BP, "Statistical Review."

141. Parra, *Oil Politics*, Fattouh, *Anatomy*, 14–15.

142. Parra, *Oil Politics*, 97–98.

143. Maugeri, *The Age of Oil*, 84.

144. Heard, "Railroad Commission Warns of Oil Troubles Ahead," *San Antonio Express*, August 29, 1970, 78.

145. "Texas Planning Full-scale Oil Production,"*El Dorado Times*, March 17, 1972, 1.

146. Nancy Heard, "Texas Oilwells Attaining Peak Output," *San Antonio Express*, March 16, 1972, 30.

147. Maugeri, *The Age of Oil*, 77.

148. Yergin, *The Prize*, 27.

149. Ibid., 541.

150. DeGolyer and MacNaughton, *Twentieth Century Petroleum Statistics*, 108.

151. Yergin, *The Prize*, 543–46.

152. Reserves (Federal Trade Commission. *International Petroleum Cartel*, Table 1, Table 8, 5–6, 23).

153. Data for 1950 (Federal Trade Commission. *International Petroleum Cartel*, Table 10, 25).

154. Hamilton, "Historical Causes of Postwar Oil Shocks," 99; Hamilton, "Historical Oil Shocks," 9.

155. Maugeri, 2006, 48.

156. "The Commission had the companies' demand forecasts for the next month, and they also had excellent inventory data, with a lag of only about a week or two. When stocks appeared to be accumulating, production would be cut back. If inventories appeared to be falling below the amount needed to support current production, production quotas [quotas] would be increased. Everybody knew that stability was the Commission's object, and therefore, nobody worried about small changes up or down" (Adelman, *Economics of Oil Supply*, 429–30).

157. de Chazeau and Kahn, *Integration and Competition*, 151.

158. Frankel, *Essentials of Petroleum*, 67.

159. de Chazeau and Kahn, *Integration and Competition*, 74.

160. Williamson and Daum, *American Petroleum Industry*, 554. See also Hamilton, "Historical Oil Shocks," 8.

161. In *Integration and Competition*, de Chazeau and Kahn conceded that post-1934 price stability "might to some extent have come to pass in a maturing domestic industry, in the absence of prorationing [quotas]" but concluded "prorationing [quotas are] is the primary reason for the vastly reduced number of crude oil price changes since 1933, as well as for the timing of those that occurred" (150–51).

162. Cited in Prindle, *Petroleum Politics*, 126.

163. Zimmermann, *Conservation in the Production of Petroleum*, 111.

164. Ibid., 113.

165. Blair, *Control of Oil*, 165.

166. Prindle, *Petroleum Politics*, 126.

167. Bradley, *Oil, Gas, and Government*, vol. *I*, 129. I have only briefly and partly described Blair's critique, which is developed in Chapter 3 of his cited work. Confronted with rampant overproduction, the domestic oil industry, former federal antitrust official Blair

noted in 1976, "probably more than any other field of business activity, has been remarkably successful in inducing the state to shore up the private means of control with the mandatory powers of government" (Blair, *Control of Oil*, 152).

168. Adelman, *Genie*, 42.

169. The FTC report contains a wealth of historical information and data on the operations of the Seven Sisters that in 1949 controlled 65 percent of the world's oil reserves and 80 percent of production excluding the United States.

170. Maugeri, *The Age of Oil*, 72.

171. Federal Trade Commission, *International Petroleum Cartel*, 376.

172. Ibid., 376–77.

5. THE BIRTH OF OPEC: 1960–1969

1. Yergin, *The Prize*, 464; Sampson, *Seven Sisters*, 121.

2. The new shares were 40 percent for BP; 14 percent for Shell; 7 percent each for Exxon, Mobil, SoCal, Texaco, and Gulf; 6 percent for Compagnie Française Pétrole; and 5 percent for a handful of independent U.S. oil companies organized into an entity called "Iricon" (Blair, *The Control of Oil*, 46).

3. Blair, *The Control of Oil*, 44–45.

4. Parra, *Oil Politics*, 89–92.

5. Yergin, *The Prize*, 512.

6. Parra, *Oil Politics*, 89–94; Yergin, *The Prize*, 510–13.

7. Yergin, *The Prize*, 513.

8. Ibid.

9. Soviet production doubled between 1955 and 1960, when it replaced Venezuela as the world's second largest producer after the United States (Yergin, *The Prize*, 515).

10. Skeet, *OPEC*, 6–7.

11. In addition to coordinating supply (Pérez Alfonzo's chief goal), the Maadi Pact signatories agreed to regularly consult "(a) improvement of contractual terms and the requirement for consultation on [administered] price change[s]; (b) an integrated approach to oil industry operations; (c) increasing refinery capacity in their countries; (d) establishment of national oil companies; and (e) national coordination of the conservation, production, and exploitation of oil resources" (Skeet *OPEC*, 15–16).

12. Yergin, *The Prize*, 521; Seymour, "OPEC Production Cutback Accord," 1. Exxon's administered price for Saudi Arab Light fell from $1.90 to $1.76 (Skeet, OPEC, 17).

13. For color on Monroe Rathbone's fateful decision see Sampson, *Seven Sisters*, 156–60; Parra, *Oil Politics*, 97; and Yergin, *The Prize*, 520–22.

14. Yergin, *The Prize*, 522.

15. Sampson, *Seven Sisters*, 162.

16. Yergin, *The Prize*, 522.

17. Ibid., 523.

18. Parra, *Oil Politics*, 101.
19. Useem, "The Devil's Excrement."
20. Parra, *Oil Politics*, 105.
21. Ibid., 106.

6. OPEC TAKES CONTROL FROM TEXAS AND THE SEVEN SISTERS: 1970-1980

1. BP, "Statistical Review," 2015.
2. Parra, *Oil Politics*, 116–117.
3. Adelman, *Genie*, 50–51.
4. Yergin, *The Prize*, 585–586.
5. Ibid. However, these desired impacts of higher crude oil prices were offset by domestic price controls imposed to combat inflation that worked the other way by encouraging consumption and discouraging new supply.
6. Parra, *Oil Politics*, 117.
7. BP, "Statistical Review."
8. Yergin, *The Prize*, 578.
9. Adelman, *Genie Out of the Bottle*, 70–71.
10. Parra, *Oil Politics*, 123.
11. Parra, *Oil Politics*, 124–125. For State's view that the Libyan demands were "reasonable" see also Adelman, *Genie*, 75.
12. Parra, *Oil Politics*, 126. Yergin, *The Prize*, 580–83.
13. Yergin, *The Prize*, 563.
14. Sampson, *Seven Sisters*, 226.
15. Parra, *Oil Politics*, 128–130; Adelman, *Genie*, 76–78; Yergin, *The Prize*, 580–82.
16. Yergin, *The Prize*, 582–83.
17. Ibid., 590–91.
18. Pump Prices dataset (nominal prices); API, *Petroleum Facts and Figures* (1959).
19. Parra, *Oil Politics*, 162.
20. Hammes and Wills, *Black Gold*, 10.
21. Sampson, *Seven Sisters*, 233.
22. Sampson, *Control of Oil*, 243.
23. Yergin, *The Prize*, 592; Parra, *Oil Politics*, 161–62.
24. Maugeri, *The Age of Oil*, 107.
25. Yergin, *The Prize*, 600.
26. Trans-Arabian Pipeline, an oil pipeline between Qaisumah, Saudi Arabia, and Sidon, Lebanon, constructed starting in 1947, opened in 1950, and operated until 1990.
27. William D. Smith, "Q. and A. on Oil Prices: A Ripple Effect, " *New York Times*, December 25, 1973, A1.
28. Unlike Arab producers, Iran was on good terms with Israel and close to the United States; as in 1967 the Shah did not join in oil boycotts, which were implemented by Arab OPEC members.

29. Para, *Oil Politics*, 81. Yergin, *The Prize*, 624.
30. Bernard Weinraub, "Shah of Iran," *New York Times*, 1973, 31, 37; Yergin, *The Prize*, 630.
31. William D. Smith, "New Rises Are Feared: Price Quadruples for Iranian Crude Oil at Auction Kuwait Oil Deal Reported," *New York Times*, December 12, 1973, 1, 64.
32. Maugeri, *The Age of Oil*, 114.
33. Parra, *Oil Politics*, 181–82.
34. Adelman, *Genie*, 110–13.
35. Robinson, *Yamani*, 96.
36. Sampson, *Seven Sisters*, 237. Libya had nationalized remaining foreign company assets in 1973, whereas Saudi Arabia had adopted a more incremental approach, signing a deal at the end of 1972 with Aramco concession companies for a 25 percent share immediately, rising to 51 percent in 1983.
37. Yergin, *The Prize*, 633.
38. Anthony Sampson wrote the embargo "provoked the most embarrassing show of European disunity since the Common Market began" (Sampson, *Seven Sisters*, 262).
39. EIA, "Monthly Energy Review," Table 3.1.
40. EIA, U.S. Field Production of Crude Oil.
41. Kalt, *Oil Price Regulation*, 9–11.
42. Yergin, *The Prize*, 659–60.
43. For an extensive analysis of oil price regulation, see Kalt, *Oil Price Regulation*.
44. Helbing and Turley, *Oil Price Controls*, 2.
45. Ibid., 3, 5.
46. The foregoing is based on Helbing and Turley, *Oil Price Controls*.
    This unintended consequence stemmed from complex government regulations established help domestic refiners who were not fortunate enough to use cheaper, price-controlled "old" oil. To equalize crude costs among all refiners, Washington created an "Old Crude Oil Entitlement Program" designed to distribute lower-cost old oil equitably. Every month FEA would use the ratio of old oil to new oil to determine a fair share for all refiners. For example, in March 1975 41 percent of the U.S. crude supply was "old" crude, so each refiner was "entitled" to purchase at least 41 percent of his crude at the controlled price of \$5.25 per barrel. Refiners could trade entitlements to this oil, with the price determined on the basis of the difference between the controlled and uncontrolled price of a barrel of oil. In March 1975, the average price per barrel of "new" domestic and imported crude was \$12.56, thus "the FEA established an entitlement price of \$7.31 for that month." Thus refiners using less than 41 percent imported oil would sell their entitlements at the \$7.31 price to refiners who used use more than 41 percent old oil. Refiners who used only old oil were "required to purchase entitlements equal to 59 percent of his input," amounting to an effective tax on that refiner of \$4.31 per barrel (59 percent of \$7.31). In this way, the "burden" of high-cost imported oil was equalized via an income redistribution program. Domestic old oil was taxed and the revenue used to subsidize the purchase of imported oil.
    Thus, Helbing and Turley concluded, "as imported oil becomes an increasing proportion of total domestic consumption, the effective domestic price of oil will increase also.

The greater U.S. reliance on foreign sources of supply, in turn, enhances the unity of the foreign oil cartel such that the United States becomes increasingly vulnerable to external pricing and producing decisions. A situation has been fostered which would perpetuate rising world oil prices in the future."

47. "Controls can inhibit markets from responding efficiently to the challenges and can be one cause of inadequate or misallocated supply" (Hamilton, "Historical Oil Shocks," 24).

48. Yergin, *The Prize*, 616–17, 692.

49. Bamberger, *Strategic Petroleum Reserve*.

50. Doren and Van, *Economic Amnesia*, 21.

51. Sampson, *Seven Sisters*, 279–82.

52. Prodi and Clô, "Europe," Table 6A citing OECD data, 97.

53. Prodi and Clô, "Europe," 97.

54. Yamakoshi, "A Study on Japan's Reaction to the 1973 Oil Crisis," 1986, 24–28.

55. For the decision to raise the target, see Scott, *History of the International Energy Agency 1974–1994*, 93. Some members, such as the United States, hold strategic stocks in the form of government-owned and government-managed reserves. Other IEA members impose compulsory stockholding requirements on oil companies. Three net exporting IEA member countries (Canada, Denmark, and Norway) do not have a stockholding obligation.

56. Bamberger, *Strategic Petroleum Reserve*.

57. Conceived by more moderate OPEC members such as Saudi Arabia, partial nationalization or "participation" in concessions with foreign oil operators was devised as a compromise between maintaining quasicolonial original concessions and full nationalization.

58. Sampson, *Seven Sisters*, 241.

59. Adelman, *Genie*, 155 endnote 12, 183.

60. Adelman, *Genie*, 155, Table 6.5.

61. Ibid., 156.

62. Yergin, *The Prize*, 646.

63. Iranian production went from 6 mb/d in October 1978 to a low of 730 kb/d in January 1979. Total OPEC production loss was lower (~ 3 mb/d) because of increases in countries such as Kuwait and Nigeria (EIA, "Monthly Energy Review," March 29 2016, Table 11.a).

64. BP, "Statistical Review," 2015; Brent prices, for world production changes (EIA, "Monthly Energy Review,"2016, Table 11.1b).

65. Verleger, *Structure Matters*, 136.

66. Yergin, *The Prize*, 688.

67. Fattouh, "Origins and Evolution," 48.

68. Yergin, *The Prize*, 688.

69. EIA, Monthly Energy Review (MER) data show Saudi production fell from 10.4 mb/d in December 1978 to 9.8 mb/d in January, 1979. However, MER data show 9.8 mb/d for most months in 1979, suggesting the January 1979 figure is an annual average rather than monthly figure. Other sources say the Saudis cut by more. Adelman (in *Genie*, 171–72), citing trade press, said Saudi Arabia cut from between 10.2 and 10.5 mb/d in early January

to about 8 mb/d in late January. Adelman wrote the Saudi cut from 9.5 mb/d to 8.5 mb/d in early April 1979 (172), illustrating the confusion involved with oil market data.

70. Parra, *Oil Politics*, 220.

71. Halloran, "Oil 'Facts' Don't Quite Match the Rhetoric," *New York Times*, March 18, 1979, E5.

72. Yergin, *The Prize*, 692.

73. Adelman, *Genie*, 178.

74. "U.S. Troops Needed in Mideast to Guard Oil Supply: Schlesinger," *Indianapolis Star*, August 17, 1979, 1.

75. Adelman, *Genie*, 178.

76. Kalt, *Economics and Politics of Oil Price Regulation*, 287. At the same time Congress imposed a Windfall Profits Tax (WPT) on oil companies to capture some of the profits anticipated when prices rose after price controls were lifted. The WPT was repealed in 1988 because it was an administrative burden for tax authorities and a compliance burden to the oil industry, it generated little or no revenue after oil prices collapsed in 1986, and it increased oil import dependence.

77. U.S. Department of the Interior, "Managing Oil and Gas Resources," 1988, 1.3.

78. Andrews, "Oil Shale," 11.

79. Yergin, *The Prize*, 694.

80. EIA, "Monthly Energy Review," Table 11.1a.

81. As the Council on Foreign Relations explains: "Shia identity is rooted in victimhood over the killing of Husayn, the Prophet Mohammed's grandson, in the seventh century, and a long history of marginalization by the Sunni majority. Islam's dominant sect, which roughly 85 percent of the world's 1.6 billion Muslims follow, viewed Shia Islam with suspicion, and extremist Sunnis have portrayed Shias as heretics and apostates." However: "Sunni and Shia Muslims have lived peacefully together for centuries. In many countries it has become common for members of the two sects to intermarry and pray at the same mosques. They share faith in the Quran and the Prophet Mohammed's sayings and perform similar prayers, although they differ in rituals and interpretation of Islamic law" ("The Sunni-Shia Divide," Council on Foreign Relations).

82. Former FBI Director Louis Freeh believes senior Iranian government leaders directed the 1996 Hezbollah bombing that killed nineteen U.S. Air Force personnel in Dhahran, Saudi Arabia (Freeh 2006). U.S. officials reportedly believe Iran was behind a massive cyberattack against Saudi Aramco computers in August 2012. For background on the latter, see Nicole Perlroth, "In Cyberattack on Saudi Firm, U.S. Sees Iran Firing Back," *New York Times*, October 23, 2012.

83. Yergin, *The Prize*, 698.

84. Ibid., 703.

85. EIA, "Monthly Energy Review," 2016, Table 11.1b.

86. Annual average prices for Brent, which unlike WTI was unaffected by U.S. price and allocation controls (BP, "Statistical Review," 2015).

87. William Safire, "The Reagan Corollary," *New York Times*, October 4, 1981.

7. OPEC'S RUDE AWAKENING: 1981–1990

1. Adelman, *Genie*, 187–90.
2. International Energy Agency, *Oil Information 2015*.
3. Total share of gas/diesel oil (excluding transportation) and residual fuel oil of total OECD oil use was 40 percent in 1971, falling to 25 percent in 1985, and 10 percent in 2013. Calculations based on International Energy Agency, *Oil Information 2015*.
4. Alaska Field EIA, Production of Crude Oil.
5. BP, "Statistical Review," 2015.
6. Maugeri, *The Age of Oil*, 137; Skeet, *OPEC*, 185.
7. Skeet, *OPEC*, 183.
8. Ibid.
9. Ibid., 185. After the March meeting Saudi Arabia unilaterally cut production from 7.5 to 7.0 mb/d, thus lowering the effective OPEC quota from 18.0 mb/d to 17.5 mb/d.
10. Skeet, *OPEC*, 184–85.
11. Strictly speaking, OPEC and other analysts estimated a "call on OPEC and inventory changes" to balance the market.
12. EIA, "Monthly Energy Review," Table 11.a. Saudi production in February 1982 was 8.4 mb/d.
13. Mabro, *Netback Pricing*, 47. Mabro's paper provides a thorough review of netback pricing and the 1986 price collapse.
14. Mabro, *OPEC and the World Oil Market*.
15. Parra, *Oil Politics*, 286.
16. Netback pricing "involved a general formula in which the price of crude oil was set equal to the ex post product realization minus refining and transport costs. A number of variables had to be defined in a complex contract including the set of petroleum products that the refiner could produce from a barrel of oil, the refining costs, transportation costs, and the time lag between loading and delivery." Fattouh, *Anatomy*, 19; Mabro, *Netback Pricing*, 10.
17. Adelman, *Genie*, 226.
18. Ibid.
19. Mabro, *Netback Pricing*, 51.
20. Adelman, *Genie*, 224–25.
21. Parra, *Oil Politics*, 286.
22. Adelman, *Genie*, 229–31.
23. A Salomon Brothers report predicted price volatility would return to high levels seen before quotas but that it would last only two to four years, after which a "meganational" cartel composed of OPEC producers and large oil companies would restore control. "Crude Oil Prices to Lead to 'Meganational' Cartel," *Journal Record*, April 8, 1986, 1–2.
24. Prakken, Statement, 1986, 55.

25. During this period, Chevron acquired Gulf, and Conoco was overtaken by DuPont, a player outside the oil business.
26. U. S. Department of the Interior, "Managing Oil and Gas Resources," 1988, 1.1.
27. Ibid., 5.
28. Federal Trade Commission, Critical Evaluation, 1987. On likely violation of trade rules, I relied on a personal communication from Theodore Kassinger, a trade attorney and former Deputy Secretary of Commerce. Proponents could assert the United States has the authority to impose a variable levy on oil imports on national security grounds, though it is debatable whether such an assertion would withstand challenges by U.S. trading partners. For example, under the North American Free Trade Agreement, the United States committed not to impose import-restricting measures on energy goods for national security reasons, except in very limited circumstances that would not apply to a levy designed to provide long-term protection and support for the U.S. oil and gas industry.
29. Calls for such a tariff resurfaced during the oil price boom in 2006 and after the 2014 price bust. The variable import tariff is likely to return in the future policy debate on oil price stability.
30. McNulty, "Bush Sees Oil Glut Undermining U.S."
31. Adelman, *Genie*, 228.
32. EIA, "Monthly Energy Review," Table 11.1a.
33. Adelman, *Genie*, 231.
34. Robinson, *Yamani*, 278.
35. The so-called "OPEC Basket" tended to trade slightly lower than WTI until 2011. Henceforth, I will refer to WTI prices unless otherwise noted.
36. Maugeri, *The Age of Oil*, 145.
37. "Signs of Change In U.S. Attitude Towards OPEC," *Middle East Economic Survey*, May 18, 1987.
38. Fattouh, *Anatomy*, 6.
39. Futures trading began in 1978 with a heating oil contracted traded in New York. Crude oil futures began trading in 1983 and by late 1990 there were ten futures contracts actively trading (Adelman, *Genie*, 193).
40. Where the New York Mercantile Exchange and International Petroleum Exchange were located, respectively. Saudi sales to the United States would be based on differential to the price of WTI oil traded on the New York Mercantile Exchange (NYMEX). Sales to Europe would be priced relative to Brent oil that traded on the International Petroleum Exchange (IPE) and sales to Asia would be priced relative to Dubai, a crude traded in the Persian Gulf. Other OPEC producers generally followed Saudi Arabia. (For an astute discussion of the evolution oil pricing see Fattouh, *Anatomy*).
41. McQuaile, "Déjà vu." This led to many OPEC countries inflating their reserves.
42. As previously noted, there were frictions between Texas and other oil-producing states such as California, which did not implement quotas, but these were minor compared with tensions between OPEC countries.

43. Fattouh, *OPEC Pricing Power*, 1.

44. Parra, *Oil Politics*, 260–62. The 1986 price collapse engineered by Saudi Arabia played only a small role in curtailing supply, although it did force some high-cost and low-volume "stripper" wells in the United States to shut in.

45. BP, "Statistical Review."

46. Energy economist Philip Verleger believes the decision by some OPEC producers like Venezuela and Kuwait to invest heavily in downstream refining capacity during this period contributed to stabile prices as these producers because by diverting—often above quota—crude supplies through refineries they were able to disguise and moderate their actions vis-à-vis other producers (Verleger, "Structure Matters," 139–40).

47. Parra, *Oil Politics*, 262.

48. Ibid., 295.

49. Maugeri, *The Age of Oil*, 146.

50. Parra, *Oil Politics*, 295.

51. EIA, "Monthly Energy Review," Table 11.1a.

52. Adelman, *Genie*, 296–97.

53. Difiglio, "Oil, Economic Growth, and Strategic Petroleum Stocks," 55.

54. Mabro, *Dialogue Between Oil Producers and Consumers*, 1–2. "Peculiar feature of oil economics, namely a very low cost floor for crude oil production and a very high price ceiling set by substitutes, mean that the setting of an oil price level is a fairly arbitrary affair. As the market does not get much guidance from economics on where the level should be, it seeks cues from elsewhere. Although nobody should interfere with the market, other than removing imperfections, and leave day-to-day price movements entirely to its operations, the question arises as to who should provide it with the signal about a desired [long run] price level."

8. OPEC MUDDLES THROUGH: 1991–2003

1. BP, "Statistical Review," 2015.

2. EIA, "Monthly Energy Review," Table 11.1a.

3. Ibid.

4. Rapidan Group estimates derived partly from EIA "Monthly Energy Review," Tables 11.1a Table 11.1b.

5. EIA, "Monthly Energy Review," Table 11.1a. EIA has since updated its historical OPEC data to include Indonesia. Future EIA data sets will also likely reflect Gabon's joining in 2016.

6. Maugeri, *Oil Politics*, 171.

7. Guisti, "OPEC Must Shift," 4; Maugeri, *The Age of Oil*, 171.

8. "Tigers Adrift," *Economist*, March 5, 1998.

9. Maugeri, *The Age of Oil*, 171.

10. Yergin, *The Quest*, 82–85.

11. The total OPEC quota was raised from 25 mb/d to 27.5 mb/d. OPEC Secretariat.

12. Bijan Zangeneh is the current Minister of Petroleum of Iran.

13. Maugeri, *The Age of Oil*, 175.

14. WTI spot crude prices, EIA data.

15. "Riyadh Cutback," *Middle East Economic Survey*, 1998.

16. Seymour, "Plus Points."

17. OPEC Secretariat data, accessed online.

18. Mabro, *Oil Price Crisis*; see also Seymour, "Plus Points."

19. Seymour, "Plus Points."

20. Until June 1998, Iran had been insisting on cuts relative to a production level of 3.9 mb/d whereas OPEC demanded Iran cut from more realistic production levels of 3.6 mb/d; Seymour, "Plus Points."

21. EIA, "Monthly Energy Review," Table 11.1a.

22. The Senate Judiciary Committee approved NOPEC in 2000 but died there. The NOPEC bill would return later as we shall see.

23. "Fuel Economy Standard," *New York Times*, 1986.

24. "Gas Guzzler Tax," U.S. EPA.

25. "Prices of Crude Oil Retreat," *New York Times*, 1996.

26. U.S. Crude Oil Imports by Country of Origin, EIA website.

27. However, not to jump ahead of ourselves, Minister Naimi's status as the Saudi decision-maker on oil policy was eroded in April 2016 when Deputy Crown Prince Mohammed bin Salman reversed his decision to agree to a production freeze that would have excluded Iran. Smith et al., "Naimi's Decision-Maker Status Weakens in Doha." Minister Naimi was then dismissed in May 2016.

28. "Crisis Management," *New York Times*, 2000.

29. EIA, "Monthly Energy Review," Table 11.1a.

30. I respectfully acknowledge those who perished in Flight 93 in Pennsylvania (outside of Washington, D.C., and New York) on that day.

31. Annual Statistical Bulletin, OPEC, 2015, Table 1.2. Total quota lowered from 25.315 mb/d to 23.894 mb/d.

32. Annual Statistical Bulletin, OPEC, 2015, Table 1.2. Total quota lowered from 25.315 to 21.998.

33. Annual Statistical Bulletin, OPEC, 2015, Table 1.2. Total quota lowered from 21.998 to 20.575; although *Middle East Economic Survey* reported it was 1.5 mb/d ("OPEC Awaits Market Reaction to Production Cut," *Middle East Economic Survey*, January 7, 2002).

34. "OPEC Awaits Market Reaction to Production Cut," *Middle East Economic Survey*, January 7, 2002.

35. EIA, "Monthly Energy Review," Table 11.1a.

36. Ibid.

37. Parra, *Oil Politics*, 337–39. I assume Parra was referring to the OPEC basket price, which at the time traded a few dollars below WTI.

9. TWILIGHT: OPEC'S POWER TO PREVENT PRICE SPIKES
EBBS AND VANISHES: 2004–2008

1. IMF's World Economic Database, 2015.
2. BP, "Statistical Review," 2015.
3. China's Growing Demand, CBO, 2006; Fisher-Vanden et al., "Electricity Shortages," 172–88.
4. China's Growing Demand, CBO, 2006; Custom Table Builder, Short-Term Energy Outlook, EIA website; BP, "Statistical Review," 2015.
5. Verleger, *Structure Matters*, 144.
6. Mabro, Introduction, 5.
7. EIA, "Monthly Energy Review," Table 11.a,
8. EIA, "Short-Term Energy Outlook," December, 2014.
9. Spot WTI prices, EIA.
10. "The New Realism," *OPEC Bulletin*, 3.
11. For example, a UBS energy analyst to an Australian Broadcasting Corporation interviewer in June 2005 "[w]hat we're seeing that Saudi Arabia is mainly the only producer at the moment with any spare capacity and that's arguably between 1 and 1.5 million barrels a day. Seasonally, demand could grow over by over 2.5 million barrels a day between the first quarter and the fourth, so it's going to be a very tight market as we go into the northern hemisphere winter." (Alberici, "Drivers Brace for High Oil Prices.") See also Farren-Price, "Middle East Producers" and Mabro, *Oil in the 21st Century*, 7.
12. Farren-Price, "Middle East Producers."
13. "Let's face it: the problem of the overhang of excess capacity upstream is going to be with us for quite a number of years to come. Higher prices could lead to a revival of growth in non-OPEC supply. But even if this does not happen due to downsized price expectations, lower non-OPEC supply would be likely to be more than offset by increased upstream investment by international oil companies in low-cost OPEC areas. . . . According to estimates we have made in *MEES*, the extent of excess production capacity in the OPEC area will still be remaining at around 6–8 mb/d in 2005–2006, even if demand rises by a robust 1.4–1.5 mb/d per annum in the interim . . . [i]n the longer term my crystal ball suggests that . . . [t]he availability of so much surplus capacity will set a cap on prices of around $20/B (Brent). Prices above that level will, in one way or another, suck in additional supply to the market" (Seymour, "OPEC Oil Prices").
14. Farren-Price, "Middle East Producers." *Middle East Economic Survey* reported: "With output at around 9 mb/d in January, Saudi Arabia is already maintaining a spare capacity buffer of 2 mb/d, and according to Oil Minister Ali Naimi, the kingdom's production capacity is planned to rise to 12.5 mn b/d in the coming years, with the aim of always maintaining reasonable spare capacity of 1.5 mb/d as a minimum."
15. Saudi Aramco Khurais Mega Project, Khurais, Saudi Arabia.

16. King, "Saudis Face Hurdle" ; Saudi Aramco Khurais Mega Project, Khurais, Saudi Arabia. Saudi estimates of total production capacity tend to be higher than those of other experts, including EIA, which estimated maximum capacity to be 10.5 mb/d at a time when Saudi Arabia claimed 11.3. Note that in a January 2005 interview (see Farren-Price, "Middle East Producers") Oil Minister Naimi implied Saudi Arabia's maximum capacity was 11.0 mb/d. The variance is not clear but could arise from field maintenance or other issues that could have temporarily removed capacity.

17. Fattouh, "Origins and Evolution," 93.

18. Fattouh, "Spare Capacity."

19. I estimate spare capacity fell from about 10 percent of global production to 6 percent, a big drop to be sure but not low. As for ample inventory capacity, see Adelman, *Genie*, 168, 172, and Yergin, *The Prize*, 711–12.

20. EIA, "Monthly Energy Review," Table 11.1a.

21. Wilen, "Drivers Not Cutting Back."

22. Spot WTI crude prices, EIA.

23. Futures prices are not an accurate predictor of actual future prices. However, since they reflect prices at which consumers and producers are able to hedge, longer dated futures prices help shape expectations of future supply and demand conditions. IEA, *Medium-Term Oil Market Report*, 2014, 25.

24. The R-squared correlation between spot and 24-month futures prices for WTI was 0.37 during the 1990s but 0.97 during the 2000s and 0.97 since 2010.

25. Mabro, "Introduction," 7.

26. Blake Clayton innovatively examined the strong historical correlation between prolonged high oil prices and mentions of running out of oil in newspapers, books, and government records (Clayton, *Market Madness*, xii–xiii).

27. Hirsch et al., "Peaking," 19, Table II-1.

28. Roberts, "Cheap Oil Is History."

29. Clayton, *Market Madness*, viii–ix.

30. Yergin, "There Will Be Oil."

31. Hirsch et al., "Peaking," 4.

32. Hubbert, *Nuclear Energy and the Fossil Fuels*, 22 (Figure 21).

33. U.S. Field Production of Crude Oil, EIA online database.

34. Hubbert, *Nuclear Energy and the Fossil Fuels*, 22 (Figure 20). Hubbert estimated the world peak to be about 12.5 billion barrels, which equates to 34 mb/d. World crude production was 78 mb/d in 2014 (EIA, "Monthly Energy Review," Table 11.1b).

35. EIA estimates world proven crude oil reserves were 1.656 billion barrels in 2014 (International Energy Statistics, EIA website). EIA estimates global crude oil production was 78 mb/d in 2014 (EIA, "Monthly Energy Review," Table 11.1b). See also EIA, "Does the world have enough oil?"

36. This includes conventional and unconventional resources. Resources 2013, IEA, 18.

37. Al-Sabah, foreword to *Oil in the 21st Century*, xi–xv.

38. These can include "directional" bets like buying low expecting to sell high. Or "relative" bets such as expecting the price of one oil contract to rise or fall vis-à-vis another.

39. Gráda, *Famines and Markets*, 3.

40. Kotsiris, *The Antitrust Case*, 452–55.

41. Smith, "World Oil," 157.

42. Meyer, "Bart Chilton." Former CFTC Commission Bart Chilton coined the term. For a discussion of massive passive behavior see Fattouh, "Origins and Evolution," 80–83.

43. Examples include the Standard & Poor's-Goldman Sachs Commodity Index (S&P GSCI) and the Dow Jones-AIG Commodity Index.

44. Smith ("World Oil," 157) noted the widely held belief, as alleged by critics of speculation during the 2007 and 2008 price run-up, that the amount of paper barrels trading in the futures market was far larger than the underlying physical market for oil. "This misconception arises when the volume of futures contract that relate to oil deliveries that extend over many months is compared to the flow of oil production on a given day. After reconciling dates, even on the busiest trading days during 2007 and 2008, the volume of futures contracts for delivery of oil in any given month was but a fraction of the underlying physical production of oil." Smith cited Ronald D. Ripple. "Futures Trading: What is Excessive?" *Oil and Gas Journal*, 106, no. 22 (2008): 24–32.

45. Masters, *Testimony*.

46. Brunetti et al., "Speculators," 3. See also Fattouh et al., *Role of Speculation*, 11–2; and "Origins and Evolution," 82.

47. Bernanke, "Oil and the Economy."

48. Fattouh et al., *Role of Speculation*, 5, citing Pirrong (1994).

49. Hamilton, *Causes and Consequences*, 232.

50. IMF, October, 2008, 91; Fattouh et al., *Role of Speculation*, 10.

51. Fattouh et al., *Role of Speculation*, 25–26.

52. IMF, October 2008, 84.

53. IEA, *Medium Term Oil Market Report*, 2009, 100.

54. Hamilton, *Causes and Consequences*, 23. See also Baumeister and Peersman, *Source of the Volatility Puzzle*, whose key finding is "the volatility puzzle in the crude oil market is mainly driven by a considerable decrease in the price responsiveness of oil supply and oil demand attaining very low levels since the mid-eighties. An important implication of these low price elasticities is that any small excess demand or supply of crude oil requires large jumps in prices to clear the global oil market."

55. U. S. Commodities Futures Trading Commission, *Interim Report on Crude Oil*, 3.

56. Bamberger, *Strategic Petroleum Reserve*, 8.

57. Ibid., 9. During fiscal year 1996, oil from the SPR was sold three times: once to pay for decommissioning of an SPR storage site, once to reduce the budget deficit, and again to offset appropriations unrelated to the SPR.

58. See chapter 8.

59. Sanger, "Politics or Policy? " online.

60. Bamberger, *Strategic Petroleum Reserve*, 4.

61. IEA, "IEA Response System," 9. See also Bamberger, *Strategic Petroleum Reserve*.

62. McNally, "'Space Mountain' Pump Prices."

63. Bamberger, *Strategic Petroleum Reserve*, 8.

64. Personal communication from John Shages, former head of the Strategic Petroleum Reserve office at the Department of Energy.

65. Bamberger, *Strategic Petroleum Reserve*, 11.

66. The former is necessarily speculative because we have no modern experience with how companies would behave if governments tried with success to stabilize prices with strategic stock releases and fills. And as for OPEC offsetting strategic stock releases, there is little history. And OPEC decisions to cut supply in response to stock releases would be complicated by the organization's infamous struggles to collectively cut supply excepting severe price drops. However, OPEC did cut production after the September 2000 SPR release.

67. Smith, "World Oil," 156.

68. Daily spot WTI price, FOB, Cushing, OK, EIA.

69. Hamilton (*Causes and Consequences*, 8) makes the general point. Price data, noted separately, are from Real Prices Viewer, Short-Term Energy Outlook, EIA website.

70. Real Prices Viewer, Short-Term Energy Outlook, EIA website. EIA shows real and nominal price data.

71. Gallup, "Gas Prices," poll accessed online.

72. Schmickle, "A Warning."

73. Jacobe, "Majority of Americans Support Price Controls."

74. Lightman and Hall, "Why a Maine GOP Senator is Taking on Oil Speculators."

75. Schmickle, "A Warning."

76. Brodie, "Lawmakers Say."

77. The Bank of Canada dismissed commodity index inflows caused high oil prices, concluding "other explanations for the increase in oil prices include macroeconomic fundamentals, such as interest rates and increased demand from emerging Asia. Of these two explanations, the one that seems most consistent with the facts explains oil-price fluctuations in terms of large and persistent demand shocks related to growth in global real activity in the presence of supply constraints" (Alquist and Gervais, "The Role of Financial Speculation," iii). See also IEA, *Medium Term Oil Market Report*, 2009, 105. For a rare official view that speculation played a large—albeit secondary—role in addition to fundamentals, see Juvenal and Petralla, "Speculation in the Oil Market." The Dallas Fed, however, concludes speculation played a small role (Plante and Yücel, "Did Speculation Drive Oil Prices?," 4).

78. IEA, *Medium Term Oil Market Report*, 2009, 96–100.

79. King and Fritsch, "Energy Watchdog Warns."

80. Fattouh, *Oil Market Dynamics*, 41, ftn 54.

81. King and Fritsch, "Energy Watchdog Warns."

82. Private sector analysts tend to believe OPEC spare capacity is held entirely by Saudi Arabia and that the kingdom's spare capacity is over 1.0 mb/d lower than IEA estimates.
83. Dombey and Blas, "Naimi tightlipped."
84. Stolberg and Mouawad, "Saudis Rebuff Bush," and Meyers, "Bush Prods Saudi Arabia."
85. Spot WTI prices, EIA.
86. "Tapping Oil Angst," *Daily Herald* (Arlington Heights, Ill.), June 22, 2008, 2.
87. Abbot, "Saudis Willing," 1, 5.
88. Dinnick, "Saudis Will Increase Oil Output."
89. Abbot, "Saudis Willing," 1, 5.
90. Editorial, "The Saudi Spigot," *Washington Post.*
91. Front Month WTI Crude Futures Prices, Bloomberg.
92. "U.S. Seizes Control of Mortgage Giants," *Washington Post.*
93. Duca, "Subprime Mortgage Crisis."
94. Custom Table Builder, Short-Term Energy Outlook, EIA
95. "Crude Oil Prices See Year of Boom and Bust," *Middle East Economic Survey.*
96. Krauss, "Where is Oil Going Next?" *New York Times,* January 14, 2009.
97. IEA, *Impact of High Oil Prices,* 60.

10. OIL'S THIRD BOOM-BUST ERA: 2009-?

1. Latta, "OPEC Acts."
2. Mouawad, "Saudis Vow."
3. OPEC press release, October 24, 2008. Saudi production from EIA, "Monthly Energy Review," Table 11.1a.
4. "OPEC Launches Output Offensive," *Middle East Economic Survey.*
5. Ibid.
6. Ibid.
7. OPEC monthly reports, secondary sources, show Iran cut production from 3.925 mb/d in September 2008 to 3.689 mb/d in January, 2009, a decline of 236,000 b/d. According to *Middle East Economic Survey,* Iran was obligated under the Oran agreement to reduce its January supply to 3.336 mb/d in January, some 589,000 b/d below September 2008's level ("OPEC Gears Up," *Middle East Economic Survey*).
8. *Monthly Oil Market Reports,* OPEC, October 2008, and OPEC, 2009, Table 14. OPEC crude oil production based on secondary sources.
9. Spot Brent crude prices, EIA.
10. In this period the reference is Brent crude oil prices, since the emergence of the U.S. shale oil boom caused the WTI marker to disconnect from global oil markets due to logistical barriers that were largely resolved by 2015. During this period market analysts tended to regard Brent crude oil as a more representative benchmark for the global crude oil prices.
11. OPEC oil revenues, EIA, 2015.

12. *Historical Spare Production Capacity*, the Rapidan Group.

13. Custom Table Builder, Short-Term Energy Outlook, EIA website.

14. EIA, "Monthly Energy Review," March 29, 2016.

15. "OPEC Talks Collapse," *Middle East Economic Survey*, 2011.

16. Ibid.

17. Latta and Itayim, "Peace Breaks Out In Vienna 2011."

18. "'Every Time We Go To Quotas,'" *Middle East Economic Survey*.

19. "Schumer Urges Saudis To Pump Up Oil," Fox News.

20. Front month Brent futures prices, Bloomberg.

21. "U.S. to Release 30 Million Barrels," Fox News.

22. Eaton and Eckstein, 241; Bamberger, *Strategic Petroleum Reserve*. Law also provides authority for more limited releases to test SPR infrastructure and procedures as well as to respond to minor emergences.

23. SPR Quick Facts and FAQs, U.S. Department of Energy.

24. Energy, Quadrennial Energy Review: Energy Transmission, Storage, and Distribution Infrastructure 2015, S-6.

25. In the case of Katrina there was no supply disruption for crude oil but instead for U.S. gasoline and other refined products. The storm devastated refining and transportation systems in Louisiana and Mississippi (Difiglio, "Oil," 55). See also "Rita and Katrina," *New York Times*.

26. Rascoe and Gardner, "Obama Takes Flak"; Broder and Krauss, "Global Oil Reserves."

27. "History of SPR Releases," U.S. Department of Energy.

28. Hall, "Oil Prices Fall," 4; Difiglio, "Oil," 56.

29. Glick, "A Look at the IEA."

30. Ibid.

31. Farley, "Amid Unrest."

32. Koyama, "IEA Oil Reserves"; "U.S. to Release," Fox News.

34. Leff, et al., "U.S. to Seek"; Shore, "Oil Price Falls."

35. EIA, "Shale in the United States."

36. Gold, "*The Boom*," 64, 83–84.

37. Ibid., 7–8, 28–29.

38. Wang and Krupnick, "U.S. Shale Gas," 11.

39. EIA, "Shale in the United States."

40. Spot Henry Hub Natural Gas futures prices, Bloomberg.

41. EIA, "Shale in the United States." Notable tight oil formations include, but are not confined to, Bakken and Three Forks formations in the Williston Basin; Eagle Ford, Austin Chalk, Buda, and Woodbine formations along the Gulf Coast; Spraberry, Wolfcamp, Bone Spring, Delaware, Glorieta, and Yeso formations in the Permian Basin; and the Niobrara formation, which, although located in multiple Rocky Mountain basins, is primarily producing oil in the Denver-Julesburg Basin.

42. Hilyard, *Oil & Gas Industry*, 119.

43. Hicks, "Development of the Bakken Resource," 32.
44. IEA, *World Energy Outlook*, 468.
45. "IEA: US Shale," *Middle East Economic Survey*.
46. IEA, *Medium Term Oil Market Report*, 2014, 11.
47. IEA's 2014 *Medium Term Oil Market Report* assumed "average IEA import prices" would drop from approximately $108 to $92 dollars per barrel between 2013 and 2019, based on a chart on page 18 in the report. In 2013 Brent averaged $111, $3 above the IEA average import price. I assume the $3 spread remains, and derived the Brent assumption by adding it to the IEA assumption.
48. IEA, *Medium Term Oil Market Report*, 2014, 58.
49. Ibid.
50. IEA, *Medium Term Oil Market Report*, 2014, 11.
51. Mabro made this observation in 2006, which was extended to 2014: "The view of the industrialized countries and their agencies, which seem to have become an implicit part of the conventional wisdom of the past 20 years, is that the role of non-OPEC is to meet as big a part of the world oil demand increment as possible and the role of OPEC is to hold in the upstream the surplus capacity buffer required to cope with small and big emergencies." (Mabro, "Introduction," 7). Mabro was speaking of the period around 2004, when market participants started focusing on dwindling spare capacity at the time. The author believes this conventional wisdom applied equally to forecasts made in 2014 and prior years.
52. OPEC, World Oil Outlook, 11.
53. BP, "Energy Outlook to 2035," 32–33.
54. McNally, "Welcome Back to Boom-Bust Oil Prices."
55. Ibid.
56. IEA, *Oil Market Report*, July and August 2014. In July demand growth was 1.4 mb/d but in August IEA revised down to 1.0 mb/d.
57. IEA, *Oil Market Report*, September 2014.
58. Ibid.
59. Ibid.
60. Brent spot prices, EIA daily data. Brent is cited here as representative of world oil prices because at the time (2011–2015) WTI prices were depressed by logistical constraints arising from surge in domestic shale oil production and a ban on crude oil exports. WTI prices were trading around $5 below Brent and had fallen below $100 on July 31, 2014.
61. "Middle East and Central Asia Regional Economic Outlook," IMF; Burgess, Lissovolik, Armenta, "EM Oil Producers."
62. McQuaile, "No Need for Panic."
63. Nasralla and Shields, "OPEC's Badri Expects Lower Target."
64. McQuaile, "Too Early for OPEC to Say."
65. McQuaile, "No Need for Panic."
66. Brent, daily price close, Bloomberg.

67. McQuaile, "No Need for Panic."

68. Brent front month futures prices, Bloomberg. Press reports and surveys suggest views about what OPEC would do at the meeting were mixed, but this price drop suggests that the decision not to cut came as a surprise to many people. MEES reported that "most analysts had predicted that OPEC would take action to trim supply, by at least 500,000 b/d if not 1 million b/d (to 29 million b/d) to counter the price slide" ("After the Hype," *Middle East Economic Survey*), but a Bloomberg survey found 58 percent of analysts expected no cut (Nightingale, "Unchanged").

69. Front month WTI futures prices, Bloomberg.

70. The Rapidan Group advised its clients in 2013 that in the event of excess oil production Saudi Arabia would not cut output but instead let oil prices drop sharply to slow new shale drilling. Mufson, "Why Gasoline Is Suddenly $3 a Gallon." See also Gold, "No End in Sight for Crude-Oil Glut," 1.

71. Naimi, "The Kingdom's Petroleum Policy," 2015.

72. Those are the words of my friend and one of my esteemed mentors Larry Goldstein, in a private communication published with his permission.

73. Seymour and Khadduri, "Nazer Rules Out Swing Producer Role For Saudi Arabia."

74. Butt, "OPEC's Caracas Summit."

75. Takieddine, "Saudi Oil Minister Affirms."

76. Osgood, "Aramco Halts Production Capacity Expansion."

77. Ibid.

78. In a speech in December 2015 Aramco CEO Amin Nasser said his goals were to "double the percentage of locally produced energy-related goods and services to 70 percent by 2021," boost the export of domestic energy goods and services to 30 percent of its output over the same time frame, and to create half a million well-paid direct and indirect jobs for Saudis (Nasser, Keynote speech).

79. Faucon and Said, "Saudi Oil Minister Denies Price War."

80. Two years earlier Minister Naimi elaborated in a speech in Washington: "The U.S. energy scene is witnessing a remarkable evolution. Newly commercial reserves of shale oil or tight oil are transforming the energy industry in America. And that's great news. It is helping to sustain the U.S. economy and to create jobs at a difficult time. I would like to put on the record here today that I welcome these new supplies into the global oil market. I hope these additional resources will add depth and bring increased stability to global-to-global oil markets. I believe these reserves will lead the U.S. into a much deeper engagement in world energy markets. And this is good news" (Center for Strategic and International Studies, "A Conversation with His Excellency Ali al-Naimi").

81. Hall, "Saudi Arabia to Drill for Shale Gas."

82. Plumer, "How Far Do Oil Prices Have to Fall?"

83. WTI spot prices, EIA. I am referring to WTI here because it is more relevant for shale companies' investment breakeven prices. However, Brent remained at this time a better benchmark for global market prices until 2016.

84. Short-Term Energy Outlook, EIA, December 2014 and February 2015.

85. Brent spot prices, EIA. See note 83.

86. "U.S. Shale Operators May Be the New Swing Producers," *World Oil*.

87. Doan and Murtaugh, "Shale Oil as World's Swing Producer."

88. FRAK Unconventional Oil and Gas Exchange traded fund share price, Bloomberg.

89. Crooks, "U.S. Shale Industry Shows Remarkable Resilience."

90. Short-Term Energy Outlook, EIA, December 2014 and March 2016.

91. Lozada, "Revamped U.S. Oil Hedges," 2015.

92. DiChristopher, Wells, and Schoen, "Oil Rout and OPEC."

93. Domanski et al., "Oil and Debt."

94. IEA, *Oil Market Report*, October 2015.

95. Custom Table Builder, Short-Term Energy Outlook, EIA.

96. Ibid.

97. Spot Brent prices, EIA. Hereafter I will revert to using WTI prices as a global benchmark.

98. Stubbington and Kantchev, "Oil, Stocks at Tightest Correlation."

99. Domanski et al., "Oil and Debt."

100. Harrington, "Oil Credit Crunch."

101. "Oil and Gas Debt—The Next Moral Hazard?" *Seeking Alpha*; Spross, "Does the Oil Crash Signal Another Financial Crisis?"

102. Torchia, "Saudi's Naimi Says Output Freeze Enough."

103. It is important to distinguish between OPEC producers—mainly Saudi Arabia—making emergency cuts after shock lows such as in 2008 or 1998–1999 or small, temporary adjustments up and down based on seasonal or market factors, on the one hand, and the willingness to surrender substantial and sustained market share in response to structural oversupply, on the other. When we speak of Saudi Arabia or OPEC managing the market, we mean the latter. Prevailing forecasts assumed Saudi Arabia would play that latter, market manager role. McNally, "Welcome Back to Boom-Bust Oil Prices."

104. OPEC spare production capacity shrank below 1.0 mb/d according to official data. Many market participants—whose perceptions strongly influence prices—regard official data to be inflated, and assume spare capacity entirely ran out.

105. From Ali bin Ibrahim Al-Naimi's remarks at the CERA Week Conference, 2016.

EPILOGUE

1. Watkins, *Oil: Stabilization or Conservation?*, 40.

2. Cho and Cheong, "Oil Security Seen at Risk."

3. "Our tally now sits at 68 major projects containing 27 billion BOE [barrels of oil equivalent]. This equates to US$380 billion of capex deferred by total project spend in real terms. As oil prices continue to fall and capital allocation tightens, we expect the list will grow further"(Wood Mackenzie, "Pre-FID 2016").

4. Percival, "Wood Mackenzie"; Smith, "Most Global Oil Projects."

5. Cho and Cheong, "Oil Security Seen at Risk," 2016.

6. IEA, *Medium Term Oil Market Report*, 2016, 44. Columbia, Egypt, and Oman are other leading examples of producers with steep decline rates. See also http://www.reuters.com /article/oil-production-kemp-idUSL5N11L26U20150915.

7. IEA, *World Energy Outlook 2013*, 464.

8. IEA, *Medium Term Oil Market Report*, 2016; IEA, "Global Oil Supply Growth Plunging," press release February 2016.

9. Mabro, "Introduction," 10.

10. See Colgan, "The Emperor Has No Clothes."

11. Ibid., 9.

12. Raval, Sheppard, and Hume, "OPEC Meets with Oil Near $50."

13. Prindle, *Petroleum Politics*, 70.

14. Reserves: Federal Trade Commission. *International Petroleum Cartel*, 5–6, 23, Table 1, Table 8. Data for 1950. Federal Trade Commission, *International Petroleum Cartel*, 25, Table 10.

15. Data from BP, *Statistical Review of World Energy* (2015), and International Energy Forum, Joint Oil Data Initiative as of 2014.

16. IEA, *Oil Market Report*, March 2016, Table 2. Saudi oil consumption shows a strong seasonal pattern, rising sharply in the summer to meet high cooling requirements. Saudi officials are very concerned about rising domestic consumption. "'I can't overemphasize the concern I have with the rising consumption of our ultimately finite oil and gas,' Aramco CEO [since May 2016, Saudi Oil Minister] Khalid Al-Falih said. If the country's appetite for oil and gas continues rising by 6 percent to 7 percent a year, he said, 'Saudi Aramco will be the big loser.' IEA's *Medium Term Oil Market Report* flagged likelihood of slower growth through 2021" (DiPaola and Carey, "Aramco Says").

17. Saudi Arabia's state-owned Aramco and France's Total started operation of a jointly owned 400,000 b/d refinery in June 2014. Aramco plans to begin commissioning a third, wholly owned 400,000 mb/d refinery called Jazan in 2018 (Saudi Aramco, "Domestic Refining and Chemicals"; YASREF, "Yasref Overview").

18. Fattouh, "More than Meets the Eye?" 19.

19. Annual average, but with large season swings because direct burning of crude oil for cooling can rise from 300,000 b/d to 1 mb/d in a year (Fattouh, "Summer Again," 8).

20. George and Bousso, "Saudi Arabia Rewrites Its Oil Game."

21. IEA, *Oil Market Report*, March 2016, Table 1. Figures for 2015. Crude supply excludes refinery gain and biofuels, but includes natural gas liquids (96.4 mb/d total supply – 2.3 mb/d biofuels – 2.2 mb/d processing gains = 91.9 mb/d. $91.9 \times .05 = 4.6$ mb/d). Elsewhere references are of spare capacity as a percentage of global demand instead of crude production, mainly due to data constraints on biofuels and refinery gain.

22. Peel and Blas, "Saudi Arabia Halts."

23. Mahdi and Carey, "Saudi Prince."

24. Monthly Oil Data Service, IEA database. Author's calculations.

25. *Barrels-at-Risk*, the Rapidan Group proprietary estimate.

26. Lawler, "Saudi Spare Oil Capacity."

27. Micklethwait et al., "Saudi Arabia Will Only Freeze."
28. Waldman, "The $2 Trillion Project."
29. A Platts blog post by Platts Energy Economist Managing Editor Ross McCracken cited a Bentek estimate that the 993 DUCs in North Dakota in August 2015 alone if brought onstream could add nearly 600,000 kb/d of Bakken crude production, notionally (McCracken, "OPEC's Big Favor").
30. Wang, "Has US Shale Rendered Spare Capacity Irrelevant?"
31. U.S. Department of the Interior, "Managing Oil and Gas Resources."
32. Loris, "Why Congress Should Pull the Plug"; David, "US Strategic Reserve."
33. Goldwyn and Billig, "Building Strategic Reserves," 520; Difiglio, "Oil," 48.
34. Mufson, "Congress and Obama Tap Petroleum Reserve."
35. Lipsky, "Economic Shifts."
36. McNally, "'Space Mountain' Pump Prices," 4.
37. Ngai, "World Bank's Oil Hedging Deal."
38. There is an even stronger political aversion to imposing direct oil taxes on consumers. Democrats lost control of the House of Representatives in 1994 in large part because of their support for a broad-based energy tax (based on energy content of fuel or British Thermal Units, BTU). The BTU tax would have added about 7.5 cents per gallon to pump prices and cost a family of four $118 per year. The experience was so painful for House Democrats who had voted for the unpopular measure in the House only to see their Senate counterparts balk and watch the measure founder, that getting "BTU'd" became a verb (Heil, "Heard on the Hill: Bar Brawl"; Broder, "Democrats Divided"; Cohen, "Gasoline-Tax Increase Finds Little Support").

    When gasoline prices rise, many leaders and elected officials are prone to consider cutting taxes. In May 2008 when gasoline prices were soaring and crude prices were hitting a record $120 per barrel, Democratic party primary candidate Hillary Clinton championed a summer-long holiday from the 18.4 cent per gallon federal gasoline tax (and 24.4 cent per gallon diesel tax), a move her primary opponent Barack Obama called a "political stunt" (Kopp, "Obama: Clinton, McCain Wrong"). Even when gasoline prices are relatively low, as they were in the summer and fall of 2015, officials are loath to raise fuel taxes. In 2015 Congress could not agree to an increase in federal gasoline taxes to fund highway construction.
39. Levi et al., "How to Handle Oil Price Volatility."
40. International Energy Forum, Joint Oil Data Initiative.
41. The United States added 160 million barrels of storage between 2010 and 2015. "Outside of the US, capacity information is scarce, although the Chinese SPR capacity has likely increased by over 200 million barrels between 2006 and 2016" (along with private company stocks, though the two are often intermingled). In 2016 alone, IEA estimates another 230 million barrels of storage capacity will be built. IEA, *Oil Market Report*, January 2016, 32–33.
42. Mabro, "Introduction," 12.
43. Mahdi, "Saudi Aramco Sees Oil Rising;" Seba, "After Motiva Split."

BIBLIOGRAPHY

Abbot, Sebastian. "Saudis Willing to Hike Crude Output." *Gettysburg Times* (Associated Press). June 23, 2008, 1, 5.

Adelman, Morris Albert. *The Economics of Oil Supply.* Cambridge, Mass.: MIT Press, 1993.

——. *Genie Out of the Bottle: World Oil Since 1970.* Cambridge, Mass.: MIT Press, 1995.

——. *The World Petroleum Market.* Baltimore: Johns Hopkins University Press for Resources for the Future, Inc., 1972.

Alberici, Emma. "Drivers Brace for High Petrol Prices." Australian Broadcasting Corporation. June 28, 2005, http://www.abc.net.au/7.30/content/2005/s1402614.htm.

Alquist, Ron, and Olivier Gervais. "The Role of Financial Speculation in Driving the Price of Crude Oil." Bank of Canada. Discussion Paper 2011-6. July 2011.

Anderson, Patrick L., Richard D. McLeilan, Joseph P. Overton, and Gary L. Wolfram. *The Universal Tuition Tax Credit: A Proposal to Advance Parental Choice in Education.* Midland, Mich.: Mackinac Center for Public Policy, 1997, 81.

Andrews, Anthony. "Oil Shale: History, Incentives, and Policy." Washington, D.C.: Congressional Research Service, 2006. https://www.fas.org/sgp/crs/misc/RL33359.pdf.

American Petroleum Institute (API). *Petroleum Facts and Figures.* 1928.

——. *Petroleum Facts and Figures.* 1959.

Associated Press. "Burns Revokes Murray Orders in Oil Field." *Scranton Republican,* May 21, 1932, 1.

——. "Commissioner Defends Stand on Oil Output." *Odessa American,* February 15, 1957, 15.

——. "Governor Murray's Executive Order Stops Oklahoma City Output." *Corsicana Daily Sun,* August 5, 1931, 13.

——. "Oklahoma Oil Lid is Twisted Tight." *Bakersfield Californian,* June 22, 1932, 7.

——. "Martial Law Declared in State Today." *Brownsville Herald,* August 17, 1931, 1, 16.

——. "Murray Checks Oil Work Within City." *Brownsville Herald,* May 6, 1932, 1.

——. "Oil Lift to W. Europe Slumps—At Crucial Time." *Lincoln Star,* February 4, 1957, 12.

———. "State Okays Boost in Oil Production." *Lubbock Avalanche-Journal*, June 16, 1967, 1, 7.

Baffes, John, M. Ayhan Kose, Franziska Ohnsorge, and Marc Stocker. *The Great Plunge in Oil Prices: Causes, Consequences, and Policy Responses.* Washington, D.C.: World Bank Group, 2015.

Bamberger, Robert. *The Strategic Petroleum Reserve: History, Perspectives, and Issues.* Congressional Research Service Report for Congress. August 18, 2009. Washington, D.C.: Congressional Research Service. http://www.fas.org/sgp/crs/misc/RL33341.pdf.

Barden, Justine. "United Kingdom Increases Oil Production in 2015, But New Field Development Declines." *Today in Energy*, Washington, D.C.: U.S. Energy Information Administration, 2016. https://www.eia.gov/todayinenergy/detail.cfm?id=25552.

Baumeister, Christiane, and Gert Peersman. *Source of the Volatility Puzzle in the Crude Oil Market.* Ghent: Ghent University, 2009.

Bernanke, Ben S. "Oil and the Economy," speech delivered at the Distinguished Lecture Series, Darton College, Albany, Ga., October 21, 2004. http://www.federalreserve .gov/Boarddocs/Speeches/2004/20041021/default.htm.

Black, Brian. *Petrolia: The Landscape of America's First Oil Boom.* Baltimore: Johns Hopkins University Press, 2000.

Blair, John Malcolm. *The Control of Oil.* New York: Pantheon Books, 1976.

BP. *Energy Outlook 2035*, January 2014.

———. *Statistical Review of World Energy*, 2014.

———. *Statistical Review of World Energy*, 2015.

Bradley, Robert L., Jr. *Oil, Gas, and Government: The U.S. Experience.* Vol. 1. Lanham, Md: Rowman & Littlefield, 1996.

———. *Oil, Gas, and Government: The U.S. Experience.* Vol. 2. Lanham, Md: Rowman & Littlefield, 1996.

Broder, John M. "Democrats Divided Over Gas Tax Break." *New York Times*, April 29, 2008. http://www.nytimes.com/2008/04/29/us/politics/29campaign.html?_r=1.

Broder, John M., and Clifford Krauss. "Global Oil Reserves Tapped in Effort to Cut Cost at Pump." *New York Times*, June 23, 2011.

Brodie, Lee. "Lawmakers Say 'Curb Immediately' to Speculators." CNBC, June 26, 2008. http://www.cnbc.com/id/25400615.

Brown, John Howard, and Mark Partridge. "The Death of a Market: Standard Oil and the Demise of 19th Century Oil Exchanges." *Review of Industrial Organization* 13, no. 5 (1998): 569–87.

Brunetti, Celso, Bahattin Buyuksahin, and Jeffrey H. Harris. "Speculators, Prices, and Market Volatility." January 7, 2011. Available at SSRN: http://ssrn.com/abstract=1736737 or http://dx.doi.org/10.2139/ssrn.1736737.

Burgess, Robert, Yaroslav Lissovolik, and Armando Armenta. "EM Oil Producers; Breakeven Pain." *Deutsche Bank*, October 2014.

Butt, Gerald. "OPEC's Caracas Summit Seeks Stable and Fair Prices, Closer Dialogue With Consumers." *Middle East Economic Survey* 43, no. 40 (2000).

Buttram, Frank. *The Cushing Oil and Gas Field, Oklahoma*. Bulletin. Norman, Okla.: Oklahoma Geological Survey, 1914.

Carrington, Damian. "Fossil fuel industry must 'implode' to avoid climate disaster, says top scientist." *Guardian*, July 10, 2015. http://www.theguardian.com/environment /2015/jul/10/fossil-fuel-industry-must-implode-to-avoid-climate-disaster-says-top -scientist.

"Cartels: Their Significance for the American Business." *The Index* 24, no. 2 (1944): 25–33.

Center for Strategic and International Studies. "A Conversation with His Excellency Ali al-Naimi, Minister of Petroleum and Mineral Resources, Kingdom of Saudi Arabia." April 30, 2013. https://csis-prod.s3.amazonaws.com/s3fs-public/legacy_files/files /attachments/133004_TS_Al_Naimi.pdf.

Chan, Nathan W., and Kenneth Gillingham, "The Microeconomic Theory of the Rebound Effect and its Welfare Implications." *Journal of the Association of Environmental and Resource Economists* 2, no. 1 (March 2015): 133–59.

Chernow, Ron. *Titan: The Life of John D. Rockefeller, Sr.* New York: Random House, 1998.

Childs, William. *The Texas Railroad Commission*. College Station, Tex.: Texas A&M University Press, 2005.

Cho, Sharon, and Serene Cheong. "Oil Security Seen at Risk by IEA on 'Historic' Spending Cuts." *Bloomberg News*, March 23, 2016. http://www.bloomberg.com/news /articles/2016-03-23/oil-security-seen-at-risk-by-iea-on-historic-investment-cuts.

Clayton, Blake C. *Market Madness: A Century of Oil Panics, Crises, and Crashes*. New York: Oxford University Press, 2015.

Cohen, Patricia. "Gasoline-Tax Increase Finds Little Support." *New York Times*, January 2, 2015. http://www.nytimes.com/2015/01/03/business/energy-environment/support-for -gas-tax-increase-still-nil-despite-falling-prices.html.

Colgan, Jeff. "The Emperor Has No Clothes: The Limits of OPEC in the Global Oil Market." November 2011. https://www.princeton.edu/~pcglobal/conferences/environment /papers/colgan.pdf.

Cooper, John C. B. "Price Elasticity of Demand for Crude Oil: Estimates for 23 Countries," *OPEC Review* 27, no. 1 (2003): 1–8.

Council on Foreign Relations. "The Sunni-Shia Divide." InfoGuide Presentation. http://www.cfr.org/peace-conflict-and-human-rights/sunni-shia-divide/p33176#! /?cid=otr-marketing_url-sunni_shia_infoguide.

Crooks, Ed. "US Shale Industry Shows Remarkable Reslience." *Financial Times*. March 15, 2015. http://www.ft.com/intl/cms/s/0/372e52bc-c98b-11e4-a2d9-00144feab7de.html #axzz43DONgBqL.

Dahl, Carol A. 1993. "A Survey of Oil Demand Elasticities for Developing Countries," *OPEC Review* 17 (Winter 1993): 399–419.

David, Javier E. "US Strategic Reserve May Be Past Its Prime: Analysts." CNBC, March 20, 2013. http://www.cnbc.com/id/100574506.

de Chazeau, Melvin G., and Alfred E. Kahn. *Integration and Competition in the Petroleum Industry*. New Haven, Conn.: Yale University Press, 1959.

Deng, Yinke. *Ancient Chinese Inventions*. New York: Cambridge University Press, 2011.

Derrick's Handbook of Petroleum, The. 2 vols. Oil City, Pa.: The Derrick's Publishing Company, 1898, reprinted 2006.

Derrick's Hand-Book of Petroleum, The: Containing the Data of All Important Events in the History of the Petroleum Region; Daily Market Quotations; Daily Average Production, and Tables of Field Developments; Runs, Shipments, Exports, Stocks, Etc., Etc. Oil City, Pa.: Derrick Publishing Company, 1884.

DiChristopher, Tom, Nicholas Wells, and John W. Schoen. "Oil Rout and OPEC Reverse Surge in Energy Jobs Market." CNBC, December 4, 2015. http://www.cnbc.com/2015/12/04/oil-rout-and-opec-reverse-surge-in-energy-jobs-market.html.

Difiglio, Carmine. "Oil, economic growth and strategic petroleum stocks." *Energy Strategy Reviews* (2014): 48–58.

Dinnick, Wilf. "Saudis Will Increase Oil Output to Cut Prices." CNN. June 23, 2008. http://www.cnn.com/2008/WORLD/meast/06/22/oil.summit/.

DiPaola, Anthony, and Glen Carey. "Aramco Says Saudis Won't 'Singlehandedly' Balance Oil Market." *Bloomberg News*, January 28, 2015. http://www.bloomberg.com/news/articles/2015-01-27/saudi-aramco-capital-investment-to-drop-more-than-expected.

Doan, Lynn, and Dan Murtaugh. "Shale as World's Swing Producer Signals 'Jagged' Oil Future." *Bloomberg News*, April 19, 2015. http://www.bloomberg.com/news/articles/2015-04-20/shale-as-world-s-swing-producer-signals-jagged-future-for-oil.

Dolson, Hildegarde. *The Great Oildorado: The Gaudy and Turbulent Years of the First Oil Rush: Pennsylvania 1859–1880*. New York: Random House, 1959.

Domanski, Dietrich, Jonathan Kearns, Marco Jacopo Lombardi, and Hyun Song Shin. "Oil and Debt." *Bank for International Settlements*. March 18, 2015. http://www.bis.org/publ/qtrpdf/r_qt1503f.htm.

Dombey, Daniel, and Javier Blas. "Naimi Tightlipped on Bush Oil Appeal." *Financial Times*, January 16, 2008.

Downey, Morgan. *Oil 101*. New York: Wooden Table Press LLC, 2009.

Duca, John V. "Subprime Mortgage Crisis." Federal Reserve History, http://www.federalreservehistory.org/Events/DetailView/55.

Eaton, Jonathan, and Zvi Eckstein. "The U.S. Strategic Petroleum Reserve: An Analytic Framework." In *The Structure and Evolution of Recent U.S. Trade Policy*, edited by Robert E. Baldwin and Anne O. Krueger, 237–76. Chicago: University of Chicago Press, 1984.

EconMatters. "Another Oil Price Shock, Another Global Recession?" April 17, 2012. http://www.econmatters.com/2012/04/another-oil-price-stock-another-global.html.

Emory, Johnson R., and Thurman W. Van Metre. *Principles of Railroad Transportation*. New York: D. Appleton and Company, 1918.

Energy Information Administration (EIA). "Does the world have enough oil to meet our future needs?" Frequently Asked Questions, last updated May 19, 2016, http://www.eia.gov/tools/faqs/faq.cfm?id=38&t=6.

——. International Energy Statistics. http://www.eia.gov/cfapps/ipdbproject/iedindex3.cfm?tid=5&pid=57&aid=6&cid=ww,&syid=2011&eyid=2015&unit=BB.

——. "Monthly Energy Review." http://www.eia.gov/totalenergy/data/monthly/.

——. OPEC Revenues Fact Sheet. March 31, 2015. https://www.eia.gov/beta/international/regions-topics.cfm?RegionTopicID=OPEC.

——. Production of Crude Oil. http://www.eia.gov/dnav/pet/hist/LeafHandler.ashx?n=pet&s=mcrfpak1&f=a.

——. "Shale in the United States." *Energy in Brief.* July 20, 2016. https://www.eia.gov/energy_in_brief/article/shale_in_the_united_states.cfm.

——. Short-Term Energy Outlook. December, 2004. http://www.eia.gov/forecasts/steo/archives/dec04.pdf.

——. Today in Energy. March 1, 2013. https://www.eia.gov/todayinenergy/detail.cfm?id=10191.

——. U.S. Crude Oil Imports by Country of Origin. http://www.eia.gov/dnav/pet/pet_move_impcus_a2_nus_ep00_imo_mbbl_m.htm.

——. U.S. Field Production of Crude Oil. http://www.eia.gov/dnav/pet/hist/LeafHandler.ashx?n=PET&s=MCRFPUS2&f=M.

Farly, Robert. "Admid Unrest in Libya, U.S. Agrees to Release Oil from Reserves." *Politifact.* June 23, 2011. http://www.politifact.com/truth-o-meter/promises/obameter/promise/447/release-oil-from-strategic-petroleum-reserve/.

Farren-Price, Bill. "Middle East Producers Set to Add New Oil Production Capacity in 2005." *Middle East Economic Survey.* January 10, 2005.

Fattouh, Bassam. *An Anatomy of the Crude Oil Pricing System.* Oxford: Oxford Institute of Energy Studies, 2011.

——. *Oil Market Dynamics Through the Lens of the 2002–2009 Price Cycle.* Oxford: Oxford Institute for Energy Studies, 2010.

——. *OPEC Pricing Power: The Need for a New Perspective.* Oxford: Oxford Institute for Energy Studies, 2007.

——. "The Origins and Evolution of the Current International Pricing System." In *Oil in the 21st Century: Issues, Challenges, and Opportunities,* edited by Robert Mabro, 41–100. Oxford: Oxford University Press, 2006.

——. "Saudi Arabia Oil Policy: More than Meets the Eye?" Oxford: Oxford Institute for Energy Studies, June 2015. https://www.oxfordenergy.org/wpcms/wp-content/uploads/2015/06/MEP-13.pdf.

——. "Spare Capacity, Oil Prices and the Macroeconomy." Oxford: Oxford Institute for Energy Studies, 2011. https://www.oxfordenergy.org/wpcms/wp-content/uploads/2011/02/Presentation35-SpareCapacityOilPricesandtheMacroeconomy-BFattouh-2006.pdf.

——. "Summer Again: The Swing in Oil Demand in Saudi Arabia." Oxford: Oxford Institute for Energy Studies. 2013.

Fattouh, Bassam, Lutz Kilian, and Lavan Mahadeva. *The Role of Speculation in Oil Markets: What Have We Learned So Far?* Oxford: Oxford Institute for Energy Studies, 2012.

Faucon, Benoît, and Summer Said. "Saudi Oil Minister Denies Price War with U.S. Shale." *Wall Street Journal.* March 4, 2015.

Federal Oil Conservation Board. *Report of the Federal Oil Conservation Board to the President of the United States.* Washington, D.C.: Department of the Interior, 1926.

Federal Trade Commission. *A Critical Evaluation of Petroleum Import Tariffs: Analytical and Historical Perspectives.* Washington, D.C.: U.S. Government Printing Office, 1987.

——. *The International Petroleum Cartel.* Washington, D.C.: U.S. Government Printing Office, 1952.

——. *Report on the Price of Gasoline in 1915.* Washington, D.C: Federal Trade Commission, 1917.

Fisher-Vanden, Karen, Erin Mansur, and Qiong (Juliana) Wang. "Electricity Shortages and Firm Productivity: Evidence from China's Industrial Firms." *Journal of Development Economics* 114, Issue C (2015): 172–188. http://EconPapers.repec.org/RePEc:eee :deveco:v:114:y:2015:i:c:p:172-188.

Fox News. "Schumer Urges Saudis to Pump Up Oil Production as Gas Prices Rise." March 2, 2012. http://www.foxnews.com/politics/2012/03/01/schumer-urges-saudis -to-pump-up-oil-production-as-gas-prices-rise.html.

——. "U.S. to Release 30 Million Barrels of Oil from Strategic Reserve." June 23, 2011. http://www.foxnews.com/politics/2011/06/23/us-to-release-30-million-barrels-oil -from-strategic-reserve.html.

Frank, Helmut J. *Crude Oil Prices in the Middle East: A Study in Oligopolistic Price Behavior.* New York, Washington, London: Praeger Publishers, 1966.

Frankel, P.H. *Essentials of Petroleum: A Key to Oil Economics.* 2nd ed. New York: Frank Cass, 1969. First edition published in 1946.

Franks, Kenny A., Paul F. Lambert, and Carl N. Tyson. *Early Oklahoma Oil.* College Station, Tex.: Texas A&M University Press, 1981.

Fratzcher, Marcel, Daniel Schneider, and Ine Van Robays. *Oil Prices, Exchange Rates, and Assets Prices.* Frankfurt: European Central Bank, 2014.

Frey, John W., and H. Chandler Ide, eds. *A History of the Petroleum Administration for War 1941–1945.* Washington, D.C.: U.S. Government Printing Office, 1946.

Gallup. "Gas Prices." http://www.gallup.com/poll/147632/gas-prices.aspx.

——. "Majority of Americans Support Price Controls." May 28, 2008. http://www.gallup .com/poll/107542/majority-americans-support-price-controls-gas.aspx.

Gately, Dermot. "OPEC's Incentives for Faster Output Growth." *Energy Journal* 25, no. 2 (2004): 75–96.

Gately, Dermot, and Hillard G. Huntington. "The Asymmetric Effects of Changes in Price and Income on Energy and Oil Demand." *Energy Journal* 23, no. 1 (2002): 19–55.

George, Libby, and Ron Bousso. "Saudi Arabia Rewrites Its Oil Game With Refining Might." Reuters, May 22, 2015. http://www.reuters.com/article/saudi-refining-evolution -idUSL5N0YC4AI20150522.

Glick, Devin. "A Look at the IEA 2011 Release of Strategic Oil Reserves." Research paper sponsored by the Institut Français des Relations Internationales. July 28, 2011. https:// bakerinstitute.org/files/276/

Gold, Russell. *The Boom: How Fracking Ignited the American Energy Revolution and Changed the World.* New York: Simon & Schuster, 2014.

——. "No End in Sight for Crude-Oil Glut." *Wall Street Journal Europe,* August 21, 2015.

Goldwyn, David L., and Michelle Billig. "Building Strategic Reserves." In *Energy & Security: Toward a New Foreign Policy Strategy,* edited by Jan H. Kalickiand David L. Goldwyn, 509–29. Washington, D.C.: Woodrow Wilson Center Press, and Baltimore, M.D.: Johns Hopkins Unversity Press, 2005.

Gráda, Cormac Ó. "Famines and Markets." Working Paper, University College Dublin, Dublin, Ireland, 2007.

Guo, Hui, and Kevin L. Kliesen. "Oil Price Volatility and U.S. Macroeconomic Activity." *Federal Reserve Bank of St. Louis Review* 87, no. 6 (November/December 2005): 669–83. https://research.stlouisfed.org/publications/review/05/11/KliesenGuo.pdf.

Hall, Kevin G. "Oil Prices Fall as U.S., Europe Tap Reserves." *Pittsburgh Post-Gazette,* June 24, 2011, 5.

Hall, Simon. "Saudi Arabia to Drill for Shale Gas This Year." *Wall Street Journal,* March 18, 2013.

Halloran, Richard. "Oil 'Facts' Don't Quite Match the Rhetoric." *New York Times,* March 18, 1979, E5.

Hamilton, James. "Historical Causes of Postwar Oil Shocks and Recessions." *Energy Journal* 6, no. 1 (1985): 97–116.

——. "Historical Oil Shocks." February 1, 2011. http://econweb.ucsd.edu/~jhamilto/oil_history.pdf.

——. "Understanding Crude Oil Prices." National Bureau of Economic Research, Working paper 14492 , Cambridge, Mass., 2008.

Hamilton, James D. *Causes and Consequences of the Oil Shock of 2007–2008.* San Diego, Calif.: UC San Diego, Department of Economics, 2009.

Hammes, David, and Douglas Wills. *Black Gold: The End of Bretton Woods and the Oil Price Shocks of the 1970s.* Available at SSRN: http://ssrn.com/abstract=388283.

Harrington, Mark. "Oil Credit Crunch Could Be Worse than the Housing Crisis." CNBC Commentary. January 14, 2016. http://www.cnbc.com/2016/01/14/oil-credit-crunch-could-be-worse-than-the-housing-crisis-commentary.html.

Harvey, Fiona. "World's Climate Pledges Not Yet Enough to Avoid Dangerous Warming– UN." *Guardian,* October 30, 2015. http://www.theguardian.com/environment/2015/oct/30/worlds-climate-pledges-likely-to-lead-to-less-than-3c-of-warming-un.

Heil, Emily. "Heard on the Hill: Bar Brawl." *Roll Call,* November 4, 2009. http://www.rollcall.com/issues/55_53/-40292-1.html.

Helbing, Hans H., and James E. Turley. "Oil Price Controls: A Counterproductive Effort." St. Louis, Mo.: Federal Reserve Bank of St. Louis, November, 1975.

Hicks, Bruce E. "Development of the Bakken Resource." Presented at the North Dakota 9-1-1 Association Meeting. Bismark, N. Dak., March 6, 2014. https://www.dmr.nd.gov/oilgas/presentations/ActivityUpdate2014-03-06ND911Meeting Bismarck.pdf.

Hilyard, Joseph F. *The Oil and Gas Industry: A Nontechnical Guide.* Tulsa, Okla.: PennWell, 2012.

Hirsch, Robert L., Roger Bezdek, and Robert Wendling. "Peaking of World Oil Production: Impacts, Mitigation, and Risk Management." Paper sponsored by the U.S. Department of Energy, National Energy Technology Lab, February 2005. http://www.netl .doe.gov/publications/others/pdf/oil_peaking_netl.pdf.

"History of the Railroad Commission, 1866–1939." Railroad Commission of Texas website, accessed February 29, 2016. http://www.rrc.state.tx.us/about-us/history/history -1866-1939/.

Hubbert, Marion King, "Nuclear Energy and the Fossil Fuels." Paper sponsored by the Shell Development Company, Exploration and Production Research Division, 1956.

Hughes, Jonathan E., Christopher R. Knittel, and Daniel Sperling. "Evidence of a Shift in the Short-Run Price Elasticity of Gasoline Demand." *Energy Journal* 29, no. 1 (2008): 113–34.

Hydrocarbons-technology.com. "Saudi Aramco Khurais Mega Project, Khurais, Saudi Arabia." http://www.hydrocarbons-technology.com/projects/khurais/.

——. "U.S. Troops Needed in Mideast to Guard Oil Supply: Schlesinger." August 17, 1979, 1.

International Energy Agency. "Energy Snapshot of the Week." Last modified August 19, 2014. https://www.iea.org/newsroomandevents/graphics/2014-08-19-energy-consumption -per-capita-and-energy-intensity.html.

——. "Global Energy Outlook: Issues and Challenges." Background Paper, September 2006. Paris: International Energy Agency. http://archive.treasury.gov.au/documents /1192/PDF/Session_2_IEA_Global_Energy_Outlook.pdf.

——. "Global Oil Supply Growth Plunging, with US Taking Biggest Hit for Now." Press Release. https://www.iea.org/newsroomandevents/pressreleases/2016/february/global -oil-supply-growth-plunging-with-us-taking-biggest-hit-for-now.html.

——. "IEA Response System for Oil Supply Emergencies 2012." Paris: International Energy Agency, 2012. http://www.iea.org/publications/freepublications/publication /EPPD_Brochure_English_2012_02.pdf.

——. *Impact of High Oil Prices on the Economy.* Paris: International Energy Agency, 2012.

——. *Medium Term Oil Market Report.* Paris: International Energy Agency, 2009.

——. *Medium Term Oil Market Report.* Paris: International Energy Agency, 2014.

——. *Medium Term Oil Market Report.* Paris: International Energy Agency, 2016.

——. Monthly Oil Data Service (MODS), database.

——. *Oil Information 2015.* CD ROM.

——. *Oil Market Report,* various monthly issues available on line. https://www.iea.org /oilmarketreport/omrpublic/currentreport/.

——. *World Energy Outlook 2011.* Paris: Organisation for Economic Co-operation and Development/International Energy Agency, 2011.

——. *World Energy Outlook 2015.* Paris: Organisation for Economic Co-operation and Development/International Energy Agency, 2015.

International Energy Forum. Joint Oil Data Initiative (JODI). Online database. https://www.jodidata.org/.

International Monetary Fund. "Middle East and Central Asia Regional Economic Outlook." October 2014.

——. World Economic Outlook Database, 2015.

Irwin, Neil, and Zachary A. Goldfarb. "U.S. Seizes Control of Mortgage Giants." *Washington Post,* September 8, 2008.

Jacobe, Dennis. "Majority of Americans Support Price Controls on Gas." May 28, 2008. http://www.gallup.com/poll/107542/majority-americans-support-price-controls-gas.aspx.

Juvenal, Luciana, and Ivan Petrella. "Speculation in the Oil Market." June 26, 2012. https://www.eia.gov/finance/markets/reports_presentations/2012PaperSpeculationInTheOilMarket.pdf.

Kalt, Joseph P. *The Economics and Politics of Oil Price Regulation.* Cambridge, Mass.: MIT Press, 1981.

Keever, Jack. "Texas Planning Full-scale Oil Production." *El Dorado Times,* March 17, 1972, 1.

King, Neil, Jr. "Saudis Face Hurdle in New Oil Drilling." *Wall Street Journal,* April 22, 2008.

King, Neil, Jr., and Peter Fritsch. "Energy Watchdog Warns of Oil-Production Crunch." *Wall Street Journal,* May 22, 2008.

Kopp, Bruce. "Obama: Clinton, McCain Wrong on Gas Taxes." WTHR Eyewitness News, online report. May 2, 2008. http://www.wthr.com/article/obama-clinton-mccain-wrong-gas-taxes.

Kotsiris, Lambros E. "An Antitrust Case in Ancient Greek Law." *The International Lawyer* 22, no. 2 (Summer 1988): 451–57.

Koyama, Ken. "IEA Oil Reserves Release and International Oil Market." Special Bulletin, Institute of Energy Economics, Japan, June 30, 2011. https://eneken.ieej.or.jp/data/3939.pdf.

Kuhn, Oliver. "Ancient Chinese Drilling." *CSEG Recorder,* 29, no. 6 (June 2004). http://csegrecorder.com/articles/view/ancient-chinese-drilling.

Latta, Rafiq. "OPEC Acts to Engineer Soft Landing." *Middle East Economic Survey,* September 15, 2008. https://mees.com/opec-history/2008/09/15/opec-acts-to-engineer-soft-landing/.

Latta, Rafiq, and Nader Itayim. "Peace Breaks Out in Vienna." *Middle East Economic Survey,* December 19, 2011. https://mees.com/opec-history/2011/12/19/peace-breaks-out-in-vienna/.

Lawler, Alex. "Saudi Spare Oil Capacity Complicates any Aramco Listing: Sources." Reuters, January 19, 2016. http://www.reuters.com/article/us-saudi-privatisation-aramco-idUSKCN0UX1Z2.

Leff, Jonathan, et al. "U.S. to Seek G8 Support for Oil Reserve Release: Kyodo." Reuters, May 16, 2012. http://www.reuters.com/article/us-usa-oil-reserves-idUSBRE84F1BQ 20120516.

Lefler, Jack. "No Oil Shortage Is Likely in U.S." *Corpus Christi Caller-Times*, June 6, 1967, 1.

Levi, Michael A., et al. "How to Handle Oil Price Volatility." *Council on Foreign Relations*, March 19, 2012. http://www.cfr.org/oil/handle-oil-price-volatility/p27667.

Lipsky, John. "Economic Shifts and Oil Price Volatility." Remarks presented at the 4th OPEC International Seminar, Vienna, Austria, March 18, 2009. https://www.imf.org /external/np/speeches/2009/031809.htm.

Lightman, David, and Kevin G. Hall. "Why a Maine GOP Senator Is Taking on Oil Speculators." *McClatchy*, June 12, 2009. https://www.mcclatchydc.com/news/nation-world/national/economy/article24541948.html.

Logan, Leonard M. *The Stabilization of the Oil Industry*. Norman, Okla.: University of Oklahoma Press, 1930.

Long, Stuart. "Suez May Help Avoid New Taxes." *Denton Record-Chronicle*, July 9, 1967, 4.

Loris, Nicolas. "Why Congress Should Pull the Plug on the Strategic Petroleum Reserve." Heritage Organization Backgrounder #3046, August 20, 2015. http://www.heritage .org/research/reports/2015/08/why-congress-should-pull-the-plug-on-the-strategic -petroleum-reserve.

Lovejoy, Wallace, and Paul Homan. *Economic Aspects of Conservation Regulation*. Baltimore: Johns Hopkins University Press, 1967.

Lozada, Lucas Iberico. "Revamped U.S. Oil Hedges May Test OPEC's Patience." Reuters, January 5, 2015. http://www.reuters.com/article/us-oil-hedging-analysis-idUSKBN0 KE0BX20150105.

Mabro, Robert. *A Dialogue Between Oil Producers and Consumers: The Why and the How*. Oxford: Oxford Institute for Energy Studies, 1991.

——. *Netback Pricing and the Oil Price Collapse of 1986*. Oxford: Oxford Institute for Energy Studies, 1987.

——., ed. Introduction to *Oil in the Twenty-First Century: Issues, Challenges, and Opportunities*. Oxford: Oxford University Press, 2006, 1–18.

——. *Oil Price Concepts*. Oxford: Oxford Institute for Energy Studies, 1984.

——. *The Oil Price Crisis of 1998*. Oxford: Oxford Institute for Energy Studies, 1998.

——. *OPEC and the World Oil Market: The Genesis of the 1986 Price Crisis*. Oxford: Oxford University Press, Oxford Institute for Energy Studies, 1986.

Mahdi, Wael. "Saudi Aramco Sees Oil Rising as Demand Catches Up with Supply." *Bloomberg News*, March 21, 2016. http://www.bloomberg.com/news/articles/2016-03-21 /saudi-aramco-sees-oil-rising-as-demand-catches-up-with-supply.

Mahdi, Wael, and Glen Carey. "Saudi Prince Says He Could Add a Million Barrels Immediately." *Bloomberg News*, April 16, 2016. http://www.bloomberg.com/news /articles/2016-04-16/saudi-prince-says-he-could-add-a-million-barrels-immediately.

Marshall, J. Howard, and Norman L. Meyers. *Legal Planning of Petroleum Production: Two Years of Proration*. Paper 4444. New Haven, Conn.: Yale Law School Faculty Scholarship Series, 1933.

Masters, Michael W. Testimony of Michael W. Masters before the Committee on Homeland Security and Governmental Affairs, United States Senate, May 20, 2008. http://www.hsgac.senate.gov//imo/media/doc/052008Masters.pdf?attempt=2.

Maugeri, Leonardo. *The Age of Oil: The Mythology, History, and Future of the World's Most Controversial Resource*. Westport, Conn.: Praeger Publishers, 2006.

McCracken, Ross. "OPEC's Big Favor to the World of Oil." S&P Global, Platts, November 2, 2015. http://blogs.platts.com/2015/11/02/opec-big-favor-world-of-oil/.

McElwee, Neil. *Oil Creek . . . The Beginning: A History and Guide to the Early Oil Industry in Pennsylvania*. Oil City, Pa: Oil Creek Press, 2001.

McKibben, Bill. "Falling Short on Climate in Paris." *New York Times,* December 13, 2015. http://www.nytimes.com/2015/12/14/opinion/falling-short-on-climate-in-paris.html?_r=0.

McNally, Robert. "'Space Mountain' Pump Prices." Testimony to the Subcommittee on Energy and Power of the House Committee on Energy and Commerce, March 7, 2012. https://energycommerce.house.gov/sites/republicans.energycommerce.house.gov/files/Hearings/EP/20120307/HHRG-112-IF03-WState-McNallyR-20120307.pdf.

——. "Welcome Back to Boom-Bust Oil Prices." On the Record, Columbia University Center on Global Energy Policy, December 17, 2015. http://energypolicy.columbia.edu/publications/commentary/welcome-back-boom-bust-oil-prices.

McNally, Robert, and Michael Levi. "A Crude Predicament: The Era of Volatile Oil Prices." *Foreign Affairs* (July/August 2011).

——. "Vindicating Volatility: Why Fluctating Prices Are Here to Stay." *Foreign Affairs*, Snapshot, November 4, 2014. https://www.foreignaffairs.com/articles/global-commons/2014-11-04/vindicating-volatility.

McNulty, Timothy J., "Bush Sees Oil Glut Undermining U.S.," *Chicago Tribune*, April 7, 1986. http://articles.chicagotribune.com/1986-04-07/news/8601250350_1_oil-prices-oil-situation-oil-production.

McQuaile, Margaret. "Déjà Vu on System for Calculating OPEC Output Quotas." S&P Global Platts, February 21, 2014. http://www.platts.com/news-feature/2014/oil/opec-guide/opec-oil-quotas.

——. "No Need for Panic Over Oil Price Plunge, OPEC Chief Says." S&P Global Platts, October 31, 2014. http://www.platts.com/news-feature/2014/oil/opec-guide/oil-price-plunge.

——. "Too Early for OPEC to Say Whether Oil Ceiling Cut Needed in November: UAE." September 23, 2014.

Meyer, Gregory. "Bart Chilton—Regulator, Rock Fan, and Raconteur." *Financial Times*, November 6, 2013.

Meyers, Steven Lee. "Bush Prods Saudi Arabia on Oil Prices." *New York Times*, January 16, 2008.

Micklewaith, John, Riad Hamade, and Javier Blas. "Saudi Arabia Will Only Freeze Oil
    Production If Iran Joins." *Bloomberg News*, April 1, 2016.
Middle East Economic Survey. "After the Hype, OPEC Meeting Ends with a Whimper."
    November 28, 2014. https://mees.com/opec-history/2014/11/28/after-the-hype-opec
    -meeting-ends-with-a-whimper/.
——. "Crude Oil Prices See Year of Boom and Bust." September 5, 2009. https://mees
    .com/opec-history/2009/09/05/crude-oil-prices-see-year-of-boom-and-bust/.
——. "'Every Time We Go to Quotas Who Bears the Brunt? Us.'" December 6, 2013.
    https://mees.com/opec-history/2013/12/06/every-time-we-go-to-quotas-who-bears
    -the-brunt-us/.
——. "IEA: US Shale to Sideline OPEC Going Forward." May 17, 2013. https://mees.com
    /opec-history/2013/05/17/iea-us-shale-to-sideline-opec-going-forward/.
——. "OPEC Awaits Market Reaction to Production Cut and Price Band Suspension."
    January 7, 2002. https://mees.com/opec-history/2002/01/07/opec-awaits-market
    -reaction-to-production-cut-and-price-band-suspension/.
——. "OPEC Gears Up for Compliance Challenge." January 12, 2009. https://mees.com
    /opec-history/2009/01/12/opec-gears-up-for-compliance-challenge/.
——. "OPEC Launches Output Offensive Against Price Slide, Stock Levels." December 22,
    2008. https://mees.com/opec-history/2008/12/22/opec-launches-output-offensive
    -against-price-slide-stock-levels/.
——. "OPEC Talks Collapse in 'Worst' Meeting." June 13, 2011. https://mees.com/opec
    -history/2011/06/13/opec-talks-collapse-in-worst-meeting/.
——. "Riyadh Cutback Accord Marks Major Step Forward Towards Market Restabilization."
    March 30, 1998. https://mees.com/opec-history/1998/03/30/riyadh-production-cutback
    -accord-marks-major-step-forward-towards-market-restabilization-but-credibility
    -doubts-persist/.
——. "Signs of Change in U.S. Attitude Towards OPEC." May 18, 1987. https://mees.com
    /opec-history/1987/05/18/signs-of-change-in-us-attitude-towards-opec/.
Mouawad, Jad. "Saudis Vow to Ignore OPEC Decision to Cut Production." *New York
    Times*, September 10, 2008.
Mufson, Steven. "Congress and Obama Tap Petroleum Reserve to Plug Hole in the
    Budget." *Washington Post*, October 28, 2015. https://www.washingtonpost.com
    /business/economy/congress-and-obama-tap-petroleum-reserve-to-plug-hole-in
    -the-budget/2015/10/27/8b9135f0-7ce0-11e5-beba-927fd8634498_story.html.
——. "Why Gasoline Is Suddenly $3 a Gallon—and Could Go Lower." *Wonkblog, Washington
    Post*, October 28, 2014. https://www.washingtonpost.com/news/wonk/wp/2014
    /10/28/why-gasoline-is-suddenly-3-a-gallon-and-could-go-lower/.
Naimi, Ali bin Ibrahim. Welcome and ministerial address at the CERAWeek 2016
    Energy Conference, Houston, Tex., February 23, 2106.
——. "The Kingdom's Petroleum Policy." Saudi-US Relations Information Service,
    April 11, 2015. http://susris.com/2015/04/11/the-kingdoms-petroleum-policy-al-naimi/

Nash, Gerald D. *United States Oil Policy, 1890–1964*. Pittsburgh: University of Pittsburgh Press, 1968.

Nasralla, Shadia, and Michael Shields. "OPEC's Badri Expects OPEC to Lower Output Target." Reuters, September 16, 2014. http://uk.reuters.com/article/opec-production -idUKL6N0RH2RO20140916.

Nasser, Amin H. Keynote speech. In-Kingdom Total Value Add program launch, Dammam, Saudi Arabia, December 1, 2015. http://www.saudiaramco.com/en/home /news-media/speeches/IKTVA-Launch.html.

Navias, Martin S., and E. R. Hooton. *Tanker Wars: The Assault on Merchant Shipping During the Iran-Iraq Conflict, 1980–1988*. London and New York: I. B. Tauris, 1996.

Nevins, Allan. *John D. Rockefeller: The Heroic Age of American Enterprise*. Vol. 1. New York, N.Y.: Charles Scribner's Sons, 1940.

——. *John D. Rockefeller: The Heroic Age of American Enterprise*. Vol. 2. New York: Charles Scribner's Sons, 1940.

——. *John D. Rockefeller. A One Volume Abridgement, by William Greenleaf*. New York: Scribner, n.d.

——. "Rita and Katrina Have Shut 23 Percent of U.S. Oil Refining Capacity." September 22, 2005.

——. "Shah of Iran Is Seen as a Spur Behind Sharp Advance: Oil Expert's View Shah of Iran Linked to Oil Price Rise Participants Listed." December 25, 1973, 31, 37.

Ngai, Catherine. "World Bank's Oil Hedging Deal for Uruguay Opens Door for More." Reuters, June 16, 2016. http://www.reuters.com/article/uruguay-oil-hedges -idUSL1N19821H.

Nightingale, Alaric. "OPEC Likely to Keep Output Unchanged Tomorrow, BI Survey Shows." *Bloomberg News*, November 26, 2014.

Nordhauser, Norman. "Origins of Federal Oil Regulation in the 1920s." *Business History Review* 47, no. 1 (1973): 53–71.

Nordhauser, Norman E. *The Quest for Stability: Domestic Oil Regulation, 1917–1935*. New York: Garland, 1979.

Nysveen, Per Magnus, and Leslie Wei. "Offshore vs. Shale: Which Will Prevail and Why?" *Oil and Gas Financial Journal*, April 9, 2015. http://www.ogfj.com/articles /print/volume-12/issue-4/features/offshore-vs-shale.html.

Olmstead, Alan L., and Paul Rhode. "Rationing Without Government: The West Coast Gas Famine of 1920." *American Economic Review* (1985): 1044–55.

OPEC Secretariat data, accessed online. http://www.opec.org/library/Annual%20 Statistical%20Bulletin/interactive/current/FileZ/XL/T12.HTM.

Organization of Petroleum Exporting Countries (OPEC). *Annual Statistical Bulletin*. Vienna, Austria: OPEC, 2015.

——. *Monthly Oil Market Report*, various months. Accessed online. http://www.opec .org/opec_web/en/publications/338.htm.

——. "The New Realism," *OPEC Bulletin* 36, no. 2 (February 2005): 3.

——. Press Release, 150th (Extraordinary) Meeting of the OPEC Conference. October 24, 2008.

——. World Oil Outlook. Vienna, Austria: OPEC, 2014.

Osgood, Patrick. "Aramco Halts Production Capacity Expansion." ArabianOilandGas .com. November 22, 2011. http://www.arabianoilandgas.com/article-9694-aramco -halts-production-capacity-expansion/.

Our Documents Initiative. "National Industrial Recovery Act." Accessed September 1, 2016. http://www.ourdocuments.gov/doc.php?flash=true&doc=66.

Panetta, Leon E., and Stephen J. Hadley. "The Oil-Export Ban Harms National Security." *Wall Street Journal*, May 19, 2015. http://www.wsj.com/articles/the-oil-export-ban -harms-national-security-1432076440.

Parra, Francisco. *Oil Politics: A Modern History of Petroleum*. London: I.B. Tauris, 2004.

Peel, Michael, and Javier Blas. "Saudi Arabia Halt $100bn Oil Expansion Programme." *Financial Times*. November 21, 2011. http://www.ft.com/intl/cms/s/0/967a332a-146d -11e1-8367-00144feabdc0.html#axzz45dVvEH7R.

Penrose, Edith T. *The Large International Firm in Developing Countries: The International Petroleum Industry*. London: George Allen and Unwin, 1968.

Percival, Geoff. "Wood Mackenzie: 'Oil Projects Risk Being Scrapped at Current Prices.'" *Irish Examiner*. July 14, 2016. http://www.irishexaminer.com/business/wood-mackenzie -oil-projects-risk-being-scrapped-at-current-prices-410174.html.

Petroff, Alanna, and Tal Yellin. "What It Costs to Produce Oil." CNN Money, November 23, 2015. http://money.cnn.com/interactive/economy/the-cost-to-produce-a-barrel-of-oil/.

Petroleum Centre Daily Record. "One Million Dollars Subscribed to the Petroleum Producers' Agency." November 6, 1872, 2.

Pettengill, Samuel B. *Hot Oil: The Problem of Petroleum*. New York: Economic Forum Co., 1936.

Plante, Michael D., and Mine K. Yücel. "Did Speculation Drive Oil Prices? Market Fundamentals Suggest Otherwise." Federal Reserve Bank of Dallas. *Economic Letter*, 6, no. 11 (October 2011).

Platt's Oilgram News. "Giusti: OPEC Must Shift." November 21, 1996, 4.

Plumer, Brad. "How Far Do Oil Prices Have to Fall to Throttle the US Shale Oil Boom?" Vox.com, December 3, 2014. http://www.vox.com/2014/12/3/7327147/oil-prices -breakeven-shale.

Prakken, Joel L. Statement. "The Economic Impact of the Oil Price Collapse." Hearing before the Subcommittee on Trade, Productivity, and Economic Growth of the Joint Economic Committee, Congress of the United States, Ninety-ninth Congress, second session, March 12, 1986. 53–55.

Prindle, David F. *Petroleum Politics and the Texas Railroad Commission*. Austin, Tex.: University of Texas Press, 1981.

Prodi, Roman, and Alberto Clô. "Europe." In *The Oil Crisis in Perspective*, edited by Raymond Vernon, 91–112. New York: Norton, 1976.

Rapidan Group, The. Barrels-at-Risk. Proprietary database.

——. Historical Spare Production Capacity. Proprietary database.

——. Monthly Crude Oil Prices 1859–2016. Proprietary database.

Rascoe, Ayesha, and Timothy Gardner. "Obama Takes Flak for Tapping Emergency Oil Reserves." Reuters, June 23, 2011. http://www.reuters.com/article/us-usa-oil-obama -idUSTRE75M44D20110623.

Raval, Anjli, David Sheppard, and Neil Hume. "OPEC Meets with Oil Near $50: What to Watch For." *Financial Times*, May 31, 2016.

Roberts, Dan. "Cheap Oil Is History. But Why?" *Telegraph*, May 24, 2008. http://www .telegraph.co.uk/news/uknews/2021948/Cheap-oil-is-history-But-why.html.

Roscoe, George B. "Oklahoma Oil Fields Under Martial Law." *Taylor* (Tex.) *Daily Press*, August 5, 1931, 1, 5.

Rostow, Eugene V. *A National Policy for the Oil Industry*. New Haven: Yale University Press, 1948.

Robinson, Jeffrey. *Yamani: The Inside Story*. New York: Atlantic Monthly Press, 1988.

Rundell, Walter, Jr. *Early Texas Oil: A Photographic History, 1866–1936*. College Station, Tex.: Texas A&M University Press, 1977.

Sabah, Sheikh Ahmad Fahad al-Ahad-al. Foreword to *Oil in the 21st Century: Issues, Challenges, and Opportunities*, edited by Robert Mabro, xi–xv. Oxford: Oxford University Press, 2006.

Salpukas, Agis. "Prices of Crude Oil Retreat, but Not Outlook for Gasoline." *New York Times*, May 1, 1996.

Sampson, Anthony. *The Seven Sisters: The Great Oil Companies and the World They Shaped*. New York: Bantam Books, 1975.

Sanger, David E. "Crisis Management; There's No Shortage of Repositioning on Oil." *New York Times*, September 24, 2000.

——. "Politics or Policy?" *New York Times*, September 23, 2000. http://www.nytimes .com/2000/09/23/us/politics-or-policy.html.

Saudi Aramco. "Domestic Refining and Chemicals." http://saudiaramco.com/en/home /our-business/maximising-value/domestic-refining-and-chemicals.html.

Schmickle, Sharon. "A Warning on Oil Speculation from NWA's Steenland." *Minneapolis Post*, June 24, 2008.

Schröter, Harm G. "Cartels Revisited: An Overview of Fresh Questions, New Methods, and Surprising Results." *Revue Économique* 63, no. 6 (November 2013): 989–1010.

Schurr, Sam, and Bruce Netschert, with Vera F. Eliasberg, Joseph Lerner, and Hans H. Landsberg. *Energy in the American Economy, 1850–1975: An Economic Study of Its History and Prospects*. Baltimore: Johns Hopkins University Press, 1960.

Scott, Richard. *The History of the International Energy Agency 1974–1994: IEA the First Twenty Years*. Vol. 3: Principal Documents. Paris: International Energy Agency, 1995.

Seba, Erwin. "Exclusive: After Motiva Split, Saudi Aramco Aims to Buy More U.S. Refineries—Sources." Reuters, March 18, 2016. http://www.reuters.com/article/us -saudi-aramco-exclusive-idUSKCN0WK2HX.

Seeking Alpha. "Oil and Gas Debt—The Next Moral Hazard?" March 23, 2016. http://
    seekingalpha.com/article/3960612-oil-gas-debt-next-moral-hazard.

Seymour, Ian. "Plus Points in New OPEC Production Cutback Accord Should Outweigh
    Initial Market Scepticism." *Middle East Economic Survey,* June 29, 1998. https://
    mees.com/opec-history/1998/06/29/plus-points-in-new-opec-production-cutback
    -accord-should-outweigh-initial-market-scepticism/.

——. "OPEC Oil Prices and Management of Excess Production Capacity." *Middle East
    Economic Survey,* June 7, 1999. https://mees.com/opec-history/1999/06/07/opec-oil
    -prices-and-management-of-excess-production-capacity/.

Seymour, Ian, and Walid Khadduri. "Nazer Rules Out Swing Producer Role for Saudi
    Arabia." *Middle East Economic Survey.* September 14, 1987. https://mees.com/opec
    -history/1987/09/14/nazer-rules-out-swing-producer-role-for-saudi-arabia/.

Shore, Sandy. "Oil Price Falls as Crude Supply Rises." Associated Press, August 29, 2012.
    http://www.huffingtonpost.com/huff-wires/20120829/oil-prices/.

Sieminski, Adam. "Effects of Low Oil Prices." U.S. Energy Information Administration
    Independent Statistics and Analysis paper presented to the Energy and Environmental
    Markets Advisory Committee, Commodity Futures Trading Commission, Washington,
    D.C., February 26, 2015.

Skeet, Ian. *OPEC: Twenty-Five Years of Prices and Politics.* Cambridge: Cambridge Uni-
    versity Press, 1988.

Smil, Vaclav. "Moore's Curse." *IEEE Spectrum* (April 2015), posted March 19, 2015. http://
    www.vaclavsmil.com/wp-content/uploads/4.MOORE_.pdf.

——. "Moore's Curse and the Great Energy Delusion." *The American* (November–
    December 2008). http://www.vaclavsmil.com/wp-content/uploads/docs/smil-article
    -20081119-the_American.pdf.

Smith, Grant. "Most Global Oil Projects Seen Working Below $60 on Cost Cuts." *Bloom-
    berg News,* July 13, 2016. http://www.bloomberg.com/news/articles/2016-07-13/bulk
    -of-global-oil-projects-seen-working-below-60-on-cost-cuts.

Smith, Grant, Stephen Bierman, and Dina Khrennikova. "Naimi's Decision-Maker Sta-
    tus Weakens in Doha." *Bloomberg News,* April 20, 2016. http://www.bloomberg.com
    /news/articles/2016-04-20/saudi-arabia-s-oil-partners-lament-naimi-s-loss-of-clout-in
    -doha.

Smith, James L. "World Oil: Market or Mayhem?" *Journal of Economic Perspectives* 23,
    no. 3 (Summer 2009): 145–64.

Spross, Jeff. "Does the Oil Crash Signal Another Financial Crisis?" *The Week,* January
    21, 2016.

Stocking, Andrew, and Terry Dinan. "China's Growing Energy Demand: Implications
    for the United States." Working Paper 2015-05, Working Paper Series, Congressional
    Budget Office, Washington, D.C., June, 2015.

Stolberg, Sheryl Gay, and Jad Mouawad. "Saudis Rebuff Bush, Politely, on Pumping
    More Oil." *New York Times,* May 17, 2008.

Stoll, Hans R., and Robert E. Whaley. "Commodity Index Investing and Commodity Futures Prices." Research paper. Owen Graduate School of Management, Vanderbilt University, Nashville, Tenn., September 10, 2009. http://www.cftc.gov/idc/groups /public/@swaps/documents/file/plstudy_45_hsrw.pdf.

Stuart, Reginald. "Fuel Economy Standard for Cars Said to Be Eased for '87 and '88," *New York Times*, October 1, 1986. http://www.nytimes.com/1986/10/01/us/fuel-economy -standard-for-cars-said-to-be-eased-for-87-and-88.html.

Stubbington, Tommy, and Georgi Kantchev. "Oil, Stocks at Tightest Correlation in Twenty-Six Years." *Wall Street Journal,* January 25, 2016. http://www.wsj.com/articles /oil-stocks-dance-the-bear-market-tango-1453722783.

Takieddine, Randa. "Saudi Oil Minister Affirms OPEC's Production Targets." *Al-Monitor*, December 6, 2013. http://www.al-monitor.com/pulse/business/2013/12/saudi -arabia-oil-minister-opec.html#.

Tarbell, Ida Minerva. *The History of the Standard Oil Company.* 2 vols. New York: McClure, Phillips & Company, 1904.

Taylor, Jerry, and Peter Van Doren. *Economic Amnesia: The Case Against Oil Price Controls and Windfall Profit Taxes.* Policy Analysis No. 561. Washington, D.C.: Cato Institute, January 12, 2006.

Texas Office of the Governor. Proclamation of Martial Law in East Texas. August 16, 1931. Accessed online at https://www.tsl.texas.gov/governors/personality/sterling -oil-2.html.

Texas State Historical Association, "Oil and Gas Industry." Accessed online at https:// tshaonline.org/handbook/online/articles/doogz.

Torchia, Andrew. "Saudi's Naimi Says Output Freeze Enough to Improve Market." Reuters, February 16, 2016. http://in.reuters.com/article/oil-meeting-saudi-idIND5N0V800X.

Tordo, Silvana, with Brandon S. Tracy and Noora Arfaa. "National Oil Companies and Value Creation." World Bank Working Paper no. 218 (2011): xi. http://siteresources. worldbank.org/INTOGMC/Resources/9780821388310.pdf, xi.

Twentieth Century Petroleum Statistics. Dallas, Tex.: DeGolyer and MacNaughton, 2005.

UPI. "Middle East War May Save Texans Millions in Taxes." *Brownsville Herald*, July 24, 1967, 6.

——. "Oil Allowable Upped Second Time in July." *Pampa Daily News*, July 13, 1967, 1.

——. "Rail Commissioner Differs With Governor on Oil Issue." *Waxahachie Daily Light*, February 7, 1957, 1.

——. "Texas Oil Allowable is Boosted to Record High." *Valley Morning Star* (Harlingen, Tex.), January 19, 1957, 5.

U.S. Commodities Futures Trading Commission. "Interim Report on Crude Oil." Washington, D.C.: U.S. Commodities Futures Trading Commission, July 2008.

U.S. Department of Energy. "History of SPR Releases." Energy.gov, Office of Fossil Energy website. http://energy.gov/fe/services/petroleum-reserves/strategic-petroleum-reserve /releasing-oil-spr.

——. "Quadrennial Energy Review: Energy Transmission, Storage, and Distribution Infrastructure." 2015.

——. "SPR Quick Facts and FAQS." Energy.gov, Office of Fossil Energy website. http://energy.gov/fe/services/petroleum-reserves/strategic-petroleum-reserve/spr-quick-facts-and-faqs.

U.S. Department of the Interior. "Managing Oil and Gas Resources in an Era of Price Instability." Washington, D.C.: U.S. Government Printing Office, 1988.

Useem, Jerry. "The Devil's Excrement." *Economist*, May 22, 2003.

U.S. Environmental Protection Agency. "Gas Guzzler Tax." https://www3.epa.gov/fueleconomy/guzzler/.

"U.S. Shale Operators May Be the New Swing Producers." *World Oil*, August 19, 2015. http://www.worldoil.com/news/2015/8/19/us-shale-operators-may-be-the-new-swing-producers.

Verleger, Philip K., Jr. "Structure Matters: Oil Markets Enter the Adelman Era." *Energy Journal* 36 (2015).

Waldman, Peter. "The $2 Trillion Project to Get Saudi Arabia's Economy Off Oil." *Bloomberg Businessweek*, April 21, 2016. http://www.bloomberg.com/news/features/2016-04-21/the-2-trillion-project-to-get-saudi-arabia-s-economy-off-oil.

Wang, Herman. "Has US Shale Rendered Spare Capacity Irrelevant?" S&P Global, Platts. September 14, 2015. http://blogs.platts.com/2015/09/14/us-oil-potential-spare-capacity/.

Wang, Zhongmin, and Alan Krupnik. "US Shale Gas Development: What Led to the Boom?" Issue Brief 13-04. *Resources for the Future*. May 2013. http://www.rff.org/files/sharepoint/WorkImages/Download/RFF-IB-13-04.pdf.

Watkins, Myron W. *Oil: Stabilization or Conservation?* New York and London: Harper & Brothers, 1937.

Weaver, Bobby D. "Cushing-Drumright Field." Encyclopedia of Oklahoma History and Culture, http://www.okhistory.org/publications/enc/entry.php?entry=CU008.

——. "Greater Seminole Field," Encyclopedia of Oklahoma History and Culture, http://www.okhistory.org/publications/enc/entry.php?entry=GR020.

Wells, Bruce. "Petroleum and Sea Power." American Oil and Gas Historical Society, http://aoghs.org/petroleum-in-war/petroleum-and-sea-power/.

White, Joe L. "Columbus Marion "Dad" Joiner and the East Texas Oil Boom." *East Texas Historical Journal* 6, no. 1 (1968): article 6.

Wilen, John. "Drivers Not Cutting Back Much as Gas Prices Soar Above $3 a Gallon." *Pittsburgh Post-Gazette*, May 15, 2007. http://www.post-gazette.com/auto/2007/05/15/Drivers-not-cutting-back-much-as-gas-prices-soar-above-3-a-gallon/stories/200705150204.

Williamson, Harold F., and Arnold R. Daum. *The American Petroleum Industry: The Age of Illumination, 1859–1899*. Evanston, Ill.: Northwestern University Press, 1959.

Williamson, Harold F., Ralph L. Andreano, Arnold R. Daum, and Gilbert C. Klose. *The American Petroleum Industry, 1899–1959: The Age of Energy.* Evanston, Ill.: Northwestern University Press, 1963.

Wood Mackenzie Corporation. "Pre-FID 2016: US$380bn of Capex Deferred." January 14, 2016. http://www.woodmac.com/analysis/PreFID-2016-USD380bn-capex-deferred.

Woods, Sam, and Raymond Brooks. "The Ship of State: Suez Impact Already Being Felt on Texas Oil With More Ahead." *Waco Tribune-Herald,* November 25, 1956, 10.

Yamakoshi, Atsushi. "A Study on Japan's Reaction to the 1973 Oil Crisis." Master's thesis, University of British Columbia, 1986.

Yanagisawa, Akira. *Impact of Rising Oil Prices on the Macro Economy.* Tokyo: Institute of Energy Economics, 2012.

YASREF. "YASREF Overview." http://www.yasref.com/about/overview.

Yergin, Daniel. *The Prize: The Epic Quest for Oil, Money, and Power.* New York: Simon and Schuster, 1991.

——. *The Quest.* New York: Penguin, 2011.

——. "There Will Be Oil." *Wall Street Journal,* September 17, 2011.

Zahran, Afshin, and Javan Nahl. "Dynamic Panel Data Approaches for Estimating Oil Demand Elasticity." *OPEC Energy Review* 39, no. 1 (2015): 53–76.

Zimmermann, Erich W. *Conservation in the Production of Petroleum: A Study in Industrial Control.* London: Oxford University Press, 1957.

INDEX

CPSIA information can be obtained
at www.ICGtesting.com
Printed in the USA
JSHW031452260622
27275JS00001B/1

9 780231 178150